D1134605

Current Topics in Human Intelligence

Volume 2

Is Mind Modular or Unitary?

List of Contributors

Numbers in parentheses indicate the pages on which the author's contributions begin.

David L. Alderton, Personnel Systems Department, Navy Personnel Research and Development Center, San Diego, California 92152 (141)

Charlotte G. Andrist, Notre Dame College, 4545 College Road, Cleveland, Ohio 44121 (1)

Jacquelyn G. Baker, University of British Columbia, Vancouver, Canada. (61)

Stephen J. Ceci, Department of Human Development and Family Studies, Cornell University, Ithaca, New York 14853 (61)

Frances A. Conners, Department of Psychology, Box 870348, University of Alabama, Tuscaloosa, Alabama 35487-0348 205-348-7913 (187)

Douglas K. Detterman, Department of Psychology, Case Western Reserve University, Cleveland, Ohio 44106 (1)

Steven W. Evans, Department of Psychology, Case Western Reserve University, Cleveland, Ohio 44106 (1)

H. J. Eysenck, University of London, Institute of Psychiatry, De Crespigny Park, Denmark Hill, London, SE5 8AF, England (83)

Robert L. Greene, Department of Psychology, Case Western Reserve University, Cleveland, Ohio 44106 (231)

Michael J. Kahana, Department of Psychology, Case Western Reserve University, Cleveland, Ohio 44106 (1)

Andrew Kertesz, Department of Clinical Neurological Sciences, University of Western Ontario, Lawson Research Institute, St. Joseph's Hospital, London, Ontario N6A 4V2, Canada (157)

Cynthia R. Knevel, Department of Psychology, Case Western Reserve University, Cleveland, Ohio 44106 (1)

Gerald E. Larson, Personnel Systems Department, Navy Personnel Research and Development Center, San Diego, California 92152 (141)

Dashen Luo, Department of Psychology, Case Western Reserve University, Cleveland, Ohio 44106 (1)

Alex Martin, Chief, Cognitive Studies Unit, Laboratory of Clinical Science, NIMN, Bldg. 10, Rm. 3D-41, Bethesda, Maryland 20892 (117)

Narina N. Nightingale, University of Wyoming, Laramie, Wyoming (61)

Mary W. Persanyi, Department of Psychology, Case Western Reserve University, Cleveland, Ohio 44106 (1)

Kathleen M. Spry, Department of Psychology, Case Western Reserve University, Cleveland, Ohio 44106 (1)

Herbert Weingartner, Department of Psychology, George Washington University, Washington, D.C. 20052 (117)

Current Topics in Human Intelligence

Volume 2

Is Mind Modular or Unitary?

Editor

Douglas K. Detterman

Case Western Reserve University

Ablex Publishing Corporation
Norwood, New Jersey

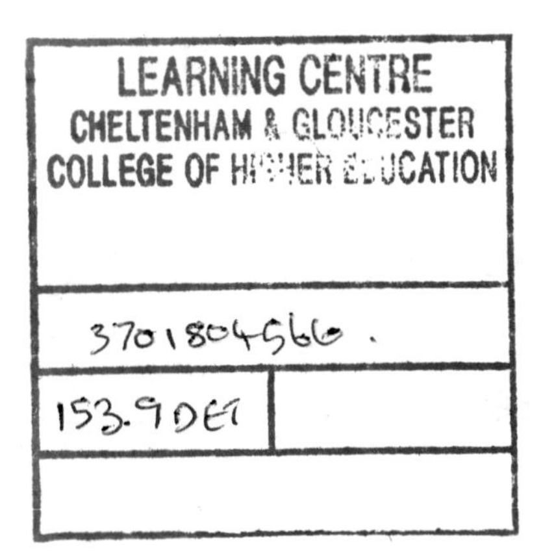

Printed in the United States of America.

ISBN: 0-89391-703-6

ISSN: 8755-0040

Ablex Publishing Corporation
355 Chestnut Street
Norwood, New Jersey 07648

Contents

Current Topics in Human Intelligence
Foreword to the Series

Douglas K. Detterman, Editor

The purpose of this series is to focus on single issues of importance to the study of human intelligence. Unlike many edited volumes, this one is designed to be thematic. Each volume will present a detailed examination of some question relevant to human intelligence and, more generally, individual differences.

The reason for beginning this series is that a forum is needed for extensive discussions of pertinent questions. No such forum currently exists. A journal does not allow an author sufficient space or latitude to present fully elaborated ideas. Currently existing edited series are not thematic but, instead, offer researchers an opportunity to present an integrative summary of their own work. Both journals and edited, nonthematic monographs are essential to the advancement of the study of human intelligence. But they do not allow collective intelligence to be brought to bear on a single issue of importance.

Why is it important to examine specific issues in detail? The answer to this question depends on an appreciation of the historical development of the study of human intelligence. For at least 40 years, and perhaps longer, the study of human intelligence has been less than highly regarded as an academic pursuit. The reasons for this attitude are many and have been discussed elsewhere. Despite the reasons, the lack of academic sanction for the study of individual differences in human intelligence has produced a discipline without a unifying paradigm. When researchers study human intelligence, it is almost always from the perspective of training in a related, but different, discipline. Disciplines which have "sacrificed" researchers to human intelligence include: cognitive, developmental, and educational psychology, behavior genetics, psychometrics, mental retardation, neuropsychology, and even experimental psychology. Each of these researchers has brought a different set of assumptions and methods to the study of human intelligence.

That so many different points of view have been applied to a single subject area has, in my opinion, brought vitality to the endeavor, a vitality currently lacking in so many areas of the social sciences. But this vitality does not arise from the isolation and fractionation which can be the result of different points of view. On the contrary, it results from the juxtaposition of these different points of view, a juxtapositioning which has occurred with increasing frequency over the last 10 years.

Therefore, it is the purpose of this series to bring different points of view together on issues of importance to understanding human intelligence. The hope is that, at the very least, researchers will find more reason to give their primary allegiance to the study of human intelligence and, at the most, the series will contribute to the emergence of a unifying paradigm.

Foreword to Volume 2: Is Mind Unitary or Modular?

The human mind is the last unexplored frontier. We know less about the mind than we do about many of the distant stars in our solar system. Even the most basic and rudimentary information about the mind evades us. For example, we do not know if the mind is unitary or modular in construction. Should the mind be regarded as a collection of separate parts operating together or should it be viewed as an integrated whole? It is amazing that we should know so little about such an important topic as how the mind is structured.

This volume is an attempt to present a spectrum of views concerning the form the mind takes, particularly with regard to individual differences. Is it modular and constructed of a number of different parts? Or, does it consist of a single mechanism of operation? These are classic, unresolved questions.

Perhaps the most famous advocate of mind as a unitary construct was Lashley who developed the principles of mass action and equipotentiality. According to these principles, the mind acted as a whole (mass action) and every part of the brain was functionally equivalent to every other (equipotentiality). Others before Lashley had argued for the doctrine of localization. For example, Broca and Wernicke had found portions of the cortex which controlled speech production and comprehension. The questions concerning anatomical structure raised by these early investigators have not yet been resolved.

The same argument concerning the structure of the mind which was argued among neuroanatomists is mirrored in classic controversies between psychometricians trying to understand human intelligence. Spearman used factor analysis to show that mental tests were highly correlated with each other. He called his positive intercorrelation *positive manifold* and took it to be evidence in support of what is called "g", or general intellectual ability. On the other hand, theorists like Thurstone and Guilford have argued that intelligence is really composed of several or many separate cognitive abilities.

The same argument where a unitary mechanism is opposed to modularity can also be found in cognitive models of human functioning. Models incorporating neural networks strongly suggest the unitary nature of human information processing. On the other hand, many theorists believe that human cognition and perception is composed of modules arranged in a hierarchy.

This classic problem of whether the mind is unitary or modular is not going to be solved in a single volume. The chapters in this book should be regarded as representations of current positions about the issue by people who have given some thought to the matter. Some of the chapters, instead of addressing the issue directly, present information that may be critical to answering the larger question. Even if none of the chapters presents a definitive answer to the question posed, they will have succeeded if they clarify and focus attention on the question of whether mind is modular or unitary.

Douglas K. Detterman
February 19, 1990

Chapter 1

*Individual Differences in the Biological Correlates of Intelligence: A Selected Overview**

Charlotte G. Andrist, Michael J. Kahana, Kathleen M. Spry, Cynthia R. Knevel, Mary W. Persanyi, Steven W. Evans, Dashen Luo, and Douglas K. Detterman

Department of Psychology
Case Western Reserve University

* This chapter was written as a class project for a biological basis of mental retardation course taught by Dr. D. K. Detterman. Individual students and the instructor were each responsible for reviewing an area of the biological literature included in this chapter. The first author was responsible for the introduction and discussion sections along with major editing and integration of the individual sections. The authors wish to thank Drs. Robert Greene, Robert Wilcott, and Joseph Fagan for their helpful comments and suggestions on the chapter.

INTRODUCTION

Cognitive scientists in a wide variety of disciplines have attempted to answer questions concerning the biological basis of intelligence for over a century (see Halstead, 1947, for review). But the relationship between the biological structure of the brain and individual differences in intelligence continues to elude scientists of today, much as it eluded the earliest investigators. The objective of the current paper is twofold: (a) To present a selected overview of literature on the biological correlates of intelligence, and (b) To evaluate the contributions of major biological correlates to our understanding of individual differences in intelligence. Selected biological correlates include gross anatomical, neurological, bio-electrical, and biochemical measures. The effects of environmental assaults on intelligence are also discussed. Research cited in the current paper is primarily limited to studies which measure general cognitive ability through standard psychometric tests. In research areas where psychometric data is not generally available, animal learning and clinical studies of populations with general cognitive deficits have been included. We begin with a brief history of the search for biological correlates of intelligence.

HISTORICAL PERSPECTIVE

Early theories of brain and cognition shared a common objective, to identify the structure of mental processing. This shared interest laid the foundation for a new discipline, psychology, or as Wundt termed it, the "physiology of the unconscious" (Boring, 1963). Initial experimental studies of cognition were based directly on the physiology of the brain. Early physiological models of brain structure and theories of intelligence are briefly reviewed below.

Early Physiological Models of Brain Structure

The study of the anatomical location of specific mental processes was first formalized through the work of Gall in the early nineteenth century (see Rosenfield, 1988, for review). Models based on the localization of specific mental functions were first challenged by Flourens in 1842 and later by Hughlings-Jackson (Jerison, 1982). Flourens, the leading neurologist of the day, argued that mental processes were a function of the brain as a whole. Hughlings-Jackson, although not completely rejecting theories of localization, challenged them on the basis of their simplicity. Hughlings-Jackson argued that the anatomical localization of specific mental processes was based on both the complexity and voluntary attributes of mental processes themselves. He argued that the more complex and voluntary a process was, the greater the number of connections it would have in the cerebral cortex and, therefore, the less localized it would be (Changeux, 1985). Flourens conceived of mental processing as completely distributed; Hughlings-Jackson proposed that mental processing was discretely distributed based on the complexity of the mental process involved (Halstead, 1947).

These initial holistic and aggregate concepts of biological structure proposed by Flourens and Hughlings-Jackson, respectively, lost support in 1881 after a heated debate and the formal adoption of the "doctrine of localization" (Rosenfield, 1988). It would not be until Karl Lashley's work on equipotentiality and mass action in the mid-20th century that any serious challenge to this conclusion would be presented (see Beach, Hebb, Morgan, & Nissen, 1960, for review).

Early Theories of Intelligence

Theories of intelligence which evolved around the turn of the nineteenth century were generally derived from early physiological models of brain structure. Investigators theorized about the nature of intelligence from two perspectives: psychometric and physiological. Three major theories of intelligence emerged: intelligence as a single higher order construct, intelligence as a holistic property of the brain, and intelligence as an aggregate or series of interconnections between mental processes.

The first major theory to be discussed is based on the concept of intelligence as a single higher order construct. Foremost among these intelligence theorists was a psychologist named Binet. He postulated that the essential feature of intelligence was judgment (Halstead, 1947). Binet not only considered judgment a separate entity, but believed that it governed the use of specific abilities. Binet developed a set of psychometric tests based on his notions of intelligence which, in modified form, is still used today for the basis of predicting intelligence.

Based on theories supporting both the 'localization of function' and intelligence as a "higher order construct," a group of researchers in the late nineteenth and early twentieth centuries attempted to localize intelligence (Halstead, 1947). Data collected from studies of brain-injured soldiers in World War I suggested to Kleist that the convex lateral surface of the frontal lobes were the seat of intelligence. Although Kleist localized intelligence in the frontal lobes, he argued that it was an aggregate of localized processes. Hitzig defined intelligence as abstract thought and localized it in the frontal lobes. His studies were based largely on work with animals and impressionist ideas concerning the nature of intelligence. Bianchi, in summarizing his work on dogs, foxes, and monkeys, maintained that the frontal lobe was the "organ of intellect." Franz used cats and monkeys to investigate loss of learning through lesion experiments. Although Franz never used the term *intelligence,* he stated that all previously learned associations seemed to be lost when connections to the frontal lobe were severed.

In his concluding comments, Halstead argues that biological intelligence represents adaptive behavior and, although not strictly localized, is primarily located in the frontal lobes.

A second major psychometric theory of intelligence to emerge in the early nineteenth century characterized intelligence as a holistic property of the entire brain (Spearman, 1904). This psychological theory of intelligence was consistent with the earlier physiological work of Flourens concerning the structure of the intellect (Halstead, 1947). Spearman's holistic theory was based on factor analytic studies of highly complex, dissimilar tests. Through his studies, Spearman was able to demonstrate that a single factor accounted for most of the variance in mental tests. Spearman termed the general factor 'g' and argued that it represented a mental "'power' or 'energy' which serves in common the whole cortex (or possibly even the whole nervous system)" (Spearman, 1927, p. 5). However, Spearman's theory also provided for the role of specific factors, which he tied to the functioning of neural groups. Although 'g' played a central part in Spearman's theory of intelligence, he believed this common source of mental energy was alternately distributed among specific neural groups.

Several comparative studies supported the holistic view of intelligence. Goltz, working at the end of the nineteenth century, was the first to note that the size of the brain lesion in dogs was directly related to the severity of the resulting dementia (Halstead, 1947). Physiologists such as Ferrier and Loeb, investigating the effects of brain lesions in dogs and monkeys during the same period, came to similar conclusions. Lashley's (1929) work also supported the holistic theory of intelligence. Through his studies of maze learning in rats, Lashley concluded that intelligence was a general capacity. He believed that learning was based on the absolute quantity of cortical tissue. Lashley aligned himself with theories of intelligence such as Spearman's which held that intelligence was a general factor determining the efficiency of the entire brain (Halstead, 1947).

An intermediate position between the localization and holistic positions was presented by a physiologist named Munk in 1890 (Halstead, 1947). Munk proposed an aggregate theory in which he hypothesized that intelligence was based on the discrete rather than continuous distribution of sensory processes. He postulated that sensory fields were interconnected and that their aggregate functioning gave rise to intelligence. Munk's theory, like physiologists' arguing for intelligence as a completely distributed property of the brain, was based on data which suggested that larger lesions produced larger deficits in animal learning. Due to the lack of physiological sophistication at the time, distinction between the two arguments was primarily theoretical. In later studies of animal learning, Thorndike came to similar conclusions to those of Munk (Halstead, 1947). Thorndike (1921) argued that intelligence was based on the interconnections which were formed between mental processes.

In the psychometric domain, Thurstone proposed a factor analytic theory of intelligence which was similar to the comparative models proposed by Munk and

Thorndike (Halstead, 1947). Thurstone (1931) hypothesized that intelligence was a general capacity to form bonds or connections among ideas. A Scottish psychologist, Thomson (1939), also hypothesized that intelligence was a series of interconnections in the brain. According to this "sampling" theory, performance on mental tasks requires the sampling of a wide variety of mental operations. Thomson proposed that the correlation between two tasks was a function of the number of overlapping bonds. The primary difference between these two theories was the number of hypothesized mental processes. Thomson proposed that mental processing reflected an infinite number of bonds; Thurstone proposed seven primary mental abilities.

Summary

Early physiological models of biological function included localization of function, holistic processing, and aggregate models (Changeux, 1985). The first major theories of intelligence mirrored these early physiological models of brain structure. Current research on the biological correlates of intelligence can also be traced to early physiological models of brain structure. Gross anatomical and bioelectrical studies of the brain have been guided by the early physiological debate of localization of function versus holistic mental processing. Both neurological and neural network frameworks were derived from the basic holistic and connectionist ideas initially proposed by Flourens and Hughlings-Jackson. Although holistic ideas of completely distributed processes were rejected on the gross anatomical level in the late 1800s, they continued to be debated on the neuronal level through the 1950s (Changeux, 1985). Biochemical studies of intelligence may help to provide construct validity to both neurological and bioelectrical measures by providing alternate information on neural processes important to intelligence. This construct validity is crucial to the eventual identification of biological substrates important to individual differences in intelligence.

INTELLIGENCE AND GROSS ANATOMICAL FEATURES OF THE BRAIN

Our review of research on the relationship between gross anatomical features of the brain and intelligence is limited to studies which use general psychometric measures to assess intelligence. Major gross anatomical measures reviewed include brain-tissue volume loss, location of lesion, volume asymmetry, and head circumference. Human studies in gross anatomical research have relied primarily on brain damaged individuals but have recently begun to include normal adults and children.

Background

Gross anatomical research has been guided, in large part, by early questions concerning localization of function versus mass action. Theories based on the formal location of mental functions date back to the early nineteenth century and the work of Franz Gall in phrenology (Changeux, 1985). Since that time, studies in gross anatomical research have attempted to localize areas in the brain which contribute to specific mental functions. Two of the most noted contributions supporting localization of mental processes were Paul Broca's 1861 discovery of a language center in the brain, and the subsequent related discovery by Carl Wernicke (Rosenfield, 1988).

Gall and Broca also studied the relationship between brain size and intelligence. Although both were strong advocates of localization in terms of specific mental functions, they argued that intelligence was correlated with total brain size (Jerison, 1982). Flourens, Goltz, Ferrier, and Munk (Halstead, 1947) supported theories based on the relationship between brain-tissue volume loss and intelligence. Theories which emphasized the importance of brain-tissue volume loss included both holistic and aggregate models of mental processing.

Adult Studies

The first major work related to brain-tissue volume loss was done by Teuber and his colleagues in the 1950s. They examined the effects of specific brain injuries on the intelligence of World War II and Korean War veterans. The research was based on preinjury intelligence test scores gathered at the time of enlistment and compared to postinjury intelligence measures. In summarizing their work, Weinstein and Teuber (1957) concluded that long-term effects of penetrating brain wounds on intelligence were small. Although some evidence was found suggesting that damage to the left parietotemporal cortex decreased general intelligence, the authors argued that results may have been due to the nature of the test. The parietotemporal area of the brain is believed to be responsible for the analysis and synthesis of auditory input (Luria, 1966). Damage to this area may have interfered with the subjects' ability to understand the test rather than general cognitive ability.

Grafman, Salazar, Weingartner, Vance, and Amin (1986) reached conclusions similar to those of Weinstein and Teuber. The authors examined the effects of site of damage and brain-tissue loss volume on intelligence in 182 Vietnam War veterans. Subjects were divided into those with both right ($n = 98$) and left ($n = 84$) hemisphere damage. Mean preinjury intelligence scores on the Armed Forces Qualification Test (AFQT) were at the 55th and 52nd percentile ($\bar{X} = 50$); postinjury Wechsler Adult Intelligence Scales-Revised (WAIS-R) Full-Scale scores were 103 and 99 ($\bar{X} = 100$) for the right and left hemisphere groups, respectively. These intelligence scores suggest that the injuries produced little to no effect on general intelligence. Preinjury intelligence and education predicted postinjury intelligence better than brain-tissue loss volume and location of the lesion.

In a more recent study Grafman et al. (1988) extended the findings of their previous paper by better defining the effects of brain-tissue volume loss and location of lesion. They reported that, while preinjury intelligence remained the best predictor of postinjury IQ, brain-tissue volume loss accounted for a significant portion of the variance after controlling for preinjury scores. Location of the lesion was not related to pre/post differences in IQ but was related to scores on certain tests of specific cognitive abilities.

Studies reported by Teuber, Grafman, and their colleagues are particularly important because they employ both preinjury and postinjury intelligence measures. Most of the findings supporting the notion that brain damage causes a decrease in levels of intelligence rely on studies comparing brain injured subjects to each other or to uninjured controls. These less powerful designs are often necessitated because of the difficulties in obtaining reliable preinjury intelligence scores.

A study by Salazar et al. (1986) examined the effects of injury to the basal forebrain on general intelligence and other cognitive measures. They compared a group of subjects with injuries to the basal forebrain with a group of uninjured controls. While statistically significant differences between the groups were found on measures of memory, reasoning, and arithmetic, the measures of general intelligence did not significantly differ between the two groups.

Milner and Petrides (1984) reviewed studies of patients with damage to the frontal lobes. The studies reviewed supported previous research indicating that brain damage affected some specific abilities (verbal fluency, faulty regulation of behavior, impaired organization, etc.). Despite specific deficits, subjects in these studies had intelligence scores in the normal range. Findings from the Milner and Petrides review are in agreement with other studies investigating the effects of frontal lobe damage on general intelligence (e.g., Stuss et al., 1983). Since preinjury scores were not available, interpretation of these results is problematic, however. *Normal* covers a wide range of intelligence scores. A significant loss in IQ could occur and still be in the normal range.

A number of studies have focused on subjects with damage to the temporal lobes. Most of these studies have looked at differences between Verbal and Performance scores on the WAIS-R. In general, studies found that groups of brain damaged and nondamaged subjects can be discriminated using this difference score (Sundet, 1986; Herring & Reitan, 1986; Bornstein & Matarazzo, 1984; Bornstein, 1984; Inglis & Lawson, 1982). While the findings in these studies consistently reveal a greater discrepancy score in brain damaged men than nondamaged men, the findings are less consistent with women. Larrabee and Haley (1986) use their own results and review others to question the validity of using the discrepancy score to discriminate subjects with unilateral brain damage from those without. The authors conclude that, although the discrepancy scores may reflect the effects of unilateral brain damage, they are not reliable predictors.

Larger than normal discrepancy scores have more recently been reported in certain patients without brain damage. Yeo, Turkheimer, Raz, and Bigler (1987) found that the degree of hemisphere volume asymmetry correlated (.45) with the difference between scores on the Verbal and Performance scales of the WAIS-R. This finding seems consistent with the previously reviewed findings of brain damaged patients. Damage to a hemisphere appears to alter and probably increase the functional volume asymmetry of the brain. While Yeo et al. (1987) found a relationship between asymmetry and the discrepancy score, they found no relationship between total brain or hemisphere volumes and intelligence. Results are in agreement with the conclusions of Stott (1983), who reviewed the literature on brain size and intelligence and found little evidence for a relationship between the two.

Developmental Patterns

McCall, Meyers, Hartman, and Roche (1983) looked for a relationship between gross anatomical measures and intelligence from a developmental perspective. They tracked the growth of the brain and cognitive development on 80 subjects from the age of 2.5 to 17. They found evidence indicating that both the physical growth of the brain and cognitive development occur in spurts. However, they found no evidence for a relationship between growth of head circumference and cognitive development.

The effects of brain damage in childhood appear to be far more equivocal than those in adulthood. Vygotsky (Luria, 1965) has cautioned that similar symptoms in children and adults can result from very different types of damage and identical types of damage can result in very different symptoms. Thus it appears that the localization of specific cognitive abilities across the developmental spectrum is very fluid. Data supporting the complexity of developmental studies have recently been reviewed by Hartlage (1985). Related methodological problems concerning localization of specific cognitive processes in children have been discussed by Bolter and Long (1985).

Despite the persistence of the idea that brain damage earlier in childhood results in smaller long-term intellectual deficits than damage later in childhood, evidence appears to be to the contrary (Chelune & Edwards, 1981; Klonoff & Low, 1974; Levin, Benton, & Grossman, 1982). Consistent with these findings are those of a more recent study by Riva and Cazzaniga (1986), where damage prior to 1 year of age was related to more global intellectual deficits, while damage after 1 year of age was not. This finding is not limited to infancy. Brink, Garrett, Hale, Woo-Sam, and Nickel (1970) found that damage prior to age 10 resulted in greater intellectual damage than damage after 10 years of age.

Another belief persisting in the neuropsychology literature is that the IQ subtest discrepancy relationship to brain damage in adults also applies in children. However, a recent study by Aram and Ekelman (1986) found no evidence to support that generalization.

There are many contradictory findings concerning the relationship between intelligence and brain damage in children. Studies have reported a relationship between general brain damage and intelligence deficits (Aram, Ekelman, Rose, & Whitaker, 1985), intellectual deficits with right hemisphere damage only (Aram & Ekelman, 1986), deficits only in scores on the Performance Scales (Winogran, Knights, & Bawden, 1983), intelligence deficits in proportion to the size of the damaged area regardless of location (Levine, Huttenlocher, Banich, & Duda, 1987), and deficits in general intelligence which return to a level equivalent to controls within a 5-year period (Klonoff, Low, & Clark, 1977). Contradictory findings such as these led Rourke, Bakker, Fisk, and Strang (1983) to suggest that one of the primary objectives of future research should be to identify subtypes of damage and subtypes of children along a developmental perspective. Rourke believes that such identification may improve our understanding of the relationship between intelligence and the brain in childhood.

Summary

Early brain damage studies of adults seemed to indicate that brain-tissue volume loss and intelligence were unrelated (Weinstein & Teuber, 1957; Grafman et al., 1986). More recent studies, however, which employed more sophisticated measurement techniques indicated that brain volume loss accounted for a significant proportion of the variance in IQ after effects of preinjury scores had been removed (Grafman et al., 1988). It seems that brain-tissue volume has a small but consistent effect on general intelligence. The Grafman et al. study (1988) suggests that brain-tissue volume loss is important in predicting outcome measures of intelligence, but site of lesion is not an important predictor. Location of function was consistently related to specific cognitive deficits but not to measures of general intelligence. Since pre- and posttest measures of intelligence were not reported in most of these studies, it is difficult to evaluate the null findings.

Results based on the relationship between brain-tissue volume, normal adults, and children show no relationship between brain-tissue measures and intelligence. Localized brain damage, on the other hand, although not associated with a decrease in general intelligence, has been associated with deficits in specific cognitive abilities (Salazar et al., 1986; Telzrow, 1985). Results from developmental studies are equivocal, probably due to the plasticity and complexity of the developing brain.

The pursuit of a relationship between the brain and intelligence through gross anatomical studies of the brain seems problematic. Research studies investigating gross anatomical features of the brain and general intelligence rely primarily on the measurement of brain-tissue volume loss in brain damaged patients. Generalizations between studies of brain damaged individuals and general brain measures in undamaged persons must be cautioned against. As Hughlings-Jackson cautioned in 1874, localization of function is not the same as localization of damage which impairs function (Sergent, 1984). Another problem with studies of gross anatomical features has to do with the level of measurement. Ambiguous findings between intelligence and gross anatomical measures may, in part, be attributed to the global measures used in these studies. Allen (1983) has suggested that questions of cognitive function are better addressed through the more sophisticated study of neural substrates.

NEURONAL STRUCTURES AND INDIVIDUAL DIFFERENCES IN INTELLIGENCE

Neurological studies investigating the biological correlates of intelligence are concerned with how individual differences in basic cognitive abilities are related to variability in cortical cellular structures. Changes in these neuronal structures have been investigated through animal research, human studies, and neural networks. Animal research has demonstrated that differential experience can systematically alter neuronal structures. These changes have been related to differences in learning ability. Although much of the work examining neuronal structures has been done with animals, human studies support similar findings. Differences in human neuronal structures have shown a relationship to low and normal levels of intelligence. The study of neural networks is a recently developed technical area based on computer architectures of neural substrates (McClelland, Rumelhart, & Hinton, 1986). Neural network models have been used to simulate the neural basis of higher-order cognitive processes.

Background

Just as Broca's views of localized mental processing were gaining ground on the holistic position of mental processing, the holistic versus localization of function controversy erupted on another level (see Changeux, 1985, for review). Fueled by Flourens's views of holistic neurological function, a debate concerning the continuity of the nerve developed. This debate began around 1870 and did not end until after 1950 with the discovery of the electron microscope. One group, supported by Golgi's discoveries related to the dendritic network, argued that the cortex was composed of a continuous 'nerve net,' and supported the concept of neurological function as a unitary action of the cerebral cortex. The other group, based primarily on Ramon y Cajal's work related to Purkinje cells, argued that nerves were discrete processing units.

Hughlings-Jackson argued that neurological function was not a unitary process but was based on the complexity of the mental process itself (Changeux, 1985). Cajal's work was the first to lend credibility to Hughlings-Jackson's modified localization or aggregate position. Lashley (1929) argued for completely distributed representations of single concepts. Although Lashley's initial work supported the unitary ideas of Flourens, he later modified his position to concede some localization and came more in line with the position held by Hughlings-Jackson (Miller, 1980). In 1949, D. O. Hebb, in his landmark publication *The Organization of Behavior,* put forward "a general theory of behavior that attempts to bridge the gap between neurophysiology and psychology" (Hebb, 1949, p. vii). In this new theory of neuropsychology, Hebb proposed that intelligence was determined by the complexity and plasticity of the central nervous system. Learning was based on changes in cell assemblies. Similar work was pursued in Russia by Vygotsky and, later, Luria (1966). These prominent neuropsychologists were the first to systematically reexamine the basic concepts of localization in terms of "function" in human mental activity.

Neuronal Structures

Neurons are made up of four distinct structures: dendrites, axons, the cell body, and the terminal button (Carlson, 1986). Dendrites are short branch-like structures that extend from the cell body of each neuron. There are usually many dendrites for each cell. The function of the dendrite is to receive signals from other neurons.

Each neuron normally has one axon, a long slender structure that transmits a signal away from its cell body to the dendrites of other neurons. Some axons are insulated by a fatty sheath called myelin. Myelin allows for the transmission of a purer signal by preventing interference from surrounding neural activity. Myelinated axons conduct electrical signals very much faster than nonmyelinated axons. Myelin is only found in vertebrates and is considered essential to higher nervous function, permitting "precise integration of information from widely separated regions" (Shepherd, 1988, p. 63).

The signal from the axon of the transmitting neuron synapses with the dendrites of other neurons at the terminal button. In the brain, these neural synaptic signals are chemical and can either excite or inhibit the firing of a cell.

Environmental Influences on Neuronal Structures

There is a large body of experimental animal literature which has demonstrated that environmental stimulation can alter the development of neuronal structures and the accessibility of existing pathways in the brain (Ferchmin, Bennett, & Rosenzweig, 1975; Harwerth, Smith, Duncan, Crawford, & von Noorden, 1986; Hubel & Wiesel, 1970). Rats raised in an isolated, impoverished environment have fewer and less distributed dendritic structures, reduced brain weight, and thinner cortices. More importantly, animals raised in impoverished environments learn maze patterns slower than rats raised in a social, stimulating environment (Chang & Greenough, 1978; Rosenzweig & Bennett, 1972, 1977). Increased synaptic activity resulting from gaining experience in complex environments has been maintained in rats (Camel, Withers, & Greenough, 1986), although effects may be more enduring for some areas of the brain than in others (Green & Greenough, 1986).

Environmental stimulation in animals has been observed to have the most influential on neuronal structures during critical periods early in development (Ferchmin et al., 1975; Harwerth et al., 1986; Hubel & Wiesel, 1970). Environmental effects are not limited to these critical periods, but continue to shape neuronal structures and their effectiveness throughout the adult animal's life (Green, Greenough, & Schlumpf, 1983; Greenough, McDonald, Parnisari, & Camel, 1986; Merzenich & Kaas, 1982). In generalizing these effects to humans, Easter, Purves, Rakic, and Spitzer (1985) state that the "prolonged synaptic malleability generated by these long-term competitive interactions may be the basis of the extraordinary ability of the human nervous system to adapt to an ever-changing external environment" (p. 510).

Thompson, Berger, and Madden (1983) have pointed out that changes observed in the neuronal structures of lower animals appear to be specific consequences of different environmental activities. For example, maze learning in rats causes dendritic branching changes at the apex of pyramidal cells, whereas an enriched environment alone produces dendritic changes on the high order branches of the basal dendrites. Thompson et al. argue that some changes may be related specifically to "'learning to learn' rather than learning a specific relationship between stimuli" (p. 471).

Overproduction of Neurons

Overproduction of cortical neurons occurs early in development in both humans and animals (Huttenlocher, 1979; Purpura, 1975). Subsequent to such overproduction is a pruning of many neurons and dendrites. This pruning is apparently facilitated by behaviorally related neural activity. The overproduction of neurons and dendrites has been demonstrated by comparing the number of neurons and dendrites across age groups in both humans and Rhesus monkeys (Huttenlocher, 1979; Purpura, 1975; Rakic, Bourgeois, Eckenhoff, Zecevic, & Goldman-Rakic, 1986). The comparison revealed that there are fewer neurons and dendrites in later developmental periods, compared to the maximum number found in early pre- and postnatal developmental periods. In their work with Rhesus monkeys, Rakic and his colleagues observed that the period of greatest overproduction coincided with the expression of functional behavioral landmarks for the cortical areas investigated, although competence in these behaviors increased beyond the period of overproduction. This suggested to Rakic et al. that maturation is related to synapse elimination and increased efficiency in the remaining pathways.

Phases of maximal dendritic development observed in laboratory animals have also been found in the cerebral cortex of the human fetus, with maximal development taking place about 1 year of age (Huttenlocher, 1979, 1984; Huttenlocher, deCourten, Garey, & Van der Loos, 1982). Purpura (1975) proposed that maximal development of dendrites takes place at "different times for different cortical neuronal organizations" (p. 113). Evidence from studies by Becker, Armstrong, Chan, and Wood (1984) and Huttenlocher et al. (1982) both support Purpura's ideas of differential dendritic development as a function of both the layer and area of the human cerebral cortex. Purpura has also pointed out that the periods of maximal dendritic growth are "susceptible to many perturbations that place the human infant at risk" (p. 114). Although the nature of those perturbations was not delineated, it seems possible that differential development of maximal dendritic growth may allow environmental insults to cause damage only to the particular processes undergoing development at the time of insult, while sparing those that develop at other times.

Speculating about the functional value of these synaptic changes, Huttenlocher (1984) suggested that the changes provide plasticity in the developing brain such that alternate structures could assume the functions of a structure that is rendered nonfunctional. As an example of plasticity in neuronal structures, Huttenlocher described the ability to correct amblyopia. Amblyopia is an eye muscle disorder in which one eye becomes dominant, rendering the underutilized eye functionally blind. Correction is made by requiring the sole use of the less functional eye until it is equivalent in strength to the dominant eye. There are temporal limits in the degree of plasticity, however. Huttenlocher observed that permanent damage to vision occurs to infants deprived of normal visual experience during the period of rapid synapse production to 8 months. Such permanent visual damage has been documented in infants with cataracts that are not removed before 6 months, whereas removal of cataracts at earlier ages along with sufficient visual stimulation results in a much better outcome for visual processes. Finally Huttenlocher pointed out that, whenever differential environments were implicated in differential outcomes for children with intellectual impairment, the greatest effects on outcome were usually observed during very early periods in development. Huttenlocher suggests that, despite the flaws in some of this research, at least part of those differential effects from environmental factors may be attributable to the greater neuronal plasticity that exists during those early developmental periods.

Dendritic Structures in the Mentally Retarded

Although causal relationships have not been established, some children with mental retardation, both with and without abnormal karyotypes, have been found to have dendritic abnormalities in the cortex. Examination of neural patterns in mentally retarded individuals has revealed fewer and less densely distributed dendrites, along with thin or absent dendritic spines, compared to those found in normal age-matched fetuses or children (Marin-Padilla, 1974). Unusual dendritic spine loss, and abnormally long thin dendritic spines, have been reported in retarded children with both normal (e.g., Purpura, 1974) and abnormal karyotypes characteristic of Down syndrome (e.g., Takashima, Ieshima, Nakamura, & Becker, 1989). Other studies of mentally retarded children have found no other dendritic abnormalities except those involving dendritic development (e.g., Huttenlocher, 1974).

In the adult mentally retarded, Huttenlocher (1974) found little or no evidence of those cortical abnormalities previously observed by himself and others in young retarded children. It was, however, pointed out that methods used to examine dendritic growth in this study were not sophisticated enough to detect abnormal dendritic development in cases where it had progressed beyond the level of a 1-year-old. Nonetheless, the failure to find dendritic abnormalities in older mentally retarded persons suggested to Huttenlocher that the abnormal neural patterns detected in mentally retarded children may represent a lag or arrest in development.

Myelination of Axons

Like the maximal development of dendritic structures, the myelination of axons is associated with specific periods during development. Unlike dendritic structures, however, once myelin is formed it is not easily affected (Manocha, 1972).

The late prenatal and early postnatal periods of maximal myelin formation have been proposed by Davison and Dobbing (1966) as a period of potential vulnerability for the human infant. The authors argued that malnutrition and others forms of environmental stress could interfere with the deposition of myelin during critical periods. It was argued that this interference could cause permanent intellectual deficits. There is an extensive body of animal research which establishes that malnutrition during critical periods substantially reduces the amount of myelin that is deposited. This research has been reviewed by Wiggins

(1982), who argues that there is little question that "the human infant is vulnerable in the same sense as laboratory animals" (p. 167).

The relationship, however, between reduced myelin formation and intellectual deficits is far from understood. Nonetheless, there is some evidence consistent with the notion that inadequate deposition of myelin is involved in the retardation of intellectual growth. Wiggins (1982) noted that nerve conduction velocities were decreased in children who suffered from diseases related to malnutrition in infancy, such as marasmus and kwashiorkor. This finding is consistent with a reduction in myelin deposits. Others have shown that children who suffered from marasmus or kwashiorkor early in life but later obtained improved nutrition did not attain the level of performance of controls on tests of intelligence (Eichenwald & Fry, 1969). More evidence is needed, however, before it can be determined that it is reduced myelin formation related to malnutrition that is specifically accountable for intellectual deficits.

Certain diseases or disorders related to myelin formation are also associated with reduced mental capacity. Phenylketonuria (PKU) is such an example. PKU is an inherited disease where infants are clinically indistinguishable from normal infants at birth except for excessive levels of phenylalanine in the blood. Without intervention, intelligence as well as motor control steadily deteriorates through the first year of life, resulting in severe mental retardation (Schaumburg & Raine, 1977). Autopsies of untreated PKU patients have shown their brains to be about two-thirds normal size, without gross cellular defects except for a marked reduction in myelination (Mange & Mange, 1980). In 1953, it was established that the disorder was related to failure to produce an enzyme needed to metabolize an amino acid. By manipulating the diet, the destructive aspects of the disorder can be reduced or prevented. In cases where dietary intervention took place only after the disease had become apparent, intelligence did not return to normal. However, PKU children who have early dietary intervention that continues until about age 6 develop normal or near normal intelligence. Discontinuation of the special diet by age 6 produces no adverse affects on intelligence despite the return of high levels of phenylalanine (Schaumburg & Raine, 1977). The period of greatest vulnerability to the damaging effects of untreated PKU is between 3 months and 3 years (Mange & Mange, 1980). Normally, formation of myelin in humans takes place during that same period (Breakefield & Cambi, 1987). Thus, the greatest amount of myelination takes place in humans over roughly the same developmental period that PKU carries its potential to cause permanent deficits in intelligence.

Neural Networks

While neurologists and physiological psychologists have been exploring the neural basis of cognitive deficiencies, other cognitive neuroscientists have been developing "neurally inspired" computational architectures. These mathematical models are designed to identify the elusive mechanisms of human intelligence. *Connectionism, neural networks,* and *parallel distributed processing* (PDP) are synonymous terms for neural models of computation. The basic principle of neural networks is that, through employing an architecture of highly interconnected processing units feeding input into each other, the computational properties are similar to those of the human brain. Many cognitive tasks which are very difficult to explain using standard models of information processing emerge as elegant by-products of the neural networks architecture. Some attributes of connectionist models relate to specific findings regarding the biological basis of intellectual function. Three particular topics will be addressed: dendritic sprouting and pruning, myelination, and mass action versus localization of function.

An interesting developmental feature of neuronal structure in humans is the rapid expansion of dendrites in the first year of life, followed by the pruning of unnecessary connections throughout later development. This tract is analogous to a network which begins with complete connectivity, and then modifies its weights until optimally differentiated patterns of activation are formed (Hopfield, 1982). Hopfield, though not relating his research to these data, points out that, to achieve optimal efficiency, a network with complete connectivity is desirable. A further development to this modeling scheme is the use of unlearning as a means of enhancing network efficiency (Hopfield, Feinstein, & Palmer, 1983).

Myelin is modeled in a neural network as a source of capacitance for each neuron. Capacitance is the ability to store charge. As yet no work has directly investigated the relationship between the presence of capacitance in a neural model and network efficiency. It would appear, however, that a presence of capacitance would allow an activation pattern to be stored temporarily until weights can be adjusted accordingly.

The mass action versus localization of function discrepancy raises some interesting questions about the nature of distribution in neural networks processing. Two questions emerge: First, how do neural networks achieve localized function? Second, how do connectionist models account for data from lesion studies which find gross anatomical differences related to differences in mental processing.

Although many connectionist models assume units which are processing at a single level, with completely distributed processing, models are free to impose constraints on processing. These constraints generally take the form of a hierarchical organization to the network (Minsky & Papert, 1969; McClelland, 1979). Hierarchies may function in top-down, bottom-up, or interactive manners (Rumelhart, Hinton, & McClelland, 1986). By imposing a hierarchical organization, one decreases the efficiency of the network but permits the execution of more complex, modular, tasks. In this sense, one might account for localized process, and provide a framework for the information-processing paradigm.

Evidence for mass action is derived from Lashley's work, which found a positive correlation between lesion size and behavioral deficit in the cortex of a rat (Lashley, 1929). Equipotentiality is partly derived from the finding that subtotal lesions of a given size will usually produce effects of the same or similar magnitude. Simulated lesion experiments suggest that even a relatively simple model, such as that proposed by Anderson and his colleagues (Anderson, Silverstein, Ritz, & Jones, 1977), can provide similar findings to those which led Lashley to propose mass action and equipotentiality, or, alternately, to results consistent with localization of function (Wood, 1978). Wood (1978, 1980) cautions that these findings implicate the difficulties in making inferences of neural organization from real lesion experiments. Dean (1980) has argued that the concepts of mass action and localization of function are not necessarily opposed. The potential involvement of several regions of the brain in a complex task and fewer regions in a simple task is an advantage, not disadvantage, of neural networks which demonstrates the consistency between concepts of mass action and localization of function (Dean, 1980).

When attempting to generalize the neural network paradigm to the biological structure of intelligence, one must be very careful. Any model proposed must be a reasonable approximation of its biological counterpart. To insure falsification, proposed models should make some predictions currently unknown to already existent models, and thus be testable. Any model born of human subject data should be tested on a new sample to reject or support its predictions. Unfortunately, most current models of neural networks lack this experimental rigor. But the understanding of the human brain requires more than a new computational architecture for implementing normative psychological processes. A search for the biological basis of intelligence calls for approaches which can elucidate individual differences in special abilities. Future research should aim to develop testable models which lend themselves to explanations of individual differences. Ultimately, the role of neural networks in facilitating our understanding of intelligence is predicated on the development of biologically viable modeling strategies.

Summary

The study of neuronal structures in the brain has revealed that important differences related to intelligence exist at very basic cortical levels. Studies have increased our understanding of the functional significance of neuronal structures, their interactions, their development, and how they bear on individual differences in human intelligence. Differences in dendritic structures have been related to environmental stimulation and learning in animals. Animal studies suggest that faster learning is associated with more complex dendritic structures. Alteration of dendritic structures is achieved most easily during early developmental periods, but alteration remains possible into adulthood. Differences in the dendritic structures of humans are consistent with the animal literature; that is, higher intelligence is correlated with fewer but more complex dendritic structures. The evidence from human studies relating variation in axonal myelination to individual differences in intelligence, though suggestive, is less compelling than the evidence regarding dendritic structures. Whether the difference observed in neuronal structures reflect a causal role in the biological basis of intelligence or simply effects related to differences in other processes is not clear.

Although important changes in neuronal structures have been associated with both development and learning, generalization of these results to the dynamic mental processing of normal, living human beings needs to be cautioned. Data have been gathered primarily from animal or clinical studies of diseased individuals through static measures such as neurosurgery or brain imaging. The application of recent noninvasive brain imaging techniques such as magnetic resonance imaging (MRI) to the study of cortical neural structures has the potential to provide extensive information about individual differences in the structure of the normal human brain. But brain imaging studies are still limited to structural information.

Dynamic neurological mechanisms have been studied through the use of mathematical modeling. These computational models are based on principles of neuronal learning and are designed to stimulate actual neural processes. Possible links between identified differences in neuronal structures and functional differences in simulated computational models have been proposed. But generalization between computational models and actual human cognition is equivocal. Computational models are not substitutes for actual mental processes, nor do they replace their true biological counterparts (Carello, Turvey, Kugler, & Shaw, 1984). For example, current models of neural networks limit themselves to accounting for psychological processes which have little variability across individuals. A more integrated framework for neural networks which employs some of the constraints of serial processing may provide a biological framework of understanding of individual differences in human intelligence.

BIOELECTRICAL MEASURES OF MENTAL PROCESSING

Neuronal processes are electrical in nature (see Andreassi, 1980, for details). One of the first noninvasive methods of studying the biological mechanisms of mental processes was to record electrical signals from the surface of the skull. The original objective of electrocortical measurement was to obtain a direct measure of mental processing (Gale & Edwards, 1983). There are at least two related methods of studying these bioelectrical signals. The first, called *electroencephalogram* (EEG), is a recording of all electrical activity from the surface of the skull. The second method, *event related potentials* (ERP), is a recording of electrical activity from the skull synchronized with the presentation of a stimulus. These electrical signals have been hypothesized to represent both speed and structural differences in underlying neural substrates (e.g., Chalke & Ertl, 1965; Giannitrapani, 1985).

Background

Reviews of the research concerned with EEG, ERP, and individual differences have been conducted by Andreassi (1980) and Gale and Edwards (1983, 1986). The most thorough review of research specifically concerned with intelligence and EEG was presented by Vogel and Broverman (1964). Though the Vogel and Broverman review appeared before much of the work on ERPs, it has become a classic because it highlights many of the methodological problems in the area.

The earliest investigators in this area hypothesized that cognitive functions could be detected through electrocortical potentials. After many years of effort on the hypothesis, however, the question of a relationship between electrocortical potentials and intelligence is still controversial (Gale & Edwards, 1983, 1986).

ELECTROENCEPHALOGRAM (EEG)

The "brain wave" or EEG was first identified in rabbits in 1875, but it was not until almost 50 years later that Berger began his work on the brain waves of humans (Andreassi, 1980). EEG studies are concerned with the measurement of underlying neuronal structures. The last decade has seen a revival of interest in studies investigating the relationship between EEG and intelligence. Giannitrapani (1969, 1985) and others (Gasser, Von Lucadon-Muller, Verleger, & Bucher, 1983; Corning, Steffy, Anderson, & Bowers, 1986) have begun to emphasize the importance of structural correlates in the identification of individual differences in intelligence.

Method of Analysis

EEG studies are based on the measurement of wave forms identified by elements of frequency, amplitude, and regularity (see Andreassi, 1980, for further details). At least seven basic wave forms have been identified and labeled with Greek letters. Each wave form is correlated with a type of mental activity (e.g., alpha waves appear during relaxation and are characterized by regularity, frequencies between 8 to 13 Hz, and high amplitude). Electrode placement is described by a system which uses a letter and a number (Jasper, 1958). The letter specifies the area of the cortex over which the electrode is placed (e.g., T—temporal, F—frontal). A subscript of z designates the midline; subscripted numbers indicate the position from the midline. At least two electrodes must be placed on the scalp for recording. One is a reference electrode, and the other is placed at a standard recording location, as described above.

Reliability

Giannitrapani (1985) tested the reliability of EEG recordings which varied in sample length, dominant hemisphere, and behavioral state of the subject. Subjects were 12 male right-handed students. The 8-second samples had an average reliability of .3, while 32-second samples had an average reliability of over .6. Giannitrapani found EEG measures on the left side of brain were more reliable and proposed that it might have something to do with the issue of brain dominance. Changes in reliabilities were also calculated as a function of increase or decrease between the baseline resting condition and six stimulus conditions. The greatest decrease in reliability was found for listening to music, while the greatest increase in reliability occurred while listening to a story.

O'Gorman and Lloyd (1985) tested the consistency of individual differences when measured by EEG. They tried to discover if the rank order of individuals in terms of some EEG measure would vary across different experimental conditions or repeated measurements. The experimental conditions they employed were: (a) resting, (b) attentive listening, and (c) mental arithmetic. The results showed some moderate inconsistency of EEG measures across sessions, and some major inconsistency across different conditions. The person-by-session interaction and person-by-condition interaction contributed 20% and 69%, respectively, to the total variance. The authors discussed the dependence of person-by-condition interaction on the range of variation in persons and conditions. If one is restricted, the other must account for more variance. They suggested it was important to either explain individual differences with reference to specific conditions or sample a variety of conditions and average measures in order to increase reliability.

Relationship Between EEG and IQ

The most thorough work on the relationship between EEG and intelligence has been done by Giannitrapani (1969, 1985). In a recent study, Giannitrapani (1985) sampled 100 normal children aged 11–13 years. The Wechsler Intelligence Scale for Children (WISC) was the primary IQ measure used. EEG tracings were recorded simultaneously from 16 scalp areas, with spectral determination from 0 to 34 Hz in 17 bands, each 2 Hz wide for each scalp area. Intelligence measures were correlated with all frequency bands of all the scalp areas. Giannitrapani also factor analyzed the WISC, and correlated factor scores with EEG scores.

Frequency components in the 9-to-23-Hz range were reliably associated with cortical functions (Giannitrapani, 1985). Significant correlations were found between EEG and both Full-Scale and subtest performance. Correlations were related to location in some instances, with significant Full-Scale, Performance, and Verbal patterns associated with activity in the central, temporal, and parietal areas. Most of these correlations were above .36 ($p < 0.001$). Significant subtest patterns were primarily associated with bioelectrical activity in the pre- and mid-frontal areas and posttemporal areas.

Giannitrapani (1985) also found that, among all the frequency bands studied, the 13-Hz activity, particularly that in the central area, seemed to be pivotal as a correlate of cognitive ability. By correlating factors extracted from WISC subtests with EEG frequencies, Giannitrapani showed that 13-Hz activity dominated the relationship with general intelligence. In the central area, the correlations between 13-Hz activity and both verbal and performance factors were all greater than 0.48 ($p < 0.0001$).

Giannitrapani identified two sets of components in each frequency band: one positively related to mental activity, the other negatively related to age. This finding made Giannitrapani think that these two sets of components were distinct and contributed separately and orthogonally to the total variance.

Gasser and his colleages (Gasser et al., 1983) have recently proposed that resting EEGs (9 to 13 Hz) should be highly related to both IQ and cognitive developmental differences in children. His study compared 25 mentally retarded subjects to a normal control group. He hypothesized that: (a) relationships would be higher in the mentally retarded, and (b) the frequency distribution of EEG activity would be more important than the topographic distribution. Results supported Gasser's hypotheses. Gasser's work is consistent with Giannitrapani's emphasis on frequency as an important predictor of individual differences in electrocortical measurement.

Corning et al. (1986) recently investigated the relationship between development and EEG. Two groups of subjects were tested twice within a 1–2 year interval. One group had been identified as developmentally delayed using EEG profiles; the other group had normal developmental profiles. Results showed a high correlation between developmental change in EEG profiles and intelligence in the developmentally delayed group. In other words, those who had matured faster tended to score higher on IQ tests. A relationship between IQ and developmental change of EEG was not identified in the normal group.

Summary

The relationship between the EEG and intellectual capacity has long been a controversial issue. Earlier studies appeared to show some positive relationship between the EEG and intelligence for children, MR persons, geriatric patients, and brain-damaged patients. Recent research has focused more on the frequency analysis of the EEG. The frequency index of EEG, particularly in some resting conditions, has been shown to consistently relate to IQ measures.

Although correlations exist between IQ and EEG, the question of what those correlations represent is unresolved. The interpretation of these findings in terms of mental processes is unclear. Emphasis in electrocortical measurement has been to "reveal the phenotype that reflects the genotype" (Gale & Edwards, 1983, p. 81). Much of the research relating EEG and intelligence is based on the assumption that intelligence is a unitary, genetically transmitted trait. Assumptions that these methods are free from environmental influences and thus more 'pure' measurements of mental processing are unfounded (Gale & Edwards, 1986). The function of neuronal structures and subsequent electrical impulses have been shown to be influenced by both pre- and postnatal environmental influences. The notion of intelligence as a unitary trait is also the subject of much current debate (e.g., Detterman, 1987; Eysenck, 1986; Jensen, 1982). Methodological advances are needed in the area of EEG which incorporate current theoretical models of intelligence into a testable framework.

EVENT RELATED POTENTIALS

Event related potentials (ERP) or *averaged evoked potentials* (AEP) were recorded from the brain as early as 1939 (Callaway, 1975). The first comprehensive recordings of average evoked responses were conducted by Adrian (1941). Extensive work on humans awaited the use of computers capable of performing rapid data acquisition and averaging. Until recently, ERPs could be collected by only a few highly specialized laboratories.

ERPs are similar to electroencephalographic (EEG) recordings from the scalp. Unlike EEG recording, ERP recording is coordinated with some stimulus event and has been primarily used for measurement of processing speed or efficiency. ERPs have been associated with a variety of cognitive functions. Early research concerning ERP has been generally reviewed by Beck (1975).

Methods of Analysis

Electrodes are placed on the scalp according to the standard topographical procedure described above (Jasper, 1958). An additional electrode is generally used to measure eye movements or ocular artifacts. These signals from ocular artifacts are termed *electro-oculograms* (EOG). As in EEG recording, at least two electrodes must be placed on the scalp. A stimulus is presented, and the electrical activity on the surface of the scalp is recorded.

A recording from any single point on the scalp contains the brain's reaction to the stimulus as well as numerous other signals from brain activity unrelated to the stimulus. These unrelated signals from the brain are noise and should be uncorrelated with stimulus onset over trials. To filter out the noise, repeated trials are recorded and averaged. Recordings of background EEG noise and EOG are generally removed from single-trial ERPs before averaging. The average signal which emerges reflects the brain's reaction to the stimulus indpendent of spurious external events (see Coles, Gratton, Kramer, & Miller, 1986, for details). ERPs can be divided into two parts. Early components occur within about the first 100 msec after stimulus presentation, while late components occur after that.

Early components. Early components can be divided into two parts. The first are called *far field components* and occur within about 10 msec of stimulus presentation and are small (< 1 microvolt). These components are called far field because they are generated at locations relatively far from the recording electrode. The origin and function of these waves is well understood. They are used in neurological diagnosis (see Callaway, 1975, for details). The second portion of the early components are called the *primary cortical evoked responses*. These components occur between 22 and 100 msec after stimulus presentation and are of larger amplitude (1–10 microvolts). They are sometimes called *near field potentials,* since small changes in electrode placement can produce substantial changes in results which suggests that recording is from locations near to the electrode. However, the exact location and function of these components is debatable.

Late Components. The source and function of late components is highly debatable. Where a particular component actually arises in the brain cannot be determined by simply recording from electrodes on the surface of the skull. Not only is there uncertainty about the origin of these electrical potentials, but there is substantial debate about their psychological meaning. Nonetheless, there are a number of identifiable waves which occur reliably at approximately the same time after stimulus presentation. Within a particular subject, these wave forms are reliable, but across subjects they are variable. Of course, if there was no variability across subjects, there would be no potential for a using ERPs to account for intelligence. According to Callaway (1975), waves between 100 and 200 msec may reflect simple attention. A positive potential at 200 msec reflects the perception of visual form. Perhaps most important for the present purposes, a positive peak at about 300 msec (P300) may be related to attention and uncertainty.

Reliability

Internal consistency. Nearly all investigators analyze their data for internal consistency. Sometimes odd and even trials are compared and other times data collection is divided into two separate sessions which can then be compared. Latency and amplitude measures are consistently found to be moderately to highly reliable (e.g., Sklare & Lynn, 1984).

Stability over time. A more demanding test of reliability is the extent to which ERP measures remain constant over time. A number of studies have been conducted which assess just this question. As an example, Lewis (1984) studied ERPs in a group of young adult males given a second test after a few hours' delay, and a group of older subjects tested a second time after a 2-month delay. Even though Lewis did not use the typical latency and amplitude measures, results were typical of those found by others. The exact form of the ERPs varied substantially from subject to subject, but the wave form of a particular subject was moderately to highly reliable over sessions, even sessions 2 months apart. The degree of reliability was a function of stimulus modality. Least reliable was auditory stimulation, with visual stimulation being somewhat better. Bimodal stimulation was most reliable. Reliability also varied by recording site.

Heritability. Related to questions of reliability is the degree to which ERPs can be considered a heritable characteristic. Osborne (1970) found that the mean correlation of 30 ordinates of the ERP function between monozygotic twins was .77, and for dizygotic twins was .53. This finding would suggest a moderate degree of heritability.

ERPs and Intelligence

There are three ways in which the relationship between ERPs and intelligence has been studied. The first work involved correlating ERP measures of latency and amplitude with psychometric intelligence. Later investigators looked at different and more sophisticated measures. A second line of research has been the comparison of groups of mentally retarded or otherwise mentally deficient groups with normal control groups with the hope of discovering differences between these groups. Finally, the third, and perhaps most promising, line of research has attempted to investigate the relationship between individual difference in ERPs and individual differences in basic cognitive tasks. Each of these lines of research will be considered in order.

ERPs and IQ

The first and most widely publicized work was done by Ertl and his colleagues (Chalke & Ertl, 1965; Ertl, 1971; Ertl & Schafer, 1969). In these studies, the ERP was recorded, and the latency of the P300 was measured and then correlated with a standard IQ measure. These studies, and many others like them, found correlations between P300 latency and IQ which ranged from about $-.3$ to $-.9$, although some investigators found no relationship whatever (e.g., Rust, 1975).

These early studies were often criticized for small numbers of subjects, failure to attend to appropriate sampling strategies, and methodology that failed to control for potential artifacts. Shucard and Horn (1972, 1973) replicated Ertl's earlier work with a more representative sample, using a wider variety of measures and under three conditions. They also gave a much larger battery of psychometric tests in an effort to determine if ERPs were more closely related to crystallized (learned) or fluid (biological) intelligence.

The results indicated that correlations between ERP measures and psychometric intelligence ranged from about −.05 to −.32, with most of the correlations around −.15 (Longer ERP latency is associated with lower IQ producing a negative correlation.) The correlation actually got higher as testing progressed to less attention-demanding conditions, leading Shucard and Horn to conclude that high IQ subjects were able to better self-regulate alertness, thereby increasing the correlation between ERPs and IQ. Like other investigators, Shucard and Horn found that the correlations between ERP and IQ were reduced when age was partialled out.

From the studies that have been conducted it seems reasonable to conclude that there is at least a small to moderate relationship between ERPs and IQ. However, the failures to replicate suggest that there are, as yet, uncontrolled and poorly understood variables which may affect the relationship. That there may be uncontrolled variables is not surprising, given that identification of components is, at best, difficult, and that methods of measuring these components are not standardized. Further, few investigators have regarded this as more than an interesting empirical relationship deserving of further study, and so theories guiding the effort have been minimal.

More recent work concerning the relationship of ERPs and IQ have looked at more sophisticated measures than simple latency and more sophisticated levels of analyses. For example, Perry, McCoy, Cunningham, Falgout, and Street (1976) attempted to use ERP composite measures derived from factor analysis to predict IQ using multiple regression. They found multiple correlations of about .38 between IQ and ERP measures in a sample of 5-year-olds which had a substantially restricted range. A similar study by Crawford (1974) found a smaller canonical correlation when a large data set obtained from Ertl was analyzed. However, Crawford's study included far fewer measures of the ERP than did the Perry et al. study, and so it is not surprising that it accounted for less variance.

In most of the previous research, investigators have found correlations between IQ and latency of the ERPs. Few correlations have been found between measures of amplitude and IQ. More sophisticated analysis of amplitude measures, however, has shown such correlations. Flinn, Kirsch, and Flinn (1977) performed Fourier analysis on ERP data collected from 64 12-year-old girls whose IQs ranged from below 80 to over 130. Fourier analysis decomposes a complex periodic function into an additive series of sinusoidal waves varying in amplitude for each wave frequency. Correlations between maximum amplitude in specified bandwidths and IQ ranged from −.38 to .41. Low frequencies (< 24 Hz) showed negative correlations and high frequencies positive correlations.

They also found that low IQ subjects had larger low frequency (< 12 Hz) amplitudes than high IQ subjects, and that high IQ subjects had larger high (> 30 Hz) amplitudes than low IQ subjects. Correlations of the low frequency amplitudes with IQ seemed to be caused only by the low IQ subjects, whereas the correlations of high frequency amplitudes seemed to be caused by the full range of IQ. Contrary to Shucard and Horn, high frequency amplitudes showed decreasing correlations with IQ over four sessions.

The study by Flinn et al. is particularly interesting because it suggests that low IQ subjects show a different pattern of ERP amplitudes than high IQ subjects, at least for a portion of the frequency spectrum. It also suggests that the relationship between ERPs and IQ will be more complex than a simple linear relationship between IQ and ERP latency.

The Hendricksons (Blinkhorn & Hendrickson, 1982; D. E. Hendrickson, 1982; Hendrickson & Hendrickson, 1980) noted that the ERP records of high IQ subjects seemed to show more components. That is, high IQ subjects had more complex wave patterns than low IQ subjects. To avoid the problem of classifying components, they used a measure which captured the complexity of the wave. This measure was the linear distance of the ERP recording for a fixed period of time. They called this the *string measure,* because it could be obtained by laying a string along the plotted ERP wave form. Correlations between IQ and the string measure ranged up to about .8.

Shagass, Roemer, and Straumanis (1981) failed to replicate the Hendricksons's results but used a small number of subjects. Haier, Robinson, Braden, and Williams (1984) noted that the complexity of the ERP wave form was a function of stimulus intensity. They measured ERPs under three levels of stimulus intensity. The findings supported their original hypothesis: They obtained a maximum correlation of .69 between the string measure and IQ for intermediate levels of stimulus intensity. The author suggest that this relationship largely results from the amplitude of the wave form between N140 and P200. They further suggest that differences in ERPs reflect 'strength of central activation,' which may be an important determinant of intelligence. Robinson, Haier, Braden, and Krengel (1984) replicated the study of Haier et al. with a smaller number of subjects and obtained similar results. Federico (1984a,b) has also replicated the kinds of relationships reported by the investigators just mentioned, though the purpose of his research was to investigate hemispheric asymmetries.

ERPS in the Mentally Retarded

A number of studies have found differences in ERPs between intellectually normal and mentally retarded or otherwise mentally disabled populations. As would be expected from research cited earlier, the mentally retarded have longer latencies (Gliddon, Busk, & Galbraith, 1975) and different amplitude patterns (Callner, Dustman, Madsen, Schenkenberg, & Beck, 1978). Even more interesting is the finding that Down syndrome (DS) subjects show larger amplitude ERP's than other mentally retarded persons and than persons of normal intelligence (Gliddon, Busk, & Galbraith, 1975; Gliddon, Galbraith, & Busk, 1975). In addition, DS persons have been shown to have a lower amplitude of short-latency auditory brainstem responses (early far-field components) when compared to mentally retarded persons of unknown etiology. Such findings as these offer promise of differentiating categories of mentally retarded persons and suggesting mechanisms of intellectual deficit.

ERPs and Basic Cognitive Tasks

Several studies have simultaneously investigated the relationship among basic cognitive tasks, ERPs, and IQ. As an example, Jensen, Schaefer, and Crinella (1981) recorded ERPs, IQ, and reaction time latencies. The ERP measure was neural adaptability. *Neural adaptability* is a measure of the amplitude difference between expected and unexpected stimulus events in the ERP wave. Neural adaptability was correlated .31 with general intelligence. In combination with reaction time measures, neural adaptability had a multiple correlation with general intelligence of .64.

A study by Naylor, Halliday, and Callaway (1985) investigated the interaction between target detection difficulty and response difficulty under various doses of methylphenidate, a stimulant. They showed that the P300 latency was increased by stimulus complexity but was unaffected by methylphenidate and response difficulty. The authors argue that this demonstrates the independence of stimulus decision and response factors in reaction time. This was certainly an elegant experiment deserving replication and extension. In fact, using ERPs to come to a better understanding of the processes operating in basic cognitive tasks may be one of the major applications of ERP technology in the future.

Summary

Amplitude and latency measures, as well as more complex composite measures (like the string measure) have been found to correlate with standard measures of IQ. The correlations obtained range from −.15 to −.80, depending on the measure and the particular experimental conditions. Statistically significant effects have been obtained sufficiently often to conclude that ERPs are correlated with IQ.

In retrospect, it is not surprising that such a relationship can be confirmed, because whatever differences can be shown behaviorally must be reflected in the brain. The important question now is why this relationship exists. Several investigators, particularly the Hendricksons, have presented testable theories of the ERP–IQ relationship. All of the theories suggest some form of neural efficiency as the basis for intelligence as reflected in ERPs.

Regardless of the correctness of these theories, ERPs offer the potential for providing information about the operation of the brain in intact, thinking human subjects. Unfortunately, it may not be possible to determine exactly what this information means, because the source of ERPs cannot be localized to a particular part of the brain. Further, recording ERPs is fraught with methodological problems which have only been touched on here. Basic problems discussed in relationship to EEG recordings concerning intelligence as a unitary, genetically transmitted trait also apply here (see summary under EEG). All of this taken together suggests ERPs will be a source of substantial controversy but may provide insights about the nature of human intelligence in the future.

NEUROMETRICS

One ambitious attempt to relate EEG and ERP to intellectual functions is John's (1977) development of neurometrics. John chose the term *neurometrics* to indicate a tool for the evaluation of neurocognitive function. As John advocated, "the goals of neurometrics are to gather accurate data sensitive to this variety of brain functions [anatomical integrity, developmental maturation, and mediation of sensory, perceptual, and cognitive processes]; to extract and quantify critical features of these datum, and to classify the resulting profiles into clusters sharing common features of these brain functions by using statistical analysis and numerical taxonomy" (John et al., 1977, p. 1393).

The idea of neurometrics was based on the assumptions that the EEG and ERP potentials contain accessible, diagnostically valuable information, and that clusters of individuals with similar electrocortical profiles could be identified. Based on electrocortical data associated with neuropathological analysis and cognitive capacity, John constructed a neurometric test battery (NB) which consisted of 20 'challenges' or conditions. The battery included various measures of habituation and dishabituation which used both auditory and visual stimuli. Auditory measurements were taken with eyes open and eyes closed. Recordings were both spontaneous and evoked.

The first step of the neurometric procedure was to obtain baseline data on all or part of the items from normal newborn infants, elementary school children, and elderly adults. Means and standard deviations were computed for each index in each group. All indices were converted to a common metric (Z score). Each individual was then evaluated with reference to normal group mean. Thus, weighted summations of the Z scores provided the quantitative and objective criterion for the severity of brain dysfunctions. It would also provide the basis for an objective diagnostic classification scheme when the orientation of the summed Z score was considered. Some methods of numerical taxonomy (e.g., factor analysis, cluster analysis, stepwise factor analysis, and multidimensional scaling) were also used in classification of individuals in terms of their shared features of brain dysfunctions. These methods played an important part in the neurometric procedure. For instance, stepwise factor analysis was applied to the detection of neurological disease, and discriminant analysis was applied to the identification of cognitively impaired patients. Numerical taxonomy of the neurometric indices was also found effective in discrimination between normal and learning-disabled children, particularly in reflecting processes more intimately related to brain function.

Summary

John energetically emphasized the significance of neurometric methods as effective criteria in the diagnosis of a wide variety of diseases and dysfunction, including neurological disease, senile deterioration, learning diability, psychosis, mental retardation, drug addiction, and malnutrition. Neurometrics may have enormous potential for identifying individual differences in cognitive functioning. The efficacy of these methods, however, has been questioned (Giannitrapani, 1985; Gasser et al., 1983). Others have praised John's comprehensive effort to bring theory to the field of electrocortical recordings (Gale & Edwards, 1986).

BIOCHEMICAL CORRELATES OF INTELLIGENCE

The following section presents an overview of biochemical processes which have been linked to intellectual functioning. Biochemical processes in the living organism are important for metabolism. Metabolism has two major components, the synthesis of complex molecules necessary for major life processes, and the breakdown of substances to gain energy. The breakdown of glucose through oxidative processes is the primary source of energy production in the brain. The relationship between intelligence and both major metabolic components has been investigated. The synthesis of complex molecules important for synaptic transmission, such as neurotransmitters and neuropeptides, has been measured through chemical concentration and drug treatment studies. Oxygen and glucose utilization have most recently been measured through radioactive isotope tracer studies of cerebral blood flow and glucose metabolism. Calcium is a crucial element in the regulation of important biochemical feedback processes in the central nervous system (CNS). The relationship between calcium concentration and intelligence is also discussed. Biochemical research on normal healthy individuals is not generally available. Studies reviewed in this section focus on aberrations in individuals with general cognitive deficits such as dementia and Down syndrome (DS).

Background

Although neurotransmitters were identified in the peripheral nervous system in 1904, many physiologists in this period actively resisted the use of biochemistry to investigate human mental processing (Changeux, 1985). Since that time, a large and growing body of literature has accumulated on the biochemical processes of the brain. This literature is based largely on two breakthroughs made in the mid-1900s. The first was the use of radioactive isotopes of chemical elements to trace the pathway of substances in the animal body in 1935; the second was the discovery of neurotransmitters in the brain in 1949.

Neurotransmitters and Neuropeptides

The activation and function of neural cortical substrates depend on chemical synapses between neurons (Hartlage, 1985). These chemical synapses use neurotransmitters and neuropeptides, which are highly localized in specific populations of neurons. Neurotransmitters are chemical substances released from the sending neuron's axons. These chemical substances activate receptors resulting in the excitation or inhibition of the postsynaptic neuron (Guyton, 1987; Shepherd, 1988). Hebb (1980) proposed that the ratio of excitation to inhibition synapses is directly related to the efficiency of the human brain. Neuropeptides are neuromodulators which are found in the synaptic region with neurotransmitters. The exact nature of their role is unknown, but these bioregulators most likely influence the growth and activity of dendritic structures.

Although several neurotransmitters and neuropeptides have been identified as important to human cognition, most studies have been based on disease or drug treatment models. The possibility of a relationship between neurotransmitters and individual differences in intelligence is just beginning to be investigated. Studies cited have focused on the neurotransmitters serotonin and acetylcholine, and on a series of neuropeptides from the pituitary which most likely regulate growth and synaptic change. The exact relationship between neural chemical processes and cognitive functioning, however, is not clear.

Chemical concentration studies. Concentration studies measure the presence of a particular chemical in the brain by calculating its concentration level from body fluid samples. The earliest studies investigated the concentration of serotonin in the urine excretion of DS individuals (McCoy & Enns, 1986). Later studies used blood serum or cerebral spinal fluid samples.

The earliest biochemical studies emphasized the role of serotonin in general cognitive disorders such as Down syndrome (McCoy & Enns, 1986). Recent serotonin studies have focused on blood platelet concentrations. According to McCoy and Enns, platelets are unique, because they are nonneuronal cells which transport and store neurotransmitter amines, primarily serotonin. The concentration levels of serotonin in blood platelets has been related to the uptake and storage rate of serotonin in the serotonergic neurons of the CNS. The classification group identified with serotonin receptors has been localized in multiple brain areas with high density in the frontal lobe of the brain. Studies have suggested that decreased calcium may be a factor in the decreased serotonin in the platelets. In reviewing studies of serotonin, McCoy and Enns point out that investigators have failed to find similar deficits associated with serotonin in other conditions of mental retardation, however. Findings suggest that low concentrations of serotonin may be specific to DS. It is not clear whether low concentrations are related to the cognitive deficit found in DS or to other deficits associated with the syndrome.

Studies have also investigated the relationship between general cognitive deficits such as Alzheimer's and Down syndrome and the cholinergic neurotransmitter system (Cummings, 1986). Cholinergic neurons release acetylcholine and provide widespread innervation of the cerebral cortex and related structures. They appear to play an important role in cognitive functions, especially memory and general cognitive decline associated dementia and Alzheimer's disease (AD; e.g., Davis et al., 1985; Maire & Wurtman, 1984; McKinney & Richelson, 1984; Coyle, Price, & DeLong, 1983; Fine, 1986). Deficits in the cholinergic system have also been identified in DS individuals. Yates and his colleagues (Yates, Simpson, Gordon, Maloney, Allison, Ritchie, & Urquhart, 1983) reported decreased activity of choline acetyltransferase and acetylcholinesterase. These enzymes are responsible for the inhibition and transfer in the synapse. Investigators have suggested that the relationship between DS and deficits in cholinergic enzymes may be correlated with general age-related changes rather than changes specific to intellectual decline (McCoy & Enns, 1986).

Concentration reductions of the neuropeptide somatostatin have been associated with cognitive impairment in depression, schizophrenia, and dementia and AD (Bissette et al., 1986; Folstein, Robinson, Folstein, & McHugh, 1985; Tamminga, Foster, Fedio, Bird, & Chase, 1987). The degree of reduction in somatostatin levels has been correlated with intellectual impairment as compared to controls (e.g., Bissette et al., 1986) and decline in cortical glucose utilization as determined by PET (e.g., Tamminga et al., 1987). Corticotropin-releasing factor is reduced in several brain areas of AD patients (Fine, 1986). Somatostatin and corticotropin-releasing factor have been primarily associated with the pituitary and growth hormones.

Drug treatment studies. Drug treatment studies measure behavioral outcome to known or hypothesized biochemical reactions and have indirectly implicated specific neurotransmitter systems. Drug treatments have long been known to affect various aspects of cognitive functioning (Wolkowitz, Tinklenberg, & Weingartner, 1985). Effects have typically been described with respect to memory, arousal, attention, and sensory thresholds, and vary with the particular drug. The mechanism for a drug's effects on cognition may be through its action on neurotransmitter systems in the brain. For example, drug treatment studies have supported the importance of the cholinergic system. Similar subtest profiles on the WAIS have been observed in normal subjects with drug-induced cholinergic deficiency and in patients with AD (Fuld, 1984). Cholinergic agents have also been used as pharmacological treatment in AD to restore deficient levels of the neurotransmitter acetylcholine (Dysken, 1987). Subsequent improvements in performance were observed.

Treatment with vasopressin and related neuropeptides from the pituitary has led to inconsistent results. While several studies have shown improvements in learning, memory, attention, and concentration (e.g., Brambilla et al., 1986; Kragh-Sorensen, Olsen, Lund, & Van-Riezen, 1986; Van-Ree, Higman, Jolles, & deWied, 1985), other studies have shown no effects (e.g., Hommer, Pickar, Crawley, Weingartner, & Paul, 1985; Sahgal, Wright, & Ferrier, 1986) or selective effects. Till and Beckwith (1985) concluded that individual difference factors are important to the understanding of drug effects.

Another important set of neuropeptides produced by the pituitary are melanocortins. Melanocortins have been seen to improve adaptational abilities, i.e., neural plasticity, of the nervous system. Age-related brain diseases may be correlated with loss of neural plasticity. Decrease of melanocortins in the system may have a role here (Gispen, Isaacson, Spruijt, & deWied, 1986). They have also been shown to have a selective cognitive influence in learning in rats (Handelmann, O'Donohue, Forrester, & Cook, 1983). Administration increased the rate of learning of visual tasks but had no effect on the rate of learning of auditory tasks.

Treatment research in the area of depression also shows drug effects on intelligence tests. In tricyclic antidepressant-induced remission of depression, significant increases have been seen in WISC Performance IQ's (average 16-point increase) and the WISC Similarities, Coding (Digit Symbol), Block Design, and Object Assembly subtests (average 3- to 4-point increases; Brumback, Staton, & Wilson, 1980, 1984a,b; Staton, Wilson, & Brumback, 1981; Brumback & Staton, 1982a,b, 1983).

Other studies have shown decreased cognitive functioning associated with drugs thought to interfere with neurotransmitter actions (e.g., Grob & Coyle, 1986; Murray, 1984; Weddington, 1982). Among these, the tranquilizers Valium and Librium are associated with serotonin, an excitatory neurotransmitter.

The fact that drugs can alter areas of cognitive functioning in an individual supports the idea of a biochemical aspect to or influence on intelligence. Improvement in cognitive functions as a result of increased levels of a deficient neurotransmitter seems to add support for the idea that drugs affect cognition via neurotransmitter mechanisms. Drug effects prompt a basic issue in the question of how biochemical processes relate to intelligence: Do deficits in neurotransmitters alter intelligence or do they alter the access to intelligence?

In conclusion, it seems that various neurochemicals have differential roles in cognition and intelligence, that these roles may be influenced by individual differences within people, and that depletion of some of these neurochemicals correlates with decreased levels of cognitive functioning. Research on subject groups without pathological conditions, such as Alzheimer's disease and Down syndrome, is especially needed. A disease has strong influence on many aspects of biochemical functioning. The influence on cognitive functioning needs to be isolated in order to determine the relationship between biochemistry and intelligence.

Oxygen and Glucose Utilization

Oxygen combines with glucose to produce energy. Oxygen utilization is measured through increased blood flow; the glucose utilization is determined by the rate at which it is metabolized. Increased cerebral blood flow and glucose metabolism are highly intercorrelated. Decreased cerebral activity due to dementia has long been associated with reduction in oxygen and glucose usage (e.g., Garfunkel, Baird, & Ziegler, 1954; Lassen, Munch, & Tottey, 1957).

Recent studies investigating the role of oxygen and glucose in cognition have used radio-labeled oxygen and glucose substrates in order to trace their pathways in the brain. Regional cerebral blood flow (rCBF) and glucose metabolism are calculated using baseline and difference comparisons of labeled substrate concentration in specific brain areas. Measurement is based on the uptake rate of the radioactive substrate which is mathematically converted to a measure of rCBF or metabolic rate. These measures in turn serve as an index of the functional activity of underlying neuronal structures.

Cerebral regional blood flow (rCBF). Oxygen is necessary for brain metabolism and the resulting production of neurotransmitters important in cognition. Blood flow increases in proportion to increased cognitive activity in order to carry oxygen to the area of the brain where it is needed. Cerebral blood flow is measured by injecting or inhaling xeon (^{133}Xe), a radio-labeled isotope of oxygen.

In traditional rCBF studies using ^{133}Xe inhalation or injection, measurement is recorded through a large number of surface detectors placed on the scalp. Researchers have recently criticized this rCBF technique, because it provides low resolution and little subcortical information (e.g., Haier et al., 1988). More recent measurement of cerebral blood flow has been conducted with the PET technique which provides higher resolution and detailed information about subcortical structures.

A recent review of rCBF studies utilizing the ^{133}Xe inhalation technique found specific regional changes in blood flow associated with dementia (Risberg, 1986). Individual differences related to blood flow within dementia have also been identified. For example, Johanson, Gustafson, and Risberg (1986) found that scores on the WAIS Block Design Subtest were similar for two groups of individuals with organic dementia. However, one group had decreases of cerebral blood flow in frontal regions, and the other had decreases in postcentral areas. The two groups differed on behaviors related to test performance, e.g., attempts at completion and rotations.

Using the ^{133}Xe inhalation technique, Brooks and his colleagues (Brooks et al., 1984) found significantly lower levels of cerebral oxygen utilization in multiple sclerosis patients with cerebral atrophy and/or in whom a significant fall in present Full-Scale IQ from estimated premorbid rates had occurred. Lower global cerebral blood flow rates have been observed in patient groups such as individuals with autism (Sherman, Nass, & Shapiro, 1984) and individuals with chronic head injury (Barclay, Zemcov, Reichert, & Blass, 1985), who typically have lower IQ scores.

Cerebral blood flow has also been associated with performance differences on cognitive tasks. For example, differential cerebral blood flow rates have been observed in recognition memory versus semantic classification tasks (Wood, Taylor, Penny, & Stump, 1980). Also, Gur and Reivich (1980) observed that, during performance of the Gestalt Completion Task, individual differences could be seen in the distribution of blood flow in both hemispheres, and that the amount of increase in blood flow in the right relative to the left hemisphere was correlated with performance on this task.

Glucose metabolism. Glucose metabolism is generally assessed using PET with ^{18}F-2-fluoro-2-deoxy-D-glucose (FDG-18) as the radioactive uptake tracer. In this procedure, the radio-tracer FDG-18 is injected intravenously. The radiotracer accumulates in the CNS cells in proportion to their glucose usage. The PET scanner can then map tracer concentrations throughout the brain. These concentrations are mathematically converted to metabolic rate, a measure of underlying neural activity.

Metabolic rate is generally measured while subjects are in a resting condition, eyes closed, and is subsequently correlated with some psychometric measure such as general intelligence. Resting brain metabolism of glucose was found to be reduced in AD patients (Haxby & Rapoport, 1986). Reduction was related to the severity of the dementia. Grady, Haxby, Schlageter, and Berg (1986) found that individual patterns of metabolic asymmetry in AD patients appear stable over time. Foster, Chase, Fedio, Patronas, Brooks, and Di Chiro (1983) found that Alzheimer patients with specific cognitive deficits had focal as well as general reduction in cerebral glucose metabolism. Chase, Fedio, Foster, Brooks, Di Chiro, and Mansi (1984) found significant correlations (all p's $< .01$) between Verbal ($r = .61$), Performance ($r = .56$), and Full-Scale WAIS IQ ($r = .68$) scores and overall cerebral glucose metabolic rates in a PET study of 17 right-handed Alzheimer's patients and 5 right-handed controls. Correlations were attributed to performance measures in the right-hemisphere and verbal measures in the left-hemisphere although inter-hemispheric correlations were not reported.

Memory loss was seen to precede reduction of brain metabolism in early Alzheimer's disease in a study by Cutler et al. (1985) which used PET to measure glucose metabolism. PET studies have also shown that metabolic reduction preceded nonmemory cognitive deficits in early Alzheimer's-type dementia (Haxby et al., 1986). Haxby and Rapoport (1985) found a relation between metabolic rate and neuropsychological deficits in patients with early AD but no relation between these measures in controls. They concluded that the relation in early AD may be caused by the underlying developing disease process.

Both hemispheric and many regional cerebral metabolic rates of glucose metabolism as measured by PET have been found to be higher in young DS individuals than in age-matched controls (Schwartz et al., 1983). Schwartz et al. (1983) did not find significant differences between the regional cerebral metabolic rate for a 51-year-old individual with DS and the mean values for middle-aged controls, however. In a study investigating the effects of both age and DS on absolute cerebral glucose metabolic rate and neuropsychological performance, Schapiro and his colleagues (Shapiro, Haxby, Grady, & Rapoport, 1986) found significant increases in glucose metabolic rate in young DS individuals as compared to young healthy controls, particularly in the parietal lobe regions. Significant age differences in metabolic rate were associated with DS but not the control group, with higher metabolic rates again found in young DS individuals. The authors also found that, although only some older individuals with DS were demented, significant age reductions in neuropsychologic variables occurred in all their subjects.

In a recent PET glucose study, Berent and his colleagues (1988) investigated the relationship between psychometric measures and cerebral metabolism in 15 patients with Huntington's disease (HD) and 14 normal volunteers. Glucose metabolism was measured in the caudate, putamen, and thalamus. Although no significant relationships were found between Full Scale WAIS-R IQ and metabolic rate, trends indicated a moderate positive relationship in the HD group (all r's $> .33$) and zero order to negative correlations in the normal group (all r's $< -.01$). Significant correlations were found between some specific cognitive tasks and metabolism in the HD group.

A recent study of glucose metabolism using PET has recorded metabolic rate while subjects were actively engaged in cognitive tasks (Haier et al., 1988). Haier and his colleagues used 30 normal right-handed men to investigate the relationship between glucose consumption in the brain and performance on three cognitive tasks. Haier and his colleagues found no significant correlations between relative metabolic rates for various brain regions and performance on the Raven's Advanced Progressive Matrices (APM). However, when comparing performance and brain absolute glucose metabolic rate, a negative correlation was found between performance on the APM and metabolic rate. In other words, higher performance was associated with less glucose consumption and lower metabolic rates. Findings suggest that subjects who achieved higher scores may have had more efficient brains. These findings are consistent with studies of young DS individuals which indicate an increase in glucose metabolism. Findings are also consistent with the neurological research of Rakic and others which suggests that subjects with higher IQs have more neuronal pruning with maturation and hence greater specificity in neural activation. Increases have not been found in older DS individuals or individuals suffering from Huntington's disease, however.

Rumsey (1985), in a PET glucose study of 18–36-year-old males with a history of infantile autism, found no diffuse or focal deficiencies in absolute resting cerebral metabolic rate of glucose in these subjects when compared with controls. Metabolic rates of glucose did not correlate with WAIS IQ in this study. These results are in contrast to the results which show deficient cerebral glucose utilization in patients with acquired lesions or diseases such as Alzheimer's. None of Rumsey's subject groups had a disease condition, such as is found in Alzheimer's. This points to the importance of understanding metabolic differences between healthy individuals and individuals with some type of disease before we can understand the relationship between metabolism and individual differences in intelligence.

Not all studies investigating relationships between glucose and cognition utilize PET scans. For example, Holmes, Koepke, and Thompson (1986) measured food intake in 24 male diabetics. Simple motor and perceptual skills were not affected by alterations in blood glucose levels, though more complex cognitive processing required significantly longer response latencies during this period of hypoglycemia. Short-term fasting (skipping breakfast) decreased subjects' late morning problem-solving performance under controlled metabolic conditions (Pollitt, Lewis, Garza, & Shulman, 1983). Observations suggest that the timing and nutrient composition of meals have an acute and demonstrable effect on behavior.

In conclusion, various clinical groups and individuals with differing cognitive strengths differ in oxygen and glucose consumption. Lower levels of oxygen correspond to lower performance on cognitive tasks. The relationship betwen glucose metabolism and cognition is not as clear. Studies have found an increase in resting glucose metabolism in young DS individuals but not in older DS individuals or individuals suffering from Huntington's disease. A recent PET glucose study conducted while normal individuals were actively engaged in cognitive tasks found an inverse relationship between glucose metabolism and intelligence (Haier et al., 1988). Glucose metabolism seems to depend on a complex interaction between developmental and cognitive parameters. Differences between healthy individuals and diseased individuals need to be further evaluated before we can understand the relationship between metabolism and individual differences in intelligence.

Calcium

The size and number of synapses have been identified as important to cognition, with larger and more numerous receptors corresponding to increased intellectual capacity (e.g., Plett, 1987). Plett gives the following overview of calcium's possible role. Learning may be a sequence of physiological events: (a) neural arousal causes an influx of calcium into the axon, (b) this causes the synaptic disk to become more curved and the dendritic spine to grow thicker, (c) this results in an increase in the overall size of the synapse, and (d) there is then a growth of new synapses and dendritic spines. This plasticity, or the ability to change the overall configuration of synapses and dendritic spines, is possibly critical in the learning process and, by extension, in the determination of level of intelligence.

Summary

Biochemical mechanisms are associated with processes that influence synaptic transmission and neural plasticity. Changes in both the structure and metabolic processes of these neural substrates have been associated with differences in general cognitive ability and learning. A knowledge base addressing the relationship between biochemical mechanisms and cognitive functioning is just beginning to be established. Biochemical studies of neurotransmitters have the potential to provide us with important insights on the nature of individual differences in cognitive processing at the synaptic level. Blood platelet studies have implicated the importance of serotonin in general cognitive functioning. Chemical concentration and drug treatment studies have also implicated the cholinergic neurotransmitter system and neuropeptides from the pituitary as important regulators of synaptic transmissions associated with cognitive processing. The role of calcium has also been implicated as important in synaptic change. However, an understanding of specific relationships between biochemical mechanisms and cognition is limited. Research investigating individual differences in intelligence and neurobiochemical processes is rare. Studies typically contrast clinical and control subject groups, and are aimed at understanding neurobiochemical processes as they relate to the various clinical conditions. Many reported results are effects of various treatment procedures. Correlations between biochemical aspects of brain functioning and general cognitive deficits such as Down syndrome and Alzheimer's disease are being seen, but generalizations of results from these clinical studies to individual differences in normal intellectual functioning must be cautioned. The selection process of clinical groups can produce spurious results with limited generalizability. The diseased brain can reflect many secondary symptoms not necessarily tied to cognitive ability.

Biochemical studies of metabolism and blood flow using isotope tracer studies may help to alleviate problems of reliability and validity in other areas of biological measurement, but these studies have their own set of problems. PET studies of glucose metabolism do not provide completely dynamic measurements of mental processing; blood flow studies which use scalp detectors provide more dynamic measurements of mental processing but have lower resolution and provide no information about subcortical structures. PET blood flow studies combine more dynamic measurement and high resolution. But PET studies are extremely expensive. The prohibitive cost has made it impossible to run large random samples of normal subjects. Studies are generally limited to small numbers of clinical or diseased individuals.

Mapping studies trace the paths and locations of specific neurotransmitters and neuropeptides. Cortical mapping studies may be unique in their ability to provide information about the relationship between inhibitory and excitatory neural synapses in the brain. But the human cognitive system is so complex that cortical mapping studies are in their infancy (Slaunwhite, 1988). There is no immediate danger that any biochemist in the area of brain chemistry will be unemployed in the near future. More basic research in cortical biochemistry is needed before specific influences on intelligence can be identified and understood. The identification of important neurobiochemical mechanisms will supplement our knowledge on the biological basis of intelligence from related areas such as neurology and bioelectrical measurement.

ENVIRONMENTAL ASSAULTS

The purpose of the present section is to summarize the current literature regarding the influence of certain environmental toxins on human intelligence. The effects of prenatal hormones, nutrition, alcohol, nicotine, lead, and mercury will be addressed specifically. Problems with research design and, therefore, interpretation of the data will be presented. Suggestions for future study are indicated.

Prenatal Sex Hormones and Intelligence

The influence of sex hormones on development in utero and on later cognitive skills has received some research attention. It is hypothesized that the differences in relative strengths of verbal and mathematical/spatial skills seen in males and females are due to the influence of sex hormones on brain development in utero. Systematic changes are seen for sex differences in brain morphology during prenatal development. A review by Kimura (1987) suggests that adult cognitive sex differences may partially be the result of these pre-natal sexual differences in brain organization at critical stages of development.

Ehrhardt, Meyer, and Heino (1979) looked at prenatal sex hormones in relation to intelligence and cognitive sex differences along with gender identity, gender role, and sexual orientation. They state that the data are inconclusive with regard to effects of sex hormones on sex differences in cognitive abilities and general intelligence. It seems logical that, if sex hormones cause prenatal differences in brain morphology, these differences could affect cognitive skills. More research needs to be done before sex hormones in utero and adult intelligence can be tied together causally.

Nutrition

The title of Kaplan's 1972 review, "Malnutrition and Deficiency," indicates that her summary of the literature argues for the negative impact of malnutrition on cognition. Further review of past literature, however, concludes that malnutrition, while a social concern, is not a cause of mental deficiency. Warren (1973) points out that the studies cited by Kaplan used either no control groups or inappropriate control groups.

Stein and Susser (1985) found that it is only in the periconception phase and the embryonic phase that dietary deficiencies affect later mental processes. These two phases encompass the time from 2 weeks prior to conception through the first trimester of pregnancy. The dietary deficiencies are specific. Iodine deficiency in the mother before conception is associated with cretinism. Uncontrolled insulin-dependent diabetes in the mother is associated with a higher risk of mental retardation. P. K. U. in pregnant women increases the risk for mental retardation in the infant. As suggested, these are very precisely defined dietary problems and not associated with a global level of malnutrition.

With regard to malnutrition, Stein and Susser found no negative effects on cognition. The issues of both acute starvation and chronic malnutrition were addressed in a reassessment of the data from the Dutch Famine Study (Stein & Susser, 1985) and in a study of the North American poor (Rush, Stein, & Susser, 1980). Neither study revealed any long-term effects of poor nutrition on cognition. Stein and Susser conclude that, except for the specific dietary problems discussed above, malnutrition, either chronic or acute, in the prenatal, fetal, or postnatal phases of life does not cause lasting depressed mental competence.

Alcohol

In the past 15 years, research has flourished in the area of maternal alcohol consumption and its effects on the fetus. Research was spurred by reports in the early 1970s describing a syndrome peculiar to offspring of alcoholic mothers (Jones, Smith, Ulleland, & Streissguth, 1973; Ulleland, Wennberg, Igo, & Smith, 1970). The syndrome is characterized by a specific malformation of the face and is associated with mental retardation. The syndrome has been well publicized and has been labeled *fetal alcohol syndrome* or FAS. Although the identification of FAS is responsible for encouraging additional research, the research is beset with difficulty, and we cannot ascribe the FAS outcome solely to the prenatal consumption of alcohol. The first major problem apparent in the research is that features described in FAS are found in the offspring of mothers with problems other than alcohol consumption. The second problem is a lack of sufficient controls in much of the research conducted to date (Zuckerman & Hingson, 1986).

Aside from the FAS syndrome, other outcomes associated with maternal alcohol consumption are intrauterine growth retardation and behavioral difficulties (e.g., attention deficit). Research indicating the effect of alcohol on these two outcomes suffers from the same insufficiently controlled research designs. One of the best controlled studies was done by Little, Mandell, and Schultz (1977). Even though variables such as maternal age, weight, parity, number of cigarettes smoked, gestational age, and sex of child were held constant in the Little study, potentially important variables such as maternal illness during pregnancy and maternal weight gain were not controlled for.

Maurer (1988) points out that another problem with studies of the effects of maternal alcohol consumption on the child's development is the difficulty in finding pregnant women who drink enough to fulfill the criteria. She states that the normal reaction to alcohol during pregnancy is nausea. Maurer further hypothesizes that, in a woman for whom this physiological change is not operating, it is possible that she is not normal physiologically, and that it may be this basic, underlying physiological difference, not the alcohol, which results in poorer outcomes for their babies.

Zuckerman and Hingson (1986) conclude in their review that very alcohol consumption (more than two drinks per day), or binge drinking, may be risky to the well being of the developing fetus. They also emphasize that it is the existence of multiple detrimental health habits which significantly increase risk, rather than abuse of any one particular substance.

Behavioral effects of prenatal alcohol consumption appear to be minimal. In short, although not clearly understood, research designs are complicated by the fact that genetic, as suggested by Maurer's hypothesis, and ongoing environmental effects may influence outcome measures. These influences make it difficult to determine whether specific amounts of maternal alcohol consumption during pregnancy are the sole cause of cognitive and/or behavior difficulties later in life.

Nicotine

There is no indication that smoking impairs long-term cognitive functioning. The relationship between mother's smoking and initial cognitive deficits in infants has only been indirectly investigated through low-birth-weight studies. Yerushalmy (1971, 1972), in a set of ingenious experiments, explored the complex role of parental nicotine use on fetal outcome. The first study found that, when looking at mortality rates of low-birth-weight babies, the highest mortality rates were for infants of nonsmoking mothers and smoking fathers. The second study found that women who didn't smoke when their baby was born, but began smoking after the birth of the baby, had the same rate of low-birth-weight infants as those who had smoked throughout the pregnancy. Similarly, women who smoked during pregnancy but stopped afterward didn't have an increased rate of low-birth-weight babies. Yerushalmy concludes that it is the smoker and not the smoking that affects infant birth weight, thus implicating genetic and/or psychological factors as important indicators of outcome.

Lead and Exposure

The effect of lead exposure on intelligence is yet another controversial domain of inquiry. The literature on the effects of lead exposure on intelligence is similar to the literature on prenatal alcohol consumption and its effects on intelligence. Severe lead exposure, just as severe alcohol exposure, can result in mental retardation, but the significance of asymptomatic lead exposure is unclear. The animal and human research seem to indicate subtle behavioral effects but no significant effects on intelligence (Holloway & Thor, 1987; Silva, Hughes, Williams, & Faed, 1988; Harvey, Hamlin, Kumar, & Morgan, 1988).

Many of the early studies suffered from major methodological difficulties, and results were often inconsistent. Gregory and Mohan (1977), in their review of nine studies, concluded that all were deficient and that no conclusions concerning intellectual consequences could be reached. Methodological problems most often cited include: use of cross-sectional designs, improper treatment of confounding variables, and inaccurate measurement of lead exposure (Ernhart, Morrow-Tlucak, Marler, & Wolf, 1987).

Although recent studies have employed more thoughtful and sophisticated designs, they have still failed to come to any agreement on the cognitive effects of lead exposure. Bellinger, Leviton, Waternaux, Needleman, and Rabinowitz (1987), in a prospective study of 249 children from birth, demonstrated that prenatal measures of blood lead level (PbB) predicts lower performance on the Bayley Mental Development Index (MDI). Across groupings of low, medium, and high prenatal PbB, a difference of almost 5 points on the Bayley was detected. Interestingly, Bellinger et al. found no evidence of a relationship between post natal PbB measures and cognitive development.

Baghurst, Robertson, McMichael, Vimpani, Wigg, and Roberts (1987) reported on a study they conducted in Port Pirie, Australia, where PbB levels were elevated due to industrial lead emissions. Baghurst et al. aimed to identify whether higher infant mortality in Port Pirie was related to lead levels in the environment. In their follow-up of 831 infants through childhood, they found equivocal evidence on the relationship between lead exposure and cognitive development. After controlling for relevant confounding factors, including HOME scores and maternal IQ, the Bayley MDI at 24 months was not significantly related to lead exposure. A noteworthy exception was observed during one-time sampling. Infants with high levels of PbB at 6 months scored significantly lower (10 points) on the Bayley at 24 months than those who had very low PbB levels.

Some researchers contend that there is no support for the link between lead exposure and IQ. Krall (1980) found no differences in WISC scores between 47 children treated for lead poisoning and their 45 sibling control group. Milar, Schroder, Mushak, Dolcourt, and Grant (1980) suggest intellectual deficits previously attributed to lead poisoning may actually be due to home environment.

Ernhart, Morrow-Tlucak, Wolf, Super, and Drotar (1989) conducted a study of lead exposure in the prenatal and early preschool periods of 242 children. They found no significant correlations between PbB level and WPPSI–IQ after controlling for appropriate confounding variables (maternal PPVT, HOME, etc.). It is noteworthy that this null finding presented itself at all time samplings of blood Pbb level (prenatal, 6 months, and preschool). Before controlling for confounds, all of the WPPSI–PbB measures were significant (except PbB at 6 months). After controlling for confounds WPPSI–PbB correlations were completely attenuated. In an earlier report, Ernhart and her colleagues (Ernhart et al., 1987) concluded that the relationship between lead exposure and measures of cognitive development were mostly dependent on the quality of the caretaking environment.

Research on the relationship between blood lead levels and later cognitive development is beset with methodological difficulties. If any relationship can be found, it seems to be present in early cognitive development of children exposed to high levels of lead prenatally, or in infancy. This would be harmonious with the foregoing review of research identifying the most active periods of brain development occurring during the first year of life (see section on neural structures). More conclusive results may be available once all of the prospective studies have analyzed data on intelligence later in childhood, when more reliable intelligence measures are available.

Summary

Studies indicate that risk research is multiply confounded. The best model currently available is one which incorporates risk as a multidimensional factor. No single factor is particularly culpable. It is extreme abuse of single agents or interactions among a variety of agents in conjunction with poor home environments (Sameroff & Chandler, 1975) which increases the likelihood of cognitive deficit.

The lack of convergent evidence between environmental assaults, other biological correlates, and intelligence points to the resilience and complexity of the developing human brain. Performance on intelligence tests is mediated by the environment, which either increases or decreases the effects of the biological correlates. The influence of any factor is a function of an individual's age, genetics, intrauterine events, birth-related events, and postnatal events.

GENERAL DISCUSSION

Measurement of the structure and function of the human brain has virtually exploded in the last few decades. Following a series of important discoveries in the mid-nineteen hundreds such as the identification of 'brain waves' in humans, the tracing of radio-labeled isotopes in the animal body, the isolation of neurotransmitters in the brain, and the discovery of the electron microscope (Changeux, 1985), studies of the brain have grown to include many diverse and highly sophisticated methodologies. Neuroscientists have made technological advances in the noninvasive study of neurological function through the use of electroencephalographic (EEG) recordings, event-related potentials (ERP), neurotransmitter mapping, and radio-tracer studies of regional cerebral blood flow (rCBF) and glucose metabolism. Mainstream neurology has developed neurosurgical techniques to analyze cell assemblies or "modules" that help establish a connection between cortical neural substrates and mental processes (Thompson, 1986).

Much of the early research on the brain characterized mental processing as either highly localized or completely distributed. But early theoretical arguments were in large part a product of the methodologies which were employed (Halstead, 1947). Most proponents of holistic processing, such as Flourens and Lashley, did their research on lower animals like birds and rats, while strong advocates of "localization of function," such as Broca and Franz, did their work on either brain-damaged humans or higher-order primates. Intermediate positions such as the one held by Hughlings-Jackson were lost in the heat of the early dichotomous debate, largely, since a technology did not exist which could distinguish between "completely" and "discretely" distributed processes (Halstead, 1947). It has only been in the last 40 years or so that technological advances have allowed neuroscientists to be beyond the old localization of function versus mass action debate. As late as 1950, the continuity of the nerve was still being debated. It was only through use of the electron microscope that the debate was finally resolved in favor of 'discretely' distributed processing (Changeux, 1985).

Beginning with neurological concepts of mental processing taken from Hebb (1949), Vygotsky (Luria, 1965), and Luria (1966), neuroscientists have been able to piece together new information on the dynamic structure of the human brain. Converging evidence has led investigators to propose that the brain is composed of a set of discretely distributed neural substrates whose function depends on the complexity of the mental process being investigated (e.g., Allen, 1983; Changeux, 1985).

In contrast, theories of individual differences in intelligence have remained amazingly stable over time. Three major psychological theories can be found in the early intelligence literature. These early psychological theories made different assumptions about the biological structure of intelligence. Assumptions were parallel to early physiological debates characterizing mental functioning as holistic, localized, or aggregates of mental processes. The similarity between early biological and psychological models is not surprising, since early psychology and physiology developed together, investigating theories of neurological function and sharing a common objective to develop a model of mental processing. Current theories of intelligence seem to mirror early psychological theories. Basic theories include: intelligence as a single propery of the brain (A. E. Hendrickson, 1982; Eysenck, 1986; Jensen, 1982), intelligence as a higher-order "executive" process (Sternberg, 1982), and intelligence as a set of orthogonal mental processes (Detterman, 1987), respectively.

Perhaps our lack of progress related to theories of intelligence can, in part, be attributed to the loss of a direct link between physiology and psychology. For a period, during the height of behaviorism, the brain and cognition were separated completely (LeDoux & Hirst, 1986). Studies of individual differences were limited to observable behavior within the context of the learning framework. Theories of intelligence were based on either psychometric data or animal learning studies, without much thought to 'cognitive processing.' The brain sciences also evolved without much mention and cognition.

With the advent of the cognitive revolution in the late 1950s, questions of "mental" processing once again became part of the legitimate domain of psychological study. But the ensuing cognitive revolution was built on information-processing rather than physiological models. Although Hebb's (1949) theory of mental processing was meant to bridge the gap between psychology and neurology, the cognitive revolution proceeded without much talk of neural substrates, neurotransmitters, or action potentials (LeDoux & Hirst, 1986). The new "cognitive" psychology was bent on replacing behaviorism. Since the brain sciences had become so closely aligned with behaviorism, neurological contributions towards the psychological study of mental processing were, for the most part, "cheerfully ignored."

Cognitive psychologists were not the only ones responsible for maintaining the separation of brain and cognition (LeDoux & Hirst, 1986). Brain scientists had little or no use for the new "cognitive" psychology. Instrumental and classical conditioning paradigms served them well. Recent technological breakthroughs in the study of brain function had been based on the link between physiological response systems and behavioral expression. The brain sciences seemed to be progressing quite well without any reference to "cognition." Just as cognitive psychologists had left neurological studies of the brain behind, neuroscientists left "cognitive" studies of neurological function behind.

In recent years, both cognitive psychology and the neurosciences have once again begun to share similar interests and objectives (LeDoux & Hirst, 1986). These shared interests are reflected in the recent merger of the two sciences to form "cognitive neuroscience." After nearly three-quarters of a century, the brain and cognition seem to be coming together again. There have also been a growing number of individual difference researchers who recognize that the study of neurological functioning has the potential to contribute an important component to our understanding of individual differences in intelligence (e.g., Vernon, 1985).

Recent technological advances in the biological measurement of the brain provide a valuable technology for investigating the biological basis of intelligence. The search for biological correlates of intelligence has been conducted on many levels through studies of gross anatomical features, neuronal structures, bioelectrical recordings, biochemical measures, and environmental assaults. But generalization of findings to theories of individual differences in intelligence must be viewed cautiously. Two major milestones have yet to be overcome: (a) methodological problems associated with the biological measurement of mental processing, and (b) the development of a theoretical framework which will link neurological studies of brain function with theories of individual differences in intelligence.

The measurement of biological correlates of intelligence is plagued with basic measurement problems. Basic issues include: reliability of measurement, validity and interpretation of results, and measurement errors related to sampling. To date, most research concerned with the biological correlates of intelligence has been based on small samples of brain damaged or diseased individuals or on animal studies. Studies including normal control groups and/or large samples are rare. Although some areas hold promise for providing detailed information on the dynamic function of the human brain, most of these studies are only beginning to address questions of individual differences in intelligence (e.g., neuronal and biochemical studies). Even in research areas where questions of individual differences have been addressed directly, methodological problems still limit the application of research findings to theories of intelligence. For example, in the area of gross anatomical function, measurement techniques are limited to global levels of measurement. These measurements are insufficient for providing detailed information on the basic neurological mechanisms of the brain. In the area of bioelectrical measurement, on the other hand, although detailed information has been gathered on the neurological function of the human brain, the interpretation of these measurements in relationship to underlying mental processes is still being actively debated (e.g., Donchin & Coles, 1988; Rabbitt, 1988). In sum, no one technique is without methodological problems. These methodological problems limit the generalizability of results to theories of individual differences in intelligence.

A second major problem limiting the generalization of neurological findings to individual differences in intelligence concerns the lack of a theoretical framework which links the two research areas. The current neuroscience literature suggests convergence on the notion of specific mental processes as highly localized (e.g., Mishkin & Appenzeller, 1987; Posner, Petersen, Fox, & Raichle, 1988; Salazar et al., 1986.) But current research investigating the biological correlates of intelligence has, for the most part, failed to incorporate neurological knowledge about brain function into a working framework of intelligence. Biological studies are all too often based on global psychometric measures of intelligence or global cognitive deficits which assume that intelligence is a unitary trait. The relationship between general intelligence and specific cognitive processes continues to go unanswered. A theoretical framework for investigating underlying biological substrates important to individual differences in intelligence needs to be generated which integrates basic processing theories of intelligence with recent technological advances in the neurosciences.

A few groups of intelligence researchers have begun to develop more theoretically based intelligence models through the use of elementary cognitive tasks. Intelligence models based on elementary cognitive processes will help to provide a more direct link between individual differences in intelligence and neurocortical function. But although these recent studies have the advantage of focusing on the relationship between basic mental processes and IQ, researchers using elementary cognitive tasks are still divided between holistic and aggregate theories of intelligence.

The Hendricksons (1980) have generated a biological theory of intelligence based on individual differences in neural efficiency. Other investigators interested in the relationship between speed and intelligence have used elementary cognitive tasks to generate theories on the biological structure of intelligence (e.g., Eysenck, 1986; Jensen, 1982). These researchers have begun to make connections between biological correlates of neural efficiency and individual differences in intelligence. But theorists who have proposed models of neural efficiency generally assume that intelligence is a single distributed process. Theories that characterize intelligence as a single distributed process fail to incorporate findings in the neurological literature which suggest that more complex cognitive tasks involve more neural substrates. More complex tasks have been shown to be more highly correlated with intelligence than simple tasks based on neural efficiency (e.g., Larson & Saccuzzo, 1989).

Detterman (1984) is another researcher who has used elementary cognitive tasks to develop a theory of intelligence. Contrary to the single factor theory proposed by Eysenck (1986) and Jensen (1982), Detterman has demonstrated that several elementary cognitive tasks, highly predictive of IQ, have low intercorrelations. Based on these findings, Detterman (1987) has suggested that intelligence is a complex system of independent processes. Using multiple regression analysis, Detterman (1984) has been able to demonstrate that elementary cognitive tasks predict IQ as highly as normative psychometric IQ tests predict each other. In an analysis conducted on WAIS-R and WISC-R standardization data,

Detterman and Daniel (1989) found that intercorrelations among IQ subtests and elementary cognitive tasks were considerably lower for high IQ groups than they were in the lower IQ ranges. Findings suggest that the interdependence of basic mental processes varies with the level of IQ. The proposition that "g" may in large part be an artifact of the interactive nature of basic processes implicates the necessity for modeling intelligence as a function of basic underlying mechanisms.

In sum, data gathered on the biological correlates of intelligence are inconclusive. The current neuroscience literature suggests convergence on the notion of mental processing in favor of aggregate models of neurological function. But studies of individual differences in intelligence have failed, for the most part, to incorporate the information gained from basic neuroscientific studies. Still, the link between the sophisticated measurement techniques in the neurosciences and basic information-processing theories of intelligence in the psychological sciences holds promise that individual differences in intelligences will eventually be understood. Findings from neuroscientific studies of brain function and psychological studies of elementary cognitive tasks, when taken together, suggest that individual differences in intelligence might be best accounted for by aggregate models of intelligence.

REFERENCES

Adrian, E. D. (1941). Afferent discharges from the cerebral cortex from peripheral sense organs. *Journal of Physiology, 100,* 159–191.

Allen, M. (1983). Models of hemispheric specialization. *Psychological Bulletin, 93,* 73–104.

Andreassi, J. L. (1980). *Psychophysiology: Human behavior and physiological response.* New York: Oxford University Press.

Anderson, J. A., Silverstein, J. W., Ritz, S. A., & Jones, R. S. (1977). Distinctive features, categorical perception, and probability learning: Some applications of a neural model. *Psychological Bulletin, 84,* 413–451.

Aram, D. M., & Ekelman, B. L. (1986). Cognitive profiles of children with early onset of unilateral lesions. *Developmental Neuropsychology, 2,* 155–172.

Aram, D. M., Ekelman, B. L., Rose, D. F., & Whitaker, H. A. (1985). Verbal and cognitive sequelae following unilateral lesions acquired in early childhood. *Journal of Clinical and Experimental Neuropsychology, 7,* 55–78.

Baghurst, P. A., Robertson, E. F., McMichael, A. J., Vimpani, G. V., Wigg, N. R., & Roberts, R. R. (1987). Port Pirie cohort study: Lead effects on pregnancy outcome and early childhood development. *Neurotoxicology, 8,* 395–402.

Barclay, L., Zemcov, A., Reichert, W., & Blass, J. P. (1985). Cerebral blood flow decrements in chronic head injury syndrome. *Biological Psychiatry, 20,* 146–157.

Beach, F. A., Hebb, D. O., Morgan, C. T., & Nissen, H. W. (1960). *The neuropsychology of Lashley.* New York: McGraw-Hill.

Beck, E. C. (1975). Electrophysiology and behavior. *Annual Review of Psychology, 26,* 233–262.

Becker, L. E., Armstrong, D. L., Chan, F., & Wood, M. M. (1984). Dendritic development in human occipital cortical neurons. *Developmental Brain Research, 13,* 117–124.

Berent, S., Giordani, B., Lehtinen, S., Markel, D., Penney, J. B., Buchtel, H. A., Starosta-Rubinstein, S., Hichwa, R., & Young, A. B. (1988). Positron emission tomographic scan investigations of Huntington's disease: Cerebral metabolic correlates of cognitive function. *Annals of Neurology, 23,* 541–546.

Bellinger, D., Leviton, A., Waternaux, C., Needleman, H. L., & Rabinowitz, M. (1987). Longitudinal analysis of prenatal and postnatal lead exposure and early cognitive development. *New England Journal of Medicine, 316,* 1037–1043.

Bissette, G., Widerlov, E., Walleus, H., Karlsson, I., Eklund, K., Forsman, A., & Nemeroff, C. B. (1986). Alterations in cerebrospinal fluid concentrations of somatostatinlike immunoreactivity in neuropsychiatric disorders. *Archives of General Psychiatry, 43,* 1148–1151.

Blinkhorn, S. F., & Hendrickson, D. E. (1982). Averaged evoked responses and psychometric intelligence. *Nature, 295,* 596–597.

Bolter, J. F., & Long, C. L. (1985). Methodological issues in research in developmental neuropsychology. In L. C. Hartlage & C. F. Telzrow (Eds.), *Perspectives on individual differences: The neuropsychology of individual differences, a developmental perspective* (pp. 41–59). New York: Plenum Press.

Boring, E. G. (1963). *History, psychology, and science: Selected papers.* New York: John Wiley and Sons.

Bornstein, R. A. (1984). Unilateral lesions and the Wechsler adult intelligence scale-revised: No sex differences. *Journal of Consulting and Clinical Psychology, 52,* 604–608.

Bornstein, R. A., & Matarazzo, J. D. (1984). Relationship of sex and the effects of unilateral lesions on the Wechsler intelligence scales: Further considerations. *Journal of Nervous and Mental Disease, 172,* 707–710.

Brambilla, F., Aguglia, E., Massironi, R., Maggioni, M., Grillo, W., Castiglioni, R., Catalano, M., & Drago, F. (1986). Neuropeptide therapies in chronic schizophrenia: TRH and vasopressin administration. *Neuropsychobiology, 15,* 114–121.

Breakefield, X. O., & Cambi, F. (1987). Molecular genetic insights into neurologic diseases. *Annual Review of Neuroscience, 10,* 535–594.

Brink, J. D., Garrett, A. L., Hale, W. R., Woo-Sam, J., & Nickel, V. L. (1970). Recovery of motor and intellectual function in children sustaining severe head injuries. *Developmental Medicine and Child Neurology, 12,* 565–571.

Brooks, D. J., Leenders, K. L., Head, G., Marshall, J., Legg, N. J., & Jones, T. (1984). Studies on regional cerebral oxygen utilization and cognitive function in multiple sclerosis. *Journal of Neurology, Neurosurgery and Psychiatry, 47,* 1182–1191.

Brumback, R. A., & Staton, R. D. (1982a). An hypothesis regarding the communality of right-hemisphere involvement in learning disability, attentional disorder, and childhood major depressive disorder. *Perceptual and Motor Skills, 52,* 1091–1097.

Brumback, R. A., & Staton, R. D. (1982b). Right hemisphere involvement in learning disability, attention deficit disorder, and childhood major depressive disorder. *Medical Hypotheses, 8,* 505–514.

Brumback, R. A., & Staton, R. D. (1983). Learning disability and childhood depression. *American Journal of Orthopsychiatry, 53*, 269–281.

Brumback, R. A., Staton, R. D., & Wilson, H. (1980). Neuropsychological study of children during and after remission of endogenous depressive episodes. *Perceptual and Motor Skills, 50*, 1163–1167.

Brumback, R. A., Staton, R. D., & Wilson, H. (1984a). Psychopharmacology in children. *New England Journal of Medicine, 311*, 473–474.

Brumback, R. A., Staton, R. D., & Wilson, H. (1984b). Right cerebral hemispheric dysfunction. *Archives Neurologica, 41*, 248–250.

Callaway, E. (1975). *Brain electrical potentials and individual differences*. New York: Grune & Stratton.

Callner, D. A., Dustman, R. E., Madsen, J. A., Schenkenberg, T., & Beck, E. C. (1978). Life span changes in the averaged evoked responses of Down syndrome and nonretarded subjects. *American Journal of Mental Deficiency, 82*, 398–405.

Camel, J. E., Withers, G. S., & Greenough, W. T. (1986). Persistence of visual cortex dendritic alterations induced by postweaning exposure to a "superenriched" environment in rats. *Behavioral Neuroscience, 100*, 810–813.

Carello, C. Turvey, M. T., Kugler, P. N., & Shaw, R. E. (1984). Inadequacies of the computer metaphor. In M. S. Gazzangia (Ed.), *Handbook of cognitive science* (pp. 229–248). New York: Plenum Press.

Carlson, N. R. (1986). *Physiology of behavior* (2nd ed.). Boston, MA: Allyn and Bacon.

Chalke, F. C. R., & Ertl, J. P. (1965). Evoked potentials and intelligence. *Life Sciences, 4*, 1319–1322.

Chang, F. L. F., & Greenough, W. T. (1978). Increased dendritic branching in hemispheres opposite eyes exposed to maze training in split-brain rats. *Society for Neuroscience Abstracts, 4*, 469.

Changeux, J. P. (1985). *Neuronal man: The biology of mind* (L. Garey, trans.). New York: Pantheon Books.

Chase, T. N., Fedio, P., Foster, N. L., Brooks, R., Di Chiro, G., & Mansi, L. (1984). Wechsler adult intelligence scale performance. Cortical localization by fluorodeoxyglucose F 18-positron emission tomography. *Archives of Neurology, 41*, 1244–1247.

Chelune, G. J., & Edwards, P. (1981). Early brain lesions: Ontogenetic-environmental considerations. *Journal of Consulting and Clinical Psychology, 49*, 777–790.

Coles, M. G. H., Gratton, G., Kramer, A. F., & Miller, G. A. (1986). In A. Gale & J. A. Edwards (Eds.), *Physiological correlates of human behavior: Individual differences and psychopathology* (Vol. 13, pp. 183–221). New York: Academic Press.

Corning, W. C., Steffy, R. A., Anderson, E., & Bowers, P. (1986). EEG "maturational lag" profiles: Following-up analysis. *Journal of Abnormal Child Psychology, 14*(2), 235–249.

Coyle, J. T., Price, D. L., & DeLong, M. R. (1983). Alzheimer's disease: A disorder of cortical cholinergic innervation. *Science, 219*, 1184–1190.

Crawford, C. B. (1974). A canonical correlation analysis of cortical evoked response and intelligence test data. *Canadian Journal of Psychology, 28*, 319–332.

Cummings, J. L. (1986). Subcortical dementia: Neuropsychology, neuropsychiatry, and pathophysiology. *British Journal of Psychiatry, 149*, 682–697.

Cutler, N. R., Haxby, J. V., Duara, R., Grady, C. L., Moore, A. M., Parisi, J. E., White,

J., Heston, L., Margolin, R. M., & Rapoport, S. I. (1985). Brain metabolism as measured with positron emission tomography: Serial assessment in a patient with familial Alzheimer's disease. *Neurology, 35,* 1556–1561.

Davis, B. M., Mohs, R. C., Greenwald, B. S., Mathe, A. A., Johns, C. A., Horvath, T. B., & Davis, K. L. (1985). Clinical studies of the cholinergic deficit in Alzheimer's disease: I. Neurochemical and neuroendocrine studies. *Journal of the American Geriatrics Society, 33,* 741–748.

Davison, A. N., & Dobbing, J. (1966). Myelination as a vulnerable period in brain development. *British Medical Bulletin, 22,* 40–44.

Dean, P. (1980). Recapitulation of a theme by Lashley? Comment on Wood's simulated lesion experiment. *Psychological Review, 87,* 470–473.

Deary, I. J., Hendrickson, A. E., & Burns, A. (1987). Serum calcium levels in Alzheimer's disease: A finding and an aetiological hypothesis. *Personality and Individual differences, 8,* 75–80.

Detterman, D. K. (1984). Understand cognitive components before postulating metacomponents, etc.: Part II. *Brain and Behavioral Science, 7,* 289–290.

Detterman, D. K. (1987). Theoretical notions of intelligence and mental retardation. *American Journal of Mental Deficiency, 92,* 2–11.

Detterman, D. K., & Daniel, M. H. (1989). Correlations of mental tests with each other and with cognitive variables are highest for low IQ groups. *Intelligence, 13,* 349–360.

Donchin, E., & Coles, M. G. H. (1988). Precommentary: Is the P300 component a manifestation of context updating? *Behavioral and Brain Sciences, 11,* 355–372.

Dysken, M. (1987). A review of recent clinical trials in the treatment of Alzheimer's dementia. *Psychiatric Annals, 17,* 178–191.

Easter, S. S., Jr., Purves, D., Rakic, P., & Spitzer, N. C. (1985). The changing view of neural specificity. *Science, 230,* 507–511.

Ehrhardt, A. A., Meyer, B., & Heino, F. (1979). Prenatal sex hormones and the developing brain: Effects on psychosexual differentiation and cognitive function. *Annual Review of Medicine, 30,* 417–430.

Eichenwald, H. R., & Fry, P. C. (1969). Nutrition and learning. *Science, 163,* 644–648.

Ernhart, C. B., Morrow-Tlucak, M., Marler, M. R., & Wolf, A. W. (1987). Low level lead exposure in the prenatal and early preschool periods: Early preschool development. *Neurotoxicology & Teratology, 9,* 259–270.

Ernhart, C. B., Morrow-Tlucak, M., Wolf, A. W., Super, D., & Drotar, D. (1989). Low level lead exposure in the prenatal and early preschool period: Intelligence prior to school entry. *Neurotoxicology & Teratology, 11,* 161–170.

Ertl, J. P. (1971). IQ, evoked responses, and Fourier analysis. *Nature, 241,* 209–210.

Ertl, J. P., & Schafer, E. W. P. (1969). Brain response correlates of psychometric intelligence. *Nature, 223,* 421–422.

Eysenck, H. J. (1986). Toward a new model of intelligence. *Personality and Individual Differences, 7,* 731–736.

Federico, P. A. (1984a). Event-related-potential (ERP) correlates of cognitive styles, abilities and aptitudes. *Personality and Individual Differences, 5,* 575–585.

Federico, P. A. (1984b). Hemispheric asymmetries: Individual-difference measures for aptitude-treatment interactions. *Personality and Individual Differences, 5,* 711–724.

Ferchmin, P. A., Bennett, E. L., & Rosenzweig, M. R. (1975). Direct contact with enriched environment is required to alter cerebral weights in rats. *Journal of Comparative and Physiological Psychology, 88,* 360–367.

Flinn, J. M., Kirsch, A. D., & Flinn, E. A. (1977). Correlations between intelligence and the frequency content of the visual evoked potential. *Physiological Psychology, 5,* 11–15.

Fine, A. (1986). Peptides and Alzheimer's disease. *Nature, 319,* 537–538.

Folstein, M. F., Robinson, R., Folstein, S., & McHugh, P. R. (1985). Depression and neurological disorders: New treatment opportunities for elderly depressed patients. 14th CINP Congress: Management of depression in late life (1984, Florence, Italy). *Journal of Affective Disorders, Suppl. 1,* 11–14.

Foster, N. L., Chase, T. N., Fedio, P., Patronas, N. J., Brooks, R. A., & DiChiro, G. (1983). Alzheimer's disease: Focal cortical changes shown by positron emission tomography. *Neurology, 33,* 961–965.

Fuld, P. A. (1984). Test profile of cholinergic dysfunction and of Alzheimer-type dementia. *Journal of Clinical Neuropsychology, 6,* 380–392.

Gale, A., & Edwards, J. A. (1983). Cortical correlates of intelligence. In A. Gale & J. Edwards (Eds.), *Physiological correlates of human behavior: Individual differences and psychopathology* (Vol. 3, pp. 79–97). New York: Academic Press.

Gale, A., & Edwards, J. A. (1986). Individual differences. In M. G. H. Coles, E. Donchin, & S. W. Porges (Eds.), *Psychophysiology: Systems, processes, and applications* (pp. 431–507). New York: The Guilford Press.

Garfunkel, J. M., Baird, H. W., & Ziegler, J. (1954). The relationship of oxygen consumption to cerebral functional activity. *Journal of Pediatrics, 44,* 64–72.

Gasser, T., Von Lucadon-Muller, I., Verleger, R., & Bucher, P. (1983). Correlating EEG and IQ: A new look at an old problem using computerized EEG parameters. *Electroencephalography and Clinical Neurophysiology, 55,* 493–504.

Giannitrapani, D. (1969). EEG average frequency and intelligence. *Electroencephalography and Clinical Neurophysiology, 27,* 480–486.

Giannitrapani, D. (1985). *The electrophysiology of intellectual functions.* New York: Karger.

Gispen, W. H., Isaacson, R. L., Spruijt, B. M., & de-Wied, D. (1986). Melanocortins, neural plasticity and aging. *Progress in Neuro-Psychopharmacology and Biological Psychiatry, 10,* 415–426.

Gliddon, J. B., Busk, J., & Galbraith, G. C. (1975). Visual evoked responses as a function of light intensity in Down syndrome and nonretarded subjects. *Psychophysiology, 82,* 416–422.

Gliddon, J. B., Galbraith, G. C., & Busk, J. (1975). Effect of duration of a preconditioning visual stimulus on visual evoked responses in Down syndrome and nonretarded subjects. *American Journal of Mental Deficiency, 80,* 186–190.

Grady, C. L., Haxby, J. V., Schlageter, N. L., Berg, G., & Rapoport, S. I. (1986). Stability of metabolic and neuropsychological asymmetries in dementia of the Alzheimer type. *Neurology, 36,* 1390–1392.

Grafman, J., Jonas, B. S., Martin, A., Salazar, A., Weingartner, H., Ludlow, C., Smutok, M. A., & Vance, S. C. (1988). Intellectual function following penetrating head injury in Vietnam veterans. *Brain, 111,* 169–184.

Grafman, J., Salazar, A., Weingartner, H., Vance, S., & Amin, D. (1986). The relationship of brain-tissue loss volume and lesion localization to cognitive deficit. *The Journal of Neuroscience, 6,* 301–307.

Gregory, R. J., & Mohan, P. J. (1977). Effect of a symptomatic lead exposure on childhood intelligence: A critical review. *Intelligence, 1,* 381–400.

Green, E. J., & Greenough, W. T. (1986). Altered synaptic transmission in dentate gyrus of rats reared in complex environments: Evidence from hippocampal slices maintained in vitro. *Journal of Neurophysiology, 55,* 739–749.

Green, E. J., Greenough, W. T., & Schlumpf, B. E. (1983). Effects of complex or isolated environments on cortical dendrites of middle-aged rats. *Brain Research, 264,* 233–240.

Greenough, W. T., McDonald, J. W., Parnisari, R. M., & Camel, J. E. (1986). Environmental conditions modulate degeneration and new dendrite growth in cerebellum of senescent rats. *Brain Research, 380,* 136–140.

Grob, C., & Coyle, J. T. (1986). Suspected adverse methylphenidate-imipramine interactions in children. *Journal of Developmental and Behavioral Pediatrics, 7,* 265–267.

Gur, R. C., & Reivich, M. (1980). Cognitive task effects on hemispheric blood flow in humans: Evidence for individual differences in hemispheric activation. *Brain and Language, 9,* 78–92.

Guyton, A. C. (1987). *Basic neuroscience: Anatomy and physiology.* Philadelphia, PA: W. B. Saunders.

Haier, R. J., Robinson, D. L., Braden, W., & Williams, D. (1984). Evoked potential augmenting-reducing and personality differences. *Personality and Individual Differences, 5,* 293–301.

Haier, R. J., Siegel, B. V., Nuechterlein, K. H., Hazlett, E., Wu, J. C., Paek, J., Browning, H. L., & Buchsbaum, M. S. (1988). Cortical glucose metabolic rate correlates of abstract reasoning and attention studied with positron emission tomography. *Intelligence, 12,* 199–217.

Halstead, W. C. (1947). *Brain and intelligence.* Chicago, IL: University of Chicago Press.

Handelmann, G. E., O'Donohue, T. L. Forrester, D., & Cook, W. (1983). Alpha-melanocyte stimulating hormone facilitates learning of visual but not auditory discriminations. *Peptides,* 4, 145–148.

Hartlage, P. (1985). A survey of developmental neurologic conditions: Implications for individual neuropsychological differences. In L. C. Hartlage & C. F. Telzrow (Eds.), *Perspectives on individual differences: The neuropsychology of individual differences, a developmental perspective* (pp. 253–270). New York: Plenum Press.

Harvey, P. G., Hamlin, N. W., Kumar, R., & Morgan, G. (1988). Relationships between blood lead, behaviour, psychometric and neuropsychological test performance in young children. *British Journal of Developmental Psychology, 6,* 145–156.

Harwerth, R. S., Smith, E. L. III, Duncan, G. C., Crawford, M. L. J., & von Noorden, G. K. (1986). Multiple sensitive periods in the development of the primate visual system. *Science, 232,* 235–237.

Haxby, J. V., & Rapoport, S. I. (1985). Asymmetry of brain metabolism and cognitive function. *Geriatric Nursing, 6,* 200–203.

Haxby, J. V., & Rapoport, S. I. (1986). Abnormalities of regional brain metabolism in Alzheimer's disease and their relation to functional impairment. *Progress in Neuro-Psychopharmacology and Biological Psychiatry, 10,* 427–438.

Haxby, J. V., Grady, C. L., Duara, R., Schlageter, N., Berg, G., & Rapoport, S. I. (1986). Neocortical metabolic abnormalities precede nonmemory cognitive defects in early Alzheimer's-type dementia. *Archives of Neurology, 43,* 882–885.

Hebb, D. O. (1949). *The organization of behavior: A neuropsychological theory.* New York: John Wiley & Sons.

Hebb, D. O. (1980). The structure of thought. In P. W. Jusczyk & R. M. Klein (Eds.), *The nature of thought: Essays in honor of D. O. Hebb* (pp. 19–36). Hillsdale, NJ: Erlbaum.

Hendrickson, A. E. (1982). The biological basis of intelligence. Part I: Theory. In H. J. Eysenck (Ed.), *A model for intelligence* (pp. 151–196). New York: Springer-Verlag.

Hendrickson, D. E. (1982). The biological basis of intelligence. Part II: Measurement. In H. J. Eysenck (Ed.), *A model for intelligence* (pp. 197–228). New York: Springer-Verlag.

Hendrickson, D. E., & Hendrickson, A. E. (1980). The biological basis of individual differences in intelligence. *Personality and Individual Differences, 1,* 3–33.

Herring, S., & Reitan, R. M. (1986). Sex similarities in verbal and performance IQ deficits following unilateral cerebral lesions. *Journal of Consulting and Clinical Psychology, 54,* 537–541.

Holloway, W. R., & Thor, D. H. (1987). Low level lead exposure during lactation increases rough and tumble play fighting of juvenile rats. *Neurotoxicology & Teratology, 9,* 51–57.

Holmes, C. S., Koepke, K. M., & Thompson, R. G. (1986). Simple versus complex performance impairments at three blood glucose levels. *Psychoneuroendocrinology, 11,* 353–357.

Hommer, D. W., Pickar, D., Crawley, J. N., Weingartner, H., & Paul, S. M. (1985). The effects of cholecystokinin-like peptides in schizophrenics and normal human subjects. New York Academy of Sciences and the Fondation Medicale Reine Elisabeth: Neuronal cholecystokinin (1984, Brussels, Belgium). *Annals of the New York Academy of Sciences, 448,* 542–552.

Hopfield, J. J. (1982). Neural networks and physical systems with emergent collective computational abilities. *Proceedings of the National Academy of Sciences of the United States of America, 81,* 3088–3092.

Hopfield, J. J., Feinstein, D. I., & Palmer, R. G. (1983). "Unlearning" has a stabilizing effect in collective memories. *Nature, 304,* 158–159.

Hubel, D. H., & Wiesel, T. N. (1970). The period of susceptibility to the physiological effects of unilateral eye closure in kittens. *Journal of Physiology, 206,* 419–436.

Huttenlocher, P. R. (1974). Dendritic development in neocortex of children with mental defect and infantile spasms. *Neurology, 24,* 203–210.

Huttenlocher, P. R. (1979). Synaptic density in human frontal cortex-developmental changes and effects of aging. *Brain Research, 163,* 195–205.

Huttenlocher, P. R. (1984). Synapse elimination and plasticity in developing human cerebral cortex. *American Journal of Mental Deficiency, 88,* 488–496.

Huttenlocher, P. R., deCourten, C., Garey, L., & Van der Loos, H. (1982). Synaptogenesis in human visual cortex: Evidence for synapse elimination during normal development. *Neuroscience Letters, 33,* 247–252.

Inglis, J., & Lawson, J. S. (1982). Sex differences in the effects of unilateral brain damage on intelligence. *Science, 212,* 603–695.

Jasper, H. J. (1958). The ten twenty electrode system of the International Federation. *Electroencephalography and Clinical Neurophysiology, 10,* 371–375.

Jensen, A. R. (1982). Reaction time and psychometric g. In H. J. Eysenck (Ed.), *A model for intelligence* (pp. 93–132). New York: Springer-Verlag.

Jensen, A. R., Schaefer, E. W., & Crinella, F. M. (1981). Reaction time, evoked brain potentials, and psychometric 'g' in the severely retarded. *Intelligence, 5,* 179–197.

Jerison, H. J. (1982). The evolution of biological intelligence. In R. J. Sternberg (Ed.), *The handbook of human intelligence* (pp. 723–791). Cambridge, England: Cambridge University Press.

Johanson, A. M., Gustafson, L., & Risberg, J. (1986). Behavioral observations during performance of the WAIS block design test related to abnormalities of regional cerebral blood flow in organic dementia. *Journal of Clinical and Experimental Neuropsychology, 8,* 201–209.

John, E. R. (1977). *Neurometrics: Clinical application of quantitative electrophysiology.* Hillsdale, NJ: Erlbaum.

John, E. R., Karmel, B. Z., Corning, W. C., Easton, P., Brown, D., Ahn, H., John, M., Harmony, T., Prichep, L., Toro, A., Gerson, I., Bartlett, F., Thatcher, R., Kaye, H., Valdes, P., & Schwartz, E. (1977). Neurometrics. *Science, 196,* 1393–1409.

Jones, K. L., Smith, D. W., Ulleland, C. N., & Streissguth, A. (1973). Pattern of malformation in offspring of chronic alcoholic women. *Lancet, 1,* 1267–1271.

Kaplan, B. J. (1972). Malnutrition and mental deficiency. *Psychological Bulletin, 78,* 321–334.

Kimura, D. (1987). Are men's and women's brains really different? Annual Meeting of the Canadian Psychological Association (1986, Toronto, Canada). *Canadian Psychology, 28,* 133–147.

Klonoff, H., & Low, M. (1974). Disordered brain function in young children and early adolescents: Neuropsychological and electroencephalographic correlates. In R. M. Reitan & L. A. Davison (Eds.), *Clinical neuropsychology.* Washington, DC: Hemisphere.

Klonoff, H., Low, M. D., & Clark, C. (1977). Head injuries in children: A prospective five year follow-up. *Journal of Neurology, Neurosurgery, and Psychiatry, 40,* 1211–1219.

Kragh-Sorensen, P., Olsen, R. B., Lund, S., & Van-Riezen, H. (1986). Neuropeptides: ACTH-peptides in dementia. *Progress in Neuro-Psychopharmacology and Biological Psychiatry, 10,* 479–492.

Krall, V. (1980). Effects of lead poisoning on cognitive test performance. *Perceptual and Motor Skills, 50,* 483–486.

Larrabee, G. J., & Haley, J. A. (1986). Another look at VIQ-PIQ scores and unilateral brain damage. *International Journal of Neuroscience, 29,* 141–148.

Larson, G. E., & Saccuzzo, D. P. (1989). Cognitive correlates of general intelligence: Toward a process theory of g. *Intelligence, 13,* 5–32.

Lashley, K. S. (1929). *Brain mechanisms and intelligence.* Chicago, IL: University of Chicago Press.

Lassen, N. A., Munch, O., & Tottey, E. R. (1957). Mental function and cerebral oxygen consumption in organic dementia. *Archives of Neurology and Psychiatry, 77,* 126–134.

LeDoux, J. E., & Hirst, W. (1986). Cognitive neuroscience: an overview. In J. E. LeDoux

& W. Hirst (Eds.), *Mind and body: Dialogues in cognitive neuroscience* (pp. 1–4). New York: Cambridge University Press.

Levin, H. S., Benton, A. L., & Grossman, R. G. (1982). *Neurobehavioral consequences of closed head injury*. New York: Oxford University Press.

Levine, S. C., Huttenlocher, P., Banich, M. T., & Duda, E. (1987). Factors affecting cognitive functioning of hemiplegic children. *Developmental Medicine and Child Neurology, 29,* 27–35.

Lewis, G. W. (1984). Temporal stability of multichannel, multimodal ERP recordings. *International Journal of Neuroscience, 25,* 131–144.

Little, R. E., Mandell, W., & Schultz, F. A. (1977). Consequences of retrospective measurement of alcohol consumption. *Journal of Studies on Alcohol, 38,* 1777–1780.

Luria, A. R. (1965). Vygotsky and the problem of localization of functions. *Neuropsychologia, 3,* 387–392.

Luria, A. R. (1966). *Human brain and psychological processes*. New York: Harper & Row.

Maire, J. C. E., & Wurtman, R. J. (1984). Choline production from choline-containing phospholipids: A hypothetical role in Alzheimer's disease and aging. Proceedings of the 7th Annual Meeting of the Canadian College of Neuro-Psychopharmacology: Perspectives in Canadian neuro-psychopharmacology. *Progress in Neuro-Psychopharmacology and Biological Psychiatry, 8,* 637–642.

Mange, A. P., & Mange, E. J. (1980). *Genetics: Human aspects*. Philadelphia, PA: Saunders.

Manocha, S. L. (1972). *Malnutrition and retarded human development*. Springfield, IL: Thomas.

Marin-Padilla, M. (1974). Structural organization of the cerebral cortex (motor area) in human chromosomal aberrations. A Golgi study. *Brain Research, 66,* 373–391.

Maurer, D. (1988). *World of the newborn*. New York: Basic Books.

McCall, R. B., Meyers, E. D., Hartman, J., & Roche, A. F. (1983). Developmental changes in head-circumference and mental-performance growth rates: A test of Epstein's phrenoblysis. *Developmental Psychobiology, 16,* 457–468.

McClelland, J. L. (1979). On the time relations and mental processes. An examination of systems of processes in cascade. *Psychological Review, 86,* 287–330.

McClelland, J. L., Rumelhart, D. E., & Hinton, G. E. (1986). The Appeal of parallel distributed processing. In D. E. Rumelhart, J. L. McClelland, & the PDP research group (Eds.), *Parallel distributed processing: Explorations in the microstructure of cognition. Volume 1: Foundations*. Cambridge, MA: MIT Press.

McCoy, E. E., & Enns, L. (1986). Current status of neurotransmitter abnormalities in Down syndrome. In C. J. Epstein (Ed.), *The neurobiology of Down syndrome* (pp. 73–87). New York: Raven Press.

McKinney, M., & Richelson, E. (1984). The coupling of the neuronal muscarinic receptor to response. *Annual Review of Pharmacology and Toxicology, 24,* 121–146.

Merzenich, M. M., & Kaas, J. H. (1982). Reorganization of mammalian somatosensory cortex following peripheral nerve injury. *Trends in Neuroscience, 5,* 434–436.

Milar, C. R., Schroder, S. R., Mushak, P., Dolcourt, J. L., & Grant, L. D. (1980). Contribution of the caregiving environment to increased lead burden in children. *American Journal of Mental Deficiency, 84,* 339–344.

Miller, E. (1980). Neuropsychology and the relationship between brain and behaviour. In A. J. Chapman & D. M. Jones (Eds.), *Models of man* (pp. 75–85). Leicester, England: The British Psychological Society.

Milner, B., & Petrides, M. (1984). Behavioural effects of frontal-lobe lesions in man. Special Issue: The frontal lobes—uncharted provinces of the brain. *Trends in Neuroscience, 7,* 403–407.

Minsky, M., & Papert, S. (1969). *Perceptrons.* Cambridge, MA: MIT Press.

Mishkin, M., & Appenzeller, T. (1987). The anatomy of memory. *Scientific American, 256,* 80–89.

Murray, J. B. (1984). Effects of Valium and Librium on human psychomotor and cognitive functions. *Genetic Psychology Monographs, 109,* 167–197.

Naylor, H., Halliday, R., & Callaway, E. (1985). The effect of methylphenidate on information processing. *Psychopharmacology, 86,* 90–95.

O'Gorman, J. G., & Lloyd, J. E. M. (1985). Is EEG a consistent measure of individual differences? *Personality and Individual Differences, 6,* 273–275.

Osborne, R. T. (1970). Heritability estimates for the visual evoked response. *Life Sciences, 9*(Part II), 481–490.

Perry, N. W., McCoy, J. G., Cunningham, W. R., Falgout, J. C., & Street, W. J. (1976). Multivariate visual evoked response correlates of intelligence. *Psychophysiology, 13,* 323–329.

Plett, T. L. (1987). The shape of intelligence. *The Sciences, 27,* 58–61.

Pollitt, E., Lewis, N. L., Garza, C., & Shulman, R. J. (1983). Fasting and cognitive function. *Journal of Psychiatric Research, 17,* 169–174.

Posner, M. I., Petersen, S. E., Fox, P. T., & Raichle, M. E. (1988). Localization of cognitive operations in the human brain. *Science, 240,* 1627–1631.

Purpura, D. P. (1974). Dendritic spine "dysgenesis" and mental retardation. *Science, 186,* 1126–1128.

Purpura, D. P. (1975). Dendritic differentiation in human cerebral cortex: Normal and aberrant developmental patterns. *Advances in Neurology, 12,* 91–116.

Rabbitt, P. (1988). Has the P300 been cost effective? *Behavioral and Brain Sciences, 11,* 388–390.

Rakic, P., Bourgeois, J. P., Eckenhoff, M. F., Zecevic, N., & Goldman-Rakic, P. S. (1986). Concurrent overproduction of synapses in diverse regions of the primate cerebral cortex. *Science, 232,* 232–234.

Risberg, J. (1986). Regional cerebral blood flow in neuropsychology. Special issue: Methods in neuropsychology. *Neuropsychologia, 24,* 135–140.

Riva, D., & Cazzaniga, L. (1986). Late effects of unilateral brain lesions sustained before and after age one. *Neuropsychologia, 24,* 423–428.

Robinson, D. L., Haier, R. J., Braden, W., & Krengel, M. (1984). Psychometric intelligence and visual evoked potentials: A replication. *Personality and Individual Differences, 5,* 487–489.

Rosenfield, I. (1988). *The invention of memory.* New York: Basic Books.

Rosenzweig, M. R., & Bennett, E. L. (1972). Cerebral changes in rats exposed individually to an enriched environment. *Journal of Comparative and Physiological Psychology, 80,* 304–313.

Rosenzweig, M. R., & Bennett, E. L. (1977). Effects of environmental enrichment or impoverishment on learning and on brain values in rodents. In A. Oliverio (Ed.), *Genetics, environment, and intelligence.* Amsterdam, Netherlands: Elsevier.

Rourke, B. P., Bakker, D. J., Fisk, J. L., & Strang, J. D. (1983). *Child neuropsychology.* New York: Guilford Press.

Rumelhart, D. E., Hinton, G. E., & McClelland, J. L. (1986). A general framework for parallel distributed processing. In D. E. Rumelhart, J. L. McClelland, and the PDP research group (Eds.), *Parallel distributed processing: Explorations in the microstructure of cognition. Volume 1: Foundations.* Cambridge, MA: MIT Press.

Rumsey, J. M. (1985). Brain metabolism in autism: Resting cerebral glucose utilization rates as measured with positron emission tomography. *Archives of General Psychiatry, 42,* 448–455.

Rush, D., Stein, Z., & Susser, M. (1980). A randomized controlled trial of prenatal nutritional supplementation in New York City. *Pediatrics, 65,* 683–697.

Rust, J. (1975). Cortical evoked potential, personality, and intelligence. *Journal of Comparative and Physiological Psychology, 89,* 1220–1226.

Sahgal, A., Wright, C., & Ferrier, I N. (1986). Desamino-d-arg-sup-8-vasopressin (DDAVP), unlike ethanol, has no effect on a boring visual vigilance task in humans. *Psychopharmacology, 90,* 58–63.

Salazar, A. M., Grafman, J., Schlesselman, S., Vance, S. C., Mohr, J. P., Carpenter, M., Pevsner, P., Ludlow, C. L., & Weingartner, H. (1986). Penetrating war injuries of the basal forebrain: Neurology and cognition. *Neurology, 36,* 459–465.

Sameroff, A. J., & Chandler, M. T. (1975). Reproductive risk and the continuum of caretaking causality. In F. D. Horowitz (Ed.), *Review of child development research* (Vol. 4, pp. 187–243). Chicago, IL: University of Chicago Press.

Schapiro, M. B., Haxby, J. V., Grady, C. L., & Rapoport, S. I. (1986). Cerebral glucose utilization, quantitative tomography, and cognitive function in adult Down syndrome. In C. J. Epstein (Ed.), *The neurobiology of Down syndrome* (pp. 89–108). New York: Raven Press.

Schaumburg, H. H., & Raine, C. S. (1977). The neurology of myelin diseases. In P. Morell (Ed.), *Myelin* (pp. 325–351). New York: Plenum Press.

Schwartz, M., Duara, R., Haxby, J., Grady, C., White, B., Kessler, R., Kay, A., Cutler, N., & Rapoport, S. (1983). Down syndrome in adults: Brain metabolism. *Science, 221,* 781–783.

Sergent, J. (1984). Inferences from unilateral brain damage about normal hemispheric functions in visual pattern recognition. *Psychological Bulletin, 96,* 99–115.

Shagass, C., Roemer, R. A., & Straumanis, J. J. (1981). Intelligence as a factor in evoked potential studies of psychopathology: II. Correlations between treatment-associated changes in IQ and evoked potentials. *Biological Psychiatry, 16,* 1031–1040.

Shepherd, G. M. (1988). *Neurobiology* (2nd ed.). New York: Oxford University Press.

Sherman, M., Nass, R., & Shapiro, T. (1984). Brief report: Regional cerebral blood flow in autism. *Journal of Autism and Developmental Disorders, 14,* 439–446.

Shucard, D. W., & Horn, J. L. (1972). Evoked potential amplitude change related to intelligence and arousal. *Psychophysiology, 10,* 445–452.

Shucard, D. W., & Horn, J. L. (1973). Evoked cortical potentials and measurement of human abilities. *Journal of Comparative and Physiological Psychology, 78,* 59–68.

Silva, P. A., Hughes, P., Williams, S., & Faed, J. M. (1988). Bloodlead, intelligence, reading attainment, and behaviour in eleven year old children in Dunedin, New Zealand. *Journal of Child Psychology and Psychiatry and Allied Disciplines, 29,* 43–52.

Sklare, D. A., & Lynn, G. E. (1984). Latency of the P3 event-related potential: Normative aspects and within-subject variability. *Electroencephalography and Clinical Neurophysiology, 59,* 420–424.

Slaunwhite, W. R. (1988). *Fundamentals of endrocinology.* New York: Marcel Dekker.

Spearman, C. (1904). "General intelligence" objectively determined and measured. *American Journal of Psychology, 15,* 201–293.

Spearman, C. (1927). *The nature of intelligence and the principles of cognition* (2nd ed.). London: MacMillan.

Staton, R. D., Wilson, H., & Brumback, R. A. (1981). Cognitive improvement associated with tricyclic antidepressant treatment of childhood major depressive illness. *Perceptual and Motor Skills, 53,* 219–234.

Stein, Z., & Susser, M. (1985). Effects of early nutrition on neurological and mental competence in human beings. *Psychological Medicine, 15,* 717–726.

Sternberg, R. J. (1982). Reasoning, problem solving, and intelligence. In R. J. Sternberg (Ed.), *Handbook of human intelligence* (pp. 225–307). Cambridge, England: Cambridge University Press.

Stott, D. H. (1983). Brain size and "intelligence." *British Journal of Developmental Psychology, 1,* 279–287.

Stuss, D. T., Benson, D. F., Kaplan, E. F., Weir, W. S., Naeser, M. A., Liberman, I., & Farril, D. (1983). The involvement of orbitofrontal cerebrum in cognitive tasks. *Neuropsychologia, 21,* 235–248.

Sundet, K. (1986). Sex differences in cognitive impairment following unilateral brain damage. *Journal of Clinical and Experimental Neuropsychology, 8,* 51–61.

Takashima, S., Ieshima, A., Nakamura, H., & Becker, L. E. (1989). Dendrites, dementia, and the Down syndrome. *Brain and Development, 11*(2), 131–133.

Tamminga, C. A., Foster, N. L., Fedio, P., Bird, E. D., & Chase, T. N. (1987). Alzheimer's disease: Low cerebral somatostatin levels correlate with impaired cognitive function and cortical metabolism. *Neurology, 37,* 161–165.

Telzrow, C. F. (1985). The science and speculation of rehabilitation in developmental neuropsychological disorders. In L. C. Hartlage & C. F. Telzrow (Eds.), *Perspectives on individual differences: The neuropsychology of individual differences, a developmental perspective* (pp. 271–308). New York: Plenum Press.

Thompson, R. F. (1986). The neurobiology of learning and memory. *Science, 233,* 941–947.

Thompson, R. F., Berger, T. W., & Madden, J. (1983). Cellular processes of learning and memory in the mammalian CNS. *Annual Review of Neuroscience, 6,* 447–491.

Thomson, G. H. (1939). *The factorial analysis of human ability.* Boston, MA: Houghton Mifflin Company.

Thorndike, E. L. (1921). Intelligence and its measurement: A symposium, I. *Journal of Educational Psychology, 12,* 124–127.

Thurstone, L. L. (1931). Multiple factor analysis. *Psychological Review, 38,* 406–427.

Till & Beckwith. (1985). Sentence memory affected by vasopressin analog (DDAVP) in a crossover experiment. *Peptides, 6,* 397–402.

Ulleland, C., Wennberg, R. P., Igo, R. P., & Smith, N. J. (1970). The offspring of alcoholic mothers. *Pediatric Research, 4,* 474.

Van-Ree, J. M., Higman, R., Jolles, J., & de Wied, D. (1985). Vasopressin and related peptides: Animal and human studies. Eighth Annual Meeting of the Canadian

College of Neuropsychopharmacology: Perspectives in Canadian neuro-psychopharmacology (1985, London, Canada). *Progress in Neuro-Psychopharmacology and Biological Psychiatry, 9,* 551–559.

Vernon, P. (1985). Individual differences in general cognitive ability. In L. C. Hartlage & C. F. Telzrow (Eds.), *Perspectives on individual differences: The neuropsychology of individual differences, a developmental perspective* (pp. 125–150). New York: Plenum Press.

Vogel, W., & Broverman, D. M. (1964). Relationship between EEG and Test Intelligence: A Critical Review. *Psychological Bulletin, 62,* 132–144.

Warren, N. (1973). Malnutrition and mental development. *Psychological Bulletin, 80,* 324–328.

Weddington, W. W. (1982). Delirium and depression associated with amphotericin B. *Psychosomatics, 23,* 1076–1078.

Weinstein, S., & Teuber, H. L. (1957). Effects of penetrating brain injury on intelligence test scores. *Science, 125,* 1036–1037.

Wiggins, R. C. (1982). Myelin development and nutritional insufficiency. *Brain Research Reviews, 4,* 151–175.

Winogran, H. W., Knights, R. M., & Bawden, H. N. (1983, February). *Neuropsychological deficits following head injury in children.* Paper presented at the meeting of the International Neuropsychological Society, Mexico City, Mexico.

Wolkowitz, O. M., Tinklenberg, J. R., & Weingartner, H. (1985). A psychopharmacological perspective of cognitive functions: II. Specific pharmacologic agents. *Neuropsychobiology, 14,* 133–156.

Wood, C. C. (1978). Variations on a theme by Lashley: Lesion experiments on the neural model of Anderson, Silverstein, Ritz, & Jones. *Psychological Review, 85,* 582–591.

Wood, C. C. (1980). Interpretation of real and simulated lesion experiments. *Psychological Review, 87,* 474–476.

Wood, F., Taylor, B., Penny, R., & Stump, D. A. (1980). Regional cerebral blood flow response to recognition memory versus semantic classification tasks. *Brain and Language, 9,* 113–122.

Yates, C. M., Simpson, J., Gordon, A., Maloney, A. F. J., Allison, Y., Ritchie, I. M., & Urquhart, A. (1983). Catecholamines and cholinergic enzymes in pre-senile and senile Alzheimer-type dementia and Down syndrome. *Brain Research, 280,* 119–126.

Yeo, R. A., Turkheimer, E., Raz, N., & Bigler, E. D. (1987). Volumetric asymmetries of the human brain: Intellectual correlates. *Brain and Cognition, 6,* 15–23.

Yerushalmy, J. (1971). The relationship of parents' smoking to outcome of pregnancy implications as to the problem of inferring causation from observed effects. *American Journal of Epidemiology, 93,* 443–456.

Yerushalmy, J. (1972). Infants with low birth weight born before their mothers started to smoke cigarettes. *American Journal of Obstetrics and Gynecology, 112,* 277–284.

Zuckerman, B. S., & Hingson, R. (1986). Alcohol consumption during pregnancy: A critical review. *Developmental Medicine and Child Neurology, 28,* 649–654.

Chapter 2

The Ecologies of Intelligence: Challenges to Traditional Views

Stephen J. Ceci
Cornell University

Narina N. Nightingale
University of Wyoming

Jacquelyn G. Baker
University of British Columbia

In 1925, a trial took place that drew world-wide attention, and shaped the future of American education. John Scopes, an unknown teacher from Tennessee, was tried for teaching evolutionary theory to his students. The battle lines were drawn between the evolutionists and the creationists, with prominent attorneys on both sides. It is doubtful that the courtroom participants understood the far-reaching ramifications of that trial. Not only did the Scope's Trial bring evolutionary theory into the public domain, it made clear the profound impact that science has on our lives. Of course, the debate was waged in the scientific community and opposing camps vied for professional allegiances well before the Scope's Trial took place. As the evidence began to mount and the debate intensified, most scientists shifted towards the Darwinian view, with the "old guard" left grasping for the remnants of the previous paradigm.

Since the Scope's Trial, scientists have been faced with new challenges and debates. For those of us interested in the scientific study of human intelligence, now is the appropriate time to confront some of the traditional notions of intelligence. Currently under debate is the issue of whether there exists a single intellectual force ("g") underlying much, if not all, cognitive performance, or if there exists a plurality of fairly independent intellects. Respected scientists supporting both views are vying for professional allegiances. As in the debates waged prior to the Scope's Trial, evidence is being compiled by both sides and the debate is intensifying. Whatever the outcome, it is certain the result of these deliberations will have important political and educational ramifications.

We favor a modular view of intelligence. Our goal in writing this paper is to provide empirical support and logical analyses for the position that there is, not one genetically determined intellectual force ("g") underlying all intelligent performance, but rather multiple genetically determined cognitive potentialities that are fairly independent of one another. While we believe there is a genetic basis for each of these potentialities, the amount of variance explained by genetics is unclear. Excellent work already exists which examines the genetic components of both general and specific intellectual abilities (see Rice, Fulker, & DeFries, 1985; Rice, Fulker, Defires, & Plomin, 1988), but at the same time this work is quite limited by the nature of the sample and the measures employed. (For example, it is unclear how much of the genetically associated variance in cognitive traits is due to the hereditary transmission of either general or specific cognitive abilities, and how much is due to the hereditary transmission of temperamental and dispositional tendencies that moderate and modulate the developing organisms's information-processing skills (e.g., impulsivity). It may be that later cognitive outcomes are related to parental cognitive profiles, because what is genetically transmitted is a personality disposition that influences the likelihood of processing certain types of information during sensitive periods of development, and this operates independently of the biological capacity to process information.) Thus, while we recognize the importance of genetic influences on cognitive potentialities, the focus of this chapter will not be to debate the amount of variance explained by genetics, but rather to discuss the nature of these genetic potentialities for cognizing (i.e., are they intellective or non-intellective), and to examine how they are (or are not) manifested.

In addition to postulating multiple cognitive potentialities, we emphasize the role of *context* in each of their crystallizations. Like muscles, cognitive potentialities must receive exercise in order to develop maximally. *Contexts* are the arenas of exercise, and certain developmental contexts are more important for the development of some cognitive potentialities than others. Thus, a home filled with age-appropriate reading material and parents who engage their children in word games may be a more valuable context for the crystallization of one type of cognitive potential (i.e., verbal fluency) than for another (i.e., visual-spatial reasoning). And the presence of such experiences may be greater during one epoch than another.

A final prong in our thinking is that it is not sufficient for one merely to have a particular cognitive potential and to be exposed to an appropriate context for its crystallization, but one must also be *motivated* to benefit from the exposure. As an example, many children have a difficult time learning the alphabet through the process of rote memorization. They are often more motivated to learn the alphabet, however, if it is set to music. We have all known children who have graced us (for hours on end) with that catchy tune and its lyrics, "Now I know my ABC's . . ."

To summarize, the three propositions that we will elaborate are as follows:

1. There are multiple cognitive potentialities that for practical purposes are independent of one another.
2. Contexts are necessary crystallizers and elicitors of these cognitive potentialities.
3. Motivation plays a key role in both the acquisition and subsequent elicitation of potentials.

As will be seen, this perspective expands upon earlier notions of intelligence that also have postulated an interaction between the organism and the environment in the crystallization of cognitive abilities. Although they will be presented independently, the three components listed above are inextricably linked.

MULTIPLE COGNITIVE POTENTIALITIES

Support for the existence of multiple potentialities underlying human "intelligence" comes from past studies that have demonstrated that cognitive abilities exhibited by individuals in one domain were superior to those they exhibited in another. Similarly, some of these studies have suggested superior cognitive complexity by low-IQ persons over high-IQ persons, at least in some domains (see, for example, Ceci & Liker, 1986; Dörner, Kreuzig, Reither, & Staudel, 1983). Other evidence supporting a modular view of human intelligence comes from the fields of education and neuropsychology. In a review of the literature from these various disciplines, Ceci (1990) concluded that the bulk of the evidence is in the direction of multiple, statistically independent, cognitive abilities. We want to stress at the outset that we take no position on the exact number of human potentialities or intellectual abilities, as others have (Gardner, 1983; Guilford, 1967;1982; Thurstone, 1938; Spearman, 1904) only that the number is more than one. Although an important question, it is beyond the scope of this paper.

The question of whether there exist multiple-independent potentialities is not new, and elsewhere we have chronicled the history of this question (Doris & Ceci, 1988). Suffice to say here that, from antiquity to the present, there have always been representatives of the *modularity* and *singularity* of mind perspectives. It is one of the oldest and most challenging debates in the study of the intellect, and in our recent history this debate has been supported on both sides through the use of factor analysis. Although Spearman (1904) and Thurstone (1947) espoused different views of intelligence, they were both able to support their theories with the use of factor analysis. As the axes being fit in a factorial analysis can be rotated, it is easy to understand how a given set of data can be interpreted in different ways. Spearman (1923), believing in the existence of a general factor of intelligence, utilized a "tetrad differences" factorial method which allows a large general factor to emerge as the first factor. Thurstone (1947), in search of the existence of several independent traits, utilized a method which yields a number of independent factors (i.e., "centroid" method) but no general first order factors.

The majority of factor analytic studies of intelligence have yielded similar factor structures, and a general factor of intelligence seems to have emerged (see Sternberg, 1985b). It could be argued that many of these studies, however, have predetermined a "g" solution by the inclusion of a set of homogeneous skills in their assessment. In addition, the meaning one attaches to the general factor is open for debate, some alleging it to be a reflection of a single underlying resource pool that is akin to a biological capacity, and others claiming it is nothing more than similar environments or personalities that influence a wide range of performances. In our view, the magnitude of the general intelligence factor will be diminished when a variety of cognitive potentialities are included in the assessment of intelligence, and when a variety of assessment contexts are employed to help distinguish between cognitive and noncognitive bases. For example, a wide range of potentialities could be identified through the use of a multimethod approach, such as the one advocated by Anastasi (1983): Standardized testing and statistical analyses would be enhanced through the use of methods such as field studies, naturalistic observations, longitudinal designs, and experimental techniques. Recently, researchers have begun to include tasks that were not traditionally included in factorists' batteries, and the result has been to document the existence of new, statistically independent, abilities, such as "wisdom," "social perception," and "practical intelligence" (e.g., Cornelius & Caspi, 1987; Sternberg, Ketron, Conway, & Bernstein, 1981; Wagner & Sternberg, 1985).

In recent years, investigators within the field of information processing also have attempted to understand the dimensions underlying human intelligence. However, their focus has centered on the *processes* underlying intelligent behavior, rather than the *products* that served as grist for the factorists' statistical mills. Using new methodological and statistical paradigms, these investigators have been able to circumvent many of the problems and circularity that plagued a previous cohort of psychometricians. As a result, some progress has been made toward a better understanding of mental processes. Recent findings hold promise for educational assessment and rehabilitative purposes.

Although many theorists have claimed that these methods aid our understanding of "g," it is not clear that this is so. For example, Hunt's (1980,1985) theory of intelligence is built on the well-established "positive manifold" of correlations between various short term memory functions and IQ. The fact that measures such as speed of encoding, verbal fluency, and retrieval parameters all correlate modestly with each other and IQ (*r*s ranging between .2–.3, for the most part) is taken as evidence for the existence of a cognitive "g" (as opposed to a "g" based on shared environments or similar temperaments). We agree with Sternberg (1985b), however, that these modest correlations, though statistically reliable and surely documenting the cross-task involvement of some common attribute—be it intellective or nonintellective—provide a tenuous basis for causal inferences regarding the nonexistence of qualitatively distinct specific abilities. For some, the common involvement across tasks may be due to something that is inherently nonintellective, such as a personality disposition that affects the crystallization of cognitive skills.

The argument that "g" is a reflection of a biologically determined resource pool that sets limits on speed and efficiency of processing and is therefore a substantial contributor to a wide array of cognitive performances becomes even shakier when one considers that, in several validation studies, the most widely used cognitive measures have not correlated with one another, let alone with more macrolevel measures of problem solving (Keating, List, & Merriman, 1985; Herrmann & Gruenich, 1985; List, Keating, & Merriman, 1985; Coles, 1978; Laufer, 1985). For example, in a study by Herrmann and Gruenich (1985), it was found that performance on nine different basic memory tasks (e.g., paired associates, digit span) was essentially uncorrelated, and Keating et al. (1985) demonstrated that three instances of mental rotation (rotating figures, faces, and letters) were uncorrelated with each other as well as with other cognitive performances such as memory and IQ.

These results led Keating and his colleagues to suggest that, by using standard experimental parameters, we may have fallen into the same trap of reification that plagued earlier factor analysts. These researchers reported that the evidence for a relationship between microlevel processing parameters such as those derived from encoding and rotation tasks was "bleak." Of 30 correlations for the adults, only 8 were statistically reliable (and for eighth graders, only 5 of 30 were statistically reliable). Moreover, the average intercorrelations for the rotation measures were only .17. Interestingly, Keating, et al. found similar magnitudes when correlating measures from diverse domains (r = .17). As if this were not bad enough, they found that, for the retrieval from memory measures, the average intercorrelation was actually negative in sign (−.13)! After summarizing these results, Keating, et al. went on to examine the relationship between these microlevel measures and measures of intelligence, and concluded:

> What of the second tier, the processing/ability connections? The evidence here is more strikingly negative. Of the six theoretically relevant correlations for eighth graders, only one is significant. . . The average verbal ability/retrieval parameter correlation is −.14; the average verbal ability/rotation parameter correlation is −.01. The theoretically less related ability/process correlations average is −.09, which is indistinguishable from the predicted correlations. . . . The virtual absence of significant correlations in the predicted directions, together with the equal likelihood of across-domain compared to within-domain correlations . . . provides clear disconfirmation of the . . . theoretically critical processing/ability relationships. . . The findings from this construct validity investigation of the connection between cognitive processing variance, as assessed in a series of standard experiments, and mental ability, as assessed by both group and individual ability tests, are unequivocally disconfirming. We examined a number of possible artifacts to explain these negative results but none were compelling. The experimental procedures and paradigms are among the most widely used. Preliminary analyses showed no anomalous patterns of errors, of effects, of experimental conditions, or of parameter reliabilities. This is indeed paradoxical, given the earlier noted propensity (though not unanimity) of positive findings in previous research. (p. 168)

In a related study, Keating and his colleagues have also reported that parameters derived from individual differences in long term memory retrieval were uncorrelated with intellectual ability measures (List et al., 1985). In that study they cautioned researchers against accepting previous claims of a relationship between retrieval parameters and IQ, since their study had various methodological advantages over those previous studies purporting to find such relationships: "Our study . . . provides strong evidence that this (traditional) method of parameter estimation confounds other cognitive processes. In our investigation, LTM retrieval efficiency correlated with verbal ability . . . when the more confounded estimate was used but was not related to individual differences in complex task performance when the less confounded estimate was used" (p. 149). Recently, Larson (1989) has provided convergent evidence for the modularity position.

In addition to the work of Keating et al. there is a growing body of related work that examines the influence of such nonintellective variables as familiarity on the relation between microlevel performance and its relationship to macrolevel measures (e.g., measures of fluid abilities) that leads to the same conclusion (e.g., Larson, Merritt, & Williams, 1988; Tetewsky, 1988). Psychologists who argue in favor of either "g" *or* multiple potentialities, based solely on evidence from psychometrics or information processing investigations, will need to go beyond off-the-rack laboratory or psychometric instruments to a more process-based approach that actively attempts to disprove the existence of alternative accounts. It would seem that a particularly valuable approach to disconfirmation would be to examine evidence from a variety of disciplines, because it is here that a failure to challenge the psychometric implications regarding g are most pronounced. We believe that, once the literature from various fields is taken into account, the support for independent multiple potentialities will become more forceful, because the *singularity of mind approach* frequently carries with it the inference that rural peoples from nonliterate cultures who perform less efficiently on information-processing tasks are not generally impaired in their cognition.

Some evidence in support of multiple potentialities comes from the neuropsychological literature—specifically, clinical studies that have demonstrated that localized brain lesions lead to the loss of specific cognitive skills. Verbal functions are a frequent subject of such clinical studies, and aphasic patients have been instrumental in providing new insights into brain functioning. In one study, Risse, Rubens and Jordan (1984) found that aphasic patients with inferior frontal lobe lesions and/or lesions of the basal ganglia were severely impaired on the aquisition and long-term retention of word lists. On the short-term memory task, however, the patients performed quite well. Conversely, patients with posterior temporoparietal lesions demonstrated no deficits when examined on either long- or short-term memory tasks. The authors suggest that there is support for a functional and neuroanatomical dissociation of short- and long-term memory systems. Additionally, neural connections in the inferior frontal lobe and the basal ganglia may be important for retrieval processes in long-term memory. Recently, Brainerd and his colleagues have shown that the storage and retrieval stages of short-term memory can be statistically disentangled; it is possible to excell on one without excelling on the other (Brainerd & Reyna, 1989). Yet, since most psychometric tasks require the interaction of both stages, they lead to a singularity view because failure on one leads to failure on the other. But this obfuscates the modularity of these stages in other tasks.

Other investigations have provided support for a neuroanatomical separation of various nonverbal cognitive skills. To give one example, a dissociation between the processing requirements of a task with an energy mask versus a patterned backward mask was recently demonstrated. The results of this study, comparing Alzheimer's patients with age-matched controls, suggests that patterned masks interrupt the integration of physical features into relational and categorical information, and that such functions may be located in the pyramidal cells of the hippocampus and layers III and V of the association cortex (Schlotterer, Moscovitch, & Crapper-McLachlan, 1983).

Clinical studies have also shown that brain damage may result in poor performance on *some* IQ subtests but not on others. In fact, clinical neuropsychologists often utilize IQ profiles as a diagnostic method in order to help localize a patient's lesion (Beaumont, 1983). In this research, there does not appear to be any area that can be regarded as an area for "g," as damage to such an area would be expected to result in similar deleterious effects on all test items having a high "g" loading. To date, such a pattern has not been found.

Although there exists a plethora of neurological evidence supporting the existence of multiple potentialities, there are reasons to resist concluding that this is evidence against the existence of a general factor. First, on logical grounds it is not only possible but probable that cognitive tasks require both some general intellectual resource pool (or "g") as well as specific skills. If so, then it is possible that the specific skills are localized in various anatomical structures of the brain. However, the general intellective resource pool might not be encapsulated within specific processing regions. Thus, localized cognitive deficits associated with specific neural lesions might be independent of the existence of "g." This might be true, especially if the particular cognitive tasks in question have relatively high individual variances. An analogy from the realm of athletics may help make this point clearer: Performance on track and field events tend to be highly correlated. Persons who can throw a javelin the furthest tend to pole vault the highest, run the fastest, and so on. Some sort of underlying general factor could be at work here, perhaps physical strength. Yet, if an athlete incurs damage to his nondominant hand, this may have the effect of diminishing performance at pole vaulting (which requires both hands) while leaving the other skills intact. Damage to the dominant hand could impair the shot-put, javelin, and pole vault while leaving running and jumping relatively unimpaired. Therefore, it is conceivable to imagine a neurological model that would allow both specific and general factors and damage to the former could mask the presence of the latter.

There have been recent attempts to discover an anatomical substrate which might be present in all areas of the cortex and be responsible for cortical function ("g" to intelligence researchers). In a recent review of the cerebral localization literature, Phillips, Zeki, and Barlow (1984) describe the search for "g," or what they describe as a:

> repetitive unit in the cortex, of known anatomical organization, which performs a basically uniform operation, but one which varies from area to area or region to region, according to differences in extrinsic connections. (p. 342)

This anatomical structure has been described by Merzenich as the "glue" which holds the cognitive map together (reported in Phillips et al., 1984). The results of studies searching for this "cortical glue" have *not* been able to find evidence in support of such a notion (e.g., Gilbert & Wiesel, 1979; Martin, Somogyi, & Whitteridge, 1983), even though reports of behavioral manifestations have at time suggested otherwise. For example, Edward Schafer (1987) reported that a parameter derived from evoked cortical potential in response to auditory clicks correlated .66 with WAIS IQ scores (corrected to .82 for range restriction). He concluded from these results that the brains of intelligent persons have evolved to adapt to unexpected events while ignoring highly regular ones, and because of its huge correlation with the size of the first principal component from the standardization sample for the WAIS, "provides a biological determinant of g factor psychometric intelligence" (Schafer, 1987, p. 240). Yet it would seem these findings do not rule out the possibility that the parameters derived from the evoked auditory potentials were themselves modulated by learned strategies associated with schooling, SES, and parenting styles. Thus, while the neuropsychological literature cannot be invoked to prove or disprove a modularity of the mind, the evidence from the localization studies is more or less congruent with a modularity interpretation. And when the supporting neuropsychological studies are joined to the cognitive studies mentioned above, the case against a large and influential "g" becomes more substantial, we believe.

While the neuropsychological literature cited above supports the notion that there are multiple potentialities, there is evidence from the psychological literature that would seem to support a *general* factor of intelligence (discussed earlier). The reason for the disparate interpretations, however, is easily explained. In any discipline, the conclusions that one can draw from a particular piece of research are limited by the questions addressed, by the tools utilized in the work, and by the subject population under investigation. While tasks that are heavily laden with verbal content, for example, are important in understanding certain abilities, it is erroneous to assume that these tasks tap some general intellectual factor that flows into all types of cognizing. What they may be measuring instead, are abilities important in an academic setting, and the general factor usually identified may be an indicant of an academic ability and/or academic experience.

Contrary to the traditional belief that information contained on IQ tests is potentially available to all children, regardless of environmental conditions (Jensen, 1980), it has been known for many decades that schooling exerts a strong influence on intelligence test performance. Thus, to the extent that individuals differ in their level of schooling, they can be expected to differ in their IQs, and this difference has little, if anything, to do with their underlying ability to detect, store, and/or retrieve information.

The most trivial example of the impact of schooling on IQ performance can be found in the small but reliable decrement in IQ that occurs during summer vacations, especially among low-income youngsters whose summer activities are least likely to resemble those found in school (Jencks, Smith, Acland, Bane, Cohen, Gintis, Heyns, & Michelsen, 1972). This finding has twice been replicated with large samples by independent investigators (Hayes & Grether, 1982; Heyns, 1978). The steady increase in both IQ and achievement test scores that accrues as the school year progresses is partly reversed during the summer vacation (Hayes & King, 1974).

One of the best documented studies of the impact of schooling actually was intended as a demonstration of cohort-sequential analysis rather than as a study of the effect of schooling per se. Baltes and Reinert (1969) randomly sampled 630 children from 48 elementary schools in Säarbrucken, Germany. Three cross-sections of 8- to 10-year-olds, who were separated in age by 4-month intervals, were administered a German version of the Primary Mental Abilities Test (Thurstone & Thurstone, 1962). The German school system requires children to be 6 years of age by April 1 as a criterion for admission to school. Therefore, it was possible to compare same-aged children who had received up to a year difference in schooling. For example, a child who was born in March and is 8 years, 2 months in May could be compared with a child who was born in April and was 8 years, 2 months in June. The former child would have received an additional year of schooling by the time he or she was 8 years old. Baltes and Reinert (1969) found a substantial correlation between the length of schooling and intellectual performance among same-aged, same-SES children. Highly schooled 8-year-olds actually were closer in IQ to the least schooled 10-year olds than they were to least schooled 8-year-olds!

There is also ample support for the view that schooling conveys positive effects on the acquisition and use of the microlevel information-processing components. For example, the ability to use depth cues in two-dimensional pictorial representations, the ability to disambiguate figure-ground pictorial representations (Children's Embedded Figure Test scores), and the ability to perceive abstract visual-spatial organizations (Block Design scores) all have been shown to be enhanced through the schooling process (Dawson, 1967; Greenfield & Childs, 1972; Kilbride & Leibowitz, 1975; Myambo, 1972; Witkin & Berry, 1975). Similarly, numerous studies have documented effects of schooling on a variety of conceptual skills. Compared to their nonschooled peers, school children are more likely to: (a) sort stimuli by form-class rather than by color, (b) group items that belong to the same taxonomic class rather than to the same thematic class, (c) demonstrate greater flexibility in shifting between domains during problem solving, and (d) spontaneously engage in more verbal descriptions of their classifications (Ceci & Liker, 1986; Gay & Cole, 1967; Hall, 1972; Greenfield, Reich, & Olver, 1966; Irwin & McLaughlin, 1970).

The results of the work discussed above suggest that what some researchers call a general factor of intelligence is actually an academic ability or set of abilities. Nowhere is this more apparent than in anthropological research of societies in which there is no Western schooling. Super's (1980) study of the !Kung San, a hunting/gathering tribe of the Kalahari Desert, is a good case in point.

The elaborate descriptions of the !Kung San men's behavior during hunts clearly demonstrate that they behave in a cognitively complex manner. These men glean clues from the environment, differentially weight the import of these clues for the hunt's success, and arrive at some decision. During one hunt, for example, a giraffe was wounded and the !Kung San needed to determine whether or not to continue the hunt. They evaluated clues such as whether a twig was splattered with the giraffe's blood before or after it was bent. If it was bent *before*, the giraffe was still standing tall while feeding on the branch and thus could have the ability to evade the hunters for several more days. On the other hand, if the branch was *already* bent when the giraffe's blood marked it, this might suggest that the animal was already craning low to the ground during feeding as a result of its injury. !Kung San hunters evaluated the pattern of crushed grasses and animal droppings in order to yield information about the giraffe. Not all the clues were equally important in the decision about whether or not the hunt should have been continued.

It is difficult not to be impressed by the !Kung San hunters' adroit problem-solving abilities, as evidence for their cognitive complexity is apparent in the ethnographies presented by Super and his colleagues. Yet, the !Kung San men perform only as well as Western *children* when they are administered IQ tests, Piagetian tests, and information-processing tasks. These findings hold true even when the tasks are adapted for the local culture (e.g., by substituting familiar vegetables for unfamiliar vegetables on the IQ test). How can one reconcile these mens' apparent complexity while hunting with their poor performance on traditional micro- and macrolevel aspects of intelligence? Under the auspices of a general factor of intelligence, these findings cannot be reconciled. They can be partially explained, however, if one views intelligence as a set of independent potentialities, each developing within a specific context. Performance in one domain (e.g., hunting) would not necessarily be expected to correlate with performance in another (e.g., verbal ability). Of course, to more fully explain these findings, one must consider the importance of *context* in the crystallization of specific abilities.

CONTEXTUAL INFLUENCES ON INTELLIGENCE

Prevailing theories of intelligence could be described as acontextual, whether they embrace one or many potentialities. In other words, the ability or abilities that an individual possesses would be expected to be apparent in any situation that requires them. A child with superior visual-spatial abilities would be expected to perform well on both the WISC-R Block Design and video games at the local arcade. A person's ability to perform a task would not be expected to vary as a function of the context in which the testing occurs. Such assumptions may be false. It is possible that intelligent behavior might be affected by the context in which a particular skill is required. Similarly, one might develop a set of highly complex abilities that are utilized in one context but not in another.

A study by Ceci and Bronfenbrenner (1985a) demonstrates the importance of context in the assessment of intelligent behavior. In this study, children of various ages were asked to remember to do things in the future (i.e., remove cupcakes from the oven in 30 minutes or disconnect a battery charger from a motorcycle battery in 30 minutes). While waiting to do these things, the children were invited to play *PacMan,* a popular video game. The data of interest concern the children's clock-checking behavior while waiting for the 30 minutes to elapse. Children behaved differently as a function of the setting in which they were studied. When observed in the familiar context of their own homes and in the company of their siblings, children appeared to "calibrate" their psychological clocks through a process of early and frequent clock-checking. These early clock-checks permitted the children to synchronize their psychological clocks with the passage of actual clock time. For example, a child might begin the waiting period by making several confirmatory checks to insure that the amount of time that has transpired is close to their subjective estimates. After several such confirmatory checks, children gain the confidence to allow their psychological clocks to "run" until nearly the end of the 30-minute period, whereupon last-minute incessant clock-watching was evidenced by scalloping.

The advantage of using a calibration strategy is that it permits children to engage effectively in other activities (playing video games), unencumbered by the need to look constantly at the wall clock. It also allows a maximum degree of precision with a minimum amount of effort (clock-checking). Thus, the use of the calibration strategy does not result in a loss of punctuality. None of the children who gave evidence of employing this strategy burned the cupcakes or overheated the motorcycle battery. Support for the assumption that children were indeed synchronizing their psychological clocks with a nearby wall clock was provided by showing that the U-shaped distribution of clock-checking was recoverable even when the wall clock was programmed to run faster or slower than real time. That is, subjects were able to adjust their subjective estimations of the passage of clock time, and, once this adjustment was achieved, they were successful at gauging the remainder of the waiting period with only a minimal amount of glancing at the clock.

In the laboratory, however, children displayed no evidence of using a calibration strategy. They, too, did not burn the cupcakes but they required nearly a third more effort. As a result, the ability to engage effectively in video game activities was lessened during the waiting period. With the exception of older boys who were asked to engage in a traditionally female sex-typed task (baking cupcakes), there was no evidence of calibration in the laboratory setting.

These data point to the influence of context on strategy use. Here, context is conceived as, not only the physical setting in which the task unfolds, but the social/cultural features, as well (e.g., the sex-role expectations of the task, the age-appropriateness of the task, the presence or absence of familiar persons, etc.). Unlike the traditional information processing conceptualization of context as something adjunctive to cognition (i.e., a social/physical address where cognitive tasks are performed), these findings suggest context should be viewed as a constituent of the cognitive task, influencing the manner in which the task is perceived and the selection of strategies for its solution. Had the investigators assessed children's competence only in the laboratory setting, they would have been led to underestimate the potential sophistication of their strategies. Conversely, had they observed children's clock-checking only in their homes, they would have missed the significance of many of the ecological contrasts that the laboratory comparison afforded.

In a similar vein, it is possible that some persons who perform rather poorly on laboratory tasks or on standardized tests of intelligence might demonstrate complex cognitive abilities in other contexts. That is, some individuals who perform poorly on an I.Q. test might demonstrate complex reasoning in the tasks that confront them in their everyday lives. Several recent studies support such a notion, and two will be discussed in further detail.

The first set of studies has been conducted during the past 5 years by Sylvia Scribner (a psychologist) and a group of anthropologists interested in industrial literacy in America. In their examination of a Baltimore dairy factory, these researchers discovered that assemblers, the men responsible for filling cases with prespecified proportions of whole milk, 2% milk, skim milk, buttermilk, and chocolate milk, made rapid assessments of nearby cases that were partially filled in order to avoid beginning an order with an empty case. Empty cases require a good deal of bending, and the workers appeared adept at selecting partially filled cases that allowed orders to be filled with the least amount of bending.

In a follow-up experiment to confirm these naturalistic observations, Scribner (1984) demonstrated the assemblers' skill at making rapid assessments of the possibilities of partially filled cases for making prespecified orders. Assemblers, as a group, were the least educated workers in the factory, yet they were more successful at making rapid assessments of partially filled cases than were more educated whitecollar workers who occassionally substituted on the assembly line when an assembler was absent. Interestingly, there was no relationship between this skill and various high school test scores (e.g., IQ, arithmetic test scores, or grades).

In a study of expert racetrack handicappers, Ceci and Liker (1986) provide evidence that parallels Scribner's (1984) findings. They demonstrated that a group of relatively uneducated but expert racetrack handicappers employed a complex, multiplicative model involving multiple interaction effects. By regressing 25 racetrack variables on experts' assessments of odds, Ceci and Liker were able to show that simple additive models failed to account for the handicappers' decisions. For instance, to successfully predict the speed with which a horse could run the final quarter-mile of a race, experts used a six-way interactive model. Use of this complex interaction term discriminated experts from nonexperts in the ability to predict odds. The correlation between experts' IQs and the beta weight for this six-way interactive term (a surrogate for cognitive complexity) was −.07. Thus, assessments of one's intelligence on a standard IQ test were irrelevant in predicting the complexity of their thinking at the races. Within either group (experts *or* nonexperts), IQ was unrelated to handicapping complexity but between groups there was an invariant finding: Experts with low IQs always used more cognitively complex, interactive models than did nonexperts possessing high IQs, and the success of the former was due in large part to the use of these complex models.

Taken together, the research reviewed (baking cupcakes, packing milk crates, and handicapping real races) suggests the need to expand earlier notions of intelligence that were developed within the psychometric and information-processing traditions. It is not only that individual differences in IQ test score variance did not account for individual differences on other forms of cognitive complexity, but the likelihood of using even microlevel cognitive strategies that underpin more complex cognition is significantly under the influence of ecological variables such as the sex-role expectations of the task and the physical setting where the task is performed. These studies call into question a prior era's unrivaled assumptions regarding the generality of intelligence and the status of *context* as a mere adjunct to cognition. They demonstrate the importance of contextual variables as an integral aspect of the perception and solution of complex problems.

MOTIVATIONAL INFLUENCES ON INTELLIGENCE

Our final proposition stresses the role of motivational variables on intelligent performance. In order to examine the role that motivation plays, let us return to the information-processing literature. There are at least two ways in which motivation may affect information processing and learning. First, encoding and long-term storage of material can be facillitated if incentives are present. Second, motivational factors may influence the likelihood that certain abilities are elicited during retrieval.

Several researchers have examined the usefulness of incentives throughout the learning process. Atkinson and Wickens (1971), for example, have suggested that incentives cause a selective attention bias towards high-incentive items in learning tasks. A study conducted by Loftus (1972) supports such a view. Subjects examined pairs of pictures (one picture in each pair was associated with high incentives), and their eye movements were monitored. As hypothesized, subjects spent more time fixating on the high incentive pictures and consequently identified more of those pictures during a recognition memory task.

Eysenck (1982) suggests that the extra attention which is given to high incentive items results in a more elaborate encoding of these items. In an earlier study, Eysenck and Eysenck (1980) presented subjects with lists of words for subsequent cued recall. No differences were found between the recall of words in the high- or low-incentive condition when either phonetic or semanitic cues were presented. In comparison, interactive effects were found between the incentive condition and whether the cue was of weak or strong association value. That is,

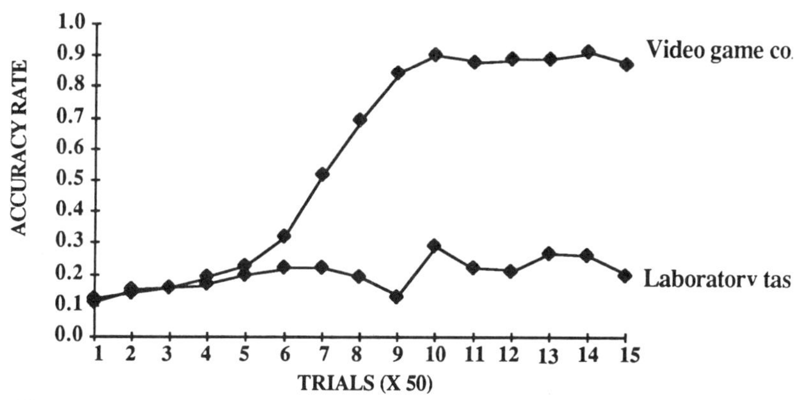

Figure 1. Children's mean proportion of accurate estimates of a moving object is game versus laboratory contexts. (Simple main effects algorithm)

weak cues were only helpful in the recall of high-incentive items, while strong cues were helpful regardless of the incentive. The authors suggest that incentives do not result in qualitative differences in processing, rather they serve to increase the extensiveness of the encoding (Eysenck & Eysenck, 1980).

Recently, it was found that incentives facilitated recall after extended retention intervals (Ward, 1985). This finding complements Eysenck's explanation of the influence of motivation on learning. Ordinarily, we would expect retrieval to become more difficult after extended retention intervals. However, words which have been elaborately encoded should be less vulnerable to decay with the passage of time.

As we mentioned earlier, motivation may also serve to elicit the expression of a particular ability. This seems to be the case in a study by Ceci and Bronfenbrenner (1985b, reported in Ceci, 1990). In an extension of their cupcake study, children were instructed to predict where, on a video terminal, an object would terminate by placing a cross on the screen at that location by moving a joystick. The object was one of three types (square, circle, triangle), two colors, and two sizes, yielding 12 combinations of features. A simple additive algorithm was written to "drive" the stimuli so that, for example, squares would go up, circles would go down, and triangles would stay horizontal. Similarly, green-colored objects would move right, and blue-colored objects would move left. Large objects would move on a lower-left-to-upper-right diagonal, while small objects would move along the opposite diagonal. There were no interactions in the algorithm. Children were given 15 sessions of 50 random trials each to provide probability feedback. Even after 750 probability feedback trials, however, their prediction accuracy was only 22% (lower lines in Figure 1).

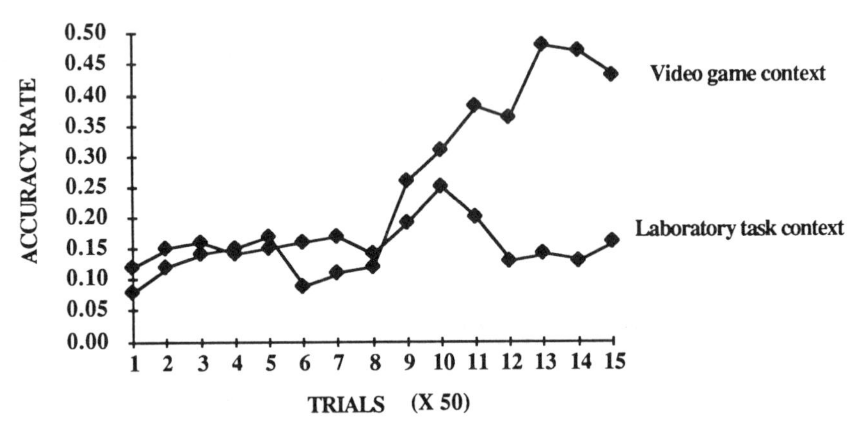

Figure 2. Children's mean proportion of accurate estimates of a moving object in game versus laboratory contexts. (Multiplicative algorithm)

Next the researchers used the same algorithm to drive a video game. The three geometric shapes were converted to a butterfly, a mosquito, and a bird. (The same colors and sizes were used.) Instead of placing a cross on the area of the video terminal where they predicted the object would terminate, children were told to place a "butterfly net" to "capture the prey," by moving a joystick. Children were awarded points for each correct capture. As can be seen in Figure 1, this shift in context resulted in drastically improved performance. After 750 feedback trials the children were near ceiling.

In an extension of this study, the investigators used a more complex algorithm to drive the objects, a curvilinear function:

$$.8 \text{ Sin}_x + .6 \text{ Sin}_y + .4 \text{ Sin}_z + 5\% \text{ error*} \quad (1)$$

Again, there was a substantial enhancement of performance when the task was embedded in the presumably more motivating video game context, though the overall levels of performance were not as high as those found with the simple additive model algorithm (see Figure 2).

These data are important in dispelling the belief that young children are "main effects" thinkers, incapable of grasping more complex, multiplicative models (see Klayman, 1984, for evidence that even college students are unable to assimilate a curvilinear function in a probability learning exercise similar to the one being discussed).

* The mapping function (over a quarter sine phase) was: x^1, y^1, z^1 = random number {0–9}, where x,y,z = maxdistance + 1.8 (0.8 sine x^1 .10 + 0.6 sine $y^1 \times .10$ + 0.4 sine $z^1 \times .10$).

Had children been tested in only the disembedded laboratory-prediction context (squares, circles, etc.), a vast underestimation of their cognitive competence would have resulted. These data indicate that children have at least some ability to understand complex models of probability when motivated. This may come as no surprise to parents who have spent many a Saturday afternoon watching their children successfully come to terms with complex video games at the local mall.

Despite the evidence demonstrating the importance of motivation on basic processing abilities (e.g., encoding and retrieval), many have argued that motivational influences are not important when examined in the context of more global measures such as IQ tests. A number of investigators have attempted to boost IQ scores through the use of both extrinsic and intrinsic motivators. Many have failed to produce any substantial gains in IQ (Maller & Zubin, 1932; Sarason & Minard, 1962).

The fact that children perform the same on an IQ test independent of the level of motivation provided by testers is both unsurprising and compatible with the argument being advanced in this chapter. We believe that the evidence on the role of motivation in the encoding and retrieval of information is quite extensive. But it is worth remembering that encoding and retrieval are *processes,* not products. A *process* can be made to function more efficiently by the use of motivation, and to the extent this is the case one would expect more knowledge to be acquired by way of these processes. Individuals who go through life highly motivated to learn vocabulary will undoubtedly learn more vocabulary than someone with an equivalent capacity for word learning but who went through life unmotivated to acquire vocabulary. Motivation allows a test of the "outer limits" of one's basic processes; providing incentives during encoding (and/or retrieval) should result in more information being encoded (or retrieved, if the information was already encoded).

It is an entirely different matter, however, to suggest that extant *products* (like IQ-relevant world knowledge, vocabulary, and spatial abilities), which themselves were the result of the efficiency of basic processes during an individual's life-time interacting with ongoing motivations, can be enhanced through the use of incentives at the time of testing. We have no supernatural expectations for the role of incentives; if they are operative at the time a process is being carried out, then we expect that process to result in a superior amount of acquisition (i.e., a superior product). On the other hand, if processes were unmotivated when they were originally undertaken to encode some specific information, there is no viable role for motivation to play at the time of their retrieval, beyond revealing the fullest picture of the previously encoded product. That is, incentives may operate at the time of encoding or at the time of retrieval, but if at the latter, they will be unable to influence the child's performance beyond what he or she has already encoded. Thus, incentives may be ineffective in elevating cognitive products (IQ) beyond the level to which they were acquired originally. A corrolarly of this position is that to the extent motivation was strong during the encoding and retrieval of information relevant to IQ performance (e.g., word learning), the resultant cognitive product (IQ or verbal fluency) will be enhanced vis-á-vis an unmotivated comparison. Incentives then are conceptualized as affecting input to the cognitive system and, given this input, output. They cannot, of course, affect the output of information that had never been input in the first place. Similarly, an individual asked to define words that have not been acquired previously will be unable to supply their meanings no matter how motivated he or she is at the time of testing.

TAKING STOCK OF OUR OPTIONS

In sum, we have argued for a view of human intelligence that is modular in nature and under the direct influence of contextual factors. Our "game plan" has been to move beyond the confines of our own discipline (that of cognitive psychology) in order to integrate findings from various fields of inquiry. After examining the evidence from such fields as anthropology, neuropsychology, education, and developmental psychology, we have concluded that there is converging support for the view that multiple independent potentialities underpin human intelligence.

By stepping outside our own discipline, we have been forced to confront some of the inadequacies of our own paradigms. One difficult but necessary consequence of this brief but interdisciplinary excursion of the literature has been our realization that traditional conceptualizations of intelligence, as embodied in the psychometric and information-processing traditions, are ill wrought. Their acontextual focus, coupled with the limited role of motivation, has led to "snapshots" of the individual as he or she negotiates tasks. These "snapshots" are frequently disconnected from important environmental contexts that served to crystallize their various cognitive potentialities.

As was demonstrated in an earlier section, contexts are not only instrumental in the formation of cognitive skills during development, they are also important as "elicitors" of already-formed cognitive skills at the time of the assessment. To disembody cognition from its crystallizing and eliciting contexts, as is characteristically done in both psychometric and information-processing approaches, is to be left with an intellectual product that represents but a single aspect of cognitive complexity, namely, the ability to perform in situations unrelated to one's life history. Such acontextual approaches provide a needlessly singular and ungenerous picture of one's cognitive capabilities. This was graphically depicted in the study of distance estimation; these childrens' performance in the laboratory context erroneously suggested an inability to employ multicausal reasoning. Similar examples are strewn throughout the anthropological literature whenever an individual is shown to be deficient on a task but can subsequently perform the very same operation when it is couched in some more meaningful context (e.g., Lave, 1977; Lave, Murtaugh, & de la Rocha, 1984).

What are we to make, then, of the moderately high correlations between IQ and school performance? Or, for that matter, how do we explain the correlations between IQ and various microlevel information processing parameters (Hunt, 1980)? As we have argued, such correlations are not surprising. School performance, IQ tests, and information-processing tasks all tap a relatively homogeneous set of the same personality and tempermamental dispositions (e.g., sitting still, being reflective, self-monitoring). For researchers who are interested in academic performance, the current battery of psychometric and information processing tasks is valuable as a means of prediction. It is unwarranted, however, to assume that these test batteries offer anything more in the way of explanation than the prediction of academic attainment. Academic attainment reflects but one of many underlying cognitive potentialities. Not until researchers begin to recognize the independence of these potentialities, and the factors by which these potentialities are elicited and crystalized, can we expect progress toward the understanding of real-world manifestations of cognitive complexity.

REFERENCES

Anastasi, A. (1983). Evolving trait concepts. *American Psychologist, 38,* 175–184.

Atkinson, R. C., & Wickens, T. D. (1971). Human memory and the concept of reinforcement. In R. Glaser (Ed.), *The nature of reinforcement.* London: Academic Press.

Baltes, P., & Reinert, G. (1969). Cohort effects in cognitive development in children as revealed by cross-sectional sequences. *Developmental Psychology, 1,* 169–177.

Beaumont, J. G. (1983). *Introduction to neuropsychology.* New York: Guilford Press.

Brainerd, C. J., & Reyna, V. (1989). Output interference theory of dual-task deficits in memory. *Journal of Experimental Child Psychology, 47,* 1–18.

Ceci, S. J. (1990). *On intelligence . . . . more or less: A bio-ecological treatise on intellectual development.* Englewood Cliffs, NJ: Prentice-Hall (Century Series in Psychology).

Ceci, S. J., & Bronfenbrenner, U. (1985a). Don't forget to take the cupcakes out of the oven: Strategic time-monitoring, prospective memory, and context. *Child Development, 56,* 175–190.

Ceci, S. J., & Bronfenbrenner, U. (1985b). *The acquisition of simple and complex algorithims as a function of context.* Unpublished manuscript, Cornell University.

Ceci, S. J., & Liker, J. (1986). A day at the races: A study of IQ, expertise, and cognitive complexity. *Journal of Experimental Psychology: General, 115,* 255–266.

Coles, G. (1978). The standard LD battery. *Harvard Educational Review, 48,* 313–340.

Cornelius, S. W., & Caspi, A. (1987). Everyday problem solving in adulthood and old age. *Psychology and Aging, 2,* 144–153.

Dawson, J. L. M. (1967). Cultural and physiological influences upon spatial-perceptual processes in West Africa, Part 1. *International Journal of Psychology, 46,* 596–597.

Doris, J., & Ceci, S. J. (1988, Spring). Varieties of Mind. *National Forum, 68,* 18–22.

Dörner, D., Kreuzig, H., Reither, F., & Staudel, T. (1983). *Lohhausen: Vom umgang mitunbestimmtheit und komplexitat.* Bern: Huber.

Eysenck, M. W. (1982). *Attention and arousal.* Berlin: Spinger-Verlag.
Eysenck, M. W., & Eysenck, M. C. (1980). Effects of monetary incentives on rehearsal and on cued recall. *Bulletin of the Psychonomic Society, 15,* 245–247.
Gardner, H. (1983). *Frames of mind: The theory of multiple intelligences.* New York: Basic Books.
Gay, J., & Cole, M. (1967). *The new mathematics and an old culture.* New York: Holt, Rinehart, & Winston.
Gilbert, C., & Wiesel, T. N. (1979). Morphology and intrcortical proojections of functionally characterized neurones in the cat visual cortex. *Nature, London, 280,* 129–130.
Greenfield, P. M., & Childs, C. P. (1972, September). *Weaving, color terms, and pattern representation: Cultural influences and cognitive development among the Zinacantecos of Southern Mexico.* Paper presented at the meeting of the International Association of Cross-Cultural Psychology, Hong Kong.
Greenfield, P. M., Reich, L., & Olver, R. (1966). On culture and equivalence. In J. S. Bruner, R. Olver, & P. M. Greenfield (Eds.), *Studies in cognitive growth.* New York: Wiley.
Guilford, J. P. (1967). *The nature of human intelligence.* New York: McGraw-Hill.
Guilford, J. P. (1982). Cognitive psychology's ambiguities: Some suggested remedies. *Psychological Review, 89,* 48–59.
Hall, J. (1972). Verbal behavior as a function of amount of schooling. *American Journal of Psychology, 85,* 277–289.
Hayes, D., & Grether, J. (1982). The school year and vacations: when do students learn? *Cornell Journal of Social Relations, 17,* 56–71.
Herrmann, D., Grubbs, L., Sigmindi, R., & Gruenich, R. (1985). Awareness of memory ability. *Human Learning, 5,* 91–107.
Heyns, B. (1978). *Summer learning and the effects of schooling.* New York: Academic Press.
Hunt, E. (1980). Intelligence as an information processing concept. *British Journal of Psychology, 71,* 449–474.
Hunt, E. (1985). Verbal ability. In R. J. Sternberg (Ed.), *Human abilities: An information processing approach.* San Francisco, CA: Freeman.
Irwin, M. H., & McLaughlin, D. H. (1970). Ability and preference in category sorting by Mano school children and adults. *Journal of Social Psychology, 82,* 15–24.
Jencks, C., Smith, M., Acland, H., Bane, M. J., Cohen, D., Gintis, H., Heyns, B., & Mitchelson, S. (1972). *Inequality: A reassessment of the effects of family and schooling in America.* New York: Basic Books.
Jensen, A. R. (1980). *Bias in mental testing.* New York: Free Press.
Keating, D. P. (1984). The emperor's new clothes: The "new look" in intelligence research. In R. J. Sternberg (Ed.), *Advances in the psychology of human intelligence* (Vol. 2). Hillsdale, NJ: Erlbaum.
Keating, D. P., List, J. A., & Merriman, W. E. (1985). Cognitive processing and cognitive ability: A multivariate validity investigation. *Intelligence, 9,* 149–170.
Kilbride, P., & Leibowtiz, H. (1975). Factors affected the magnitude of the Ponzo perspective illusion among the Baganda. *Perception & Psychophysics, 17,* 543–548.
Klayman, J. (1984). *Learning from feedback in probablistic environments.* Unpublished manuscript. Chicago: University of Chicago Graduate School of Management.

Larson, G. (1989). Cognitive correlates of general intelligence. *Intelligence, 13,* 5–31.

Larson, G., Merritt, C., & Williams, S. E. (1988). Information processing and intelligence: Some implications of task complexity. *Intelligence, 12,* 131–147.

Laufer, E. (1985, March). *Domain-specific knowledge and memory performance in the work place.* Paper presented at the Annual Meeting of the Eastern Psychological Association. Boston.

Lave, J. (1977). Tailor-made experiments and evaluating the intellectual consequences of apprenticeship training. *The Quarterly Newsletter of the Institute for Comparative Human Development, 1,* 1–3.

Lave, J., Murtaugh, M., & de la Rocha, D. (1984). The dialectic of arithmetic in grocery shopping. In B. Rogoff & J. Lave (Eds.), *Everyday cognition: Its development in social context.* Cambridge, MA: Harvard University Press.

List, J., Keating, D., & Merriman, W. (1985). Differences in memory retrieval: A construct validation investigation. *Child Development, 56,* 138–151.

Loftus, G. R. (1972). Eye fixations and recognitions and recognition memory for pictures. *Cognitive Psychology, 3,* 525–551.

Martin, K. A. C., Somogyi, P., & Whitteridge, D. (1983). Physiological and morphological properties of identified basket cells in the cat's visual cortex. *Experimental Brain Research, 50,* 193–200.

Maller, J. B., & Zubin, J. (1932). The effect of motivation upon intelligence test scores. *Journal of Genetic Psychology, 41,* 136–151.

Myambo, K. (1972). Shape constancy as influenced by culture, Western education, and age. *Journal of Cross-Cultural Psychology, 3,* 221–232.

Phillips, C., Zeki, S., & Barlow, H. (1984). Localization of function in the cerebral cortex. *Brain, 107,* 328–361.

Rice, T., Fulker, D. W., & Defries, J. C. (1985). Multivariate path analysis of specific cognitive abilities in the Colorado Adoption Project. *Behavior Genetics, 16,* 107–125.

Rice, T., Fulker, D. W., Defries, J. C., & Plomin, R. (1988). Path analysis of IQ during infancy and early childhood and an index of the Home Environment in the Colorado Adoption Project. *Intelligence, 12,* 27–45.

Risse, G. L., Rubens, A. B., & Jordan, L. S. (1984). Disturbances of long-term memory in aphasic patients: A comparison of anterior and posterior lesions. *Brain, 107,* 605–617.

Sarason, I., & Minard, J. (1962). Test anxiety, experimental instructions, and the Wechsler Adult Intelligence Scale. *Journal of Educational Psychology, 53,* 299–302.

Schafer, E. (1987). Neural adaptability: A biological determinant of g factor intelligence. *Behavioral and Brain Sciences, 10,* 240–241.

Schlotterer, G., Moscovitch, M., & Crapper-McLachlan (1983). Visual processing deficits as assessed by spatial frequency contrast sensitivity and backward masking in normal ageing and Alzheimer's disease. *Brain, 107,* 309–325.

Scribner, S. (1984). Studying working intelligence. In B. Rogoff & J. Lave (Eds.), *Everyday cognition: Its development in social context.* Cambridge, MA: Harvard University Press.

Spearman, C. (1904). 'General intelligence' objectively determined and measured. *American Journal of Psychology, 15,* 206–221.

Spearman, C. (1923). *The nature of "intelligence" and the principles of cognition.* London: Macmillan.

Sternberg, R. J. (1985a). *Human abilities: An information processing approach.* San Francisco, CA: Freeman.

Sternberg, R. J. (1985b). *Beyond IQ: A triarchic theory of human intelligence.* Cambridge, England: Cambridge University Press.

Sternberg, R., Ketron, J., Conway, B., & Bernstein, M. (1981). People's conceptions of intelligence. *Journal of Personality & Social Psychology, 41,* 37–55.

Super, C. M. (1980). Cognitive development: Looking across at growing up. *New Directions for Child Development: Anthropological Perspectives on Child Development, 8,* 59–69.

Tetewsky, S. J. (1988). *An analysis of familiarity effects in visual comparison tasks and their implications for studying human intelligence.* Unpublished doctoral dissertation, Yale University.

Thurstone, L. L. (1938). *Primary mental abilities.* Chicago, IL: University of Chicago Press.

Thurstone, L. L. (1947). *Multiple factor analysis.* Chicago, IL: University of Chicago Press.

Thurstone, L. L., & Thurstone, T. G. (1962). *Test of primary mental abilities* (rev. ed.). Chicago, IL: Science Research Assoc.

Wagner, R., & Sternberg, R. J. (1985). Practical intelligence in real-world pursuits. *Journal of Personality & Social Psychology, 49,* 436–458.

Ward, C. A. (1985). *Effects of incentive motivation on memory performance of children.* Unpublished master's thesis, SUNY Cortland.

Witkin, H., & Barry, J. (1975). Psychological differentiation in cross-cultural perspective. *Journal of Cross-Cultural Psychology, 6,* 322–334.

Chapter 3

Intelligence: The One and the Many

H. J. Eysenck

Emeritus Professor of Psychology
University of London

1. INTELLIGENCE: ONE OR MANY?

In Greek philosophy, the problem of the one and the many was a fundamental one. Is nature unitary or diverse? Can we step into the same river twice? Is all matter made up of atoms? The specter of this question haunted Greek thinking, and it also seems to haunt modern theorists of intelligence. The battle between Spearman's (1927) *g* and Thurstone's (1938) primary mental abilities is just one example of this, but it goes back to a similar difference of view point characterizing the respective theories of Sir Francis Galton (1892, 1943), and Alfred Binet (1903, 1907). In modern times Jensen (1984) might be used as representative of the unitary theory, Guilford (1967) of the modular one.

There are of course many psychologists who hold an intermediary position, acknowledging the existence both of a general factor of intelligence and also the existence of independent group or primary factors (Vernon, 1979; Eysenck,

1939, 1979; Cattell, 1971; Burt, 1940, and many others). Even Thurstone (Thurstone & Thurstone, 1941) and Spearman (Spearman & Jones, 1950) finally agreed that the description of cognitive ability needed both a general factor and group factors, leaving group factors as a residual, whereas Thurstone would extract the general factor from the intercorrelations between his primaries.

In the continuum running from the one to the many, this compromise solution, while in good accord with the facts, is widely disregarded by textbook writers, educational psychologists, and many others, who still argue along the original Thurstone lines (Thurstone, 1938) and pretend that there is really no evidence for a general factor of intelligence. Guilford (Guilford & Hoepfner, 1971) has adopted this cause by advocating his "model of the intellect," which suggests the existence of 120 independent abilities, although, as Eysenck (1979) has pointed out, the data simply do not support his interpretation. The allegedly independent tests are highly correlated, and all correlate quite highly with IQ tests. Furthermore, the statistical methods used (targeted rotation methodology) has been severely criticized by almost all reviewers (e.g., Horne & Knapp, 1973) and would be difficult to defend. Nevertheless, his model features in practically all textbooks, and the criticisms are usually not given the prominence they deserve. The Zeitgeist clearly does not favor the concept of a general factor of intelligence, or even the very notion of *intelligence* in the sense in which the term was used by Galton, Spearman and others.

In actual fact the continuum from *g*, through Thurstone's seven or so factors, and Ekstrom's (1979) and Horn's (1978) 20–30 factors, to Guilford's 120 abilities can be continued well beyond this point, to the advocacy of a complete *specificity doctrine*. This doctrine is a relic of primitive behaviorism, which taught that abilities are specific, learned elements of behavior, and that mental tests are merely measures of whether a person has learned certain bits of behavior or not. This notion is based on two beliefs. (a) Human mental abilities, and individual differences in these abilities, consist of nothing more than a repertoire of specific items of knowledge and specific skills acquired through learning and experience. (b) Psychometric tests of IQ and mental abilities measure nothing other than some selected sample of the total repertoire of knowledge and skills considered important by the test constructor. According to this behavioristic view of mental specificity, IQ tests are useful in terms of predictive validity only because they measure specific knowledge and skills that constitute part of the criterion behavior to be predicted by the test scores. This doctrine has a respectable ancestry, dating back to Thorndike (1903), perhaps the most important advocate of the S-R model of behavior. The specificity hypothesis was formally stated by Thorndike, Bregman, Cobb, and Woodyard (1926) as follows: "The hypothesis which we present and shall defend asserts that in their deeper nature the higher forms of intellectual operation are identical with mere association or connection forming, depending upon the same sort of physiological connections but requiring *many more of them*. By the same argument the person whose intellect is greater or higher or better than that of another person differs from him in the last analysis in having, not a new sort of physiological process, but simply a larger number of connections of the ordinary sort" (p. 415; emphasis in original). In other words, intelligence is a function of the number of S-R connections one has formed. This view is in many ways similar to that of Thomson (1939), whose "sampling theory" maintains that each mental test calls upon a sample of the bonds which the mind can form, and that some of these bonds are common to two tests and cause their correlation. These "bonds," of course, are similar in nature to Thorndike's S-R connections, and the theory can be restated in a more mathematical form (Maxwell, 1972) to form a basis for factor analytic algorithms.

Both theories, however, pose a very important question. They go back, essentially, to Locke and his notion of the mind as a *tabula rasa,* on which experience could write anything it pleased. Intelligence, on this conception, would be the number of things written on the *tabula rasa* by experience, that is, the number of bonds or S-R connections. This is often taken as an absolute statement of environmentalism, but this is historically incorrect. Neither Locke, nor Thorndike, nor Thomson was a 100% environmentalist, and clearly the nature of the *tabula rasa* itself determines very much what and how much can be written on it, and how long the writing will endure. The *tabula rasa* may be made of wax, easy to write on and easy to erase; it may be made of granite, like the tablets which Moses brought back from Mount Sanai; it may be made of papyrus, of sand, of slate, or paper, or wood or any other material, and similarly the writing instruments may vary from chisel to ball point, from chalk to finger. The nature of the tablet itself, therefore, determines to a very large extent the degree to which experience can write on it, and what the fate of the writing will be.

The theory, both in its original and in its modern form, is too imprecise to permit of any direct testing; neither Thorndike nor Thompson specified the physiological processes involved, which are hence purely notional. However, the theory is clearly subject to disproof if we can find high correlations between measures of the hypothetical bonds, on the one hand, and measures which cannot by any stretch of the imagination be so considered, such as the latency and amptitude of evoked potentials on the EEG (Eysenck, 1982). The fact that such correlations have been found seems to ring the death knell for any such pluralistic theory.

The specificity doctrine is now much more widely adopted in relation to personality than to intelligence. Mischel (1968) is probably the best known advocate of the specificity doctrine, disguised as "situationism," but even here it cannot be said to have achieved academic respectability (Eysenck & Eysenck, 1980; Magnusson, 1981). This has not prevented it from achieving great practical importance in several court cases which resulted in the banning of IQ testing for various educational purposes. Jensen (1984) quotes a number of the judicial pronouncements in these cases and indicates their reliance on the specificity doctrine. He also quotes testimony given by Leon Kamin, quoted by one of the judges, as follows: "IQ tests measure the degree to which a particular individual who takes the test has experience with a particular piece of information, the particular bits of knowledge, the particular habits and approaches that are tested in these tests" (p. 94). The fact that these beliefs are anachronistic and contrary to all the evidence has not apparently led to their being discarded; the Zeitgeist still favours views which deny the importance of the general factor of intelligence, or even of primary abilities, and their genetic origin.

2. DIFFERENT CONCEPTIONS OF INTELLIGENCE

When broad disagreements of this kind appear in a science, the possibility should always be considered that the differences are not only or mainly due to conflicting empirical evidence, but may be due to differential concepts and definitions, unrecognized by proponents of the various different theories. To some extent this seems to be true in this case, and it may be advantageous to discuss this point in some detail. Hebb (1949) and Vernon (1979) have distinguished between *three* conceptions of intelligence, labeled (not very meaningfully) as "intelligence A," "intelligence B," and "intelligence C." Intelligence A is conceived as *biological* intelligence underlying all cognitive processes and differences therein. Intelligence B is *social* intelligence, that is, intelligence A applied to everyday life affairs, and inevitably mixed up with a large number of different noncognitive factors, such as personality, socioeconomic status, education, experience, and so on. Last, intelligence C refers to the *psychometric* measurement of intelligence by means of IQ tests. Figure 1 shows roughly and in diagrammatic form the relationship between these three concepts. IQ tests of course may differ from one another in various ways, some coming closer to the measurement of crystalized ability, others to that of fluid ability. Finally, we may have more direct physiological tests of intelligence. These concepts are indicated by subscripts, (g_f, g_c, and g_p in Figure 1). The figure of course expresses in itself a conception of the structure of intelligence which would not be acceptable to believers in the specificity doctrine, as they would deny the existence of intelligence A. Nevertheless, as a first approximation it is clear that, if some psychologists are arguing about intelligence A, others about intelligence B, and others yet about intelligence C, without recognizing that they are discussing different concepts, then clearly no agreement will be reached. It is the first step towards clarification to recognize these differences, and not to enter into irrelevant arguments concerning them.

The respective relations between intelligence A, IQ, and intelligence B are shown diagrammatically as the series of Euler circles in Figure 2. Intelligence A, or biological intelligence, will be seen to be the most central, and also the most circumscribed. IQ is very much dependent on intelligence A, but includes various environmental factors, such as education, learned strategies, and so on,

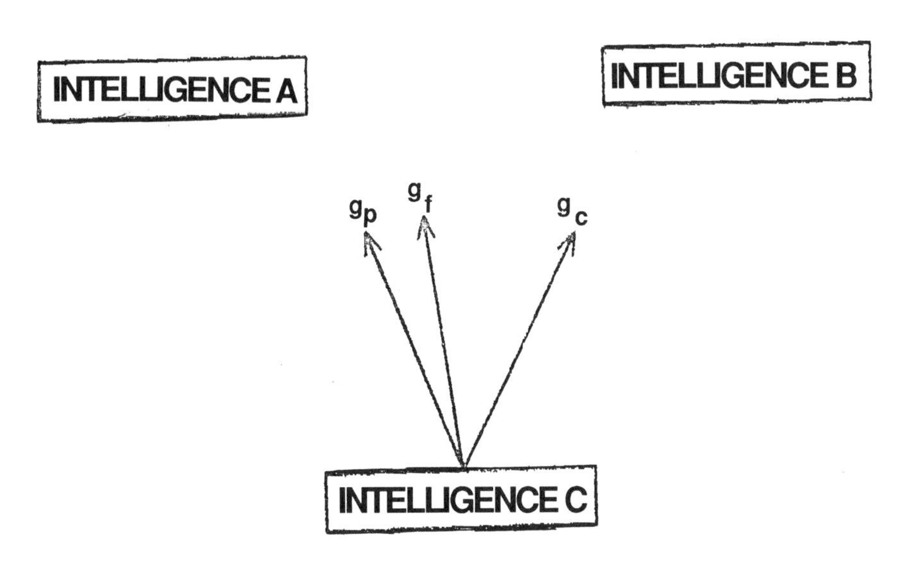

Figure 1. Diagram Illustrating Intelligence A, Intelligence B, and Intelligence C.

which are independent of intelligence A. Intelligence B, finally, is even more inclusive than IQ; although still based on intelligence A, it contains many more extraneous and irrelevant factors than does IQ, which would seem on this basis to give a fairly adequate but by no means perfect measure of intelligence A.

It will be clear from what has been said so far that those who advocate the concept of general intelligence (Galton, Spearman, Jensen) are talking mainly about intelligence A, whereas the believer in a specificity doctrine are much more concerned with intelligence B. Those who defend the notion of a general factor as well as of a fair number of group or primary factors usually talk about intelligence C, such as, the factor analytic study of test results (Eysenck, 1985). Let us consider these different concepts in some more detail.

Factor analysis plays an important part in the debate about the one and the many, but before turning to this, it may be useful to look at a more modern version of the doctrine of the many, which has been identified with the concept of adaptation, and has been very much elaborated from the early form of the theory stated by Dewey (1957). Among the authors subscribing to this theory we might name Berry (1981), Charlesworth, (1976), Cole (1979–1980), Keating (1984), Gordon and Terrell (1981), Neisser (1979), and Sternberg and Salter (1982). The

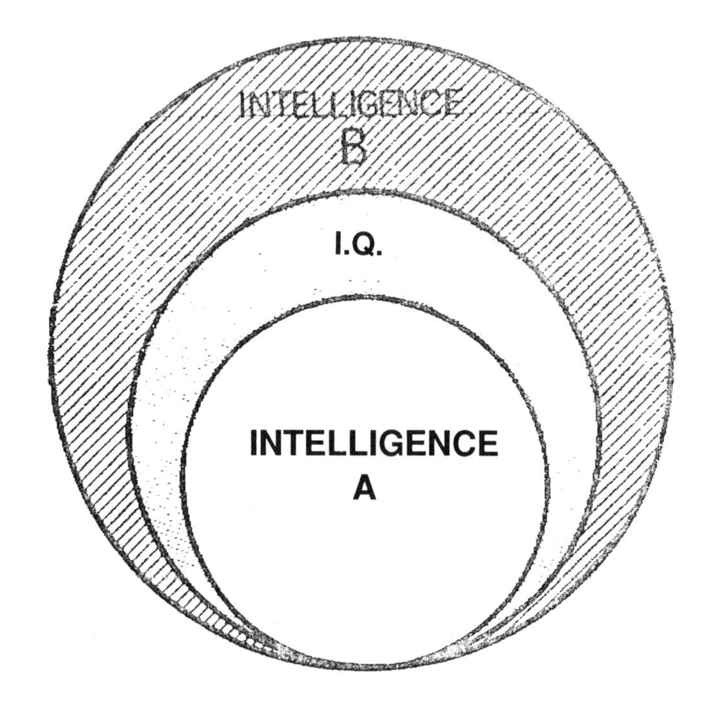

Figure 2. Euler Circles Showing Greater Inclusivity of Intelligence B, and Central Position of Intelligence A.

latest statement of this view is contained in Sternberg's (1985) "Beyond IQ," and we will turn to this for a brief statement of the theory.

Sternberg states the theory as part of his "triarchic" theory of human intelligence, namely as part of what he calls a "contextual sub-theory of intelligence." He begins by telling us that there is a need to study intelligence in relation to real-world behavior. He views intelligence as mental activity directed towards purposes, adaptations to, and selection and shaping of, real-world environments relevant to one's life. Adaptation, he maintains, consists of trying to achieve a *good fit* between oneself and one's environment. When adaptation is not possible or desirable, the individual may attempt to *select* an alternative environment with which he or she is able to attain a better contextual fit. When adaptation and selection are for some reason impossible, environmental shaping may be used, that is, an attempt to reshape one's environment so as to increase the fit between oneself and that environment.

As Sternberg points out, this view of intelligence implies that, because what is required for adaptation, selection, and shaping may differ across persons and groups, as well as across environments, intelligence may not be the same thing from one person or group to another, nor is it exactly the same thing across environments. Equally, intelligence is not likely to be exactly the same thing, at different points in the life span, as what is required, for contextual fit will almost certainly differ, both for children versus adults, and for adults at one age level versus adults of another age level. The contextual aspect of intelligence, therefore, is idiographic in nature.

This view of intelligence may be criticized for being so highly overinclusive as to make the concepts of intelligence meaningless. Sternberg admits (p. 54) that the contextualist view is highly inclusive in the sense that it includes within the realm of intelligence characteristics that might be typically placed in the realms of personality or motivation; other variables clearly included are education, specific items of knowledge, skills and strategies acquired in the course of one's life, and quite generally many of the factors contributed by parental socioeconomic status. In other words, intelligence as conceived in this theory is almost synonymous with behavior; it has no separate status as a scientific concept and obviously requires to be analyzed into components such as intelligence A, personality variables, motivational factors, educational achievements, and so on. This, surely, is another variant of the "many" doctrine (although Sternberg acknowledges the existence of *g*), and the very fact that the elements involved are uncorrelated and indeed unrelated means that the concept has no scientific meaning.

It is of course an interesting and important question to ask how intelligence A, personality factors like neuroticism, extroversion and psychoticism, educational achievements, learned strategies, and so forth, combine to determine adaptation, but to call the accidental and haphazard combination of these factors *intelligence* is certainly to go well beyond the usual meaning of the term, as used either popularly or by scientists, and to make impossible the scientific analysis of it. Intelligence A is a meaningful scientific concept; intelligence B as the contextualist views it is not.

Let us consider a specific example. Neuroticism and intelligence are for all practical purposes orthogonal and uncorrelated. Nevertheless, as far as intelligence B is concerned, it seems on a priori grounds very likely that the strong emotional reactivity of the high-neuroticism scorer will interfere with his or her social adjustment and his or her work adjustment, regardless of his or her intelligence. At the high IQ range, Oden (1968) has shown that, in the follow-up of Terman's gifted children, the majority made excellent life adjustments, but a small group failed to do so and did not live up in their work record to their early promise. It was found that practically all of these failures had been rated as emotionally unstable, or in some other way high N, by their teachers when they were young. In other words, their intellectual promise was not fulfilled because of interference by emotional factors.

Similar results have been reported in mentally defective groups (O'Connor, 1952; Tizard & O'Connor, 1951) where social adjustment and work adjustment were much more determined by emotional instability or stability, than by IQ. Heron (1951, 1954, 1955) also worked with work adjustment and found in normal IQ subjects a relative independence between cognitive and emotional factors, and evidence for the importance of emotional factors for all work adjustment.

These and many other data that could be quoted show clearly that the identification of social adjustment with "intelligence" is scientifically meaningless and quite unjustifiable. To analyze the situation regarding adaptation, we must separate out the many different strands which determine social, family, and work adaptations, and measure them independently. To call this conglomerate intelligence simply makes confusion worse confounded, and makes it impossible to obtain a proper definition of intelligence.

Eysenck (1979) has found it helpful to compare the concepts of intelligence A, intelligence B, and intelligence C with a more firmly established scientific concept, namely, temperature. Psychologists are often accused of differing from practitioners of the "hard sciences" by having multiple conceptions like these, but it is possible to identify temperature A, temperature B, and temperature C in a very similar manner. Temperature A, to somewhat simplify matters, according to Bernouilli's original theory, is the physical speed of movement of molecules or atoms. Temperature B is heat as experienced by human beings, which is determined to some extent of course by temperature A, but also by a variety of other factors such as the so-called "chill factor," that is, the movement of air, by exercise, by food and by drink consumed by the individual in question, by fever, and by many other similar factors. No scientist would consider temperature B to be a meaningful scientific concept; he or she would want to study the various elements that go into it, see how they combine, but certainly look upon them as quite separate elements.

Temperature C, corresponding to intelligence C, refers to the different methods of measuring temperature A. We have the mercury-in-glass thermometer, depending on the change in volume of the mercury with increase in heat; the constant-volume gas thermometer, depending on the reactance of the welded junction of two fine wires; resistance thermometers, depending on the relation between resistance and temperature; thermal couples, depending on the setting up of currents by a pair of metals with their junction at different temperatures; etc. Nelkon and Parker (1968), in their text on advanced level physics, point out that "temperature scales differ from one another, and no one of them is any more "true" than any other, and that our choice of which to adopt is arbitrary, so it may be decided by convenience" (p. 186). Thus, when a mercury-in-glass thermometer reads 300°C, a platinum-resistance thermometer in the same place and at the same time will read 291°C! There is no meaning attached to the question of which of these two values is "correct," just as it is meaningless to ask whether an IQ produced by the Wechsler test is more "correct" than a different IQ produced by Binet.

It will, I think, be clear that the Sternberg contextualist definition of intelligence is unacceptable. It is not intended here to go into the other parts of his triarchic model, that is, the experiential subtheory of intelligence, and the componential subtheory; they clearly do not deal with intelligence as normally conceived, but are rather theories of adaptation or indeed behavior in general. As such they may well be of interest to psychologists, but we will here be restrained in our discussion to consider intelligence only.

3. DOES FACTOR ANALYSIS PROVIDE A SOLUTION?

After this excursion, we may return to our consideration of traditional psychometric methodology and ask whether factor analysis has not succeeded in clearing up this issue. The question is a very relevant one, because in a sense factor analysis was created in order to answer precisely this type of question. Clearly it has failed to do so, because the debate is still continuing. One of the reasons for this unsatisfactory state of affairs may be that factor analysis has been and still is subject to many criticisms (Lenk, 1983; Reventsdorf, 1980). To take but one example, it is usually assumed that factors are similar or identical for different populations, as long as these are not selected in such a way as to alter the variance of the test scores. Yet this does not appear to be so. Lienert (1963), Lienert and Croft (1964), and Eysenck and White (1964) have shown that, when a sample is subdivided as high and low on neuroticism, respectively, and factor analysis is carried out on the matrix of intercorrelations between cognitive tests in each of these groups, there is a very significant reduction in the number of factors in the neurotic as compared with the nonneurotic group. Thus, clearly, neuroticism, which is a personality variable orthogonal to *g*, apparently affects the factor structure of IQ tests in important ways. Similarly, Wewetzer (1958) showed that, when a class of children was subdivided on the basis of high or low IQ, more factors were obtained among the bright than among the dull. Clearly, the number and type of factors discovered depends on the make-up of the group, and as this is hardly ever controlled in any fashion, factor structures must necessarily differ from sample to sample.

Possibly even more important is an objection to the effect that factor analysis is usually applied to correlations between scores on tests, usually arrived at by summing the number of correct answers for each subject. However, it is clear that identical scores on a test may be obtained by different individuals obtaining correct answers on quite different problems (Eysenck, 1953, 1967, 1982). Thus, to take an imaginary example, the typical plodder might obtain correct answers until the level of difficulty made it impossible for him or her to continue. Such a person might have no incorrect answers in the range of difficult levels with which he or she was able to cope. An impulsive person, on the other hand, might have several incorrect answers at difficulty levels where he or she would be expected to be able to obtain correct answers, but, unlike the plodder, he or she might abandon some problem which was within his or her ability to solve. A third

Table 1. Problems in Increasing Order of Difficulty: Scoring Patterns of Three Imaginary Subjects on a 10-Item IQ Test

	1	*2*	*3*	*4*	*5*	*6*	*7*	*8*	*9*	*10*	*Score*
Plodder:	r	r	r	r	r	r	a	a	a	a	6
Impulsive:	r	r	r	r	w	r	w	r	w	w	6
Nonmotivation:	r	a	r	r	r	s	r	a	r	a	6

Key: r = right
w = wrong
a = abandoned

person, perhaps poorly motivated, might abandon some easy problems, although he or she might be able to solve these, and solve more difficult ones. All three might obtain identical scores, as shown in Table 1, but can it really be maintained that their problem-solving behavior was identical?

Considerations of this kind suggested that the proper unit of analysis is not the test score, but the outcome of each individual item, whether solved correctly, solved incorrectly, or abandoned. In addition, solution time for each item seemed an important element in IQ measurement. Eysenck (1953) formulated the hypothesis that the outcome of such a study would indicate three major and relatively independent factors, namely *mental speed,* such as the speed of mental processing; persistence or continuance, such as, the tendency to continue searching for a solution for a lengthy period of time; and *error checking,* the tendency to put down wrong solutions due to the failure to check the solution properly against some standard. This hypothesis was investigated by the writer in conjunction with Furneaux (1952, 1961) and White (1982), with results which indicated that three such relatively independent factors could indeed be identified, and an elaborate algorithm was written to put this theory into a mathematical form. It would take us too far to discuss it in detail, but it may be noted that only speed of mental processing is a genuinely cognitive variable; both persistence and error-checking seem to indicate the influence of personality factors on IQ test scores (Eysenck, 1982).

Speed of mental processing has indeed turned out to be a vital component of success in intelligence test items. Figure 3 (Eysenck, 1953) illustrates some results from work undertaken by Furneaux (1961), in which time and log time, respectively, for solving items at different difficulty levels were plotted for different subjects. *A* illustrates the typical relationship between solution time and difficulty level, and *B* shows the log time relationships for three hypothetical individuals, alpha, beta, and gamma. It was empirically found that these regressions were linear when only correctly solved items were considered, and it seemed clear that speed at the 100% correct solution level (baseline) could give accurate predictions for much more complex problems with much lower proportions of correct solutions. This finding became fundamental to the theory of

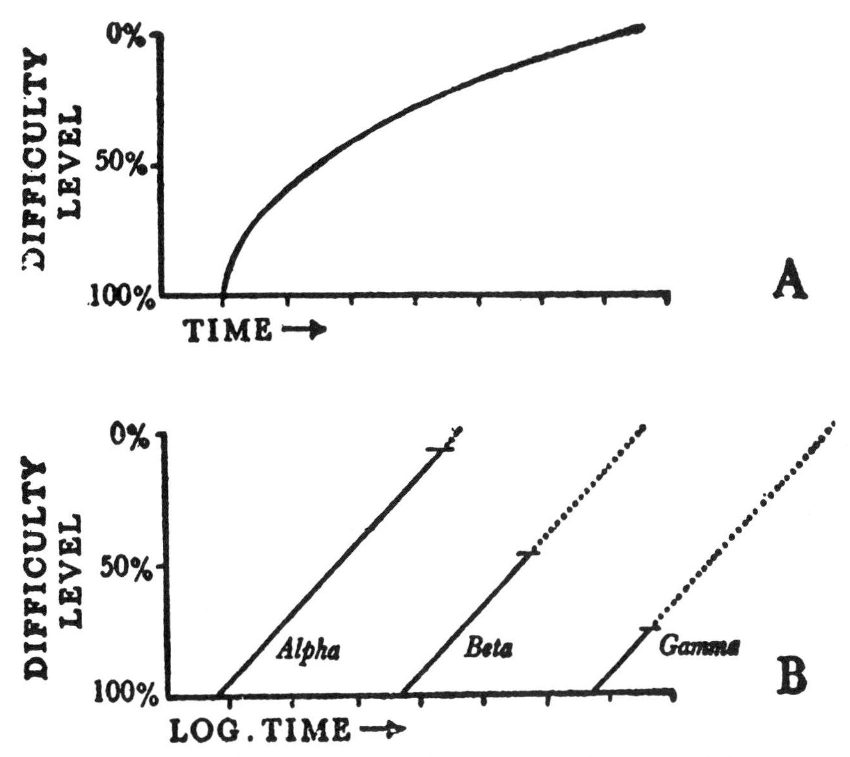

Figure 3. Relation between Difficulty Level of Items and Time for Solution (A) and Log Time for Solution (B). (From Eysenck, 1953).

intelligence briefly outlined elsewhere (Eysenck, 1987a). Such a theory would predict, as indeed had Galton (1892, 1943), that very simple measures of speed of information processing, such as choice reaction times, inspection times, and so on, should be excellent measures of intelligence A, and correlate highly with IQ tests, that is, to the degree that the two Euler circles overlap.

We will return to the empirical investigation of this prophecy later on; here let us note merely that it is completely incompatible with the contextualist theory because such simple tests of speed of mental processing are at the difficulty level where every subject would succeed in the task, given sufficient time; in other words, there is no question but that the "bonds," or S-R connections supposedly underlying the ability to carry out the task, have already been formed, and none of the "contextualist" factors invoked by Sternberg seem to be in the slightest degree relevant. On the basis of these various hypotheses one would have to predict a zero or very low correlation; if a reasonably high correlation could be found, this would indicate the essential falsity of the contextualist theory.

Do the difficulties inherent in factor analysis, and discussed above, make it impossible to use this technique to solve the problem of the one and the many? There are certain properties of the matrices of observed correlations between many very different types of cognitive tests which suggest that such a pessimistic conclusion would be premature. The first and most important is the observation in practically every case of a "positive manifold," such as, the observation that all correlations are positive when each test is scored in the direction of greater achievement. The specificity theory certainly cannot explain this phenomenon, there being no reason why in any given group specific elements should not be negatively correlated. It is perfectly reasonable to expect that the person who devotes much of his or her time to learning ancient and modern languages would be prevented from devoting much time to learning facts about music, or painting. The person devoting much time to the acquisition of mathematical skills would have that much less time to devote to a study of poetry and the drama. Primary mental abilities might possibly be acquired in this fashion, but it is not reasonable to anticipate the emergence of a general factor, as seems to be implied by the existence of the "positive manifold."

Equally ubiquitous is the observation that such matrices of intercorrelations have a *low rank*, and if the tests are carefully chosen so as to avoid undue overlap, the rank may be one of *unity*. In the Thurstone and Thurstone (1941) study, many rather similar type tests were included, and the matrix approximating rank one was achieved by correlating the primary factors which eliminated the similarities between the tests. For the reasons already given, as well as problems of sampling, chance error, inadequate selection and so on, the approximation to rank one is of course seldom perfect, but the low rank of most of the matrices observed does strongly suggest the existence of a general factor.

It is not suggested, of course, that this general factor explains all the observed particulars of the subjects' performance. As already noted, we need to postulate a number of rather smaller group factors, such as Thurstone's verbal comprehension, verbal fluency, number, spatial visualisation, memory, reasoning, and perceptual speed, or perhaps the more numerous factors postulated by Horn (1978), or the somewhat different factors isolated in the German-speaking regions (Jager, 1967; Meili, 1964), but of course the common variance for all these factors combined does not add up to the total variance observed, and a certain amount of specificity is left for each test, thus perhaps satisfying the specificity theorists to some extent at least. Nevertheless, it is their denial of a general factor (or indeed of any ability factors even of the primary kind) which characterizes their theorizing, and there is little doubt that factor analysis studies, with all their imperfections, have destroyed the empirical underlay for any such wide-ranging specificity theories.

Why, then, can we not rest content with the factor analytic results? The answer is that by suitable rotations we can always reallocate the variance in any way we choose, and we can do that, as Guilford (1967) has shown, by adopting a theory which excludes a general factor, and by targeting rotations in a suitable manner. To most statisticians this will not seem a reasonable way of proceeding, and it does contradict the principles of simplicity and Occam's razor, but it might be replied by those intent by all means to reject any postulation of *g* that such general principles are arbitrary and should not confine our theorizing. In a similar way, Guilford has argued that, when simple structure and orthogonality are incompatible, orthogonality should be preserved and simple structure be given up, contrary to Thurstone's own preferences on this point. It is possible to say that Guilford and his followers are behaving in a rather arbitrary manner, rejecting widely accepted principles of rotation and making their hypotheses essentially untestable (Eysenck, 1988). Nevertheless, clearly a more definitive demonstration of the importance of *g* seems desirable, and to that we must next turn.

Other answers to the problem of the one and the many could perhaps be found by looking at the evidence from behavioral genetics. If, as seems very clear from the evidence, there is a strong genetic element in causing individual differences in mental ability (Eysenck, 1979; Vernon, 1979), then might one not be able to use that evidence in an attempt to settle the rotational question? Unfortunately, this is not so; the problem remains exactly the same. The total amount of heritability attaching to a given set of tests can be concentrated in a single factor, or distributed over several factors, in the same way as test variance can be so distributed, and no answer will be found along these lines. This should, indeed, be obvious from a consideration of the way in which heritability is defined, and this attempt at finding a solution does not really add to our store of knowledge. Is it then impossible to deduce from the various theories consequences which would be incompatible with one or the other, and which might serve as crucial experiments for distinguishing between these theories?

4. TWO PARADIGMS OF INTELLIGENCE, REACTION TIME, AND IQ

It may be useful to return to the originators of the two major paradigms of intelligence, namely, Galton and Binet. There are three major differences between their conceptions of intelligence. The first one relates indeed to the problem which we are considering at the moment, namely, the scientific usefulness of a concept of intelligence as a unitary quality of the mind. Galton certainly believed wholeheartedly in this view, but for Binet intelligence was essentially a statistical artifact, merely the average of a number of more or less independent abilities. Thus a way of raising the problem of the one and the many appears right at the beginning of our modern attempts to measure intelligence and to formulate theories concerning it (Eysenck, 1985). The second point on which they differed, namely the inheritance of intelligence, favored by Galton but of no great importance for Binet, has also been with us for a long time, but as pointed out above, does not really throw much light on the problem of the one and the many.

The third difference between these theorists is of more direct interest. It concerns the best methods to be used for the measurement of intelligence. Galton, clearly having biological intelligence (intelligence A) in mind, looked for simple physiological indices, such as reaction times, and the early work of Burt (1909) and Spearman (1904) followed his advice in large part, concentrating on tests of sensory discrimination, inspection time, etc., with some success. Binet, on the other hand, used the well-known type of test associated with his name, that is, problem solving of one kind or another, memory tests, following instruction, learning, and other social skills involving educational and cultural factors. As is well known, Binet won the day, and practically all modern IQ tests follow his example. There was some debate later on about the relative advantages of "speed" and "power" tests (Berger, 1982), with the former following Galton in the sense of including simple problems which could be solved by any testee, given enough time, and the latter following Binet in using problems which could not be solved by all testees, even given infinite time. In fact very high correlations were found between these different types of tests, suggesting that the differentiation between them was somewhat unreal, but this was not thought to lead to a solution of the "one and the many" problem.

A number of studies were actually carried out using reaction times (McFarland, 1928), and these showed significant correlations between reaction time and intelligence, although the size of the correlation varied from one study to the other, and none were very high. Interest was lost in this approach, probably due to the success of the Binet-type test, until relatively recently interest began to revive in this type of test (Roth, 1964; Eysenck, 1967). Since then, several geographically differentiated schools have carried out large numbers of tests along these lines, particularly the Erlangen School in Germany, the Jensen School in the United States, and the Australian School in Adelaide (Eysenck, 1987a).

There are essentially five different types of paradigms which have to be distinguished in talking about evidence from reaction times. The first of these is *simple reaction time,* in which a signal which may be auditory, visual, or somatosensory causes the subject to lift his or her finger off a button (button A) and move it to another button (button B) which may or may not be in continguity with the signal (e.g., the button may be adjacent to a lamp which lights up). Decision time (DT) is the time from the signal coming on to the lifting of the finger off button A; movement time (MT) is the time from the lifting of the finger off button A to the depression of button B. Correlations between simple DT or MT and IQ are negative but quite low; a correlation of $-.2$ would perhaps be typical of many reported data.

The second paradigm is *choice reaction time,* in which an array of two, four, eight, or more possible stimuli are presented to the subject, whose finger is on button A; when one of the stimuli is activated, movement from button A to an appropriately placed button B has to be made. Choice DT and MT are nearly always measured in a visual paradigm, with the response button being adjacent to the lights which constitute the stimulus array. Reaction times in this paradigm obey Hick's (1952) law; such as, they increase linearly with the increase in the $\log_2$ of the number of stimuli (bits of information). Correlations here are substantially higher than "simple" DT and MT, with −.4 being perhaps a typical value. Variability in the response has also been correlated with IQ, with values varying around −.4 to −.5. Jensen (1982a, b) has suggested that there is an increase in choice RT with an increase in the number of stimuli, but this is not invariably found (Longstreth, 1984; Carroll, 1987; Barrett, Eysenck, & Lucking, 1986); similarly, claims have been made for the slope of the Hick regression line, and the evidence suggest that correlations of between −.3 and −.4 can be obtained using this variable. Barrett et al. (1986) have suggested caution in using Hick's law, as between 10% and 20% of their subjects were found to give results not in accord with this law; their exclusion considerably increased the observed correlations.

The third paradigm enlarges the *complexity* of the simple and choice reaction time experiment by the inclusion of short-term memory scan elements (Sternberg, 1966), long-term memory access features (Posner, Boies, Eichelman, & Taylor, 1969), or simple education of relations, as in a study by Frearson and Eysenck (1986), who presented an eight-light array in which three lights would be lit simultaneously, and the subject had to press the button next to the light which was the "odd man out," that is, was separated from the other two by a greater distance than they were separated from each other. Correlations with these paradigms are around −.5 but may go up to −.6 and higher.

A fourth paradigm allied to these, and more widely used, is the so-called "inspection time" paradigm (IT), the evidence concerning which is summarized by Brand (1981) and Brand and Deary (1982). Correlations with this paradigm, in which two lines of greatly differing lengths are exposed in a tachistoscope for a very short period of time, followed by a backward masking stimulus, range around −.5, when the score is the shortest period of time at which correct guesses are around the 97.5% mark.

The fifth paradigm makes use of very simple *perceptual motor tasks,* such as card-sorting (Oswald, 1971), the speed of pronouncing 20 letters presented to the subject on a sheet of paper (Lehrl & Frank, 1982), or the drawing of connecting lines between consecutive numbers irregularly spaced on a sheet of paper (Oswald & Roth, 1978). Some of these tests, as well as an early version of the IT test, were already used by Burt (1909), but it is only recently that they have been used as measures of IQ by the Erlangen School. Correlations with IQ for these tests vary around −.5 to −.6, with even higher correlations being occasionally reported (Eysenck, 1987a).

The estimates of correlations obtained between RT and IQ above are not meant to be taken too literally. The reported coefficients in the literature vary widely from very low to very high, and only rather subjective estimates like those given above are possible at the moment. The reasons for this are as follows:

1. Some studies include retardates, others do not, and their inclusion clearly produces much larger correlations than would be produced in their absence. It seems likely that retardates suffer specific deficits which make it inadvisable to include them in any study that aims at estimating the correlation between RT and IQ, and consequently, in the estimates given above, studies using retardates have been omitted.
2. Given that the inclusion of retardates *increases* the range of talent grossly, and hence leads to an overestimation of the correlation between RT and IQ, the use of students as subjects considerably *reduces* the range of talent, and hence leads to an underestimation of the true correlation. It is necessary in every case to correct the observed correlations for range of IQ; if this is not done, no meaningful comparisons can be made with the data.
3. The type of intelligence test used may have an influence on the results. Nonverbal tests, for instance, tend to give higher correlations with RT than do verbal tests (Barrett et al., 1986), and altogether the special make-up of the IQ test may determine varying degrees of association with RT.
4. The actual mode of presentation of the RT stimuli, the arrangement of the array, the modality used, the intensity of the stimuli, and so on, may affect the outcome, and little has been done unfortunately in the way of studying the importance of these parameter values. It is difficult to compare meaningfully studies which differ with respect to any of these variables.
5. Longstreth (1984) has pointed out a number of experimental considerations that ought to be considered in interpreting or even designing experiments in this field, and students should certainly be familiar with the major theoretical positions that have been adopted by experimental psychologists (Smith, 1968; Welford, 1980).

For all these reasons it is impossible to present any final estimates of the relationship between RT and IQ, but the values suggested above are probably indicative of the correct order of magnitude, but might be somewhat lower or higher depending on variations in the many parameters just mentioned. It should be noted, in addition, that multiple correlations using several different types of scores, such as choice RT, variability, and slope, tend to give significantly higher correlations with IQ due to the fact that the intercorrelations between the RT variables are not usually very high. Such multiple correlations should of course always be shrunk in order to reduce capitalizing on error variance. It would seem safest if the weights of the multiple R determination were determined prior to undertaking the experiment, on the basis of previous work; in this way we can rely on excluding this process of error capitalization.

One other point needs to be considered, and that is that the "true" correlation between RT and IQ is considerably higher than the values quoted, due to the fact that there is considerable day-to-day variability in RT measurement. Test-retest reliability for most of the paradigms considered is only around .8; this means that observed correlations should be corrected for attenuation. Such corrections are of course only of theoretical value; if we wish to use such RT tests as measures of intelligence for practical purposes, then this unreliability constitutes a very real disadvantage. However, from the theoretical point of view it is important to know what the "true" correlation is, and for that purpose corrections of attenuation should always be taken into account. When this is done, we find that correlations between RT and IQ, using the best combination of scores under optimal conditions, and correcting for attenuation, will be between −.7 and −.8. These values are almost of the same order as those observed between different IQ tests, or even higher; this is an important finding which should not be lost sight of in any discussion of the nature of intelligence.

These results are difficult to reconcile with any theory of intelligence which does not posit the existence of a very strong and indeed dominant general factor. It is certainly not compatible with the specificity doctrine, because quite obviously the specific events leading to proficiency on RT paradigms would be completely different from those leading to proficiency on IQ tests; yet as we have seen, RT correlates almost as highly with IQ test as these correlate with each other!

Equally, a doctrine like Guilford's, or even the early Thurstone belief that primary factors alone are responsible for the total variance in the intercorrelation matrix between IQ tests, is equally incompatible with these findings. If we were indeed dealing with seven or more independent abilities, then there is no theoretical reason to anticipate that RT tests should correlate with typical IQ measures, which on that hypothesis would be artifactual averages of independent factors. Clearly the facts as discussed above present insuperable difficulties to theories which exclude *g* from consideration.

A theory which best fits the circumstances would seem to be one which regards mental speed as fundamental to all cognitive processes, and as being the biological substratum of cognitive ability (Eysenck, 1967, 1987a; Frearson, Eysenck, & Barrett, 1990). At the moment, no other theory seems to be capable of explaining the observed facts, and hence it may be suggested that intelligence A may be identified with speed of information processing as measured by the various reaction time paradigms discussed above (Eysenck, 1987a). We may readily concede that, for intelligence B, that is, the application of intelligence to everyday life problems, other factors such as personality, education, cultural influences, socioeconomic status, and so on, may have to be added, but as we have already argued, these are noncognitive and should not be identified as constituting the meaningful scientific concepts of intelligence. Figure 4 illustrates this conception.

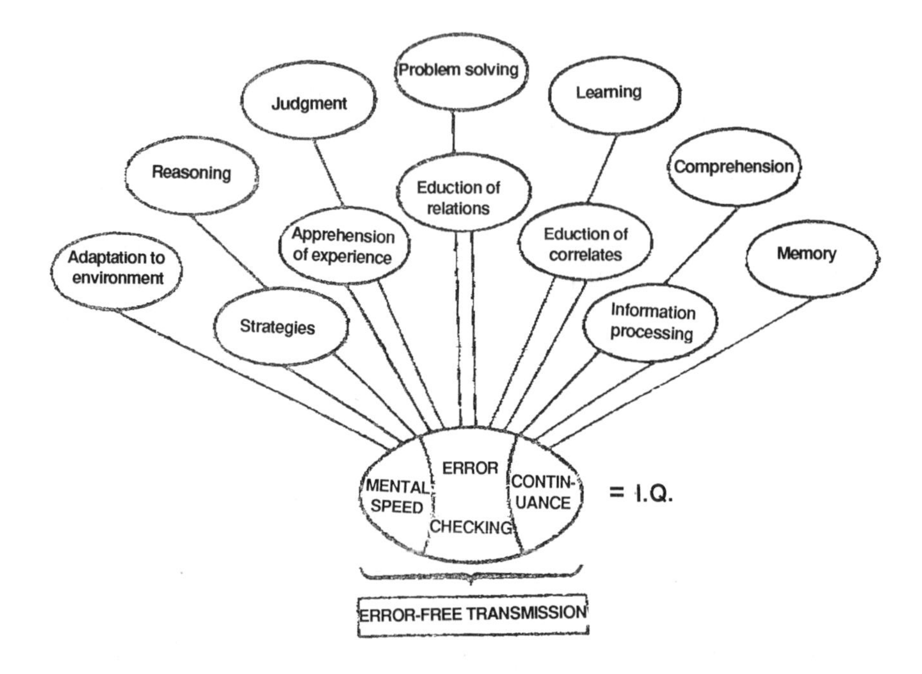

Figure 4. Relations between Fundamental Biological Property of the Cortex (Errorless Transmission of Information), IQ, and Intelligence B.

5. THE PHYSIOLOGY OF INTELLIGENCE: THE EVOKED POTENTIAL

We come to a similar conclusion when we consider another type of evidence, namely, that coming from psychophysiology (Eysenck & Barrett, 1985). Here the early work of Ertl (1971, 1973) and Ertl and Schafer (1969) pioneered the use of evoked potentials on the EEg as measures of intelligence, using the latency and the amplitude of the evoked responses as correlates of IQ. Callaway (1975) has reviewed this early literature and has shown that model correlations in the neighborhood of .3 can be obtained between latency (negative), amplitude (positive), and variability of responses (negative) and IQ. This demonstration follows the Binet-type paradigm, in that older children show shorter latencies, greater amplitudes, and lesser variability, thus making possible the application of Binet's mental age argument to physiological measures.

These early studies were essentially atheoretical, and the correlations were not high enough to be of any practical value. However, in recent years several paradigms based on theoretical considerations have been advanced, and much higher correlations have been recorded as a consequence. A detailed discussion of these paradigms is given elsewhere (Eysenck & Barrett, 1985); particularly noteworthy are the Hendrickson (1982) paradigm, the Schafer, Amochaev and Russell (1981) paradigm, and the Robinson (1982) one.

These paradigms are quite different from each other, at first sight, although it may be possible to reconcile them on a theoretical basis. However, all give high correlations between certain aspects of the AEP (average evoked potential) and IQ, to a degree even exceeding that found in the preceding section between RT and IQ.

It may be helpful to discuss two of these paradigms (Schafer and Hendrickson) in some detail; the Robinson one is too complex to lend itself to a brief statement. To begin with the Schafer paradigm, several studies in recent years have shown the influence of selective attention (Picton & Hilward, 1974) expectancy (Squires, Wickens, Squires, & Donchin, 1976; Schafer et al., 1981), and information processing work load (Israel, Wickens, Chesney, & Donchin, 1980) on the amplitude of AEPs.

Schafer (1982) postulated the concept of "neural adaptability" based on these facts, suggesting greater adaptability in higher IQ subjects. He, Schafer and Marcus (1973), and others have found correlations with IQ, which corrected for range, yielded coefficients around 0.80! (see also Schafer et al., 1981). This is a remarkably high coefficient for a correlation between a purely physiological measure, and a psychological one.

The Hendricksons (1982) worked on the hypothesis that, when information is processed through the cortex, errors may occur, and that the IQ for given individuals may be a function of errorless transmission, in the sense that the more errors occur during transmission, the lower will be the IQ of the individual concerned. They measured the occurrence of errors essentially by variability in the average evoked potential (negative) and the complexity of the resulting average traces (positive), and found surprisingly high correlations of .83 in 219 schoolchildren of roughly normal range of ability. The IQ test used was the WAIS, and Table 2 shows the correlations of the individual subtest with an evoked potential measure, which combines variability and complexity. Also shown are the loadings of the different subtests on a general factor extracted from the intercorrelation between the WAIS subtest, both uncorrected and corrected for attentuation. Figure 5 shows typical AEP traces for bright and dull children; the differences in complexity will be obvious. (See also Eysenck & Barrett, 1985.)

We can adduce the same argument here as we did in relation to RT, namely, that only a theory which acknowledges the existence of *g* can account for these intercorrelations. It seems clear that whatever is central to all the subtests of the WAIS, that is, the general factor underlying the Binet-type measures used in the Wechsler scale, is also measured by the AEP scores. No reliance on specificity or primary mental abilities can possibly explain the observed intercorrelations.

Table 2. Correlations with Composite, AEP Measure, and Factor Loadings

WAIS Subtests	*Uncorrected*	*Corrected*	*Uncorrected*	*Corrected*
Information	−0.68	−0.71	0.78	0.82
Comprehension	−0.59	−0.66	0.73	0.82
Arithmetic	−0.65	−0.73	0.78	0.88
Similarities	−0.71	−0.76	0.82	0.88
Digit Span	−0.59	−0.70	0.68	0.81
Vocabulary	−0.68	−0.70	0.79	0.81
Digit Symbol	−0.35	−0.36	0.50	0.52
Picture Completion	−0.57	−0.63	0.68	0.75
Block Design	−0.54	−0.58	0.71	0.77
Picture Arrangement	−0.46	−0.57	0.58	0.71
Object Assembly	−0.44	−0.55	0.58	0.72

The AEP Composite Measure = −0.77
The Spearman rho between the *Uncorrected* correlations and loadings = 0.95
The Spearman rho between the *Corrected* correlations and loadings = 0.93

However, this argument can be put in a more convincing statistical form in the following way. If the factor loadings of the 11 subtests of the WAIS indicate the correlations of each with the general factor defined by the total test itself, and if the correlations of each subtest with the AEP, as is here hypothesized, indicate the correlations of each test with the physiological substratum of intellectual ability, then it should follow that these two sets of variables should be *proportional* to each other; that is, a test with a high loading on *g* should also have a high correlation with the AEP, and conversely a test having a low loading on the *g* factor should have a low correlation with the AEP. The observed correlation is +0.95, which becomes +0.93 when corrected for attentuation, that is, the unreliability of the different Wechsler subtest. This correlation is not significantly different from unity, and is surprisingly high, considering that the range of *g* loadings is much smaller than chance would have created, due to the fact that all the Wechsler subtest have been carefully selected as being good measures of *g!* This finding (Eysenck & Barrett, 1985) is in good agreement with the hypothesis already suggested, namely, that the AEP as so measured is a good, and may be an excellent, measure of the biological basis underlying cognitive ability (intelligence A). It is difficult to explain the observed data on any alternative basis, and we might regard this finding as the most clear-cut support for the Galtonian theory of a general factor of intelligence (Eysenck, 1982). It would clearly be desirable to carry out a similar study with the various RT measures, using the coefficient of proportionality as an indication of the centrality of RT as a measure of intelligence A. A first attempt to do so (Hemmelgarn & Kehle, 1984) obtained a correlation of 0.83 for 12 WISC-R subtests and an RT test, correlating loading with RT correlations.

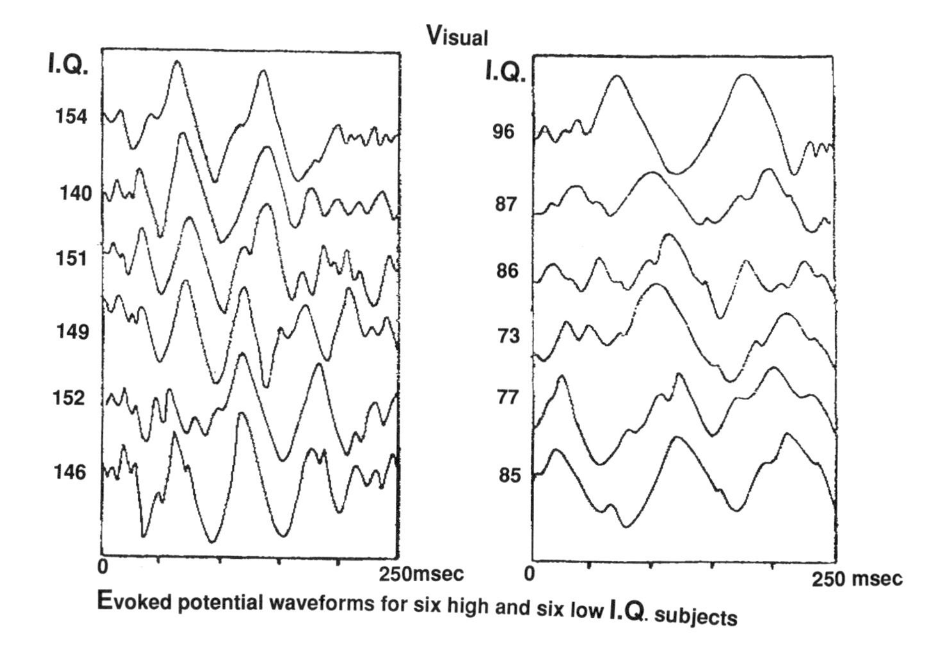

Figure 5. Evoked potential waveforms for Six High- and Six Low-IQ Subjects.

It might be thought that there is here a contradiction in theory, in that RT experiments would seem to make *mental speed* fundamental to intelligence A, whereas the Hendricksons's theory would seem to make *errors in transmission* so responsible. This is not so. Eysenck (1987a) has argued that the occurrence of many errors in transmission will *cause* a slowing down in the speed of reaction, so that the errors in transmission hypothesis would be fundamental to the speed of mental processing findings. It is not here suggested that this hypothesis is necessarily true; it is merely argued that it constitutes a possible reconciliation between the findings of these two rather divergent sets of experiments.

6. INTELLIGENCE AND BIOCHEMISTRY: MENTAL ENERGY

It will be seen that our account has been essentially a *reductionist* one, starting with psychometric *g*, going on to the postulation of mental speed factor, measured by RT tests, and finally postulating differences in number of errors in information processing through the cortex, measured by AEPs. Is it possible to go one step further along this line and identify biochemical features which might be responsible for the features of this scheme? An early candidate for this role was glutamic acid, the role of which was emphasized by Zimmerman and Ross (1944), who reported that feeding of glutamic acid to dull young rats resulted in a considerable improvement in maze-learning ability. Another group of workers, also at Columbia University, reported beneficial effects on the performance of rats in complex reasoning problems (Albert & Warden, 1944). This work was extended to mentally retarded children, with results which suggested that glutamic acid might increase their IQ if measured by standard intelligence test; however, not all investigations have given favorable results, as indicated in a review by Hughes and Zubek (1956). Many animal experiments, too, have given negative results, very probably because positive results have only been achieved with dull rats, so that experiments using average or bright rats are strictly irrelevant to the theory.

These empirical data are supported by theoretical considerations. Zimmerman, Burgemeister, and Putnam (1949) have argued that the improvement in learning ability might be due to the facilitatory effect of glutamic acid upon certain metabolic processes underlying neural activity. Thus it is known that glutamic acid is important in the synthesis of acetylcholine, a chemical substance necessary for the production of various electrical changes appearing during neural transmission. It has been found that the rate of acetylcholine formation could be increased four to five times by adding glutamic acid to dialyzed extracts in rat brain (Nachmansohn, John, & Walsh, 1943). In addition, Waelsch (1951) has shown that the concentration of glutamic acid in the brain is disproportionately high, as compared with the concentration of other amino acids, or with its concentration in other body tissues. It alone, of all the amino acids, is capable of serving as a respiratory substrate of the brain in lieu of glucose. And finally, Sauri (1950), experimenting on rats, discovered that the acid exerts its main action on the cerebral cortex, lowering the threshold of excitability.

All these results clearly point to the importance of glutamic acid in cerebral metabolism. Its effectiveness in dull rats only suggests that the cerebral metabolism of the dull rats is defective in some way, while that of average and bright rats is normal, allowing glutamic acid to facilitate or improve the defective cerebral metabolism of the dull animals while having no particular effect on the normal metabolism of the bright ones. This suggestion is strengthened by the fact that Himwich and Fazekas (1940), in a careful study of tissue preparations from the brain of mentally retarded persons, were able to show that these tissues were incapable of utilizing normal amounts of oxygen and carbohydrates. In other words, the cerebral metabolism in these mentally retarded patients was defective.

More recent work, summarized by Spitz (1986), has thrown considerable doubt on the empirical basis of this theory, but the theory has led to some extremely interesting developments. A number of empirical correlations between biochemical parameters and results of conventional mental tests have been reported by several investigators. Weiss (1982, 1984, 1985) has brought together much of this literature, and has based his theoretical conception of a biochemical analogue of Spearman's "mental energy" (Spearman, 1927) on this work. Thus IQ has been found correlated with the activity of brain choline acetyltransferase to the extent of .81 (Perry et al., 1978), with brain acetylcholinesterase to the extent of .35 (Soinine et al., 1984), and erythrocyte glutathione peroxidase to the extent of .58 (Sinet, Lejeunne, & Jerome, 1979). Cerebral glucose metabolism rates have also been found correlated with IQ to the extent of about .60 by De Leon et al. (1983), and Chase, Foster, Brooks, Di Chiro, and Mausi (1984). These studies, admittedly, were not intended to clarify the physiological background of normal intelligence, but to throw light on the metabolic causes of premature senescence and cognitive losses in Alzheimer's disease, Down's syndrome, and Parkinson's disease. However, it is doubtful if there are any qualitative differences between Alzheimer's disease and normal aging (Mann, Yates, & Maroynink, 1984), and this disease may be viewed as one tail of a continuous distribution. Furthermore, these correlations with IQ have also been confirmed in healthy comparison groups (Soininen et al., 1984; De Leon et al., 1983, Chase et al., 1984), and hence these results must be regarded with respect.

Mutatis mutandis, the theory offered by Weiss is not dissimilar to that of Zimmerman already referred to. As Weiss (1985) points out, the brain consumes glucose as a normal, exclusive source of energy. Although the human brain represents only 2% of body weight, its energy consumption is about 20% of total energy requirement (Hoyer, 1982). Compared with the high rate of utilization, the energy stores in the brain are almost negligible, and the brain is consequently almost completely dependent on the continuous replenishment of its glucose supplies by the cerebral circulation (Reinis & Goldman, 1982). Weiss goes on to argue that it would defy most fundamental laws of thermodynamics if individual differences in brain power did not find their counterparts in individual differences of brain energy metabolism. This argument is powerfully strengthened by the fact that two research groups (De Leon et al., 1983; Chase et al., 1984) report significant correlations of around .60 between regional cerebral glucose metabolism rates and a number of IQ tests, including memory capacity and mental speed, in both the Alzheimer's and control groups (Chase et al., 1984). By positron emission tomography of radio active fluorine, it became possible to quantify glucose metabolism in milligrams per 100 grams of brain tissue per minute. Now, since both IQ and glucose metabolism grades are far from perfectly reliably measured, these correlations must be regarded as very high indeed, suggesting strong degrees of dependence of intelligence on cerebral glucose metabolism.

Weiss takes the argument a good deal further, but this is not the right place to follow a complex biochemical argument, or to indicate possible criticism in detail. The small number of normal cases tested, the unknown reliability of the biochemical assays, and the failure of the authors mentioned to address the central issue of Weiss's argument (understandable because of their orientation towards medical problems of aging) combine to make it desirable for a new, large-scale investigation to be carried out along the same lines, but emphasizing proper large samples of normal adults covering the full range of IQ. However that may be, the data are certainly impressive in suggesting that glucose, glutamic acid, and other biochemical agents responsible for the energy supply of the cortex, and connected with the production of neurotransmitter substances, have a vital causal role to play in intelligence A, and may be the ultimate source of that "mental energy" which is the underlying biological substrate of Spearman's *g*. It cannot at the moment be claimed that the search has ended with these tantalizing findings, but it may be claimed that it has not only begun, but has already made possible the postulation of specific testable theories. Clearly, the matter requires to be taken further, and this in turn requires cooperation between many different disciplines, ranging from psychology and neurology to biochemistry and tomography. Such collaboration is difficult to achieve, but without it we can hardly hope to achieve the final explanation of intelligence A in biological terms.

7. PERSONALITY AND THE PROBLEM OF THE ONE AND THE MANY

So far we have dealt entirely with intelligence, partly because the theoretical conflict has mainly ranged around this concept, and partly because a great deal of evidence is now available which we have suggested is capable of settling the dispute once and for all. However, in the personality field too, meaning by this at the moment those aspects of individual differences not primarily concerned with cognitive factors (temperament), a similar battle has been raging between those who, like Cattell (1957; Cattell & Schaier, 1961), Cattell, Eber, and Tatsouka (1970), and Guilford (1975; Guilford, Zimmerman & Guilford, 1976) believe in the primacy of simple traits (primary factors), whereas others, such as Eysenck (1970; Eysenck & Eysenck, 1985) lay greater emphasis on superfactors of much greater generality, such as neuroticism, extroversion, and psychoticism. Quite generally, British authors have tended to emphasize more general, higher order concepts, while American authors have tended to stress more the large number of simple traits or "source factors" as Cattell calls them. It would be interesting to study the causes of these national differences, which emerge equally clearly in the personality as in the intelligence field, but of course this is not the place to do so.

The arguments in favor of the concept of superfactors, corresponding to *g* in the intelligence field, have been summarized in considerable detail by Eysenck and Eysenck (1985), and these arguments of course resemble those adduced for intelligence in previous sections of this chapter. It is not denied that, in addition to these superfactors, a certain amount of variance must be attributed to group or primary factors, and also to specific factors; what is asserted is simply that the superfactors are of much greater generality, much greater psychological importance, and can at the moment be defined much more objectively.

As an example of this degree of objectivity, consider the difference in replicability of the Eysenck and the Cattell factors. Some of the criticisms of Cattell's work have been detailed elsewhere (Eysenck, 1972), and they will only be stated very briefly now, in a comparison with the results of work on the Eysenck factors.

In the first place, the Cattell factors have very low reliabilities, whereas second order factors can be measured much more reliably. In the second place, Cattell's primary factors are often based on very low factor loadings for individual items, whereas factor loadings are uniformally much higher for the Eysenck factors. In the third place, Cattell's factors have been impossible to replicate in a large number of studies carried out in the United States, Canada, Germany, Scandinavia, and the United Kingdom; in none of these was it possible to obtain Cattell's 16 factors, or anything remotely resembling them. On the other hand, the Eysenck factors have been replicated in 25 different countries, with indices of factor comparison averaging around .98 (Barrett & Eysenck, 1984). The different cultures compared were much more divergent than those on which the replication of the Cattell studies were attempted, including, for instance, Uganda, Nigeria, Japan, Mainland China, and various socialist countries, as well as South American, European, and English-speaking countries; nevertheless, near-identical factors were extracted in all these countries. It would seem that, if replicability is an important consideration, then the superfactors are much more replicable than are lower order trait factors.

It may be objected that possibly many first-order factors, even though not very valid, may capture more of the valid variance than do second-order factors, however reliable. Reynolds and Nichols (1977) have carried out a large-scale experiment to test this view, using the CPI as a measuring instrument. They found that all the valid variance was accounted for by two superfactors of extraversion and neuroticism; the variance contributed by the many scales of the CPI did not contribute at all. Theoretically, this may seem a paradoxical result, as one might have expected that the additional variance contributed by the primaries should add to the total validity of the superfactors, but this would only be so if the regression weights for different populations were identical. As they are not, the primaries may subtract from, rather than add to, the validity of the scales. The question is an important one, and it is regrettable that there are not more studies of this kind to indicate whether the answer provided by Reynolds and Nichols has wider validity, and does not only apply to the CPI, and to the particular criteria used by them. The evidence, however, does indicate that we should not assume, as many psychometrists do, that many unreliable factors are better than a few reliable ones.

Another important consideration is the longitudinal consistency of personality test scores. Conley (1984) has surveyed the available literature on P, E, and N and has found marked consistency even over quite long periods (up to 50 years). No such data are available for simple traits and primary factors, and until it can be shown that they too are equally consistent we must conclude that the evidence again favours higher-order conceptions or "type" factors.

Another important aspect is the fact that firm biological foundations have been found for the superfactors (Eysenck, 1967, 1981), while there is a dearth of such theories linking constitution and behavior as far as primary personality traits are concerned. By the same token, the biological view would suggest that behavior patterns similar to P, E, and N would be observable in animals, and the work of Chamove, Eysenck, and Harlow (1972) and of Garcia-Sevilla (1984) has shown that this is indeed so. This link between the biological foundations and behavior is of course suggested by the fact that personality traits show strong determination by genetic factors (Fulker, 1981; Eaves & Young, 1981) which can only be mediated by physiological, hormonal, and other biochemical intermediaries. The absence of any theories of this kind regarding the Cattell, Gough, MMPI, and other factors must make their position more hazardous, and less established. A much more detailed discussion of these points can be found elsewhere (Eysenck & Eysenck, 1985).

These are not the only points that could be mentioned, but for a brief discussion it may suffice as far as the major considerations relating to the issue of the one and the many in personality research are concerned. Here too, just as in the case of intelligence, we find strong evidence to suggest that superfactors like P, E, and N are much better established than the so-called primaries or traits usually preferred by North American psychologists, although of course none would deny that, within the personality sphere, a certain amount of variance is left over for such traits, and for specificity. It is merely asserted that these higher order factors are of very considerable importance in the description of personality and have a much more assured standing than do factors at a lower level of generality.

Briefly, it may be useful to mention here that, as in the case of intelligence, so here also, biochemical factors may be causally instrumental in mediating differences in personality on such superfactors as neuroticism. If, indeed, predispositions to neurosis are largely inherited (Fulker, 1981), it is to be expected that further advances in understanding the process of incubation of anxiety will come from an understanding of individual differences in neurobiological factors such as neurohormones. Apart from peripheral endocrine functions, hormones are present in the CNS and affect emotions by the modulation of activity in the limbic system. It is known that at least patients with panic attacks have limbic abnormalities (Ritzman, Colburn, Zimmerman, & Krivoy, 1984); particularly relevant are ACTH and some of the endogenous opioids for anxiety, as well as cortisol for depression. A detailed analysis of these relationships is given elsewhere (Eysenck & Kelley, 1987), and it would not be possible to go into detail here. It may be mentioned, however, that vasopressin (AVP) is also involved in the mediation of extinction and incubation of anxiety, and has modulatory properties on neuronal activities in the limbic system and effects on resistance to extinction in aversive conditioning paradigms. As an example of the type of correlation which may be found, consider the finding by Jacquet (1978) that plasma levels of beta-endotrophin covary perfectly with ACTH, and CSF levels of endorphins are highly correlated (.67) with neuroticism as measured on the Eysenck Personality Questionnaire (Post, Pickar, Ballenger, Naher, & Rubinow, 1984).

Similarly, high correlations have been found between introversion and monoamine oxydase, suggesting an intimate and probably causal relationship between behavior and neurohormones. A survey of the evidence on this, and other correlations between biochemical and psychological factors, is given by Zuckerman, Ballenger, and Post (1984), and no detailed discussion of the issues involved can be given here. Note merely that, in the field of personality, as in the field of intelligence, deductions as programmed have been successful in demonstrating quite strong relations between hormonal and physiological events, on the one hand, and individual differences in personality and behavior, on the other.

8. CONCLUSIONS

This concludes our brief discussion of the many complex and difficult issues involved in the debate between the one and the many. Ultimately, of course, the issues can only be resolved by discovering the degree to which a given set of theories is useful or useless, and relates to a progressive or regressive research program (Lakatos, 1968). The evidence both for intelligence and for personality indicates very clearly at the moment that the general factor of mental ability and the superfactors P, E, and N in the personality field all form part of a progressive research program and cannot be dismissed, neglected, or left out of account in any scientific account of individual differences.

REFERENCES

Albert, K., & Warden, C. J. (1944). The level of performance in the white rat. *Science, 100,* 476.

Barrett, P., & Eysenck, S. B. G. (1984). The assessment of personality factors across 25 countries. *Personality and Individual Differences, 5,* 615–632.

Barrett, P., Eysenck, H. J., & Lucking, S. (1986). Reaction time and intelligence: a replicated study. *Intelligence, 10,* 9–40.

Berger, M. (1982). The "scientific approach" to intelligence: An overview of its history with special reference to mental speed. In H. J. Eysenck (Ed.), *A model for intelligence* (pp. 13–14). New York: Springer.

Berry, J. W. (1981). Cultural systems and cognitive styles. In M. Friedman, J. P. Das, & N. O'Connor (Eds.), *Intelligence and learning.* New York: Plenum.

Binet, A. (1903). *L'etude experimentale de l'intelligence.* Paris: Schleicher, Frenes.
Binet, A. (1907). *La psychologie du raisonnement.* Paris: Alcan.
Brand, C. R. (1981). General intelligence and mental speed. In M. Friedman, A. Das, & N. O'Connor (Eds.), *Intelligence and learning.* New York: Plenum.
Brand, C. R., & Deary, L. J. (1982). Intelligence and "inspection time." In H. J. Eysenck (Ed.), *A model for intelligence.* New York: Springer.
Burt, C. (1909). Experimental tests of general intelligence. *British Journal of Psychology, 3,* 94–177.
Burt, C. (1940). *Factors of the mind.* London: University of London Press.
Callaway, E. (1975). *Brain electrical potentials and individual psychological differences.* London: Grune & Stratton.
Carroll, J. B. (1987). Jensen's mental chronometry: Some comments and questions. In S. Modgil & C. Modgil (Eds.), *Arthur Jensen: Consensus and controversy* (pp. 297–307). Lewes, England: Falmer Press.
Cattell, R. B. (1957). *Personality and motivation structure and measurement.* Yonkers, NY: New Worlds.
Cattell, R. B. (1971). *Abilities, their structure, growth and action.* Boston, MA: Houghton Mifflin.
Cattell, R. B., Eber, H. W., & Tatsouka, M. M. (1970). *Handbook for the sixteen personality factor questionnaire.* Champaign, IL: Institute for Personality and Abilities Testing.
Cattell, R. B., & Scheier, I. N. (1961). *The meaning and measurement of neuroticism and anxiety.* New York: Ronald.
Chamove, A. S., Eysenck, H. J., & Harlow, H. F. (1972). Personality in monkeys: Factor analysis of rhesus social behaviour. *Quarterly Journal of Experimental Psychology, 24,* 496–504.
Charlesworth, W. R. A. (1976). Human intelligence as adaptation: An ethological approach. In L. B. Resnick (Ed.), *The nature of intelligence.* Hillsdale, NJ: Erlbaum.
Chase, R. N., Foster, N. L., Brooks, R., Di Chiro, G., & Mausi, L. (1984). Wechsler adult intelligence scale performance: cortical localization by fluorodeoxyclucose F18-positron emission tomography. *Archives of Neurology, 41,* 1244–1247.
Cole, M. (1979–1980). Mind as a cultural achievement: Implication for IQ testing. In *Annual Report of the Research and Clinical Center for Child Development.* Sappore, Japan: Hokkaido University, Faculty of Education.
Conley, J. J. (1984). The hierarchy of consistency: A review and model for longitudinal findings on adult individual differences in intelligence, personality and self-opinion. *Personality and Individual Differences, 5,* 11–26.
De Leon, M. J., Ferris, S. H., George, A. E., Christman, D. R., Fowler, J. S., Gentes, C., Reisberg, B., Gee, B., Emmerich, M., Yonekura, Y., Brodie, J., Kricheff, I. I., & Wolf, A. P. (1983). Positron emission tomographic studies of aging and Alzheimer's disease. *American Journal of Neuroradiology, 4,* 568–571.
Dewey, J. (1957). *Human nature and conduct.* New York: Modern Library.
Eaves, L. J., & Young, P. A. (1981). Genetical theory and personality differences. In R. Lynn (Ed.), *Dimensions of personality* (pp. 129–179). London: Pergamon.
Ekstrom, R. B. (1979). Review of cognitive factors. *Multivariate Behavioural Research Monograph, 79*(2), 7–56.

Ertl, J. (1971). Fourier analysis of evoked potential and human intelligence. *Nature, 230,* 525–526.
Ertl, J. (1973). IQ, evoked potential responses and Fourier analysis. *Nature, 241,* 209–210.
Ertl, J., & Schafer, E. (1969). Brain response correlates of psychometric intelligence. *Nature, 223,* 421–422.
Eysenck, H. J. (1939). Primary mental abilities. *British Journal of Educational Psychology, 9,* 270–275.
Eysenck, H. J. (1953). *The uses and abuses of psychology.* London: Pelican.
Eysenck, H. J. (1967). Intelligence assessment: A theoretical and experimental approach. *British Journal of Educational Psychology, 37,* 81–98.
Eysenck, H. J. (1970). *The structure of human personality* (3rd ed.) London: Methuen.
Eysenck, H. J. (1972). Primaries or second-order factors: A critical consideration of Cattell's 16 PF battery. *British Journal of Social and Clinical Psychology, 11,* 265–269.
Eysenck, H. J. (1979). *The structure and environment of intelligence.* New York: Springer.
Eysenck, H. J. (1981). *A model for personality.* New York: Springer.
Eysenck, H. J. (1982). *A model for intelligence.* New York: Springer.
Eysenck, H. J. (1985). The theory of intelligence and the psychophysiology of cognition. In R. J. Sternberg (Ed.), *Advances in the psychology of human intelligence* (Vol. 3). Hillsdale, NJ: Erlbaum.
Eysenck, H. J. (1987a). Speed of information processing, reaction time, and the theory of intelligence. In P. A. Vernon (Ed.), *Speed of information processing and intelligence* (pp. 21–68). Norwood, NJ: Ablex Publishing Corp.
Eysenck, H. J. (1987b). Thomson's "bonds" or Spearman's "energy": Sixty years on. *The Mankind Quarterly, 27,* 257–274.
Eysenck, H. J. (1988). The concept of "intelligence": Useful or useless? *Intelligence, 12,* 1–16.
Eysenck, H. J., & Barrett, P. (1985). Psychophysiology and the measurement of intelligence. In C. R. Reynolds & V. Wilson (Eds.), *Methodological and statistical advances in the study of individual differences.* New York: Plenum.
Eysenck, H. J., & Eysenck, M. W. (1980). Mischel and the concept of personality. *British Journal of Psychology, 71,* 191–209.
Eysenck, H. J., & Eysenck, M. W. (1985). *Personality and individual differences: A natural science approach.* New York: Plenum.
Eysenck, H. J., & Kelley, M. J. (1987). The interaction of neurohormones with Pavlovian A and Pavlovian B conditioning in the causation of neurosis extinction and incubation of anxiety. In G. Davey (Ed.), *Cognitive processes and pavlovian conditioning in humans* (pp. 251–286). London: John Wiley.
Eysenck, H. J., & White, O. (1964). Personality and the measurement of intelligence. *British Journal of Educational Psychology, 34,* 197–202.
Frearson, W. M., & Eysenck, H. J. (1986). Intelligence, reaction time and a new "odd-man-out" RT paradigm. *Personality and Individual Differences, 7,* 807–817.
Frearson, W., Eysenck, H. J., & Barrett, P. (1990). The Furneaux model of human problem solving: Its relationship to reaction time and Intelligence. *Personality and Individual Differences, 11,* 239–257.

Fulker, D. W. (1981). The genetic and environmental architecture of psychoticism, extraverson and neuroticism. In H. J. Eysenck (Ed.), *A model for personality* (pp. 88–122). New York: Springer.

Furneaux, D. (1952). Some speed, error, and difficulty relationships within a problem solving situation. *Nature, 170,* 37.

Furneaux, D. (1961). Intellectual abilities and problem solving behaviour. In H. J. Eysenck (Ed.), *Handbook of abnormal psychology* (pp. 167–192). New York: Basic Books.

Galton, F. (1892). *Heredity genius: An enquiry into its laws and consequences.* London: Macmillan.

Galton, F. (1943). *Inquiries into human faculty.* London: Dent.

Garcia-Sevilla, L. (1984). Extraversion and neuroticism in rats. *Personality and Individual Differences, 5,* 511–532.

Gordon, E. W., & Terrell, M. D. (1981). The changed social context of testing. *American Psychologist, 36,* 1167–1171.

Guilford, J. P. (1967). *The nature of human intelligence.* New York: McGraw-Hill.

Guilford, J. P. (1975). Factors and factors of personality. *Psychological Bulletin, 82,* 802–814.

Guilford, J. P., & Hoepfner, R. (1971). *The analysis of intelligence.* New York: McGraw-Hill.

Guilford, J. S., Zimmerman, W. S., & Guilford, J. P. (1976). *The Guilford-Zimmerman temperament survey handbook.* San Diego, CA: Edits.

Hebb, D. (1949). *The organization of behavior.* New York: Wiley.

Hemmelgarn, T. E., & Kehle, T. J. (1984). The relationship between reaction time and intelligence in children. *School Psychology International, 5,* 77–84.

Hendrickson, D. E. (1982). The biological basis of intelligence. Part II: Measurement. In H. J. Eysenck (Ed.), *A model for intelligence.* New York: Springer.

Heron, A. (1951). *A psychological study of occupational adjustment.* Unpublished Ph.D. thesis, University of London.

Heron, A. (1954). The objective assessment of personality among factory workers. *Journal of Social Psychology, 39,* 161–185.

Heron, A. (1955). The objective assessment of personality of female unskilled workers. *Educational, Psychological Measurement, 15,* 112–126.

Hick, W. (1952). On the rate of gain of information. *Quarterly Journal of Experimental Psychology, 4,* 11–26.

Himwich, H. E., & Fazekas, J. F. (1940). Cerebral metabolism in Mongolian idiocy and phenylpyruvic oligophrenia. *Archives of Neurology and Psychiatry, 44,* 1213–1218.

Horn, J. L. (1978). Human ability systems. In P. B. Baltes (Ed.), *Life-span development and behaviour* (Vol. 1, pp. 211–256). New York: Academic Press.

Horn, J. L., & Knapp, J. R. (1973). On the subjective character of the empirical base of Guilford's structure of intellect model. *Psychological Bulletin, 80,* 33–43.

Hoyer, G. (1982). The young adult and normally aged brain. Its blood flow and oridatial metabolism. A review—Part 1. *Archives of Gerontology and Geriatrics, 1,* 101–116.

Hughes, K. R., & Zubek, J. P. (1956). Effect of glutamic acid on the learning ability of bright and dull rats: 1. Administration during infancy. *Canadian Journal of Psychology, 10,* 132–138.

Israel, J. B., Wickens, C. D., Chesney, G. L., & Donchin, E. (1980). The event related brain potentials as an index of display monitoring workload. *Human Factors, 22,* 211–224.

Jacquet, Y. F. (1978). Opiate effects after adrenocorticotropin or B-endorphin injection in the periaqueductal grey matter of rats. *Science, 201,* 1032–1034.

Jager, A. O. (1967). *Dimensionen der Intelligenz.* Gottingen, Germany: Hogrefe.

Jensen, A. R. (1982a). Reaction time and psychometric *g*. In H. J. Eysenck (Ed.), *A Model for Intelligence* (pp. 93–132). New York: Springer.

Jensen, A. R. (1982b). The chronometry of intelligence. In R. J. Sternberg (Ed.), *Advances in the psychology of human intelligence* (Vol. 1, pp. 255–310). London: Erlbaum.

Jensen, A. R. (1984). Test validity: *g* versus the specificity doctrine. *Journal of Social and Biological Structures, 7,* 93–118.

Keating, D. P. (1984). The emperor's new clothes: The "new look" in intelligence research. In R. J. Sternberg (Ed.), *Advances in the psychology of human intelligence* (Vol. 1). Hillsdale, NJ: Erlbaum.

Lakatos, L. (1968). Criticism and the methodology of scientific research programmes. *Proceedings of the Aristoletian Society, 69,* 149–186.

Lehrl, S., & Frank, H. G. (1982). Zur humangenetischen Erklarung der Kurzspeicher-Kapazitat als die zentrale individuelle Derterminante von Spearman's Generalfaktor der Intelligenz. *Grundlagenstudien aus Kybernetik und Geisteswissenchaften, 23,* 177–186.

Lenk, W. (1983). *Faktoren analyse: Ein Mythos?* Weinheim, Germany: Beltz.

Lienert, G. (1963). Die Faktorenstruktur der Intelligenz als Funktion des Neurotizismus. *Zeitschrift fur Experimentelle und Angewandte Psychologie, 10,* 1401–159.

Lienert, G., & Croft, R. (1964). Studies on the factor structure of intelligence in children, adolescents and adults. *Vita Humana, 7,* 147–163.

Longstreth, L. E. (1984). Jensen's reaction time investigations of intelligence: A critique. *Intelligence, 8,* 139–160.

McFarland, R. A. (1928). The role of speed in mental ability. *Psychological Bulletin, 25,* 595–612.

Magnusson, D. (Ed.). (1981). *Toward a psychology of situations: An international perspective.* Hillsdale, NJ: Erlbaum.

Mann, D. M., Yates, P. D., & Marcynink, B. (1984). Relationship between pigment accumulation and age in Alzheimer's disease and Down's syndrome. *Acta Neuropathologica, 63,* 72–77.

Maxwell, S. E. (1972). Factor analysis: Thomson's sampling theory recalled. *British Journal of Mathematical and Statistical Psychology, 25,* 1–21.

Meili, R. (1964). Die faktorenanalytische Interpretation der Intelligenz. Schweizer Zeitschrift fur Psychologie, 23, 135–155.

Mischel, W. (1968). *Personality and Assessment.* London: Wiley.

Nachmansohn, D., & John, H. N. (1943). Effect of glutamic acid on the formation of acetylcholine. *Journal of Biological Chemistry, 150,* 485–486.

Neisser, V. (1979). The concept of intelligence. *Intelligence, 3,* 217–227.

Nelkon, M., & Parker, P. (1968). *Advanced level physics.* London: Heinemann.

O'Connor, N. (1952). The prediction of psychological stability and anxiety-aggressiveness from a battery of tests administered to a group of high-grade mental defectives. *Journal of Genetic Psychology, 46,* 3–18.

Oden, M. H. (1968). The fulfilment of promise: 40 year follow-up of the German gifted groups. *Genetic Psychology Monograph, 77,* 3–93.

Oswald, D. W. (1971). Uber Zusammenhange zwischen Informationsverarbeitung, Alter und Intelligenzstruktur beim Kartensortieren. *Psychologische Rundschau, 27,* 197–202.

Oswald, D. W., & Roth, E. (1978). *Der Zahlen-Verbindungs-Test (ZVT).* Gottingen, Germany: Hogrefe.

Perry, E. K., Tomlinson, B. E., Blessed, G., Berman, K., Gibson, P. H., & Perry, P. N. (1978). Correlation of cholinergic abnormalities with senile plaques and mental test scores in senile dementia. *British Medical Journal, 2,* 1957–1959.

Picton, T. W., & Hilward, S. A. (1974). Human auditory evoked potentials: effects of attention. *Electroencephalography and Clinical Neurophysiology, 36,* 191–199.

Posner, M. L., Boies, S., Eichelman, W., & Taylor, R. (1969). Retention of visual and name codes of single letters. *Journal of Experimental Psychology, 81,* 10–15.

Post, R. M., Pickar, P., Ballenger, J. C., Naher, D., & Rubinow, P. R. (1981). Endrogeneous opiates in cerebrospinal fluid: relationship to mood and anxiety. In R. N. Post & J. C. Ballenger (Eds.), *Neurobiology of mood disorder.* London: Williams and Wilkinson.

Reinis, S., & Goldman, J. M. (1982). *The chemistry of behaviour.* New York: Plenum.

Reventsdorf, D. (1980). *Faktorenanalyse.* Stuttgart, Germany: Kohlhammer.

Reynolds, C. N., & Nichols, R. C. (1977). Factor rates for the CPI: Do they capture the valid variance? *Educational and Psychological Measurement, 34,* 907–915.

Ritzman, R. F., Colburn, D. L., Zimmerman, R. G., & Krivoy, W. (1984). Immonyophyseal hormones in tolerance and physical dependence. *Pharmacology and Therapy, 23,* 281–312.

Robinson, D. L. (1982). Properties of the diffuse thalamocortical system, human intelligence and differentiated vs. integrated modes of learning. *Personality and Individual Differences, 3,* 393–405.

Roth, E. (1964). Die Geschwindigkeit der Verarbeitung von Information und ihr Zusammenhang mit Intelligenz. *Zeitschrift fur angewandte und experimentelle Psychologie, 11,* 616–622.

Sauri, J. J. (1950). Accion del acido glutamico en el sistema nerviosa central. *Neuropriquiatrica, 1,* 148–158.

Schafer, E. (1979). Cognitive neural adaptability: A biological basis for individual differences in intelligence. *Psychophysiology Neurosciences, 16,* 199.

Schafer, E. (1982). Neural adaptability: A biological determinant of behavioural intelligence. *International Journal of Neuroscience, 17,* 183–191.

Schafer, E. W. P., Amochaev, A., & Russell, M. J. (1981). Knowledge of stimulus timing attenuates human evoked cortical potentials. *Electroencephalography and Clinical Neurophysiology, 52,* 9–17.

Schafer, E., & Marcus, M. (1973). Self-stimulation alters human memory brain responses. *Science, 181,* 175–177.

Sinet, P. M., Lejenne, J., & Jerome, H. (1979). Trisomy 21 (Down's syndrome), glutathione peroxidase, hexose monosphate shunt and IQ. *Life Sciences, 24,* 29–33.

Soininen, H. S., Jolkkonen, J. T., Reinihainen, K. J., Holonen, T. O., & Riekkinen, P. J. (1983). Reduced cholinesterase activity and somatostatics-like immunoreactivity in the cerebrospinal fluid of patients with dementia of the Alzheimer's type. *Journal of Neurological Science, 63,* 167–172.

Smith, E. E. (1968). Choice reaction time: An analysis of the major theoretical positions. *Psychological Bulletin, 69,* 77–110.

Spearman, C. (1904). General intelligence, objectively determined and measured. *American Journal of Psychology, 15,* 201–293.

Spearman, C. (1927). *The ability of man.* London: Macmillan.

Spearman, C., & Jones, H. (1950). *Human ability.* London: Macmillan.

Spitz, H. H. (1986). *The raining of intelligence.* Hillsdale, NJ: Erlbaum.

Squires, K. C., Wickens, C., Squires, N. K., & Donchin, E. (1976). The effect of stimulus sequence on the waveform of the cortical event related potential. *Science, 193,* 1142–1146.

Sternberg, S. (1966). High speed scanning in human memory. *Science, 153,* 652–654.

Sternberg, R. J., & Salter, W. (1982). Conception of intelligence. In R. J. Sternberg (Ed.), *Handbook of human intelligence.* Cambridge, England: Cambridge University Press.

Sternberg, R. J. (1985). *Beyond IQ.* Cambridge, England: Cambridge University Press.

Thomson, G. H. (1939). *The factorial analysis of human ability.* London: University of London Press.

Thorndike, E. L. (1903). *Educational psychology.* New York: Teachers College.

Thorndike, E. L., Bregman, E. O., Cobb, M. V., & Woodyard, E. I. (1926). *The measurement of intelligence.* New York: Teachers College.

Thurstone, L. L. (1938). *Primary mental abilities.* Chicago, IL: University of Chicago Press.

Thurstone, L. L., & Thurstone, T. G. (1941). *Factorial studies of intelligence.* Chicago, IL: University of Chicago Press.

Tizard, J., & O'Connor, N. (1951). Predicting the occupational adequacy of certified mental defectives: An empirical test and rating. *Occupational Psychology, 25,* 205–211.

Vernon, P. E. (1979). *Intelligence, heredity and environment.* San Francisco, CA: Freeman.

Waelsch, H. (1951). Glutamic acid and cerebral functions. In M. L. Auson, J. T. Edsall, & K. Bailey (Eds.) (pp. 310–339). New York: Academic Press.

Weiss, V. (1982). *Psychogenetik: Humangenetik in Psychologie und Psychiatrie.* Jena, Germany: Fischer.

Weiss, V. (1984). Psychometric intelligence correlates with interindividual different rates of lipi peroxidation. *Biomedical and Biochemical Acta, 43,* 755–763.

Weiss, V. (1985). From the genetics of memory span and mental speed towards the quantum mechanics of intelligence. *Personality and Individual Differences, 7,* 737–749.

Welford, A. T. (Ed.). (1980). *Reaction times.* New York: Academic Press.

Wewetzer, K. H. (1958). Zur Differenz der Leistungstrukturen bei verschiedenen intelligenzgraden. *Bericht des 21 Kongresses der deutschen Gesselschaft fur Psychologie.* Gottingen, Germany: Hogrefe.

White, P. O. (1982). Some major components in general intelligence. In H. J. Eysenck (Ed.), *A model for intelligence* (pp. 44–90). New York: Springer.

Zimmerman, F. I., Burgemeister, B. B., & Putnam, T. J. (1949). Effect of glutamic acid on the intelligence of patients with mongolism. *Archives of Neurology and Psychiatry, 61,* 275–287.

Zimmerman, F. I., & Ross, S. (1944). Effect of glutamic acid and other amino acids on maze learning in the white rat. *Archives of Neurology and Psychiatry, 51*, 446–451.

Zuckerman, M., Ballenger, J. C., & Post, R. N. (1984). The neurobiology of some dimension of personality. *International Review of Neurobiology, 25*, 391–436.

Chapter 4

Modules, Domains, and Frames: Towards a Neuropsychology of Intelligence

Alex Martin
Department of Neurology
Uniformed Services University of the Health Sciences

Herbert Weingartner
Department of Psychology
George Washington University

The tendency has always been strong to believe that whatever received a name must be an entity or being, having an independent existence of its own. And if no real entity answering to the name could be found, men did not for that reason suppose that none existed, but imagined that it was something peculiarly obtuse and mysterious.
John Stuart Mill*

* With thanks to S. J. Gould.

In the introduction to *Brain Mechanisms and Intelligence* (1929) Karl Lashley noted that "the whole problem is in confusion. It is uncertain whether we are justified in dealing with intelligence as a single function, as an algebraic sum of all functions, or as the sum of a few selected ones" (p. 11). The central concern of the present collection of studies underscores the rather troublesome fact that, now, 60 years after Lashley voiced his concern, there is still apparent confusion, or at least continued debate, over whether *intelligence* should be considered unitary or, using currently popular terminology, modular in design. As interested observers but not active members of the intelligence research community, it is somewhat disheartening to discover that the obligatory introductory section of many current theoretical papers on the nature of human intelligence does not differ substantially from Lashley's 1929 review. Thus, using the terminology recently offered by Howard Gardner (1983), psychological investigation of intelligence continues to be dominated by the long-standing debate between the "hedgehogs" who argue for a single unitary intelligence ("g") and the "foxes" who deny the existence of "g" and instead view intelligence as being composed of a set of relatively independent mental abilities and functions.

While we need not review this history (the interested reader is referred to Carroll, 1982), it is important to note that this controversy has been largely rooted in and directly tied to the history of test measurement theory, the development of specific types of statistical procedures and their modification (e.g., factor analysis), and the interpretation of the results of such procedures. Moreover, with extremely rare exception, the target database for these analyses has been the performance of normal individuals on collections of mental abilities tests (see Dennis, 1985a, b, for an exception to this dominant trend).

A central problem with this approach, again recognized by Lashley in his seminal book, is that the concept of intelligence viewed in this way becomes essentially a statistical or mathematical abstraction. As a result, the decision over whether or not intelligence should be considered as primarily a unitary function depends less on the data being analyzed than on the particular type of statistical analysis being employed. The hazards inherent in this approach were exemplified by L. L. Thurstone's vigorous debate with Charles Spearman and Cyril Burt concerning which mathematical procedure, principal component or rotated axes, was the "correct" method for defining factors (see Gould, 1981). If there is a lesson to be learned from their interchange, it is that such arguments can never be settled, simply because the statistical procedures are themselves neutral, there being no intrinsic or a priori reason for deciding which is better. Mathematically, each is correct. Moreover, even if it could be agreed that a particular statistical technique was the "correct" method of analysis, argument would still occur over the interpretation of the ensuing factors, including the meaning of the first principal component or so-called "g" factor (compare, for example, Jensen's 1985 interpretation, to one offered by Detterman, 1984). Again, debate over the meaning of mathematical abstractions is unlikely to foster progress without external sources of evidence that the factors represent something more than mathematical abstractions in the first place. Thus, viewed within this context, it appears that the test theory/psychometric approach limited to the performance of normal individuals has reached an impasse which renders it incapable of resolving the issue of whether intelligence is unitary or modular.

In recognition of these difficulties, a number of investigators have more recently adopted an information-processing approach to the study of intelligence, or at least that aspect of intelligence as a "thing inside the head" (e.g., Hunt, 1983; Sternberg, 1984; Jensen, 1985). Broadly defined, this approach views the mind or brain as an abstract information-processing mechanism. The principal underlying assumption of this approach is that task performance can be broken down into specific processing components which occur in a preset temporal order. Thus, within this framework, individual differences in cognitive ability are related to the speed or efficiency of a particular information-processing component, or the facility with which a set of these components interact. With regard to the nature of intelligence, it is assumed that the final goal would be to uncover and define the universal sequence of events or processes which intervene between the presentation of any cognitive task and the individual's final response. The identification and description of this set of processes would thus constitute an extremely general problem-solving mechanism, executive processor, or "g."

Although, not surprisingly, information-processing advocates have not arrived at an agreed upon typology of critical components, these investigators all appear to share the common underlying assumption that tests of mental ability require the utilization of a core or universal set of elementary cognitive operations (e.g., Hunt, 1983; Sternberg, 1984). It has been further suggested that the speed and efficiency with which these core processes are carried out may ultimately be reducible to a single physiological mechanism (Jensen, 1985).

In general, we are sympathetic to the information-processing approach to the extent that it has brought to the forefront the fact that the tasks used to measure intelligence are multidetermined. That is, rather than being pure measures of cognitive ability, they are in fact divisible into subcomponents. However, it is our contention that this approach has placed undue emphasis on the "processes" of cognition (i.e., information transformations), with little concern for the ways that different types of information are "represented." Moreover, this neglect of the nature of the representation may be viewed as an unavoidable consequence of limiting investigation to normal individuals, and to an ignorance or hasty dismissal of biological principles in general and, more specifically, of the effects of brain injury on human performance and ability.

The one noteworthy exception to this state of affairs is Howard Gardner's model of multiple intelligences (1983). The model we will propose is close in spirit, if not detail, to his. Briefly, we take as a starting point the position that the evidence from human neuropsychology heavily endorses a modular view of intelligence. Thus, the debate between the foxes and hedgehogs has been decided in favor of the foxes. We will argue that the study of cognition in individuals with pathological brain states indicates that the mind/brain is composed of relatively independent cognitive "organs." As an analogy, although all would agree that the body normally works as an integrated whole, it is in fact composed of a number of different systems (circulatory, respiratory, digestive, etc.), each of these systems is divisible into separate structures or organs, and our understanding of these organs is dependent, in turn, on an analysis of their component parts. We would submit that the human brain is at least as complex as the body, and that it follows a similar design with respect to being differentiated in functionally meaningful components. Furthermore, these components or organs are defined, not by what information analysis process they perform, but rather by the type of information they were designed to deal with. Therefore, a model of intelligence must take into account the existence of relatively independent cognitive organs or domains for handling qualitatively distinct types of mental representations such as lexical, mathematical, object, and spatial.

A crucial assumption of this view is that any cognitive (and ultimately, physiological) mechanism which has evolved to process a particular type of information is, *by its very design, incapable of performing some other type of processing demand.* In this sense, the language "organ" is as different from the spatial "organ" as the heart is from the liver. Thus, for example, although we would agree with the proponents of the information-processing approach that the processes subsumed under the rubric of "working memory" are crucial for understanding task performance, we reject the notion of a single working memory. Rather, we would submit that each cognitive domain has its own working memory component specifically designed to deal with the particular cognitive code that defines the operation of the domain in question (e.g., lexical versus spatial). Thus, these working memory systems are not interchangeable.

Neglect of the evidence for independent cognitive domains has, in our view, led to the misleading conception of a general process or set of processes which may be identified as intelligence. It is this position that we firmly reject. Therefore, although we will not attempt to identify each type of cognitive domain (that is, state how many there are or what each does), we would insist that none of them can be identified as intelligence. We view intelligence as the example, par excellence, of the process of reification. Once one accepts the fiction of intelligence as a biological structure, the fruitlessness of attempting to uncover its elementary processes becomes obvious.[1]

---

[1] Biological definitions of intelligence have been offered that attempt to equate intelligence with some measure of total neuronal information-processing capacity (e.g., Diamond, 1978; Jerison, 1982). For example, in Jerison's encephalization model, information-processing capacity is defined with regard to cortical surface size, which, in turn, is nearly perfectly correlated with total brain weight. Importantly, however, this correlation holds only across species, there being no orderly relationship between cortical surface and gross brain size within a species. Thus, these models do not, and can not, address individual differences in cognitive abilities.

In the following sections, we will offer a model of "intelligence" largely based on study of the breakdown of cognition following brain damage. Our central goal will be to provide a broad framework for conceptualizing intellectual abilities without invoking the need for a unitary intelligence, central processor, or general problem-solving mechanism.

TOWARDS A NEUROPSYCHOLOGICAL MODEL

Basic Postulates

1. Mind/Brain identity. By this we merely wish to make explicit the position that all mental phenomena, from the simplest sensations to the most complex thoughts, whether consciously perceived or not, have a physical substrate, brain. Moreover, these mental phenomena are caused by the operation of this physical system. This notion of causality is critical, because we will argue that highly specific (i.e., discretely localized) changes in this physical matter cause highly specific and predictable changes in cognition. We are well aware that statements of this form have contributed, in part, to one of the central and most intractable problems in philosophy, the mind–body or mind–brain problem. Thus, if mental events are caused by brain processes, then what exactly are these events? As recently explicated by John Searle (1984), a suitable answer is that mental phenomena or events are simple characteristics or features of brains. Thus, as Searle has argued, mentation is both caused by and, at the same time, is a feature of brains. This, of course, leads to another vexing problem; namely, if there is a causal relationship between mental and physical phenomena, then how can one be a characteristic of the other? Searle's solution to this puzzle lies in an analysis of causation. Causal relationships do not necessarily need to imply dualism. That is, although we are inclined to think of causation as implying two discrete events (i.e., if A causes B, then A and B are separate entities), this is not necessarily so. There are, in fact, a multitude of causal relations in nature that do not involve two separate entities, but rather two levels of analysis of a single entity or system ; the levels of micro- and macroproperties. Borrowing one of Searle's examples, a macrolevel global property of water is liquidity, which, in turn, can be causally explained by the nature of the interaction between H_2O molecules. Therefore, in the same way that liquidity is both a surface or global feature of water and is also caused by the behavior of the microlevel molecules, a mental event is both a feature of the brain and the result of its microlevel components.

2. Brain is a highly differentiated structure. Biological structures are composed of visibly identifiable components, and the existence of these separate entities is nearly always indicative of functional significance. Thus, when confronted with a structure that is clearly divisible into physically different regions, it is reasonable, and proper, to ask what the significance of this design may be.

Following this line of reasoning, we may also assume that the greater the physical diversity the greater the functional diversity.

In this regard, brain is characterized by an extreme degree of diversity at all levels of analysis of its physical structure; from the micro- (neuronal) to macro- (hemispheric) level. Therefore, while proponents of "g" may attempt to seek support for their position in the fact that all neurons seem to function in a similar manner, it is not true that all neurons are alike. To the contrary, brain is characterized by an ever-increasing list of neuronal cell types which can be classified according to their morphological features, primarily the shape of the cell body and dendritic pattern. For example, a partial list of neurons identified in the human cerebral cortex includes pyramidal, spiny stellate, basket, chandelier, double bouquet, and spider web cells (Peters & Jones, 1984). Although the functional significance of each cell type remains to be clarified, they do have different topological distributions across the cortex. This variability of cell type spatial distribution defines the next level diversity—cytoarchitectonics. Thus, observed differences in the horizontal (layers) and vertical (columns) arrangement of neurons have been used to segment the cerebral mantle into distinct regions. For example, Brodman's maps of the cortical surface distinguished 44 separate regions (Kemper & Galaburda, 1984). Finally, each cerebral hemisphere can be partialed into four distinct lobes, and the hemispheres themselves can be distinguished by gross differences in physical form, i.e., a larger temporal planum on the left, more prominent frontal cortex on the right.

This brief sketch of physical diversity focused only on the cerebral cortex because of its central role in human cognition. However, subcortical regions clearly play a role in most, if not all, facets of cognitive behavior. As might be expected, these subcortical structures are also characterized by extreme diversity from their micro- to macrolevel of analysis. Thus, we find distinct patterns of neuronal organizations which define complex nuclei. Collections of these nuclei are organized into larger structural units (e.g., thalamus, hypothalamus) which, in turn, form the components of the major divisions of the mammalian brain; the my-, met-, mes-, di-, and telencephalons. Finally, communication between these various subcomponents and levels is carried out via a complex web of interconnecting pathways.

In parallel with this structural diversity, brain is characterized by an equally complex chemoarchitecture. To date, eight canonical neurotransmitter substances have been identified, along with 25 or more neuroactive peptides which modulate neuronal interaction (Schwartz, 1981). In addition, these neurotransmitters and modulators also have unique spatial distributions which allow for the mapping or localization of discrete neurochemical systems within the brain (Nieuwenhuys, 1985).

Although our knowledge of the functional significance of these differences is far from complete, it is clear that brain is characterized by an extreme degree of morphological and biochemical diversity. It is this diversity that provides the physical substrate for the organs of cognitions and their subcomponents.

3. Evolution and the principle of modular design. Having argued for mind/brain identity and outlined the great physical diversity of the human brain, one may ask whether there are any compelling biological reasons why such diversity should exist, and, more importantly, why this diversity should be indicative of highly specialized, relatively independent, cognitive mechanisms. After all, one could argue that this physical diversity represents highly interdependent subprocesses of some general problem solving mechanism that we refer to as intelligence. If so, however, we need to address how such a system evolved.

Herbert Simon (1962) proposed a particularly compelling rationale for why biological structures must be composed of relatively independent subsystems. His argument was simply that evolution could not have occurred within the time frame that is has without the existence of stable intermediary forms. To illustrate this argument, Simon offered the parable of two watchmakers, Hora and Tempus. Both made equally fine watches. However, Hora prospered while Tempus did not.

> The watches the men made consisted of about 1000 parts each. Tempus had so constructed his that if he had one partly assembled and had to put it down—to answer the phone say—it immediately fell to pieces and had to be reassembled from the elements. The better the customers liked his watches, the more they phoned him, the more difficult it became for him to find enough uninterrupted time to finish a watch.
>
> The watches that Hora made were no less complex than those of Tempus. But he had designed them so that he could put together subassemblies of about ten elements each. Ten of these subassemblies, again, could be put together into a larger subassembly; and a system of ten of the latter subassemblies constituted the whole watch. Hence, when Hora had to put down a partly assembled watch in order to answer the phone, he lost only a small part of his work, and he assembled his watches in only a fraction of the manhours it took Tempus.

A similar argument concerning the nature and evolution of complex systems was put forth by David Marr (1976, 1982) as the *principle of modular design*. Briefly stated, all systems are composed of subsystems that are as nearly independent of one another as the overall function of the system will allow. As in Simon's formulation, Marr argued that, if such independence did not exist, then even a small change in one part would change the entire system. Thus, in order for evolution to occur in a nonmodular scheme, each change would need to be accompanied by numerous and simultaneous changes throughout the entire system. Modular design thus allows for the possibility of modifying or creating new subsystems without necessitating change in all other subsystems (for a detailed discussion of this issue see also Marshall, 1984).

What evidence do we have that some type of modular organization characterizes human cognition? In other words, what is the evidence that mind is decomposable into relatively independent systems? From our perspective the most compelling support for this position comes from observation and study of individuals with pathological brain states. Specifically, data from adults who, as a result of acquired brain damage, may be rendered markedly impaired in only single, highly circumscribed function or ability, and conversely, cases of so-called idiot savantism, in which a highly specialized function or skill may develop against a background of depressed performance in all unrelated abilities (see Chapter 7).

THE MODEL

Intelligence will be viewed within the context of a hierarchically organized system consisting of three major subdivisions; modules, domains, and frames.

Modules. These units will be considered the smallest psychologically realized components of cognitive behavior. Their characteristics are based largely on the criteria set forth by Fodor in *Modularity of Mind* (1983).[2] Within this framework, the primary candidates for modules are highly specialized input transducers that perform encoding operations, and output mechanism that produce discrete motor operations. Most importantly for our present considerations, the input units are specialized according to what types of information they act upon, not by the function they achieve. In other words, a number of different modules may all perform a similar information-processing task but are differentiated by the type of information that the processing task is performed upon. The operation of these units is innately determined, and may be describable by, although not necessarily equal to, a formal set of rules. In other words, the natures of the input and output of a module would suggest a particular transformation that, in turn, would suggest that the component operates *as if* it were under the control of these rules. Finally, the operation of these modules is assumed to be mandatory and automatic. That is, once they receive information, they reflexively perform their operation to completion. As a result, their operation is largely uninterruptable or modifiable, once begun.

Domains. The above-described modules are assumed to be organized into systems that are responsible for different types of knowledge representation. Candidate examples at this level would be assemblies of modules responsible for lexical/semantic, visuospatial, object recognition, and mathematical abilities and skills. For example, the domain of object recognition would include the interaction of modules responsible for processing different visual features (e.g., color, size, and, for familiar objects, constraints on the spatial organization of their components parts). As with the modules, the workings at this level would be rule bound; examples of which might include those proposed to govern visual object recognition (see Ullman, 1984) and syntactic analysis (see Chomsky, 1980).

[2] Our intent here is not to review or critique Fodor's position. For excellent critical discussion of *The Modularity of Mind*, see Marshall (1984), Putnam (1984), Shallice (1984), and Schwartz and Schwartz (1984).

Of particular importance is that the rules governing modules and domains are instantiated by predetermined physiological architectures (i.e., neuronal networks). A central feature of each of these networks is that they are specialized to perform a particular function, and that the network that performs this function is, *by virtue of its design, incompatible with the performance of some other function*. Thus, a grammar module could not perform the functions of a color perception module, and the assembly of modules responsible for determining what an object is (i.e., recognition) would be ill suited for specifying its location in space. As Lashley (1937) suggested, it is the incompatibility of the operation of these neuronal systems that requires them to be physically separated in the brain. Hence, localization of function.

For our present purposes, the critical feature of the outcome of the domain level would be to provide the minimum amount of stimulus-dependent information necessary to support reasoning, problem solving and the activation of other cognitive processes commonly associated with intelligence. Thus, within the context defined by a particular problem, these systems would provide the processing necessary to answer specific questions about the various components of the information presented. For example, what is it? where is it? and, for more familiar, routine, and overlearned applications—what do I do with it?

Each of these domains would constitute an independent representational and processing system with dedicated attentional and memorial resources. It is these domains that would be most closely aligned with the kinds of intelligence described by Gardner (1983). Therefore, the type of material presented (e.g., linguistic, visuospatial, mathematical) would activate the domain-specific representations and processes needed to support highly specific problem-solving routines. However, many problems, especially those that may be most closely associated with our everyday definition of intelligence, require either the application of previously acquired knowledge and cognitive operations to novel or unusual circumstances or the creation of novel arrangements or sequences of cognitive operations. Moreover, the essence of many of the more difficult types of problems often associated with intelligent behavior is that the nature of the representation needed is often not readily apparent. This would include problems that could be solved by multiple means (e.g., mathematically or visuospatially) with one solution being more efficient than the other. To answer the "what do I do?" question under these conditions requires a level of processing outside the capabilities of domains.

Frames. As previously noted, this is the highest level of organization. From a neuroanatomical viewpoint, the notions of modules and domains were designed to capture the functioning and organization of the flow of information from the primary sensory receiving areas to parietal and temporal association cortices at one end of a continuum and the organization of discrete motor programs at the other end. What is lacking in this formulation is conceptualization of the type, and nature, of the mechanisms responsible for the overall control, regulation, and guidance of behavior. In keeping with a number of recent formulations (see, for example, Goldberg & Bilder, 1987; Grafman, 1989; Shallice, 1982, 1984; Stuss & Benson, 1986) we view these macro-organizational units as the central and defining aspect of frontal lobe functioning. These units will be referred to as *frames*.

Frames are proposed to represent temporally organized sequences that provide the overall structure or schema for planning and carrying out courses of action and for guiding thought. As such, these structures are best viewed as control processes that integrate the information received from the cognitive domains and regulate and guide behavior towards a specified goal. An important feature of this control is the selection of task appropriate information and the inhibition of competing responses that may be activated by the overall environmental context. For example, successful problem solving often requires the ability to formulate a number of alternative solutions and to apply these possibilities in an organized, step-by-step fashion. This process of switching between alternative solutions requires, in turn, the ability to inhibit previously generated responses. It is just these types of processes, namely, the ability to shift from one strategy to another or from one type of representation to another, and the active inhibition of competing responses, that are often impaired following injury to the frontal lobes (see Stuss & Benson, 1984, for detailed review).

EVIDENCE FOR DOMAINS FROM THE STUDY OF DEMENTIA

Of all of the various syndromes and disorders produced by brain injury and disease, it has been the dementias, and in particular, Alzheimer's disease (AD), that has become most closely associated with a "loss of intelligence." Therefore, if one wanted to search for neuropsychological evidence for "g," patients suffering from AD might be the ideal target sample for such an enterprise. In fact, AD has been traditionally considered the prime example of a "global" disorder. That is, a disease characterized by progressive deterioration of a wide variety of previously acquired cognitive functions and skills with differences between patients attributed to differences in the degree or stage of dementia. Not surprisingly, this type of formulation has tended to reinforce the association of AD with a general decline in intellectual ability.

Recent evidence, however, has provided a strong challenge to this global deteriorative stage model. Specifically, it has been demonstrated that AD is associated with neuropathology in only select regions of the brain, and that the performance of these patients can be characterized by rather specific patterns of impaired and intact functions and abilities (e.g., Butters, Granholm, Salmon, & Grant, 1987; Weingartner, Grafman, Boutelle, Kay, & Martin, 1983). Moreover, in certain individuals, highly specific and contrasting patterns of deficits can be observed that can reveal the organization of specific domains of functioning and their interaction (see Martin, 1990, for detailed review of the neurobehavioral

Table 1. Psychometric Test Performance

	Patients		
	W	*C*	*F*
Wechsler Adult Intelligence Scale			
Verbal IQ	92	92	86
Performance IQ	79	80	68
Full-Scale IQ	86	86	77
Wechsler Memory Scale			
MQ	62	62	64

and neuropathological evidence in support of this claim). In this section we will provide evidence for the existence of domains using examples obtained from study of patients during the relatively early stages of AD.

Psychometric data obtained from three patients meeting established criteria for the diagnosis of probable AD are presented in Table 1. For ease of exposition, each patient has been labeled according to his or her most prominent symptom. Thus, Patient W had severe word-finding difficulties, Patient C had relatively greater difficulty on visuospatial/constructional tasks, and Patient F suffered from a problem in selecting the appropriate frame for guiding behavior and inhibiting competing responses. Note that the patients, especially patients W and C, could be considered to be equally "demented" based on their performance on the Wechsler Intelligence (WAIS) and Memory scales. Thus, in keeping with their diagnoses of AD, these patients had relatively moderate to severe deficits in various aspects, of cognition and memory. Yet, as we will see, these patients exhibited highly specific and unique patterns of deterioration in contrasting domains of functioning (a detailed description of Patients W and C can be found in Martin, 1987).

To appreciate the nature of their difficulties, consider the simple problems presented in Figure 1. In both instances the patients were presented with line drawings. In one situation they were required to simply name the object represented, and in the other to draw a copy of the material presented. Difficulties on tasks of naming ability and visuospatial/constructional skill, along with problems remembering and recalling new information, are the most common types of deficits in Alzheimer patients, the majority of whom present with deficits in all three of these domains of functioning. However, as illustrated in Figure 2, performance on these tasks can also be strikingly dissociated in patients with progressive dementing disorders. In fact, patients with relatively focal patterns of impairment involving these and other domains of functioning may compromise as much as 15% to 20% of AD cases during the relatively early stages of the disease process (see Martin, 1990, for review). Thus, patient W was able to produce a perfectly accurate and normal copy of the complex geometric figure

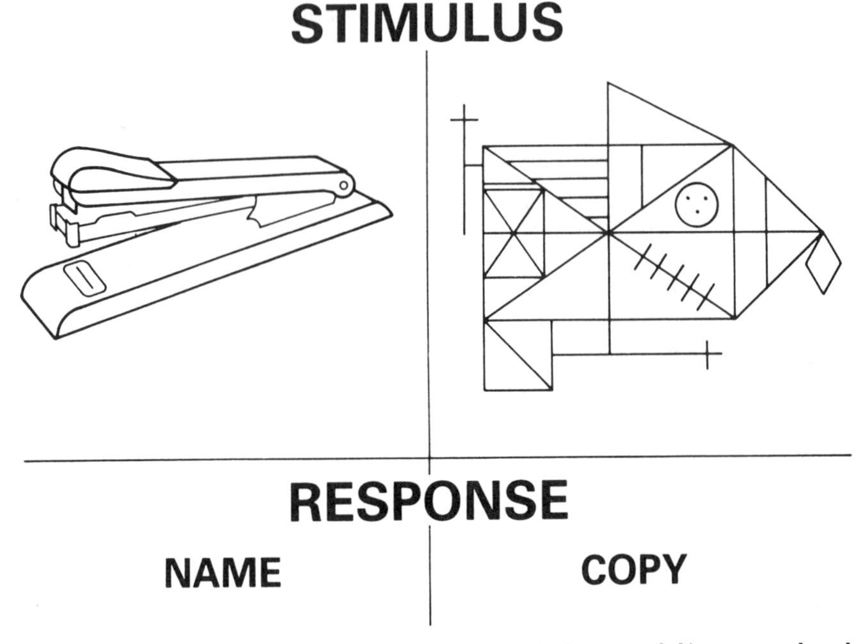

Figure 1. Prototypical stimuli for naming and visuospatial/constructional tasks. The stapler is from the Boston Naming Test and the design is the Rey-Osterrieth Complex Figure.

(Rey-Osterrieth Complex Figure; Osterrieth, 1944) while being severely impaired when required to provide the names of objects (Boston Naming Test; Kaplan, Goodglass, & Weintraub, 1976). Patient C, in contrast, produced the opposite pattern of impaired and preserved abilities.

As would be expected, these differences were reflected in other measures of spatial ability and semantic knowledge. For example, patient W performed normally on visuospatial problem solving tasks (e.g., 33/36 correct on the Ravens Coloured Progressive Matrices; scaled score of 11 on the WAIS Block Design subtest) but not on tasks requiring utilization of previously acquired semantic information (e.g., impaired ability to generate lists of semantically related items,

Figure 2. Copies of the Rey-Osterrieth Complex Figure. Numbers in parentheses indicate number of line drawn objects from the Boston Naming Test correctly named (maximum score = 85). A. Patient W and others with relatively circumscribed word-finding difficulty. B. Patient C and others with relatively circumscribed visuospatial/constructional deficits.

A **Patient W**

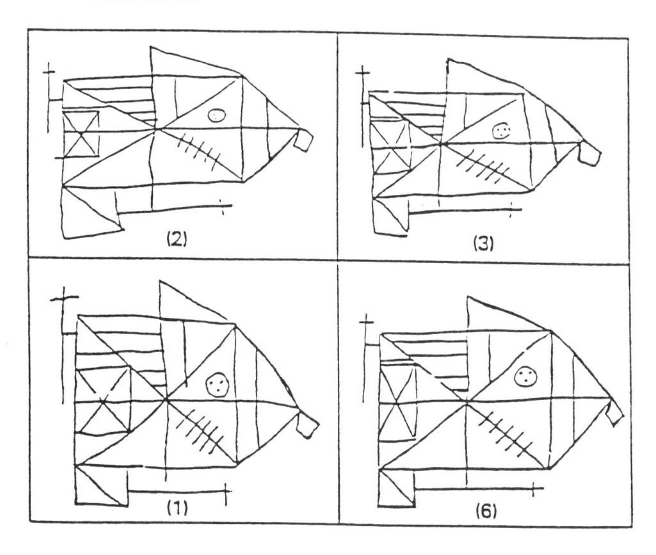

B **Patient C**

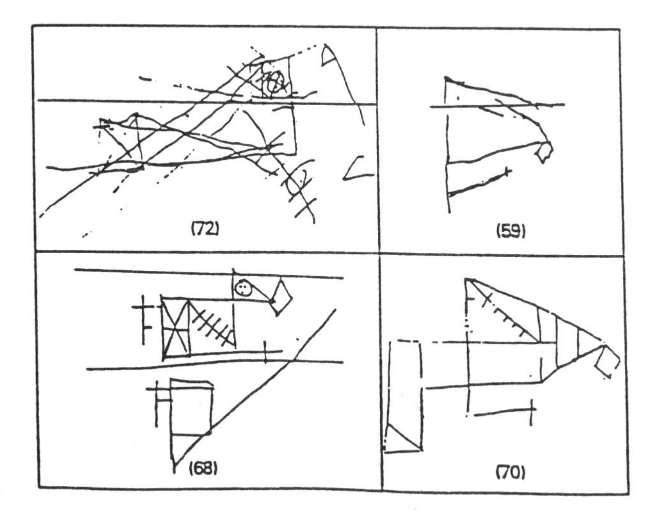

loss of knowledge of specific functionally and physical attributes of objects, impaired ability to utilize semantic knowledge to aid in puzzle construction—scaled score of 5 on the WAIS Object Assembly subtest). Patient C, in contrast performed normally on the tests of semantic knowledge while experiencing considerable difficulty with all measures of spatial problem solving (e.g., 23–36 correct on the Ravens Coloured Progressive Matrices; scaled score of 5 on WAIS Block Design).

The contrasting or double dissociations seen in these and other patients with AD can be interpreted as indicating that, in some individuals, this disease may produce a pattern of relatively domain-specific deterioration of cognitive skills. Specifically, longitudinal study of these patients has documented continued deterioration which was largely confined to a single domain of cognitive functioning (e.g., lexical/semantic or visuospatial). Moreover, this domain-specific progression can continue over a period of several years before the onset of the classic picture of more generalized, global deterioration during the latter stages of the disease process (Martin, Brouwers, Lalonde, Cox, & Fedio, 1987).

On one level of analysis, namely, neuropathological, these patterns of domain-specific deterioration in early stage AD patients simply reflect the fact that, for currently unknown reasons, the disease process appears to be limited to relatively circumscribed regions of the neocortex in these individuals. This hypothesis is based primarily on findings from studies utilizing positron emission tomography (PET scanning, an imaging technique that reveals patterns of glucose utilization in various regions of the brain). Thus, for example, AD patients with relatively focal word-finding deficits are characterized by a corresponding pattern of hypometabolism limited primarily to the left temporal lobe, while those with severe and relatively focal visuospatial deficits exhibit hypometabolism of the parietal lobes, especially within the right hemisphere (Foster et al., 1984; Martin et al., 1986).

The information provided by these recent studies of patients with Alzheimer's disease and other progressive dementias seems to be at odds with any unitary formulation of intelligence. Rather, the picture emerging from the study of the dementias is most consistent with the notion that mind is composed of a number of independent cognitive organs that are, in turn, dependent on the integrity of select regions of the human brain. When this substrate is damaged, the common consequence is not a loss of ability cutting across all, or even a large number, of intellectual domains, but rather a pattern of circumscribed dysfunction limited to single functional domains. In fact, even in patients with AD, the observed dissociations are not limited to gross distinctions between broadly conceived cognitive systems (e.g., semantic versus spatial), but rather can produce pockets of preserved functioning that can provide important clues to the nature of the internal subcomponents of these systems.

For example, detailed testing of Patient W indicted he did not suffer from a total inability to retrieve and utilize semantic word knowledge. In fact, his performance was surprisingly intact on abstract verbal reasoning tasks requiring the generation of the appropriate semantic category label when provided with exemplars (e.g., he achieved a scaled score of 11 on the WAIS Similarities subtest). Similarly, he was found to have retained considerable knowledge about objects he could no longer name. However, this knowledge was limited to base category and superordinate category membership. He could accurately indicate that a picture of a hammer was man-made rather than living, and that it belonged to the category *tools*. However, at the same time he was unable to answer simple yes/no questions concerning the specific attributes and features of tools that he could no longer name. Thus, when confronted with pictures of tools that he had correctly grouped together and labeled as *tools*, he could not indicate which had moving parts, which were used to cut, which were used to hold things, etc. These findings suggest that the naming difficulty seen in these patients may be due to a selective loss of knowledge concerning specific attributes that serve to distinguish highly related objects. These and similar studies have, in turn, led to the development of models concerning the normal organization of the lexical/semantic system (Martin, 1987; Martin & Fedio, 1983; Schwartz, Marin, & Saffran, 1979; Warrington, 1975).

In a similar fashion, study of patient C revealed that his constructional deficit was not total. For example, as illustrated in Figure 3, this patient, who, as noted

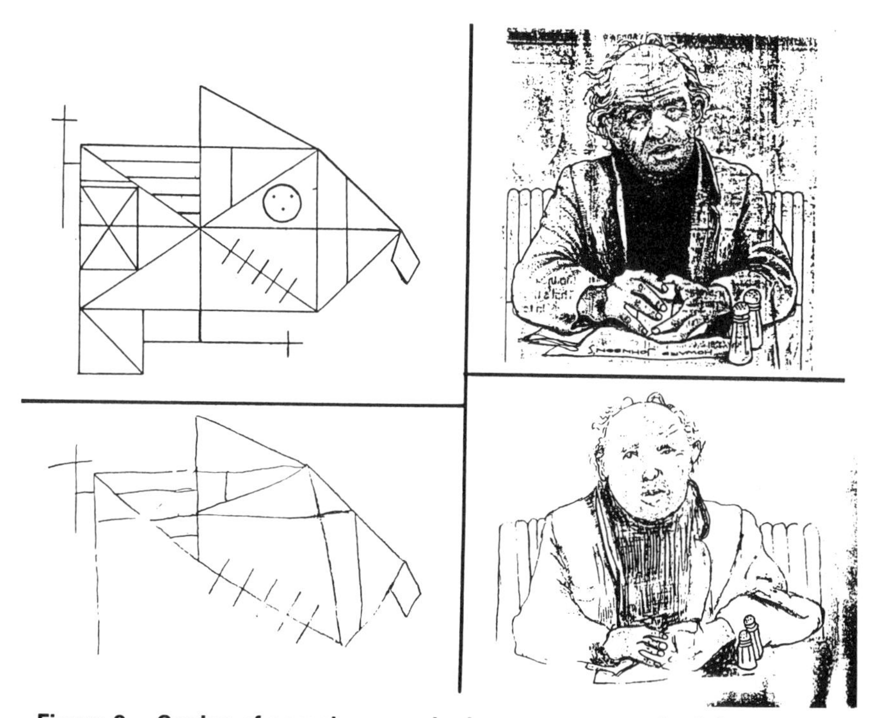

Figure 3. Copies of complex meaningless versus meaningful material produced by patient C.

previously, had an intact lexical/semantic system, retained the ability to produce exceptionally good reproductions of real objects. However, his ability to copy novel material was grossly abnormal. Detailed study of this and similar patients has suggested that this constructional deficit is due to a relatively pure impairment of spatial analysis. As a result attempts to copy novel or nonrepresentational designs suffered from an inability to accurately place component parts in their correct spatial orientation. This problem, in turn, may be due to the fact that, by definition, there are no a priori constraints on the spatial location and interrelationships between the component parts of nonrepresentational designs. Real objects, in contrast, are characterized by rather severe constraints on the relative location of parts. More recent study of a new patient with a similar dissociation between copying novel or meaningless versus meaningful material has provided additional evidence that preserved copying of meaningful material is dependent on the ability to utilize previously acquired object representations to guide construction (Kampen & Martin, 1989). Thus, the ability of these patients to solve simple constructional tasks was wholly dependent on the nature of the representational systems needed (object-based, semantically driven for meaningful material, versus spatial- or data-driven for novel material).

A PROBLEM WITH FRAMES

Although the contrasting patterns of preserved and impaired ability exhibited by these patients certainly raise a host of questions, they do seem to provide rather compelling evidence for the independence of specific domains of cognition and memory. In contrast, to these striking differences, a common feature shared by these patients was an appreciation of the requirements of each problem or task (e.g., name, copy) and an awareness of their inability to perform as well as they had in the past. Thus, the patients knew what was needed but no longer had the resources to perform the specific operations called for. With regard to our previously discussed framework, these patients appear to have retained the proper frame for performance but lacked the tools (domain-specific cognitive operations) to adequately perform. However, as mentioned previously, certain patients, especially those who have sustained injury or disease to the frontal lobes, can present with a very different picture of impairment.

Patient F, who was also assigned a provisional diagnosis of AD, shared several features in common with the previously discussed case, Patient C. For example, she had severe visuospatial/constructional difficulties, as documented by an inability to solve any of the WAIS Block Design problems (scaled score = 0), or copy the Rey-Osterrieth complex figure (1 of 36 components correctly reproduced). Again, like Patient C, Patient F's access to previously acquired lexical/semantic knowledge remained relatively intact. However, unlike the two previously discussed cases, this patient's behavior was prominently characterized by a breakdown in response selection and control, as manifested by a general tendency to perseverate previously generated responses and a failure to inhibit competing modes of responding. For example, she experienced great difficulty in producing a specified sequence of rapidly alternating hand movements and was unable to inhibit responses on a series of go:no-go tasks (e.g., press to the blue signal, do not press to the yellow signal). These and related difficulties are not uncommon following damage to the frontal lobes.

This general tendency towards a lack of inhibition and perseveration were strikingly apparent when she was asked to draw objects from memory or to copy visual material placed before her (see Figure 4). Although Patient F was well aware that the task called for a drawing response and not writing or naming, she was consistently unable to maintain the correct frame of reference and seemingly incapable of inhibiting the lexical/semantic system from gaining control. As such, her behavior suggested a loss of the ability to select the appropriate representational mode and adequately monitor, regulate, and guide her performance. As may be seen after damage to the frontal regions, these tendencies persist even though the patient can verbalize the correct mode of responding, thus suggesting a dissociation between consciously guided control processes and overt performance. A particularly revealing feature of her reproductions was the attempted utilization of lexical/semantic representations to substitute for spatially organized components of the object she was attempting to reproduce. This strategy could be viewed as a highly "intelligent" solution to the problem at hand, given the severely limited spatial processing resources that remained at her disposal.

While independent evidence of frontal pathology was not available for this case, we would suggest that this pattern of perseveration and impaired response inhibition may have been due to frontal lobe pathology in addition to more posterior parietal involvement in this case. However, regardless of the anatomical correlates, the behavior of this patient provided a striking demonstration of one type of dissociation that may occur between specific cognitive domains and some of the processes necessary for their correct and appropriate utilization.

DOMAINS OF MEMORY

Evidence for the existence of distinct memory domains comes from studies of normal individuals that show that different types of memories can be differentially effected by different types of manipulations. Evidence from these studies has, however, rarely turned out to be strong and unequivocal. What has strengthened the evidence supporting the existence of specific types of memory processes is the enormous literature that is now available providing convergent data from the study of pathologies of memory. This type of research has been developed in two different ways. As illustrated above, in some studies different domains may be studied in a single patient in comparison to normal controls. Many studies

Figure 4. Attempt by Patient F to copy a picture of a flower from the Boston Naming Test.

have successfully used this strategy to provide strong evidence for the existence of different types of memory functions based on the fact that we can see dramatic disruptions of some types of memory functions and not others.

Another approach has been to directly compare groups of patients with different neurological disorders defined on the bases of both neuroanatomical and neurochemical data (e.g., AD patients versus those suffering from Korskoff's disease; Weingartner et al., 1983). Based on such comparisons, it is possible to show that memory may fail in very different ways in different patient groups that nominally demonstrate the same extent of memory pathology. In the case of amnesic patients, many investigators have shown in a very convincing manner that, while these patients may not be able to directly tell us about their most recent experiences, and therefore may be said to have severely impaired episodic or declarative memory, other aspects of their memory functioning are completely spared. For example, the reactions of amnesics to sets of stimuli that they have previously confronted in the recent past can be shown to be very different from what it would have been if this stimulus situation were being presented to them for the first time. These amnesic patients can demonstrate memory priming, they can learn rules and procedures, and they are capable of being conditioned in various ways to different kinds of stimuli. On the other hand, these same patients appear to have no conscious recollection of having learned this material, been exposed to it, experienced it. This type of evidence is strong convergent support for the notion that memory is not a unitary process and is, in fact, divisible into distinct domains.

Another convergent and powerful approach for uncovering memory domains is to use different types of drugs as tools for producing reversible brain lesions in normal controls. The strength of this approach is that, unlike the study of patients with irreversible lesions, drug manipulations in normals allows one to use each subject as his own control. Using this approach, convergent evidence for the psychobiological specificity of the types of processes that may be selectively impaired in AD versus nondemented amnesic patients has been obtained from studies that directly compare the memory effect of two different classes of drugs administered to normal individuals. For example, with increasing doses of any benzodiazepine, such as diazepam, marked deficits in attention and in episodic memory occur. Yet despite this dense amnesia, access to previously acquired semantic knowledge, procedural, and priming memory are left intact (Lister & Weingartner, 1987; Wolkowitz et al., 1987). In at least a dozen studies accomplished in several laboratories, it is possible to show that the pattern of memory impairment seen in benzodiazepine-treated subject mimics precisely the specific features of the memory failures seen in amnesic patients. That is, learning and memory can occur, but only when tested under conditions that do not require direct access and awareness of information stored in memory. In contrast, the administration of an anticholinergic drug, scopolamine, to normal control subjects produces a very different pattern of impairment. Scopolamine produces decrements in attention, episodic memory and knowledge memory (Caine, Weingartner, Ludlow, Cudahy, & Wehry, 1981). In fact, there is a direct relationship between the extent of impairment in recent memory and the ability of subjects to access their previously acquired knowledge from long-term memory. It is this failure to efficiently access previously acquired knowledge which makes it difficult for subjects to effectively encode ongoing experiences, which, in turn, results in rapid forgetting of recent experience. One of the reasons why it is very intriguing that scopolamine, an anticholinergic drug, impairs knowledge as well as episodic memory in normal humans is that this models that pattern of cognitive deficits in AD patients, and it is the cholinergic system that is severely disrupted in this progressive dementing disorder. In fact, treating subjects who may be at risk for a dementia of an Alzheimer's type, or patients where accurate diagnosis of the source of their mental dysfunction remains a puzzlement, may prove to be of diagnostic value. We know that AD patients, when treated with an anticholinergic agent, respond just like normals. That is, they demonstrate an exaggeration of the dementia like symptoms that are already in place. However, this occurs with a far smaller dose than needed to demonstrate disruption in normal individuals.

These two drugs then, diazepam and scopolamine, may provide pharmacologic models of two very different clinical syndromes. Moreover, they may have mechanistic implications of our understanding of these disorders (Wolkowitz et al., 1987). They also illustrate how, by simply indexing changes in recent memory, important mechanisms that are responsible for alterations in cognitions can be revealed.

CONCLUSION

In the preceding sections we have attempted to sketch a model of cognitive functioning based on some of the classes of deficits that have been documented following injury and disease to the human brain. From our vantage point the dissociations of cognition and memory exhibited by these patients provide strong evidence that intelligence is not a seamless, unitary, entity, but rather a collection of independent domains of functioning with specific and dedicated processes in support of their regulation and control. In our view the central lesson to be learned from these patients is that, at least in certain cases, processes that are normally so highly interrelated as to appear seamless can become uncoupled by injury to the brain.

It has been maintained that a fundamental precondition for what philosophers of science refer to as a "special science" (that is, something other than physics) is a clear notion of the component parts that constitute the target of investigation. Moreover, it is assumed that these parts or units are not arbitrarily defined, but rather correspond to the actual or real components as present in nature. That is, they are of a natural kind. Thus the success of such a science depends heavily on the establishment of agreed upon criteria for determining these components, or as Plato would have it, "finding nature's natural joints." However, as Pylyshyn (1984) has warned, "natural joints are not easy to find . . . and they cannot be specified in advance." We maintain that the patterns of cognitive impairment resulting from brain injury and disease can serve as a strong criterion, or litmus test, for the existence of the hypothesized structures and processes of cognition, that is, for establishing the existence of units of a natural kind.

For those who accept some notion of the modularity or multiple intelligences, we would hope that the information generated by the study of brain-damaged individuals will be utilized as sources of external validation for the hypothesized components and subcomponents of various cognitive domains. For those individuals who continue to argue for a unitary conceptualization of intelligence, we would hope that they can generate a formulation rich enough to incorporate the types of neuropsychological evidence that we have discussed.

REFERENCES

Butters, N., Granholm, E., Salmon, D. P., & Grant, I. (1987). Episodic and semantic memory: A comparison of amnesic and demented patients. *Journal of Clinical and Experimental Neuropsychology, 9,* 479–497.

Caine, E. D., Weingartner, H., Ludlow, C. L., Cudahy, E. A., & Wehry, S. (1981). Qualitative analysis of scopalamine-induced amnesia. *Psychopharmacology, 74,* 74–80.

Carroll, J. B. (1982). The measurement of intelligence. In R. J. Sternberg (Ed.), *Handbook of human intelligence* (pp. 29–120). New York: Cambridge University Press.

Chomsky, N. (1980). *Rules and representations.* New York: Columbia University Press.

Dennis, M. (1985a). Intelligence after early brain injury I: Predicting IQ scores from medical variables. *Journal of Clinical and Experimental Neuropsychology, 7,* 526–554.

Dennis, M. (1985b). Intelligence after early brain injury II: Scores of subjects classified on the basis of medical history variables. *Journal of Clinical and Experimental Neuropsychology, 7,* 555–576.

Detterman, D. K. (1982). Does "g" exist? *Intelligence, 6,* 99–108.

Diamond, S. J. (1981). Intelligence. In *Neuropsychology: A textbook of systems and psychological functions of the human brain* (pp. 375–416). London: Butterworths.

Fodor, J. A. (1983). *The modularity of mind.* Cambridge, MA: MIT Press.

Foster, N. L., Chase, T. N., Mansi, L., Brooks, R., Fedio, P., Patronas, N. J., & Di Chiro, G. (1984). Cortical abnormalities in Alzheimer's disease. *Annals of Neurology, 16,* 649–654.

Gardner, H. (1983). *Frames of mind.* New York: Basic Books.

Goldberg, E., & Bilder, R. M., Jr. (1987). The frontal lobes and hierarchical organization of cognitive control. In E. Perecman (Ed.), *The frontal lobes revisited* (pp. 159–187). New York: The IRBN Press.

Gould, S. J. (1981). *The mismeasure of man.* New York: W. W. Norton.

Grafman, J. (1989). Plans, actions, and mental sets: Managerial knowledge units in the frontal lobes. In E. Perecman (Ed.), *Integrating theory and practice in neuropsychology* (pp. 93–138). Hillsdale, NJ: Erlbaum.

Hunt, E. (1983). On the nature of intelligence. *Science, 219,* 141–146.

Jensen, A. R. (1985). The nature of the black-white difference on various psychometric tests: Spearman's hypothesis. *Behavioral and Brain Sciences, 8,* 193–218.

Jerison, H. J. (1982). The evolution of biological intelligence. In R. J. Sternberg (Ed.), *Handbook of human intelligence* (pp. 723–791). New York: Cambridge University Press.

Kampen, D., & Martin, A. (1989). The role of object knowledge in constructional skill: A case report. *Journal of Clinical and Experimental Neuropsychology, 11,* 90.

Kaplan, E., Goodglass, H., & Weintraub, S. (1976). *Boston naming test* (experimental edition). Boston, MA: Boston Veterans Administration Medical Center.

Kemper, T. L., & Galaburda, A. M. (1984). Principles of cytoarchitectonics. In A. Peters & E. G. Jones (Eds.); *Cerebral cortex, Vol. 1* (pp. 35–57). New York: Plenum Press.

Lashley, K. S. (1929). *Brain mechanisms and intelligence.* Chicago, IL: The University of Chicago Press.

Lashley, K. S. (1937). Functional determinants of cerebral localization. *Archives of Neurology and Psychiatry, 38,* 371–387.

Lister, R. G., & Weingartner, H. (1987). Neuropharmacological strategies for understanding psychobiological determinants of cognition. *Human Neurobiology, 6,* 1–10.

Marr, D. (1976). Early processing of visual information. *Philosophical Transactions of the Royal Society of London, B275,* 483–524.

Marr, D. (1982). *Vision.* San Francisco, CA: W. H. Freeman and Company.

Marshall, J. C. (1984). Multiple perspectives on modularity. *Cognition, 17,* 209–242.

Martin, A. (1987). Representation of semantic and spatial knowledge in Alzheimer's patients: Implications for models of preserved learning in amnesia. *Journal of Clinical and Experimental Neuropsychology, 9,* 191–224.

Martin, A. (1989). The neuropsychology of Alzheimer's disease: The case for subgroups. In M. Schwartz (Ed.), *Modular deficits in dementia.* Cambridge, MA: Bradford Books/MIT Press.

Martin, A., Brouwers, P., Lalonde, F., Cox, C., & Fedio, P. (1987). Alzheimer's patient subgroups: Qualitatively distinct patterns of performance and subsequent decline. In R. J. Wurtman, S. H. Corkin, & J. H. Growdon (Eds.), *Alzheimer's disease: Advances in basic research.* Cambridge, MA: Center for Brain Sciences and Metabolism Charitable Trust.

Martin, A., Brouwers, P., Lalonde, F., Cox, C., Teleska, P., Fedio, P., Foster, N. L., & Chase, T. N. (1986). Towards a behavioral typology of Alzheimer's patients. *Journal of Clinical and Experimental Neuropsychology, 8,* 594–610.

Martin, A., & Fedio, P. (1983). Word production and comprehension in Alzheimer's disease: The breakdown of semantic knowledge. *Brain and Language, 19,* 124–141.

Nieuwenhuys, R. (1985). *Chemoarchitecture of the brain.* New York: Springer-Verlag.

Osterrieth, P. (1944). Le test de copie d'une figure complexe. *Archives de Psychologie, 30,* 206–356.

Peters, A., & Jones, E. G. (1984). Classification of cortical neurons. In A. Peters & E. G. Jones (Eds.), *Cerebral cortex* (Vol. 1, pp. 107–122). New York: Plenum Press.

Pylyshyn, Z. W. (1984). *Computation and cognition: Toward a foundation for cognitive science*. Cambridge, MA: MIT Press.

Putnam, H. (1984). Models and modules. *Cognition, 17,* 253–264.

Schwartz, J. H. (1981). Chemical basis of synaptic transmission. In E. R. Kandel & J. H. Schwartz (Eds.), *Principles of neural science* (pp. 106–120). New York: Elsevier North-Holland.

Schwartz, M. F., Marin, O. S. M., & Saffran, E. M. (1979). Dissociation of language function in dementia: A case study. *Brain and Language, 7,* 277–306.

Schwartz, M. F., & Schwartz, B. (1984). In defense of organology. *Cognitive Neuropsychology, 1,* 25–42.

Searle, J. (1984). *Minds, brains and science*. Cambridge, MA: Harvard University Press.

Shallice, T. (1982). Specific impairments of planning. *Philosophical Transactions of the Royal Society of London B, 298,* 199–209.

Shallice, T. (1984). More functionally isolable subsystems but fewer "modules"? *Cognition, 17,* 243–252.

Simon, H. A. (1962). The architecture of complexity. *Proceedings of the American Philosophical Society, 106,* 467–482.

Sternberg, R. J. (1985). Human intelligence: The model is the message. *Science, 230,* 1111–1118.

Stuss, D. T., & Benson, D. F. (1984). Neuropsychological studies of the frontal lobes. *Psychological Bulletin, 95,* 3–28.

Stuss, D. T., & Benson, D. F. (1986). *The frontal lobes*. New York: Raven Press.

Ullman, S. (1984). Visual routines. *Cognition, 18,* 97–159.

Warrington, E. K. (1975). The selective impairment of semantic memory. *Quarterly Journalof Experimental Psychology, 27,* 635–657.

Weingartner, H., Grafman, J., Boutelle, W., Kaye, W., & Martin, P. (1983). Forms of memory failure. *Science, 221,* 380–382.

Wolkowitz, O. M., Weingartner, H., Thompson, K., Pickar, D., Paul, S. M., & Hommer, D. W. (1987). Diazepam-induced amnesia: A neuropharmacological model of an "organic amnesic syndrome." *American Journal of Psychiatry, 144,* 25–29.

Chapter 5

The Structure and Capacity of Thought: Some Comments on the Cognitive Underpinnings of g*

Gerald E. Larson
David L. Alderton

Testing Systems Department
Navy Personnel Research and Development Center
San Diego, CA

BACKGROUND

Cronbach (1957), in a now-famous address, stressed that experimental methods could be used to build construct validity into test theory. The desired result of this

* An earlier (and shorter) version of this chapter was presented as a poster at the American Educational Research Association annual meeting, April 1988, New Orleans, LA.

The opinions expressed in this chapter are those of the authors, are not official, and do not necessarily reflect the views of the Navy Department.

merger was a mental process explanation of test results. Despite Cronbach's proposal, progress in the experimental tradition has, in certain respects, sidestepped fundamental issues in correlational or psychometric psychology. The construct of general intelligence (or the *g* factor) exemplifies this continued schism. The *g* factor is typically measured as the first principal component in a common factor analysis of a diverse battery of cognitive tests, or as the most general factor in a hierarchical analysis (Jensen, 1987a). Psychometric data support the conclusion that *g* provides most of the predictive power of aptitude batteries (Humphreys, 1979; Hunter, 1983a; Jensen, 1984; McNemar, 1964; Thorndike, 1985; Vernon, 1950). Hunter (1986), for example, notes that the massive databases gathered by the U.S. Employment Service and the armed forces clearly suggest that it is general cognitive ability rather than specific cognitive aptitudes that predict job performance. The importance of *g* may thus explain the difficulty in finding tests which have differential validity from one criteria to another (Humphreys, 1979; Hunter, 1986; Vernon, 1950).

Jensen (1987a) has broadened the discussion by demonstrating that *g*, in addition to having significance for vocational screening, is related to a number of biological indices and performance on elementary reaction time tasks. He has argued, for example, that the *g*-loading of individual tests (i.e., the strength of association between a single test and the general factor of its parent battery) is associated with heritability, inbreeding depression, hybrid vigor, and correlations with evoked potentials of the brain—variables linking psychology to biology and evolution. More recently, Spitz (1988) has reported that mentally retarded subjects score the lowest on tests that are the best measures of *g*. Collectively, these findings argue unequivocally that an analysis of *g* could help clarify the nature of socially important individual and group differences.

While *g*, or variance *shared across tasks*, is thus a central issue in psychometrics, the experimental tradition most often involves the study of single tasks or aptitude constructs. Many single task studies, by design, further compartmentalize performance into a lawful set of processing stages or components. The final cognitive models, while fulfilling the experimenter's purpose, are not suited for cross reference and thus do not easily explain task intercorrelations. As an example, the correlational literature indicates that a moderately strong relationship exists between mathematical and spatial abilities. Information-processing descriptions of math and spatial tasks, however, have few common components that would explain the convergence of these aptitudes (Briars, 1983; Lohman & Kyllonen, 1983). As a second example of the problems that *g* creates for cognitive models, research on inductive reasoning has shown that, even when "cross-referenced" performance models are explicitly constructed, it is still difficult to demonstrate that same-named components are more highly correlated with one another (convergent validity) than with components baring different names (differential validity) (Alderton, Goldman, & Pellegrino, 1985; Sternberg & Gardner, 1983; Whitely, 1980). Differential correlations between specific components and *g* have also proved elusive. The challenge, then, is to determine whether experimentally derived views of task performance are of any use in understanding the fundamental basis of test validity, such as, *g*.

TOWARD A COGNITIVE VIEW OF GENERAL INTELLIGENCE

It is almost certainly critical to observe that *g* is empirically related to a dimension of cognitive task complexity. Marshalek, Lohman, and Snow (1983), for example, compared radex and hierarchical models of ability and concluded the two frameworks suggest the identical conclusion; "the actual correlation between a test and *g* approximates the apparent complexity of its required cognitive operations" (p. 108). Also, the predictive validity of general cognitive ability is positively correlated with the complexity of the criterion task (Hunter, 1983b). That complexity has a ubiquitous role is further demonstrated by data on reaction times. Cohn, Carlson, and Jensen (1985) compared the performance of psychometrically gifted and nongifted subjects on a number of reaction time (RT) tasks. They report a correlation of .94 between the complexity of the RT task (as indicated by mean latency) and the magnitude of group differences in performance.

A critical question, then, is whether current cognitive theories can explain how *g* manifests in relatively more complex tasks. Following Sanders (1983), we recognize two major cognitive frameworks of performance: structural (or linear stage) models, and working memory (or energy resource) capacity models. The structure and capacity models support different explanations for the relationship between task complexity and *g*.

1. Structural Theories of *g*

Structures include the concepts of processing stages (Sternberg, 1969), components (Sternberg, 1980), and other descriptors for the elementary functional units of cognition. These elementary components are coordinated by executive or metacognitive routines (Hunt, 1980; Sternberg, 1980). The two-level component/metacognitive hierarchy suggests at least two possible structural theories of *g*.

1.1. In component-based theories, psychometric *g*, representing the common statistical variance of diverse tests, simply reflects the existence of common elementary performance components *within* the correlated tasks (Detterman, 1986; Sternberg & Gardner, 1983). For example, two tasks might correlate simply because they both require a similiar memory retrieval operation. A componential argument certainly seems compatible with the finding that more cognitively complex tasks exhibit the strongest interrelationships. As Hunt (1986) notes, "The more complex two tests, the more they would be likely to depend on common elementary components, and hence the higher the correlation between them" (p. 105). Also, the more complex tasks, which sample more of the universe of possible components (Vernon, 1985), provide the best single estimates of *g*.

The componential research most relevent to *g* has focused on reasoning skills (e.g., Alderton, et al., 1985; Bethell-Fox, Lohman, & Snow, 1984; LeFevre & Bisanz, 1986; McConaghy & Kirby, 1987; Sternberg, 1977; Sternberg & Gardner, 1983), the logic being that, since reasoning tests are good predictors of *g*, individual differences in the components of reasoning may also be an important source of differences on general intellectual ability. This research has typically employed confirmatory model testing. Confirmatory research is hypothesis driven in that measures of theory-based processing components are obtained in the course of the research, then entered into a multiple regression equation to predict a global performance score. The accuracy of this prediction serves as a test of the model. Thus far, however, no persuasive componential model of reasoning has emerged, for two principal reasons. First, results have been inconsistent with respect to the relative importance of various component processes. While Sternberg (1977), for example, reported that high-ability subjects spent more time on the encoding component of reasoning tasks, later studies (e.g, Bethell-Fox et al., 1984; Sternberg & Gardner, 1983) failed to replicate this finding. The second problem for models of reasoning is that, while they stress *quantitative* differences in performance components, there are also pronounced *qualitative* differences between high- and low-ability groups. These qualitative differences, perhaps driven by factors such as the subject's knowledge base (LeFevre & Bisanz, 1986) and short-term memory capacity (Bethell-Fox et al., 1984; McConaghy & Kirby, 1987) suggest that global strategies or capacities, rather than a particular set of elementary components/dimensions, underly reasoning (and by extension, *g*). In conclusion, model-driven research has been somewhat unsuccessful in partitioning surrogate measures of *g* into multiple components that explain a wide range of individual differences.

A more general problem for component-based theories of *g* is the lack of a taxonomy of components which are uncorrelated with one another, and differentially correlated with psychometric task performance. (Witness the problems with Guilford's "Structure of Intellect" model; see Brody & Brody, 1976.) The latter follows since any whole (a psychometric test) should correlate with its parts (relevant cognitive processes), but not other measures. As yet there are no such component taxonomies with promising convergent/divergent validities vis a vis psychometric batteries. The literature further indicates that many elementary cognitive measures are intercorrelated (Jackson & McClelland, 1979; Keating & Bobbitt, 1978; Kyllonen, 1985; McGue, Bouchard, Lykken, & Feuer, 1984; Lansman, Donaldson, Hunt, & Yantis, 1982; Paul, 1984; Vernon, 1983; Vernon, Nador, & Kantor, 1985; also see Cooper & Regan, 1982), raising doubt about theories which suggest process independence.[1] Finally, it is simply not obvious that common components produce correlations across broadly diverse tasks. The theory would appear to have difficulty explaining how a visual encoding task like Inspection Time correlates with Vocabulary scores (Lubin & Fernandez, 1986), and how a "verbal correlate" like speed of letter naming (Hunt, Lunneborg, & Lewis, 1975) correlates with scores on Raven's Progressive Matrices (Ford & Keating, 1981).

In summary, we see little empirical support for the view that *g* reflects orthogonal components that overlap across tasks. There is also scant evidence that *g* stems from one or two key components, to the exclusion of other types of behaviors.

1.2 Metacognitive theories. We noted above that group differences in test scores often seem related to *qualitative* performance differences (see, for example, Brown, Bransford, Ferrera, & Campione, 1983; Lohman & Kyllonen, 1983; Underwood, 1978). This might suggest a strategy-based or "metacognitive" explanation for *g,* since metacognition is mental self-government (e.g., Sternberg, 1985). One could hypothesize that more complex tasks are amenable to a relatively greater variety of possible approaches, and that *g* reflects the general tendency to employ efficient strategies across diverse tasks. It is unclear, however, whether this hypothesis is an explanation or merely a platitude. That is, when tasks are novel, the spontaneous choice of an effective approach seems to raise as many questions as it answers—for example, just how do higher ability subjects (even as adolescents: see Spitz, 1982) "know" which strategy to employ?

A study by Haygood and Johnson (1983) provides an interesting example of the greater spontaneity and flexibility of "intelligent" problem solvers given novel tasks. Haygood and Johnson employed the Sternberg (1966) memory-search task, in which subjects are asked to memorize a set of single digits (0–9) called the *positive set.* Next, subjects are asked whether the positive set includes a series of individually presented test digits. Performance is measured via reaction time (RT) to test items. A seldom-emphasized aspect of the task is that, as more digits are added to the positive set, fewer remain in the out-group or *negative set.* As the ratio shifts, the advantage of switching focus to the negative set increases, because there are relatively fewer digits to work with. For example, a subject can verify that an item is a member of a small negative set faster than he or she can determine that it is a member of a much larger positive set—yet both methods can produce the correct answer. Of interest is Haygood and Johnson's finding that subjects who scored high on a general intelligence test

[1] The reader should note that correlations between component scores are not really a surprising product of componential analysis. As Chase (1978) pointed out, processing independence should not be confused with statistical independence. He gives the example of state of arousal, which can affect performance on all stages together and lead to substantial correlations of component times.

(Raven Progressive Matrices) were also quicker to shift to a negative set focus and thereby take advantage of the difference in set sizes. Thus, their study provides evidence of strategy differences associated with *g*, but the basis for the relationship remains open to speculation.

We feel that, while the causal pathway is undoubtedly complex, strategies should be viewed as a *product* of many things (including *g*, past experiences, and temperament), rather than as a fundamental *cause* of ability differences. For one thing, even when subjects are induced to solve the same problem by the same method, pronounced skill differences remain. In a study by Lyon (1977), for example, subjects were required to impose a common memory strategy on lists of digits. Lyon found that individual differences in memory performance were scarcely affected, suggesting that such differences reflect more basic processes (see Dempster, 1981; Ellis, Meador, & Bodfish, 1985). Another important question is what happens to the validity of tests when strategies are standardized. Though little work was been done in this area, Embretson (1987) found that both the construct and predictive validity of spatial tests were improved following test-related training. Again, her results suggest, not only that nonstrategic sources of important individual differences exist, but also that nonstrategic variance is the real basis of test validity. To return to the topic of *g*, however, it would be informative to determine the proportion of variance accounted for by the *g*-factor of a test battery before and after training to reduce individual differences in test-taking strategies. If the *g*-factor is *more* pronounced following training, it would suggest that strategies are largely a confound in relation to general intelligence.

Until such studies are done, however, there will continue to be numerous reasons to believe that a strategy-based explanation cannot account for *g*. First, it is difficult to imagine how strategies could systematically elevate performance across the whole spectrum of tasks which are correlated with *g*. Vocabulary, for instance, is a good index of *g* (Jensen, 1980). Though Sternberg and Powell (1983) have argued that strategies (or metacognitive processes) are important in the acquisition of verbal information, it seems intuitively the case that word acquisition (at least in childhood) also involves incidental or non-strategy-driven learning. The correlation of certain elementary cognitive tasks with intelligence also seems difficult to explain from a strategy perspective. Findings with the *inspection time* paradigm are illustrative. Inspection time (IT) tests require the subject to discriminate between rapidly presented stimuli, usually lines. For example, the subject might be shown two horizontal lines of unequal length and asked whether the longer line was on the right or the left. During testing, the duration of time the subject sees the lines is gradually reduced, until the experimenter has determined the viewing time necessary for a criterion level of accuracy. Of interest here is the rather suprising fact that the IT task, as simple as it is, correlates with intelligence (Brand & Deary, 1982; Nettelbeck, 1987). Moreover, there is evidence that strategies disrupt rather than explain the IT–intelligence relationship (Egan, 1986; Mackenzie & Cumming, 1986). This suggests that intelligence is comprised of certain "fixed" capacities in addition to acquired strategies or tendencies.

Such capacities may, in fact, actually *drive* strategy choice on some tasks. Of interest is Bruner, Goodnow, and Austin's (1956) description of *cognitive strain*. According to Bruner et al., as tasks become more difficult, the combination of task-imposed strain (from the external information load) and strategy-imposed strain will at some point exceed subjects' capacities. When capacity is exceeded, subjects may switch to a less strainful strategy, even if such a strategy is also less efficient (see Bethell-Fox et al., 1984; Malin, 1979; McConaghy & Kirby, 1987). Therefore, individual differences in memory capacity (discussed below) may partially create intelligence-related differences in problem-solving strategies by determining the point on the complexity continuum at which strategies must be altered.

***Conclusions about structural theories of* g.** Structural descriptions of intelligence typically emphasize the elementary stages or components of cognition, and/or the orchestration of these elementary components by metacognitive routines. We have examined possible structural theories of *g* and concluded that they are unacceptable, based on current data. Among other things, advocates of component-based theories have failed to demonstrate appropriate convergent/divergent validities for processing scores, and advocates of metacognitive theories have failed to (a) acknowledge the interaction between strategies, task complexity, and subject capacities; and (b) demonstrate that the existence and validity of *g* are vitiated when subjects are trained to use common strategies.

2. Working Memory/Resource Capacity Theories of *g*

Resources is a term sometimes applied to the finite pool of energizing forces deployed in cognitive tasks (Gopher & Donchin, 1986; Wickens, 1984). In engineering psychology, increases in operator workload require increased resource investment (e.g., Wickens, 1979). Performance breaks down when the resource pool is exhausted. The concept of *workload* may also apply to mental test items. For example, if task complexity stems in some measure from problem size (the number of problem elements and their transformations: see Bourne & Dominowski, 1972), it is partly because the problem-solving workspace (e.g., short-term or working memory) is a limited capacity system.

A memory capacity theory of *g* may explain why more intelligent subjects are able to solve highly complex problems. For example, Kotovsky, Hayes, and Simon's (1985) analysis of the Tower of Hanoi problem indicates that increased memory load is a major reason why some versions of the task are more difficult than others. Mulholland, Pellegrino, and Glaser (1980) found that the difficulty of geometric analogy problems was related to the number of elements required by the problem. Each operation for defining and transforming elements was said to take up space in memory, with the aggregate being related to errors and increased solution time in a multiplicative rather than additive manner. The interaction implies competition for common memory resources. Hitch's (1978) experiments on mental arithmetic indicated that errors occur due to memory loss, which itself is a function of a number of operations. An analysis of spatial abilities by Lohman (1979) indicated that tasks which require simultaneous memory demands and data transformation are more intellectually demanding than tasks requiring either one alone. Limitations in memory capacity have also been related to deficits in reading skill (Baddeley, Logie, & Nimmo-Smith, 1985; Daneman & Carpenter, 1982), performance on figural matrices (Stone & Day, 1981), difficulty of letter series problems (Kotovsky & Simon, 1973), and reasoning from new information (Light, Zelinski, & Moore, 1982). Also pertinent is a study by Jensen and Figueroa (1975), who found that performance on backward digit span is more highly related to IQ than performance on forward digit span. One might speculate that greater problem size (e.g., processing and/or memory demands) under the backward condition causes the incremental loading on intelligence.

Earlier in this chapter we cited an analysis by Marshalek et al. (1983), who examined extensive psychometric data and concluded that more complex tests are clearly the best measures of *g*. The above results indicate that these complex "*g*-loaded" tasks are, in turn, characterized by their imposition of a relatively greater dynamic memory load. Together, therefore, the evidence invites some type of "memory capacity" theory of intelligence (to be described below).

WHY DO INDIVIDUALS DIFFER IN CAPACITY?: VOLUME THEORIES VERSUS PROCESS THEORIES

Two general types of capacity theories are predominant in the literature; (a) volume theories, and (b) process (or functional capacity) theories. Volume theories are just that; that is, they equate capacity with either the breadth of some hypothetical workspace, or the size of an energy resource pool by which the conscious mind is invigorated. In process theories, however, working memory capacity is determined by the efficiency of information handling. Examples are presented below.

1. A Volume Theory—Attentional Resources

Hunt has hypothesized that "short term memory capacity . . . is not a direct measure of a structure used in problem solving; rather, it is an indirect test of the availability of the attentional resources required for . . . thought" (1978, p. 117).

Thus, individuals may vary in their ability to supply an activating resource which enlivens short-term memory representations and powers their transformations. Various other authors also equate capacity with attentional resource volume, either explicitly (e.g., Logan, 1980; Stankov, 1983) or by juxtaposition (e.g., Gopher & Donchin, 1986; Schneider, Dumais, & Shiffrin, 1984). A fundamental problem with such comparisons is the intangibility of the *resource* construct itself. As Navon (1984) states, the resource concept is vague and malleable enough to enjoy the convenient status of an existential claim. It is a useful metaphor, which, like *mental energy,* seems to describe human capacity limitations (see Gopher & Donchin, 1986). The two metaphors, however, share weaknesses as well. Jensen (1987a) has noted that the energy metaphor has been particularly unfruitful in generating empirical investigations, and the same must be said of *resources.*

Construct intangibility is also a problem for other volume metaphors, such as *computational space* (Pascual-Leone, 1970). For this reason, process theories are preferable, because they are phrased in terms of measurable behaviors rather then hypothetical entities.

2. A Process Theory—Process Speed

Correlational relationships between mental speed (e.g., reaction time variables) and scores on complex intellectual tests have been widely reported (e.g., Barrett, Eysenck, & Lucking, 1986; Carlson & Jensen, 1982; Carlson, Jensen, & Widaman, 1983; Jensen, 1982, 1987a,b; Nettlebeck & Kirby, 1983; Smith & Stanley, 1983; Vernon, 1983; Vernon et al., 1985). Moreover, the lack of content specificity in many of these relationships suggests that they are largely a function of *g* (e.g., Larson, Merritt, & Williams, 1988; Smith & Stanley, 1987; Vernon, 1983). To operationalize the *g*/speed relationship, Jensen (1982, 1987a) and others have proposed theories of working memory capacity, the general version of which suggests that: (a) A source of difficulty in intellectually demanding tasks is that numerous aspects of a problem must be simultaneously remembered and mentally transformed or manipulated. (b) If data transformations are slow, data (e.g., memory traces) must be refreshed prior to their decay, resulting in an additional processing burdon. When operations are rapid, a *functionally* greater working memory capacity results, because a greater proportion of the workspace can be devoted to solving the task at hand, as opposed to preventing data loss. This also follows from Kahneman: "Severe time-pressure necessarily arises in any task which imposes a significant load on short-term memory, because the subject's rate of activity must be paced by the rate of decay of the stored elements" (1973, p. 26). (c) Therefore, speed of processing should predict aptitude for complex intellectual tasks by determining the functional capacity/efficiency of a generic working memory system.

We believe that progress in the scientific study of *g* requires the advancement of process theories of mental capacity. Because such theories are phrased as behavior-in-action, they can ultimately be empirically tested, and, if necessary, modified or discarded. The challenge to be faced, then, is to develop a process theory that explains all the major ability intercorrelations, including the intercorrelations between theoretically important *factors* such as the fluid and crystallized dimensions of intelligence. In the next section we present a revised process theory, with the fluid/crystallized relationships used as a test case.

A REVISED CAPACITY THEORY

To summarize the chapter to here, we have examined possible cognitive sources of psychometric *g*, and have thus far argued for the following points: (a) general intelligence (*g*) is reflected in the ability to solve increasingly complex intellectual problems; (b) the importance of task complexity seems best explained by a theory of "intelligence as capacity;" but (c) current capacity theories are mostly rough sketches in need of completion. For example, such theories are unclear on the processes by which crystallized ability variables such as vocabulary wind-up correlating with both fluid intelligence and *g*. Thus, in this final section we would like to suggest a needed revision of capacity theories that better incorporates both problem-solving (fluid) and knowledge-acquisition (crystallized) aspects of intelligence.

To explain the intercorrelation of fluid and crystallized intelligence, we start from the view that knowledge is the physiological consolidation of subjectively transient thoughts or mental objects in working memory. We therefore propose that individual differences in *g* reflect some capacity for the immediate generation of these mental objects that also enhances their physical permanence. In other words, (a) fluid intelligence, or working memory capacity, involves the temporary qualities of mental objects such as their rate and reliability, while (b) crystallized intelligence (or acquired knowledge) reflects their permanent consolidation. Therefore, (c) *g* resides in the communality of the rate/reliability and the permanence of mental objects.

The nature of this communality should be discoverable once the tools of cognitive neuroscience are further developed. Though we cannot yet demonstrate a specific physical mechanism for *g*, we may speculate that mental objects are the subjective, emergent aspect of a series of neural configurations in the cortex. Their consolidation as memory probably occurs through the development of a semipermanent bioelectric pattern in the form of a neural circuit (Bechtereva, 1978; Kissin, 1986; Thompson, 1986). Memory retrieval at a later date would involve the reactivation of the circuit (see John, 1972). Thus, some unknown individual differences variable in the transient neural reconfigurations, corresponding to the stream-of-thought, could produce later knowledge-based differences in the quality/quantity of stable, organic circuits. One example of such an individual difference variable is spontaneous background discharge in the system—if high during the formation of a neural circuit, such discharge (or *noise*) could impede the consolidation and thus the retention of the neural trace. Of interest is a neurophysiological study by Haier et al. (1988), who reported that subjects scoring high on a general intelligence test (Raven's Advanced Progressive Matrices) had *low* brain energy utilization while taking the test. Haier et al. suggest that subjects who perform well on intelligence tests may have more efficient neural circuits, possibly because of less extraneous activity. Their hypothesis is in line with the position we have presented.

To summarize our views on *g*, we propose that fluid intelligence is the capacity of working memory to reconfigure as the stream-of-thought required by task-related demands. The success of this "reconfiguration process" is a determining factor in the permanence of the object or trace, thereby explaining the correlation between fluid and crystallized intelligence. We believe that investigations along these lines are of fundamental importance for solving the riddle of *g*.

REFERENCES

Alderton, D. L., Goldman, S. R., & Pellegrino, J. W. (1985). Individual differences in process outcomes for verbal analogy and classification solution. *Intelligence, 9,* 69–85.

Baddeley, A. D., & Hitch, G. (1974). Working memory. In G. H. Bower (Ed.), *The psychology of learning and motivation: Vol. 8* (pp. 47–89). New York: Academic Press.

Baddeley, A. D., Logie, R., & Nimmo-Smith, I. (1985). Components of fluid reading. *Journal of Memory and Language, 24,* 119–131.

Barrett, P., Eysenck, H. J., & Lucking, S. (1986). Reaction time and intelligence: A replicated study. *Intelligence, 10,* 9–40.

Bechtereva, N. P. (1978). *The neurophysiological aspects of human mental activity.* New York: Oxford University Press.

Bethell-Fox, C. E., Lohman, D. F., & Snow, R. E. (1984). Adaptive reasoning: Componential and eye movement analysis of geometric analogy performance. *Intelligence, 8,* 205–238.

Bourne, L. E., & Dominowski, R. L. (1972). Thinking. *Annual Review of Psychology, 23,* 105–130.

Brand, C. R., & Deary, I. J. (1982). Intelligence and "inspection time." In H. J. Eysenck (Ed.), *A model for intelligence.* New York: Springer-Verlag.

Briars, D. J. (1983). An information processing analysis of mathematical ability. In R. F. Dillon & R. R. Schmeck (Eds.), *Individual differences in cognition. Vol I* (pp. 181–204). New York: Academic Press.

Brody, E. B., & Brody, N. (1976). *Intelligence: Nature, determinants, and consequences.* New York: Academic Press.

Brown, A. L., Bransford, J. D., Ferrera, R. A., & Campione, J. C. (1983). Learning, remembering, and understanding. In J. H. Flavell & E. M. Markham (Eds.), *Handbook of child psychology* (pp. 77–166). New York: John Wiley & Sons.

Bruner, J. S., Goodnow, J. J., & Austin, G. A. (1956). *A study of thinking*. New York: John Wiley.

Carlson, J. S., & Jensen, C. M. (1982). Reaction time, movement time, and intelligence: A replication and extension. *Intelligence, 6,* 265–274.

Carlson, J. S., Jensen, C. M., & Widaman, K. F. (1983). Reaction time, intelligence, and attention. *Intelligence, 7,* 329–344.

Chase, W. G. (1978). Elementary information processes. In W. K. Estes (Ed.), *Handbook of learning and cognitive processes. Vol. 5: Human information processing*. Hillsdale, NJ: Erlbaum.

Cohn, S. J., Carlson, J. S., & Jensen, A. R. (1985). Speed of information processing in academically gifted youths. *Personality and Individual Differences, 6,* 621–629.

Cooper, L. A., & Regan, D. T. (1982). Attention, perception, and intelligence. In R. J. Sternberg (Ed.), *Handbook of human intelligence* (pp. 123–169). New York: Cambridge.

Cronbach, L. J. (1957). The two disciplines of scientific psychology. *American Psychologist, 12,* 671–684.

Daneman, M., & Carpenter, P. (1982). Cognitive processes and reading skills. *Advances in Reading/Language Research, 1,* 83–124.

Dempster, F. N. (1981). Memory span: Sources of individual and developmental differences. *Psychological Bulletin, 89,* 63–100.

Detterman, D. K. (1986). Human intelligence is a complex system of separate processes. In R. J. Sternberg & D. K. Detterman (Eds.), *What is intelligence?* (pp. 57–61). Norwood, NJ: Ablex Publishing Corp.

Egan, V. (1986). Intelligence and inspection time: Do high-IQ subjects use cognitive strategies? *Personality and Individual Differences, 7,* 695–700.

Ellis, N. R., Meador, D. M., & Bodfish, J. W. (1985). Differences in intelligence and automatic memory processes. *Intelligence, 9,* 265–273.

Embretson, S. E. (1987). Improving the measurement of spatial aptitude by dynamic testing. *Intelligence, 11,* 333–358.

Ford, M. E., & Keating, D. P. (1981). Developmental and individual differences in long-term memory retrieval: Process and organization. *Child Development, 52,* 234–241.

Gopher, D., & Donchin, E. (1986). Workload—A examination of the concept. In K. R. Boff, L. Kaufman, & J. P. Thomas (Eds.), *Handbook of perception and human performance. Vol. II: Cognitive processes and performance*. New York: John Wiley.

Haier, R. J., Siegel, B. V., Nuechterlein, K. H., Hazlett, E., Wu, J. C., Paek, J., Browning, H. L., & Buchsbaum, M. S. (1988). Cortical glucose metabolic rate correlates of abstract reasoning and attention studied with positron emission tomography. *Intelligence, 12,* 199–217.

Haygood, R. C., & Johnson, D. F. (1983). Focus shift and individual differences in the Sternberg memory-search task. *Acta Psychologica, 53,* 129–139.

Hitch, G. J. (1978). The role of short-term working memory in mental arithmetic. *Cognitive Psychology, 10,* 302–323.

Humphreys, L. G. (1979). The construct of general intelligence. *Intelligence, 3,* 105–120.
Hunt, E. (1978). Mechanics of verbal ability. *Psychological Review, 85,* 109–130.
Hunt, E. (1980). Intelligence as an information processing concept. *British Journal of Psychology, 71,* 449–474.
Hunt, E. (1986). The heffalump of intelligence. In R. J. Sternberg & D. K. Detterman (Eds.), *What is intelligence?.* Norwood, NJ: Ablex Publishing Corp.
Hunt, E., Lunneborg, C., & Lewis, J. (1975). What does it mean to be high verbal? *Cognitive Psychology, 7,* 194–227.
Hunter, J. E. (1983a). *The dimensionality of the General Aptitude Test Battery (GATB) and the dominance of general factors over specific factors in the prediction of job performance for the U.S. Employment Service* (Uses Test Research Report No. 44). Washington, DC: U.S. Department of Labor, Employment and Training Administration, Division of Counseling and Test Development.
Hunter, J. E. (1983b). *Test validation for 12,000 jobs: An application of job classification and validity generalization analysis to the General Aptitude Test Battery* (Uses Test Research Report No. 45). Washington, DC: U.S. Department of Labor, Employment and Training Administration, Division of Counseling and Test Development.
Hunter, J. E. (1986). Cognitive ability, cognitive aptitudes, job knowledge, and job performance. *Journal of Vocational Behavior, 29,* 340–363.
Jackson, M. D., & McClelland, J. L. (1979). Processing determinants of reading speed. *Journal of Experimental Psychology: General, 108,* 151–181.
Jensen, A. R. (1980). *Bias in mental testing.* New York: Free Press.
Jensen, A. R. (1982). Reaction time and psychometric "g." In H. J. Eysenck (Ed.), *A model for intelligence* (pp. 93–132). New York: Springer-Verlag.
Jensen, A. R. (1984). Test validity: g versus the specificity doctrine. *Journal of Social and Biological Structures, 7,* 93–118.
Jensen, A. R. (1987a). The g beyond factor analysis. In J. C. Conoley, J. A. Glover, & R. R. Ronning (Eds.), *The influence of cognitive psychology on testing and measurement.* Hillsdale, NJ: Erlbaum.
Jensen, A. R. (1987b). Process differences and individual differences in some cognitive tasks. *Intelligence, 11,* 107–136.
Jensen, A. R., & Figueroa, R. A. (1975). Forward and backward digit span interaction with race and IQ: Predictions from Jensen's theory. *Journal of Educational Psychology, 67,* 882–893.
John, E. R. (1972). Switchboard versus statistical theories of learning and memory. *Science, 177,* 850–864.
Kahneman, D. (1973). *Attention and effort.* Englewood Cliffs, NJ: Prentice-Hall.
Keating, D. P., & Bobbitt, B. L. (1978). Individual and developmental differences in cognitive-processing components of mental ability. *Child Development, 49,* 155–167.
Kissin, B. (1986). *Psychobiology of human behavior: Conscious and unconscious programs in the brain.* New York: Plenum.
Kotovsky, K., Hayes, J. R., & Simon, H. A. (1985). Why are some problems hard? Evidence from Tower of Hanoi. *Cognitive Psychology, 17,* 248–294.

Kotovsky, K., & Simon, H. A. (1973). Empirical tests of a theory of human acquisition of concepts for sequential patterns. *Cognitive Psychology, 4,* 399–424.

Kyllonen, P. C. (1985). *Dimensions of information processing speed* (AFHRL TP 84-56). Brooks Air Force Base, TX: Air Force Human Resources Laboratory.

Lansman, M., Donaldson, G., Hunt, E., & Yantis, S. (1982). Ability factors and cognitive processes. *Intelligence, 6,* 347–386.

Larson, G. E., Merritt, C. R., & Williams, S. E. (1988). Information processing and intelligence: Some implications of task complexity. *Intelligence, 12,* 131–147.

LeFevre, J., & Bisanz, J. (1986). A cognitive analysis of number-series problems: Sources of individual differences in performance. *Memory and cognition, 14,* 287–298.

Light, L. L., Zelinski, E. M., & Moore, M. (1982). Adult age differences in reasoning from new information. *Journal of Experimental Psychology: Learning, Memory, & Cognition, 8,* 435–447.

Lohman, D. F. (1979). *Spatial ability: A review and reanalysis of the correlational literature* (TR-8). Palo Alto, CA: School of Education, Stanford University.

Lohman, D. F., & Kyllonen, P. C. (1983). Individual differences in solution strategy on spatial tasks. In R. F. Dillon & R. R. Schmeck (Eds.), *Individual differences in cognition* (Vol I, pp. 105–136). New York: Academic Press.

Logan, G. D. (1980). Short-term memory demands of reaction time tasks that differ in complexity. *Journal of Experimental Psychology: Human Perception and Performance, 6,* 375–389.

Lubin, M. P., & Fernandez, J. M. (1986). The relationship between psychometric intelligence and inspection time. *Personality and Individual Differences, 7,* 653–657.

Lyon, D. R. (1977). Individual differences in immediate serial recall: A matter of mnemonics? *Cognitive Psychology, 9,* 403–411.

Mackenzie, B., & Cumming, S. (1986). How fragile is the relationship between inspection time and intelligence: The effects of apparent-motion cues and previous experience. *Personality and Individual Differences, 7,* 721–729.

Malin, J. T. (1979). Information-processing load in problem solving by network search. *Journal of Experimental Psychology: Human Perception and Performance, 5,* 379–390.

Marshalek, B., Lohman, D. F., & Snow, R. E. (1983). The complexity continuum in the radex and hierarchical models of intelligence. *Intelligence, 7,* 107–127.

McConaghy, J., & Kirby, N. H. (1987). Analogical reasoning and ability level: An examination of R. J. Sternberg's componential method. *Intelligence, 11,* 137–159.

McGue, M., Bouchard, T. J., Lykken, D. T., & Feuer, D. (1984). Information processing abilities in twins reared apart. *Intelligence, 8,* 239–258.

McNemar, Q. (1964). Lost: Our intelligence? Why? *American Psychologist, 19,* 871–882.

Mulholland, T. M., Pellegrino, J. W., & Glaser, R. (1980). Components of geometric analogy solution. *Cognitive Psychology, 12,* 252–284.

Navon, D. (1984). Resources—a theoretical stone soup? *Psychological Review, 91,* 216–234.

Nettelbeck, T. (1987). Inspection time and intelligence. In P. A. Vernon (Ed.), *Speed of information processing and intelligence.* Norwood, NJ: Ablex Publishing Corp.

Nettelbeck, T., & Kirby, N. H. (1983). Measures of timed performance and intelligence. *Intelligence, 7,* 39–52.

Pascual-Leone, J. (1970). A mathematical model for the transition rule in Piaget's developmental stages. *Acta Psychologica, 32,* 301–345.

Paul, S. M. (1984). *Speed of information processing: The semantic verification test and general mental ability.* Unpublished doctoral dissertation, University of California, Berkeley.

Sanders, A. F. (1983). Towards a model of stress and human performance. *Acta Psychologica, 53,* 61–97.

Schneider, W., Dumais, S. T., & Shiffrin, R. M. (1984). Automatic and control processing and attention. In R. Parasuraman & D. R. Davies (Eds.), *Varieties of attention.* New York: Academic Press.

Smith, G. A., & Stanley, G. (1983). Clocking g: Relating intelligence and measures of timed performance. *Intelligence, 7,* 353–368.

Smith, G. A., & Stanley, G. (1987). Comparing subtest profiles of g loadings and correlations with RT measures. *Intelligence, 11,* 291–298.

Spitz, H. H. (1982). Intellectual extremes, mental age, and the nature of human intelligence. *Merrill-Palmer Quarterly, 28,* 167–192.

Spitz, H. H. (1988). Wechsler subtest patterns of mentally retarded groups: Relationship to *g* and to estimates of heritability. *Intelligence, 12,* 279–297.

Stankov, L. (1983). Attention and intelligence. *Journal of Educational Psychology, 75,* 471–490.

Sternberg, R. J. (1977). *Intelligence, information processing, and analogical reasoning.* Hillsdale, NJ: Lawrence Erlbaum.

Sternberg, R. J. (1980). Sketch of a componential subtheory of human intelligence. *The Behavioral and Brain Sciences, 3,* 573–614.

Sternberg, R. J. (1985). *Beyond IQ: A triarchic theory of human intelligence.* New York: Cambridge University Press.

Sternberg, R. J., & Gardner, M. K. (1983). Unities in inductive reasoning. *Journal of Experimental Psychology: General, 112,* 80–116.

Sternberg, R. J., & Powell, J. S. (1983). Comprehending verbal comprehension. *American Psychologist, 38,* 878–893.

Sternberg, S. (1966). High speed scanning in human memory. *Science, 153,* 652–654.

Sternberg, S. (1969). The discovery of processing stages: Extensions of Donders' method. In W. G. Koster (Ed.), *Acta Psychologica, 30:* Attention and Performance II, 276–315.

Stone, B., & Day, M. C. (1981). A developmental study of the processes underlying solution of figural matrices. *Child Development, 52,* 359–362.

Thompson, R. F. (1986). The neurobiology of learning and memory. *Science, 233,* 941–947.

Thorndike, R. L. (1985). The central role of general ability in prediction. *Multivariate Behavior Research, 20,* 241–254.

Underwood, G. (1978). *Strategies of information processing.* New York: Academic Press.

Vernon, P. A. (1983). Speed of information processing and general intelligence. *Intelligence, 7,* 53–70.

Vernon, P. A. (1985). Individual differences in general cognitive ability. In L. C. Hartlage & C. F. Telzrow (Eds.), *The neuropsychology of individual differences.* New York: Plenum.

Vernon, P. A., Nador, S., & Kantor, L. (1985). Reaction times and speed-of-processing: Their relationship to timed and untimed measures of intelligence. *Intelligence, 9,* 357–374.

Vernon, P. E. (1950). *The structure of human abilities.* London: Methven.

Whitely, S. E. (1980). Modeling aptitude test validity from cognitive components. *Journal of Educational Psychology, 72,* 750–769.

Wickens, C. D. (1979). Measures of workload, stress, and secondary tasks. In N. Moray (Ed.), *Mental workload.* New York: Plenum Press.

Wickens, C. D. (1984). Processing resources in attention. In R. Parasuraman & D. R. Davies (Eds.), *Varieties of attention.* New York: Academic Press.

Chapter 6

Modularity and Localization

Andrew Kertesz, M.D., F.R.C.P.(C)

Department of Clinical Neurological Sciences
University of Western Ontario
Lawson Research Institute
St. Joseph's Hospital
London, Ontario

The majority of neuroscientists have no difficulty accepting the idea that certain functions are related to certain structures in the brain. Some would, however, qualify that only physiological functions are structure bound, not psychological ones (Bullock, 1965). The issue of functional–anatomical relationship can be crystallized to the major questions of: (a) what is considered a neuropsychological function, (b) what are the anatomical structures necessary to carry out such a function in the normal brain, and (c) what other structures can compensate if certain parts of the brain are damaged. Central to all these issues is that, after brain damage, the observed function does not reflect the simple equation of normal function missing, therefore identifiably relating to the lesion, but often represents a new functional state of reorganization of the brain. Underlying the complex phenomena of reorganized function are the various issues of substitution, brain redundancy, vicarious function, diaschisis, regeneration, regrowth, and retraining. Most serious investigators accept Jackson's (1878) warning that only lesions, and not functions, can be localized. Goldstein's (1948) rejoinder was that the question is not, "Where is a definite function localized?" but "How does a lesion modify the function of the brain so that a definite symptom comes to the fore?"

Not every structure in the brain has the same degree of specificity, and each species is different to the extent that certain functions are related to certain areas of the brain and to how other areas can compensate for the loss of function. In addition to the interspecies differences there are substantial differences that may be common to certain biological groups, such as gender or age groups, but these group differences are often overshadowed by interindividual differences. One of the major distinctions between certain functions that are considered to be more modular than others, that involve "central" or diffusely distributed cognition, is the extent that they are bound to certain brain structures (Fodor, 1983). In this chapter, some of those functions will be reviewed that have the most established structural determinants, with a critique of the empirical evidence and methodology.

Considerable changes in the technology of localization of lesions in vivo have taken place in the last two decades, along with theoretical developments in cognitive processing. The appearance of in vivo techniques of localization, such as computerized tomography (CT), magnetic resonance imaging (MRI), positron emission tomography (PET), and single photon emission computerized tomography (SPECT), provide localizing information about functional and structural alterations, at the same time as the neuropsychological examination of the patient is carried out. For more than 100 years since Broca's epoch-making clinicopathological correlation relating the faculty of articulated language to the frontal lobe, neurologists relied on the postmortem examination of patients who were assessed during life, often long before they came to autopsy. The problems with this method are numerous, and some will be discussed below. Recent, in vivo, antemortem localization added a wealth of new empirical evidence relating structures to function, and some cerebral organization.

HOLISTIC VS. MODULAR FUNCTION

The unitary theory of brain function was formulated by Flourens and others as "sensorium commune" in the 19th century, implying that all functions were connected in some fashion. A large number of psychologists followed Lashley's (1938) consideration of the brain as a "unitary processor" (the black box) which consisted of more or less equipotential components. These components are equipotential because they are widely available for substitution. Although behaviorists do not deny the connection between brain and behavior, some express disinterest in brain structure. An extreme form of denial is that of the mentalist or dualist, who considers the mental process to be independent from brain activity. Information-process modelers tend to fall into a similar trap to some extent. To them, the functional modeling assumes a much greater importance than the "hardware" of brain tissue and its connections (Mehler, Morton, & Jusczyk, 1984). The role of structure is only an abstraction, and the limitations imposed by the anatomy on processes are not usually considered. Although some deny that the knowledge of anatomy can contribute at all to the knowledge of mental processes, the extent of function related neuronal tissue and the location of connections between them are important to cognitive modeling. One cannot be useful without the other.

The holistic view of intelligence and behavior was challenged by 19th-century anatomists who systematized the gyri and developed techniques to trace cortical connections and long tracts. They also began to assign function to them, at times on the basis of empirical evidence, other times in a speculative fashion. Phrenology was a fanciful, mosaicist view of cerebral function, which was based on external landmarks on the skull. Scientific support for the localization of function came from the physiologists of the second half of the 19th century who observed the close relationship of cortical points stimulated and movements in animals (Fritsch & Hitzig, 1870), extirpation of occipital cortex and loss of vision (Munk, 1881), and clinicians who correlated language impairment with the left perisylvian brain region (Broca, 1861). Associationist psychology, reflex physiology, and the method of clinicopathological correlation also contributed to the theoretical background of localization of function. Reflex physiology has been often used to illustrate how "everything is connected to everything." The idea of cerebral centers of language and other cognitive function interconnected by a complicated neural pathway has been under attack ever since diagrams of various processes and their interconnections have been superimposed on drawings of brains. Head (1926) discredited the "diagram-makers," and they practically disappeared from the neurological literature for a period. Processing models and diagrams, however, have made a recent comeback in cognitive psychology, with terminology borrowed from computer and linguistic sciences. These diagrams often bear some resemblance to those created after clinicopathological correlations in the last century. They try to account for every possible step and route and modality in processing. Another trend in cognitive psychology is the fractionation of function to ever-increasing numbers of smaller and more specialized modules (Ellis & Young, 1988).

DEFINING A FUNCTION

The definition of what a function is is difficult and arbitrary at the best of times. Clinicians, physiologists, and psychologists have different concepts about the same behavior. Certain psychological concepts of function may not be appropriate to describe actual brain function or connectivity. On the other hand, anatomy and physiology alone may not provide even the questions, let alone the answers, about behavior.

Recent advances in cognitive modelling are an important step in the interpretation of functional deficits. They are based on the principles of information processing and permeated by the computer metaphor. Fractionation, or staging of function, and cognitive modelling, however, have many methodological and conceptual problems. Models that are consistent with known physiology and anatomy are rarely constructed. Complex behaviors are often fractionated further, and what is considered a separate function may have the same underlying mechanism. Most of these new "modules of function" are defined in terms of computer science or artificial intelligence, and these constructs may have little, if any, relationship to a real psychological, or even less to a physiological, function (Crick, 1989). Alternative theories are elaborated to interpret functions and are changed to fit the empirical facts. Reduction of a complex behavior to its components is fraught with the hazard of losing the meaning and biological significance of the behavior to the organism. From the point of view of localization, more complex behaviors are likely to have widespread input and will be affected by lesions in many areas. Minutely fractionated functions, on the other hand, are likely to be the component of many complex behaviors and less likely to be localizable, if at all.

Fractionation of function often implies (although not necessarily so) that a serial activation of the processes takes place. However, recent physiological and theoretical considerations suggest that mental processes operate in parallel and not in a series (Hinton & Anderson, 1981; McLelland & Rumelhart, 1986). Discrete, manipulable, modular units of cognition presumably have similar counterparts in a neural organization, but so far there is no evidence that a great deal of fractionation of function through cognitive modelling has relevance to physiological organization. There has been doubt expressed whether the human world of perception and processing of input can be analyzed into independent elements (Dreyfus, 1979). Attempts to segregate perception from central processing have not always proved to be successful. Expectancy and previous knowledge, in other words the *precept,* greatly influence how stimuli are perceived. "Top down" processing, or the influence of memory associations on perception, goes on to a much greater extent than most modular functional models provide for.

Some hypothetical functions such as word retrieval or phonemic assembly (which may be the normal function that is impaired when the deficit phenomena of phonemic paraphasia is elicited) may be distributed in a diffuse fashion through the language area as they seem to be affected by lesions from many locations within the perisylvian cortex of the left hemisphere. Widespread distribution of certain cognitive functions, such as visuospatial ability, directed attention, and memory, indicate their contribution to many other processes.

Others, such as problem solving, intelligence, or judgment, defy efforts to localize them. Some of these even await definitions that are commonly agreed upon. Large neuronal networks are obviously necessary in much of the performance of complex cognitive tasks, and even those who are interested in functional–anatomical correlations are staying away from the concept of gyri or even lobar structures subserving such functions.

The analysis of behavior after a lesion should be supplanted by studies in normals to confirm conclusions about the function of a lesioned organism. The functional analysis of normal cognitive systems supplies an important, but limited, background to test the damaged or reorganized functions in patients. A detailed analysis of a function is necessary to the understanding of complex ways a lesion can affect it. The accurate, up-to-date measurement of deficit is an essential prerequisite for meaningful localization. Much of the older clinicopathological literature of more complex cognitive function is handicapped by a rather rudimentary description of the psychological deficits.

Theories of normal psychological processes, on the other hand, may benefit from taking into consideration the ways in which these can be disrupted. Clinical and anatomical constraints should be quite helpful in cognitive modelling to bring it closer to reality. It is obvious that complex cellular systems that interact must be interconnected, and this occurs most readily if cells are close together. Functional contiguity may be more important than geographic contiguity in the cortex. Topographical association of cells may also be important for specifying them genetically (Cowey, 1979; Edelman, 1987).

The behavior observed after the lesion, however, is often not analyzable in terms of normal function. As long as caution is used in the interpretation of pathological behavior as a model of brain function, the gap can be bridged with the help of some extrapolation and converging evidence from other methodologies.

SINGLE CASE VS. GROUP STUDIES, SYMPTOMS VS. SYNDROMES

A great deal of neurologically oriented cognitive theory has been elaborated on the basis of single case reports in the last 10 years. The dangers of generalizing from single case reports for or against localizing certain functions, or the modularity of function, are great. The human brain is complex, not only functionally, but also in terms of individual variability in many biological factors. There are many cases in the literature when a single case or a few selected cases are documented to show that a lesion in a certain location does or does not produce the symptoms expected. However, important biological factors, such as the time elapsed from the injury, for example, may be ignored, or inadequately considered in the interpretation of the behavior observed. Therefore, the wrong conclusions may be drawn. Nevertheless, since experimental series of lesions are often not available to investigate the function of an area, single, well-documented case reports that are followed with several examinations and have good lesion localization can be very informative. Special statistical techniques controlling for other factors influencing behavior have been developed to make single case studies more scientifically acceptable, but these also need some controls or groups of similar subjects for comparison (Kazdin, 1982).

Group studies, on the other hand, may obscure individual differences and specific functions. Detailed exploration or experimentation is also difficult to carry on in large groups. Group studies are necessary, however, to generalizing the findings and to prove that the observations are not by chance or due to some other factor than that which is being examined. Both group studies and single case studies are useful, provided scientific criteria are met. Advocating one at the expense of the other does not seem to be productive.

The analytical examination of isolated behaviors, defined by current theory, has gained support recently against the approach based on syndromes, or behaviors affected together by lesions in the brain. Clinicians, on the other hand, generally attempt to deal with syndromes as they occur in the patient, even though they may undertake symptom analysis that goes beyond the syndromes. Isolated or pure psychological phenomena, representing single modules of function, are difficult to find and to test and even more difficult to localize. Often one function is emphasized only to establish a theoretical point and other symptoms are ignored. It is often impossible to draw the line between a pure function and a syndrome of related functions. In the clinicopathological paradigm of localization, it is common to start with lesions in a certain location and determine the number of deficits related to them.

The major advantage of syndromes is that they are localizable, whereas symptoms are not. The syndrome vs. function controversy is exemplified by a series of articles on the Gertsmann syndrome (Benton, 1961; Strub & Geschwind, 1983). The combination of agraphia, acalculia, finger agnosia, and right-left confusion has caught on among clinicians as a useful syndrome. The rationale and justification, as well as its appropriateness has been questioned and the discussion which resulted can be applied to other syndromes in localization studies. Intuitive clinical taxonomy can and should be reexamined with modern statistical methods. Clinical taxonomies of aphasias have also been attacked for being arbitrary and based on a prejudicial conceptual framework, but numerical taxonomy with cluster analysis has shown that grouping of patients based on performance scores is not only clinically, but also statistically, valid (Kertesz, 1979). Different taxonomies have been used for clinical localization than for functional analysis, but to increase our knowledge about the brain and its function, integration of the two levels is most desirable.

The taxonomy issue is a crucial one in many aspects of localization. Many discrepancies are simply related to the same terminology applied to different behaviors, such as the different definitions of transcortical motor aphasia. Sometimes the opposite also occurs and similar behaviors are grouped differently; therefore, the conclusions are contradictory. An example of this is the use of the term *jargon* for the stereotypies of global aphasia, instead of restricting it to fluent Wernicke's aphasia. These disagreements may come about because a phenomenon is poorly defined and only described qualitatively. Even when standardized tests are used, classifications differ, because the criteria for each syndrome or deficit are different. Despite some of these differences, as long as the behavior criteria are clearly defined on the basis of standardized measurements, various groups can be compared with reasonable efficiency, and correlation with lesion sites has been successful and convincingly consistent for many syndromes of higher cerebral function.

HOW MUCH IS FUNCTION LOCALIZABLE?

Some early investigators, such as Goltz (1881), have concluded that the cerebral cortex is the organ of intelligence which is permanently impaired by large lesions, but smaller focal lesions cannot cause permanent or selective deficits. Subsequent stimulation and lesion studies have contradicted this to some extent and added a great deal of new information (Phillips, Zeki, & Barlow, 1984). Some of the discrepancies were attributed to species differences. There has been an increased amount of anatomical, physiological, and clinical evidence suggesting modular function in the cerebral cortex. The extent to which a function can be localized in the brain is variable. There are certain functions about which there is relatively little argument concerning localization to a certain cytoarchitectonic area. These are the primary sensory and motor areas, including the cortical areas for special sense such as hearing and vision, that are clearly responsible for perceiving the environment and initiating, coordinating, and maintaining movements. Head (1926) emphasized the distinction between the localizable function of motion, sensation, and vision, which have a clear relationship to body parts, muscles, sensory inputs, and stimuli, and "disorders of speech or similar high grade functions" that have "no such relation to parts of the body or their projection in space."

The correlation of the columnar organization of visual cortex with visual feature analysis (Hubel & Wiesel, 1968; Mountcastle, 1957) is a prime example of the modern knowledge of neurophysiological organization of the primary and secondary neocortex. However, much of the actual matching of cortical physiology with functions remains controversial (Phillips et al., 1984). Even the localization of primary motor functions is the prerolandic cortex has been the subject of a great deal of argument, especially concerning the extent to which a part of a movement or the actual whole can be localized. Stimulation and ablation studies indicated that fairly complex functional units seem to be affected together (Zulch, Creutzfeldt, & Galbraith, 1975).

Intercortical and intercerebral connections follow a certain pattern that distinguishes between primary and other cortical areas, according to Flechsig (1901), who specifically established, on the basis of myelogenetic studies, that it is the secondary and tertiary association areas that are interconnected rather than the primary ones. Although recently there has been some evidence that modifies Flechsig's rule, this remains an important principle of cortical localization. More modern emphasis was placed on cortical connections and the mechanisms of disconnections in the production of the neurobehavioral syndromes by Geschwind (1965). This kind of connectionism has been further developed by the concepts of cortical fields and their multiple activation, where the covariance of these fields that will produce functional and behavioral changes, rather than their simple connections (Phillips et al., 1984).

Lesions in animals were less successful in reproducing the selectivity of certain cortical columnar organizations. For instance, a large lesion of the striate cortex that is known to have a preponderance of orientation-selective cells through electrophysiological studies lead only to slight increase in the threshold for the discrimination of orientations (Pasik & Pasik, 1980). In other words, behavioral studies do not always replicate physiological ones, indicating that physiological function may be different from reorganized function after a lesion.

The anatomical definition of cortical areas is difficult and depends on the techniques used, such as cytoarchitectonics, and even then there is a lot of controversy. Primary areas have fairly uniform cytoarchitecture, but recent investigations indicated that even the primary areas are not uniform in function (Zeki, 1983). Similarly, the cytoarchitecture of the primary auditory area is not at all uniform, and the primary auditory area maps show a great deal of parallel organization that one would expect from secondary or tertiary cortices (Merzenich, 1981).

Cerebral maps are probably not fixed, passive representations, as some recent work has shown a great deal of plasticity in the somatosensory cortex (Merzenich, Kaas, Wall, Nelson, Sur, & Feldman, 1983). Representation in the cortex is probably dynamic, changing with time and antecedent activity involving attentional mechanisms of the amount.

The search for certain cortical modules that would be unifying in their function, despite of the changeability and plasticity of cerebral maps, provided certain principles of cortical organization that represent the anatomical and functional basis of a psychological function. The anatomy of a cortical module as a piece of neural tissue subserving a function is conceptualized as similar to the printed circuits in a computer (Szentagothai, 1978). There may be as many different modules as there are sensory systems. The reality of such cortical modules has been established to some extent in the "barrels" in lamina 4 of the somesthetic cortex of rats (Woolsey & Van Der Loos, 1970). On the other hand the "orientation" columns in the visual cortex do not have an obvious anatomical demarcation, but they are only defined by electrophysiological response to functional stimuli (Hubel & Wiesel, 1968).

The representation of function in the brain has received a boost by the demonstration that discrete grouping of cells in the somatosensory cortex respond to particular sensory modalities (Mountcastle, 1957). However, the representation of function appears to be far from uniform in the sensory areas. Sensory maps appear to be constant over long periods in a single animal, but there were differences between animals (Merzenich et al., 1983). The correlation between neural events and subjective experience is difficult to establish. Arguments for the so-called "grandmother cell" that would respond to only one type of stimulus exclusively (Barlow, 1972) have been replaced by the concepts of networks responding to certain stimulation, which are also variable and show a great deal of plasticity. From the perceptual network, the associate areas process this information, which is then assigned a psychological precept, such as a color, shape, or an individual's face, according to what memories or precepts are available to modify the perception. The integration of this perceptual process with the "top down" processing seems to be the primary function of the secondary and perhaps tertiary association areas. Recent considerations of cortical function suggest that there is more information about a stimulus in an assembly of cells than in any one of them because of the possible patterns of covariations among the cells (MacKay, 1978). This explains how multiple sensory maps that have been demonstrated by physiologists would integrate sensation, or how sensation and motor function, or even perception and memory, would be coordinated.

Secondary association regions adjacent to the primary cortical areas are less closely specified to carry out certain function, and large areas of the brain commonly called *tertiary association areas* seem even less clearly related to any particular function, and show a great deal of evidence of plasticity and interchangeability. Some of these tertiary association areas are said to have at least a hemispheric functional specialization. The unique role of some left hemisphere tertiary association areas in language has been well established since Broca, even though there is some recent evidence for oral and visual comprehension of concrete nouns and even some automatic speech output in the right hemisphere which may not be as speechless as was formerly thought. This knowledge is obtained from hemispherectomies (Smith, 1966), corpus callosum sections (Zaidel, 1976) and the study of patients with large lesions destroying the left hemisphere (Kertesz, 1979).

Polysensory cortical areas or tertiary association areas are likely to mediate crossmodal matching, although recent studies indicated that, at least in the monkey, the amygdala has important crossmodal function (Murray & Mishkin, 1985). Anatomical evidence indicates that each sensory system projects through a series of cortical fields, from primary sensory area to the temporal lobe in the insular region, which are closely connected with elements of the limbic lobe that consolidates memory (Turner, Mishkin, & Knapp, 1980). The concepts of cortical fields has replaced the rigid mosaicism of cortical centers, but their extensive subcortical connections have only been recently appreciated.

More recent computer modeling of brain function resulted in simulation of some language function, such as comprehension and response (Arbib & Caplan, 1979) and the more recent construction of "NET-talk," which simulated English pronunciation by providing an internal feedback mechanism (the so-called *hidden elements*) that allowed a Boltzmann machine to correct the initially faculty attempts to pronounce a novel word (Sejnowski & Rosenberg, 1987). An interesting feature was a degree of redundancy or plasticity which allowed considerable "lesioning" of the network without impairing its function.

Opponents of cerebral localization have been pointing out the numerous difficulties with the concept of centers of function. The evidence for widespread cerebral activation in cortical functions has been accumulating physiologically (Mountcastle, 1978; Barlow, 1981). The reticular activating system, the ubiquitous thalamocortical projections, and the multiplicity and redundancy of limbic and cortical connections indicated that central nervous system activity is complex and much of the brain may be activated even for simpler acts of cognition. These physiological notions have been confirmed lately by the multiple areas that are shown to be activated on the CBF technique in reasonably well-defined stages of the mental activity (Ingvar & Schwartz, 1974; Raichle, Herscovitch, Mintun, Martin, & Power, 1984). Indirect measures of function, such as EEG, event-related averaged potentials, or the distribution of neurotransmitters, also support the diffuse and interactive nature of cerebral activity.

Nevertheless, the observation that lesions in the same location were associated with the same deficit in some behavior encouraged many to draw conclusions about how the brain functions. This principle received further support from modern neuroscience, the combination of lesion experiments with histochemical and physiological techniques (Mishkin, 1978; Goldman-Rakic, 1988) and recent imaging techniques that actually display functional changes on line with cognitive processing, such as PET, SPECT, or electrophysiology (reviewed below).

One of the major problems in localization is whether or not the performance observed should be attributed to the damaged area that functions without some of its lost components, or to other functionally related or even unrelated structures which take over from the damaged one. An example of this would be the difficulty in constructional tasks observed in right hemisphere lesions. One cannot be certain whether this is related to poor performance of the damaged right hemisphere, or to the performance of the left hemisphere, which is left to its own devices, without the usual right-sided input for the task. At times after a lesion, not only a deficit or negative symptoms are observed, but also new behavior or positive symptoms may appear. Positive symptoms may represent elements of neural activity that had been controlled or suppressed by the structure destroyed by the lesion. Sometimes a second lesion even promotes recovery by this mechanism (Irle, 1987).

The sudden removal of large areas of functioning brain in stroke or experimental lesions may produce distant effects in functionally connected neural structures. This has also been known as *diaschisis* since von Monakow (1914). Slowly growing tumors, on the other hand, often displace tissues with relatively little functional deficit. Rapidly expanding tumors produce distant effects by edema, hemorrhage, and vascular occlusion. Therefore, in many instances, lesions of the same size or location will not produce the same deficit unless the study is strictly controlled for etiology. This principle is often violated in many studies of functional localization in neuropsychology. Occasionally, different etiologies will produce the same deficit but with different localization. An example of this is the appearance of transcortical sensory aphasia and Wernicke's aphasia in cases of Alzheimer's disease with diffuse neuronal degeneration (at least not localizable with our present methods to the same extent as a focal infarct).

Other biological factors may cause similar lesions to produce different deficits. A major difference is the age of the organism. When a child sustains brain damage, the plasticity of the brain allows for compensation by the homologous hemisphere or other structures as long as the lesion is not a progressive one. Hemispherectomy in a young child (Basser, 1962) or damage to the prepubertal brain results in almost complete recovery, indicating the possibility of hormonal influence on plasticity. Certain aphasic syndromes, such as fluent or Wernicke's aphasia, appear to be more frequent in older age. Whether this is related to anatomical differences in the vasculature affected or continuing functional lateralization remains controversial (Brown & Jaffe, 1975; Kertesz & Sheppard, 1981).

Sex differences in cerebral organizations are considered to be significant by some studies. It is assumed that language may be more bilaterally distributed in women; therefore, lesions may have a different effect in different sexes (McGlone, 1977). Recent epidemiological studies of aphasia tend not to support this contention (Kertesz & Sheppard, 1981). This is not to deny that there may be important psychological sex differences, but evidence from clinical studies is not supportive of sex differences in intra- or interhemispheric brain organization.

Handedness is considered an important factor in cerebral dominance for certain functions. Left-handers may have somewhat different cerebral organization, not just mirroring right-handers but also including important qualitative differences which may result in certain lesions producing different deficits in left- than in right-handers. Gloning, Gloning, Haub, and Quatember (1969) suspected that left-handers are likely to become aphasic regardless of which hemisphere is damaged, but we found less left-handers among our aphasics than expected from the general population, even in the acute stage (Kertesz, 1979). In the chronic stage, one would expect to see less left-handed aphasics because of the suggested better recovery from the deficit (Gloning et al., 1969).

Individual differences in brain organization may be associated with structural differences as well. Anatomical differences between individuals are often observable, but they are difficult to quantitate. Some follow a pattern such as the 65:15 ratio of larger planum temporale on the left vs. on the right (Geschwind &

Levitsky, 1968). Perhaps this accounts for the variable-extent superior temporal lobe lesions affect behavior. Hemispheric anatomical asymmetries are just a beginning in our consideration of the anatomical variables in localization. The complex gyral pattern of the human brain also shows a great deal of individual variation. The importance of this variation becomes evident when a neurosurgeon is called upon to stimulate or excise a portion of the cortex. Electrical stimulation, which is often conceived to achieve pinpoint localization of function in the cortex, often elicits the same behavior from widespread areas (Ojemann & Whitaker, 1978).

Deficits caused by a lesion are often unstable. The early deficit that may be related to edema, cellular reaction, transient ischemia, and so on, is followed by a great deal of early spontaneous recovery in trauma or stroke. The chronic deficit is related, not only to a loss of function, but to compensatory changes by the whole brain or homologous areas or neighboring areas during subsequent stages of recovery. The deficit with acute lesion cannot be considered in the same category as the recovered state although the lesion persists. These two instances lead to conflicting conclusions about localization. Therefore, in every attempt to correlate deficit with lesions, the time from onset is crucial. Failure to consider this variable is a major source of confusion in this field.

The criticism that a performance observed after a lesion has little to do with the function of the lesioned area applies to other methods of localization, such as electrical stimulation of the brain, the local application of neurotransmitters, or recording from single units, as they are connected to the whole system, and the response is the function of other structures as well (Glassman, 1978). To a certain extent, this consideration remains important in the interpretation of any method, but it does not justify the elimination of any approach in the search for causality, an important principle in science.

Behavior in a complex nervous system may be disturbed because the whole system or only a component of it is affected, with similar results, provided that the impaired component is crucial enough in the performance of a function. This, however, could mean that the same phenomenon is observed from lesions at different locations. The possibility of the organism using alternate structures for a function, or the "redundancy" of organization, would also account for variously located lesions producing the same deficit. That the same function is represented at various levels of the nervous system is the well-known principle of "hierarchical" representation, and it probably accounts for some of the recovery or reorganization seen after lesions of the CNS rather than the "taking over" by completely unrelated structures or *vicarious functioning*.

The general principles developed by many researchers in the anatomical correlations of complex network functions were summarized by Mesulam (1981): "(1) components of a single complex function are represented within distinct but interconnected sites which collectively constitute an integrated network for that function; (2) individual cortical areas contain the neural substrate for components of several complex functions and may therefore belong to several partially overlapping networks; (3) lesions confined to a single cortical region are likely to result in multiple deficits; (4) severe and lasting impairments of an individual complex function usually require the simultaneous involvement of several components in the relevant network; and (5) the same complex function may be impaired as a consequence of a lesion in one of several cortical areas, each of which is a component of an integrated network that function." These principles are general enough to explain many of the findings in lesion localization studies, and they are also applicable to stimulation studies.

THE METHODOLOGY OF FUNCTION—LESION CORRELATION

Clinicoanatomical correlation remains a well-established method that is further advanced by the development of new microscopic techniques. The study of human cytoarchitectonics and myeloarchitectonics diminished considerably after the 1920s in favor of experimental neuroanatomy in animals bolstered by autoradiography and axonal tracers, such as horseradish peroxidase (HRP). Recent advances in pigment cytoarchitectonics, and the application of silver stains to anterograde and retrograde degeneration of tracts in human lesions, opened new opportunities to study human cerebral connectivity and cortical organization in postmortem anatomical material (Sanides, 1962; Galaburda & Mesulam, 1983). The accuracy of postmortem localization makes the method the standard to which others are compared. Autopsy examination of the human brain allows topographical localization of gyral and sulcal structures, and fibre tracts and the accurate determination of the extent of lesions. In addition to gross photography, the myelin and cellular stains allow microscopic analysis of neuronal structures and lesions.

The major disadvantage of the autopsy method is that the brain usually becomes available only long after the patients have been examined clinically. Only occasionally is it possible to have the postmortem examination of the brain shortly after a detailed, clinical examination or some experimental analysis (Landis, Regard, Bliestle, & Kleihues, 1988) was performed. Patients who die after a cerebral event are usually so severely affected that they could not be examined in the acute premortem illness in any detail. If they die after a downhill course, such as in the case of a brain tumor, by the time they come to autopsy, the brain is severely distorted and will not reflect the original state which was previously studied. Although many circumscribed lesions have come to autopsy, the corresponding clinical examinations have often been scanty and incomplete. Unfortunately, the reverse is also true. When the clinical examination has been conducted in great length, the patient often recovers; when death eventually occurs for some other reason, permission to carry out a postmortem examination is not granted, or the patient dies in another location, or, even if the brain is available, aging and new lesions are added, and the opportunity to establish correlation is lost.

Naturally occurring lesions may or may not respect anatomical boundaries, and their interpretation in terms of just what is involved is a difficult methodology and requires considerable experience. A lesion may destroy an actual area that subserves a function, it may disconnect two areas that are part of the network, or it may change behavior by damaging longitudinal pathways that transverse the area affected by pathology (the transit effect). *Diaschisis* refers to the remote suppressive effect on functionally connected areas that otherwise remain intact anatomically. This consideration, of course, applies to lesion localization by other modalities as well and increases the complexity of interpretation enormously.

Neurosurgical resection of tumors and surgery for epilepsy, and at times operation on penetrating head injuries, provide a variable measure of localization. Tumor resection is not the most suitable material, because slowly grown tumors compress the brain in an insidious fashion and often there is a great deal of compensation for the slowly incurred deficit. In fact, this may result in false negative conclusions concerning the role of certain areas in the brain. Malignant tumors infiltrate the brain tissue beyond resection, and it is often difficult to determine how far they actually exert their influence. The distant effects of edema, vascular insufficiency, and displacement of the tissues are difficult to quantitate on surgical explorations. Epilepsy surgery is often performed in scarred brains, and the removed tissue may not be functional at all. The extent of the excision is difficult to quantitate because of the limitation of the exposure and the variability and distortion of the surface anatomy.

Hemispherectomies have been used to eradicate malignant tumors in adults (Smith, 1966) and for the excision of severely scarred epileptogenic tissue in infants and children. Some of these were extensively studied. Left hemispherectomies in adults produced global aphasia, but they retained emotional and automatic utterances, articulated even at a sentence level, and some comprehension of single nouns. The limitations on studying adult hemispherectomies are the rarity of the operation (most surgeons do not consider it worthwhile) and the usually relentless spread of the neoplasm into the other hemisphere. Infantile hemispherectomies have been well studied, indicating almost complete recovery of function on either side. However, sophisticated language measures have indicated less than normal development in verbal *IQ* and in grammatical competence in children who had a left hemispherectomy in their infancy (Dennis & Whitaker, 1976).

Callosotomy performed for intractable epilepsy provides an opportunity to study the function of each hemisphere (Sperry, Gazzaniga, & Bogen, 1969). In this respect, the method is not a surgical resection but a disconnection of two functional areas. The results have illuminated many right hemisphere functions, including a certain capacity of comprehending language (a more detailed review can be found in Gazzaniga, 1970). Some of the operations have been less than complete, as recent MRI studies have indicated, and this may have led to some false conclusions concerning function. On the basis of one left hemispherectomy and two commissurotomies, Zaidel (1976) estimated the vocabulary of the right hemisphere to be at or above the level of a 10-year-old child. Gazzaniga (1983) in subsequent studies felt that the normal right hemisphere has less language than was originally thought. The performance of these patients after commissurotomies could be attributable to early left hemisphere damage resulting in the organization of language functions or transfer to the right hemisphere.

More recent experiments with split-brain patients indicated that some degree of intrahemispheric transfer takes place outside the corpus callosum. Even in split-brain patients, the left hemisphere dominance exerts itself and interprets nonverbal responses from the right hemisphere into whatever verbal framework the left hemisphere experiences have constructed. Gazzaniga and LeDoux (1978) postulated that a number of mental systems, emotional, motivational, and perceptual, are monitored by the verbal system. This "verbal self looks out and sees what the person is doing and from that knowledge it interprets reality." This concept of verbal self-control is somewhat similar to Freud's theory of the ego as it is applied to language dominance. Thus, the left hemisphere not only interprets the word for us in terms of language but also integrates our mental functions in a purposeful consciousness, which is the essence of our existence.

Cortical stimulation developed for epilepsy surgery is a major contribution to cerebral localization. Initially, it was used by physiologists to map the function of the cerebral cortex in animals, and subsequently neurosurgeons, such as Otto Foerster in the 1920s, who tried to identify cortical function with stimulation in preparation for their excisions. Sensory, motor, and language areas can be spared using this technique. Penfield and Roberts (1959) mapped the language areas, and Van Buren, Fedio, and Frederick (1978), Ojemann and Whitaker (1978), and Ojemann and Mateer (1979) have added further information concerning cortical localization. These studies have shown that, indeed, Broca's area was very important for producing the most consistent naming difficulty. They also found a rather peculiar mosaic of language function, where a couple of millimetres made a great deal of difference determining what functional alterations were obtained on the stimulation. For instance, one site would interfere with one language but not the other, and a very small change in the location of the electrodes would reverse the situation. Language appeared to be concentrically organized around the Sylvian fissure rather than following the anteroposterior dichotomy of the lesion studies. Right hemisphere stimulation disrupted face recognition, labelling of emotional expression, and line orientation (Mateer, 1983).

The advantage of the method is that it can be applied in the awake, cooperative patient who can perform selected functions during stimulation. In this respect, it resembles other so-called functional methods of localization, such as cerebral blood flow and positron emission tomography. However, stimulation interferes with functions, interrupts or alters them, and, less frequently, elicits positive phenomena. In this respect, it is more like the lesion method, but stimulation involves a much smaller area, allowing a greater resolution for mapping. Several functions can be examined by repeated stimulation of the same area. Limitations of the technique include the logistics of a lengthy surgical procedure, difficulty reproducing the stimulation on the same spot, and the brevity of tasks that can be employed during the short period of stimulation (maximum about 12 seconds). The subjects usually have epilepsy or tumors with reorganized brains, and the conclusions may not always be generalizable.

Electroencephalography is a physiological method of localization that utilizes the small electric potentials generated by neuronal activity that can be detected by surface electrodes on the scalp or on the brain surface during operations. Electroencephalograms have been used for more than 60 years. However, the method suffers from relatively low specificity, since the electric potential changes often present a summation of remote effects. The localization of cognitive function in aphasia with EEG has been reported by Marinesco, Sager, and Kriendler (1936) and Tikofsky, Kooi, and Thomas (1960). Galin and Ornstein (1972) observed suppression of the alpha rhythm in the dominant hemisphere during verbal tasks, and in the nondominant side during spatial tasks. An attempt to assess intercortical connections was made by measuring the degree of correlation between pairs of electrodes, called *cortical coupling* (Callaway & Harris, 1974). Recently, sophisticated, computer-based statistical methodology has been used to display functional alterations and their location.

Event-related potentials (ERP) became possible through averaging computers. Differences in ERP lateralization were observed by using verbal and nonverbal stimuli (Buchsbaum & Fedio, 1970), words vs. nonsense syllables (Shelburne, 1972), and contextual meaning (Brown, Marsh, & Smith, 1973). Long latency *ERPs* are sensitive to task relevance and expectancy. The 300 msec positive component is called *P300,* which is considered endogenous and less dependent on stimulus characteristics. A potential which precedes movement or cognition is called the *contingent negative variation.* This has been correlated with hemispheric dominance and has been useful in various cognitive studies (Low, Wada, & Fox, 1973). Another example of negative potentials associated with processing is the *N400 potential,* which is related to the occurrence of context incongruity in serial semantic tasks (Kutas & Hillyard, 1980; Neville, Kutas, & Schmidt, 1982).

Cerebral ERP are technically difficult because of the many artefacts that interfere with the study. Some of these technical difficulties have been discussed by Desmedt (1977). Another problem with the method is the time restriction on the stimuli. The stimulation has to be very short and have a definite onset, duration, and offset, in order to be connected with cerebral event. In a way, it is the opposite to cerebral blood flow studies (see below), which require more sustained cerebral activity to be analyzed. The major advantage of the technique is that it reflects a physiological event connected with actual cerebral processing, although the resolution of localization is poor and the potentials are usually over a large area of the scalp and the brain.

Computerized tomography (CT) represents a significant breakthrough in radiology of the central nervous system. The latest generation scanners even show some grey and white matter differentiation and allow us to see changes in density, such as brain edema. Contrast enhancement with radio-opaque material, such as organic iodine, increases the visualization of vascular structures and the increased vascularity around an acute infarct. However, CT does not show lesions as early as magnetic resonance imaging, and the early changes tend to be not as distinct as the ones obtained several weeks poststroke. One of the reasons for negative localization with a clear-cut clinical syndrome could be related to the timing of the CT scan. Hemorrhages are quite dramatic, and brain tumors are also shown superiorly on CT scans. Old infarcts are quite distinct, with sharp margins and lower densities than the surrounding brain. Enlargement of the ventricles and sulci also provide an accurate measurement of atrophy.

The correlation of lesions with behavioral studies began as soon as the CT equipment became available. These studies differ in the quality of the scans, the sophistication of localization, the number of patients included, the actual neuropsychological measurements used, and the definition of the syndromes. One of the most important considerations, which is missing from some of the studies, is the time from onset. Some patients with large lesions may have recovered considerably, and this may lead to the conclusion that the area involved plays no role in a function. It is especially misleading to mix acute and chronic patients. CT studies, nevertheless, have contributed to a great deal to our knowledge about localization of lesions in syndromes of language and nonverbal cognitive impairment.

The major advantage of a CT scan is its ability to localize lesion with high anatomical resolution, especially in the late model scanners. CT scanning is especially useful in chronic lesions, where the edges of infarcts are well outlined, and in horizontal cuts, which are usually oriented 15 degrees above the orbitomeatal line. CT scans are now available in most major centers, and the method has become standard for neurological investigation. The scanning time is brief, and there is no discomfort associated with it. A clinical indication is needed for scanning, because of radiation and repeated, frequent exposures to x-rays are considered harmful. Cortical landmarks may not be seen, and one has to use ventricular and bony landmarks for anatomical orientation. Variations in head position, head size, ventricular size, extent of atrophy, and cerebral asymmetries are important to consider in accurate localization. The variation in the sulcal and gyral pattern, and the depth of the cortex in the central portions of the brain, is often underestimated in CT studies.

Magnetic resonance imaging (MRI) is the latest modality, and it provides the most accurate localization of lesions without invasive radiation. The technique uses the inherent magnetic properties of spinning atomic nuclei by placing the structure to be imaged in a large magnet and applying short-wave radio-frequency pulses to produce a resonance signal that can be quantified and computerized (Doyle et al., 1981). Superior anatomical detail can be achieved with excellent grey and white matter differentiation and an accurate outline of the edge of the brain from CSF spaces. The brain can be imaged in coronal and sagittal sections, in addition to the horizontal one, which is the usual plane obtained in other modalities. This imaging flexibility, combined with anatomical accuracy, has already established MRI as a useful clinical and research tool. The apparent lack of biohazard allows it to be used to study normals without clinical indications, as well as a more frequent repetition of imaging in patients than is possible in other modalities which use ionizing radiation (Sweetland, Kertesz, Prato, & Nantau, 1987).

Various pulse sequences can be used to probe the metabolic and molecular environment of various regions of the brain, and this makes the technique much more dynamic than the CT scan. Currently, two major pulse sequences are used. One, called *inversion recovery* (IR), emphasizes grey and white matter differences and provides excellent anatomical detail. The second is called *spin echo* (SE), which is utilized to detect edema and other metabolic changes associated with lesions. SE sequences are often superior to CT scanning in the early detection of cerebral infarct, thus reducing the false negative rate obtained on CT in the first 2 or 3 days of a stroke. The technique is particularly suited to detect demyelinating plaques and some other degenerative diseases in addition to early strokes.

Cerebral blood flow (CBF) technique utilizes the physiological and pathological alterations in regional blood supply. The technique is based on estimating the clearance of radioactive isotopes from various regions of the brain through surface detectors. The values are expressed as percentages of the hemispheric average. Increases of blood flow are assumed to be associated with increased neuronal, and therefore, functional activity. A sustained repetitive task, of at least 3–5 minutes' duration, is required for activation. The color-coded images of CBF have become popular in illustrating that the brain is activated in multiple locations when, for instance, a person reads or the right hemisphere also "lights up" when one speaks. The resting pattern shows precentral high and postcentral low flows (Ingvar & Schwartz, 1974). Simple repetitive movements of the mouth, hand, or foot augment CBF in the contralateral sensorimotor area, supporting the topography of the cortical homunculus.

The important advantage of the technique is that it reflects physiological metabolic change accompanying psychological function and can be used to study normal processes. It must be remembered, however, that these changes are not directly measuring neuronal events. These techniques are best suited for the study of sustained repetitive acts of cognition. Lesions, such as infarcts producing a deficit, may appear as areas of low flow with an area of "luxury perfusion" of high flow surrounding them. The major disadvantage is a relatively poor resolution of the noninvasive Xenon inhalation method. It only measures blood flow on the surface. The more accurate intraarterial injection is rarely used, because it is invasive and requires the indications of an angiogram. A more recent modification of the technique combines 133 Xenon inhalation with computerized tomography, achieving three-dimension representations in slices similar to those in PET scanning (see SPECT section below).

Positron emission tomography (PET) measures oxygen and glucose metabolism by using a positron-emitting isotope and a computerized tomographic scanner. It can also be used to study regional blood flow. This complex and expensive technique is available only in a few centers equipped with a particle accelerator (cyclotron) and a team of nuclear physicists, radiopharmacists, computer experts, isotope specialists, clinicians, and experimental psychologists. The positron labeled metabolites, such as 18F-Deoxy-glucose, must be given immediately at their source because of their short half-life. The nature of tracer kinetics requires that the physiological activity studied has to be sustained for 20–40 minutes. Metabolic scanning with PET confirmed the differences in hemispheric activation between the verbal and visuospatial task performance (Mazziotta & Phelps, 1984). Recently, a bolus administration of oxygen-15 has shortened the period of observation and allowed repeated measurements in the same subjects in one session (Raichle et al., 1984). A new device, the "super-PET-1," is capable of a temporal resolution of less than 1 minute (Ter-Pogossian et al., 1984). This opens up the possibility of following brief physiological events in the brain in the future. The major disadvantages are the large expense, general unavailability, poor anatomical resolution, uncertainties between the temporal sequence of cerebral events and the isotope kinetics in time, and influence of unrelated cerebral activity.

Regional blood flow can also be estimated by using a single photon emission computerized tomography (SPECT) technique that is much less expensive than PET scanning (Hill, 1980). Although it is the latest of the functional localizing methods, because of its lesser cost and general more availability, experience with the SPECT is rapidly accumulating. Single photon tracers can be used to measure blood flow, blood volume, and blood brain barrier integrity. The anatomical resolution is relatively poor, and the methodology has many pitfalls.

MODULAR FUNCTION WITH CONSISTENT LESION LOCALIZATION

It would be impossible to review all the modular functions and their structural correlations. Instead, a few examples will be used to highlight our current state of knowledge in language and visual processing.

Spoken language incorporates many subfunctions, which have been categorized by linguists as articulation, fluency, syntax utilization, phonological processing, lexical retrieval, linguistic prosody, pragmatics, etc. The function of articulated language has been much studied since Broca, particularly by neuropsychologists, linguists, neurologists, and speech pathologists with a physiological bent. Speech output is an important function, although it differs substantially, whether it is in response to questions (responsive speech), extemporaneous expression of ideas (monologue), or repetition. Nevertheless, all these phenomena tend to be involved at the same time with the clinical syndrome of Broca's aphasia with a certain frequency that allows us (a) to study them systematically, (b) to localize the lesion that causes a syndrome, (c) to study the extent of the lesion that produces permanent damage, and (d) to implicate structures that may contribute to substitution or reorganization. When a brain-damaged patient speaks effortfully with hesitations, pauses, word-finding difficulty, phonemic errors (substitutions, deletions, transpositions, anticipations), word errors (semantic substitution), unintelligible utterances, impaired syntax (agrammatism), relatively preserved comprehension, and automatic speech, a clinical syndrome of Broca's aphasia can be reliably defined by standardized test scores (Kertesz, 1979) or careful clinical description (Goodglass & Kaplan, 1972; Levine & Sweet, 1983). It is evident from the number of symptoms listed above that many modular, dissociable central processes contribute to the syndrome, but that none of these have reliable localization, only the syndrome as a whole.

Severe persisting Broca's aphasia is associated with large lesions that include, not only Broca's area, but also the inferior parietal and often the anterior temporal region (Mohr, 1976; Kertesz, Harlock, & Coates, 1979). Small lesions involving Broca's area only are compatible with good recovery. Small Broca's area lesions often produce a minor motor aphasia (called *cortical motor aphasia, pure motor aphasia,* or *verbal apraxia*) (Mohr, 1976; Kertesz, 1979). Pure motor aphasia, or verbal apraxia, has been associated with anterior subcortical, as well as opercular and insular cortical lesions (Levine & Sweet, 1983). Subcortical lesions produce atypical aphasias which may vary clinically, depending on their anteroposterior location and the extent of involvement of various subcortical structures, such as the caudate or the putamen, and the connecting white matter, such as the anterior capsule and the subcallosal fasciculus (Naeser et al., 1982).

More fractionated functions, such as syntactical processing, are much more difficult to localize if at all, and so far attempts to do so have not been successful. The available evidence suggests that extension of the lesions to the inferior parietal lobule and the central region of the rolandic cortex, above the Sylvian fissure, are the prerequisites of persistent agrammatic aphasia.

The study of lesions in fluent aphasia has revealed, not only a cortical location, but also thalamic involvement. Neologistic jargon output is associated with lesions of both the superior temporal and inferior parietal regions (Kertesz, 1979). Thalamic lesions, on the other hand, produce fluctuating jargon aphasia alternating with relatively nonfluent speech (Mohr, Watters, & Duncan, 1975). Repetition is often preserved (Cappa & Vignolo, 1979). Conduction aphasia is associated with lesions in the arcuate fasciculus, as well as in the insula (Damasio & Damasio, 1983). Transcortical sensory aphasia is associated with inferior temporo-occipital lesions (Kertesz, Sheppard, & MacKenzie, 1982).

Right hemisphere function appears to be much less well localized than that on the left side. This conclusion was first suggested from cortical excision studies by Semmes, Weinstein, Gheyt, and Tenber (1960) and later received support from a CT study by Kertesz and Dobrowolski (1981). Line bisection, drawing, block design, and Raven's scores were not significantly different among frontal, central, subcortical, parietal, and occipital lesions. The anteroposterior lesion localization of emotional and processing components in the right hemisphere, analogous to the aphasias in the left (Ross, 1981), has not been fully supported (Cancelliere & Kertesz, 1989). Lesion size was certainly a contributing variable. In the study by Hier, Moudlock, and Caplau (1983), left neglect motor impersistence and anosognosia tended to occur with rather large lesions extending beyond the right parietal lobe. On a few occasions, small, deep lesions also produced behavioral abnormalities comparable to the larger superficial cortical lesions.

Some of the clinical evidence also points in the direction of selective deficits with focal lesions even in perceptual areas, such as the patient, described by Zihl, Von Cramon, and Mai (1983), who was unable to detect motion, although able to read and see forms, or another patient of Pearlman, Birch, and Meadows (1979), who was selectively impaired in color discrimination but unimpaired in the perception of depth, movement, and reading.

Visual agnosia is classified usually to perceptive and associative varieties, as well as optic aphasia, and more recently various combinations of visual recognition defects have been described with some variations of the lesion localization. Some patients are impaired on simple shape-matching tasks and have difficulty identifying objects. In addition to these patients, there are those who can match shapes but who are impaired at identifying and matching objects under usual viewing conditions (Warrington & Taylor, 1973; Humphreys & Riddoch, 1984). There are patients who can describe details of a picture but have difficulty integrating complex pictures or differentiate a figure from the ground (Landis, Graves, Benson, & Hebbeu, 1982). A similar phenomena was considered *simultanagnosia* by Wolpert (1924) and Kinsbourne and Warrington (1963). Patients with apperceptive visual agnosia tend to have large bilateral lesions, usually related to carbon monoxide poisoning. Patients with associative agnosia more often have unilateral lesions, and patients with *semantic access agnosia* have been described with generalized atrophy. In reviewing the localization of lesions in visual agnosia, most of the cases had a large left-, and smaller right-sided lesion (Kertesz, 1988). All the autopsied cases were bilateral. Recently various forms of prosopagnosia or inability to recognize faces were further defined as having specific impairment of recognizing the emotional expressions of faces

(Damasio, Damasio, & Tranel, 1986). Lesions in prosopagnosia are also bilateral when they come to autopsy, except the recently published case of Landis et al. (1988), where the left-sided lesion was negligible, and the well-documented deficit was clearly related to the right-sided abnormality, which is often the case in publications with CT localization. The various forms of color recognition problem and achromatopsia also appear to have well-localized occipital lesions, particularly achromatopsia, which may be unilateral, and the lesion may be restricted to one quadrant of the striate cortex, usually the right inferior portion (Damasio & Damasio, 1983).

Recent PET studies of activity related changes in cerebral blood flow using short half-life oxygen-15 and a technique of subtraction of control tasks confirmed certain notions of localization. They also provided evidence for localization of certain functions that has not been possible on the basis of clinicopathological lesion analysis (Peterson, Fox, Posner, Mintun, & Raichle, 1988). Areas related to motor output and articulation were the sensory motor cortex at the lower end of the rolandic fissure and near Broca's area, which is by itself not surprising. Bilateral Sylvian activation was confirmed, and also the lack of specificity for language, because the activation also occurred when subjects moved their mouths and tongues without speaking. The left inferior frontal area was considered to participate in processing semantic associations (a verb with a noun). The anterior cingulate gyrus appeared to be part of an anterior attentional system indicated by monitoring lists of words for a semantic category. Auditory processing activated bilaterally the primary auditory cortex, but it was specific for words on the left temporoparietal cortex and in the anterior-superior temporal region.

These studies also confirmed the notions that visual information appears to access to *output coding* without phonological recoding in the posterior temporal cortex. In other words, Wernicke's area was not necessarily activated in reading. Their finding of semantic processing the frontal regions, rather than in the posterior temporal regions, is also different from previous notions (Geschwind, 1965). In addition, they found simple repetition was independent from semantic association, confirming in a sense the original Wernicke-Lichtheim model (Lichtheim, 1885). Activation for semantic association did not appear to be modality specific, and it appeared to be coupled with output activation, especially in the median frontal and anterior cingulate regions.

In another report by the same group (Posner, Petersen, Fox, & Raichle, 1988) the results indicated that the ventral occipital lobe processes the visual word form (e.g., passively looking at visually presented nouns), and the left lateral frontal lobe is involved in semantics used in coding word associations but not requiring motor or verbal output (e.g., noting but not speaking words in a specific class from a presented list). The supramarginal gyrus appears to process phonological tasks (e.g., determining whether words rhyme), whereas the anterior cingulate region is activated when the brain selects language or other information for action (e.g., naming presented words). The data suggest that a posterior system processes early visual images, and that anterior attention systems select information for output.

CONCLUSION

It may be concluded that Jackson's statement remains, with some modification, axiomatic. One can only localize lesions or physiological and metabolic changes accompanying behavior, but not function. Should we abandon, therefore, the study of lesion–behavior correlation, as some people are suggesting? The answer for many of us is "no," because, as Phillips et al. (1984) have stated, "the original method, that of studying and trying to explain the deficits of function associated with specific lesions, is still capable of yielding interesting results, and is in a sense the final arbiter; if you cannot show the expected deficits of function after a local lesion, you probably have not got the right answer about what function that local region performs." Lesion evidence is useful to localize syndromes and at times determines the sites from which a symptom can be produced. Converging evidence from physiological studies and deficit analysis indicates that the concepts of modularity of function and modular localization of the brain are not only tenable but are essential in order to understand how functions are integrated and participate in more diffusely distributed processes. A theory of cognition has to be based on available physiologic, anatomic, and psychological evidence. Evidence from clinicopathological localization has a great deal to offer in both constraining cognitive modeling towards biological reality and providing a basis upon which further physiological and psychological facts can be interpreted.

It is likely that only a certain portion of the building blocks of cortical organization are specific for certain perceptual or integrated processes, and that even these appear to be dynamically changeable. A greater degree of substitution and functional shifting exists in other parts of the brain which deal with more complex integrative processes. However, localization of function must occur in an anatomical and physiological sense for every behavioral and psychological event. How much of this localization is stable and reproducible, and within which anatomical regions the shift occurs, is of particular interest in neurobiology.

REFERENCES

Arbib, M. A., & Caplan, D. (1979). Neurolinguistics must be computational. *Brain and Behavioral Science, 2,* 449–783.

Barlow, H. B. (1972). Single units and sensation: a neuron doctrine for perceptual psychology? *Perception, 1,* 371–394.

Barlow, H. B. (1981). The Ferrier lecture: Critical limiting factors in the design of the eye and visual cortex. *Proceeding of the Royal Society, London, 212,* 1–34.

Basser, L. S. (1962). Hemiplegia of early onset and the faculty of speech with special reference to the effects of hemispherectomy. *Brain, 85,* 427–460.

Benton, A. L. (1961). The fiction of the "Gerstmann syndrome." *Journal of Neurology, Neurosurgery and Psychiatry, 24,* 176–181.

Broca, P. (1861). Remarques sur le siege de la faculte du langage articule suivies d'une observation d'amphemie (perte de la parole). *Bulletin et Memoires de la Societe Anatomique de Paris, 36,* 330–357.

Brown, J., & Jaffe, J. (1975) Hypothesis on cerebral dominance. *Neuropsychologia, 13,* 107–110.

Brown, W. S., Marsh, J. T., & Smith, J. C. (1973). Contextual meaning effects on speech-evoked potentials. *Behavioral Biology, 9,* 755–761.

Buchsbaum, M., & Fedio, P. (1970). Hemispheric differences in evoked potentials to verbal and nonverbal stimuli in the left and right visual fields. *Physiology and Behavior, 5,* 207–210.

Bullock, T. H. (1965). Physiological bases of behavior. In J. A. Moore (Ed.), *Ideas in modern biology* (pp. 32–56) New York: Natural History Press.

Callaway, E., & Harris, P. R. (1974). Coupling between cortical potentials from different areas. *Science, 183,* 873–875.

Cancelliere, A., & Kertesz, A. (1990). Lesion localization in acquired deficits of emotional expression and comprehension. *Brain and Cognition, 13,* 133–147.

Cappa, S. F., & Vignolo, L. A. (1979). "Transcortical" features of aphasia following left thalamic hemorrhage. *Cortex, 15,* 121–130.

Coltheart, M., Sartori, G., & Job, R. (1987). *The cognitive neuropsychology of language.* London: Erlbaum.

Cowey, A. (1979). Cortical maps and visual perception: The Grindley Memorial Lecture. *Quarterly Journal of Experimental Psychology, 31,* 1–17.

Crick, F. (1989). The recent excitement about neural networks. *Nature, 337,* 129–132.

Damasio, A. R., & Damasio, H. (1983). Localization of lesions in achromatopsia and prosopagnosia. In A. Kertesz (Ed.), *Localization in neuropsychology* (pp. 417–428). New York: Academic Press.

Dennis, M., & Whittaker, M. A. (1976). Language acquisition following hemidecortication: Linguistic superiority of the left over the right hemisphere. *Brain and Language, 2,* 472–482.

Desmedt, J. E. (1977). Some observations on the methodology of cerebral evoked potentials in man. In J. E. Desmedt (Ed.), *Attention, voluntary contraction and event-related cerebral potentials* (Progress in Clinical Neurophysiology, Vol. 1). Basel: Karger.

Doyle, F. H., Gore, J. C., Pennock, J. M., Bydder, G. M., Orr, J. S., Steiner, R. E., Young, I. R., Burl, M., Clow, H., Gilderdale, D. J., Bailes, D. R., & Walters, P. E. (1981). Imaging of the brain by NMR. *Lancet, 2*(8237), 53–57.

Dreyfus, H. L. (1979) *What computers can't do: The limits of artificial intelligence* (2nd ed.). New York: Harper & Row.

Edelman, G. M. (1987). *Neural Darwinism: The theory of neuronal group selection.* New York: Basic.

Ellis, A. W., & Young, A. W. (1988). *Human cognitive neuropsychology*. Hove, England: Erlbaum.

Flechsig, P. (1901). Developmental (myelogenetic) localisation of the cerebral cortex in the human subject. *Lancet, ii,* 1027–1029.

Fodor, J. A. (1983) *The modularity brain*. Cambridge, MA: MIT Press.

Fritsch, G. T., & Hitzig, E. (1870). Uber die elektrische Erregbarkeit des Grosshirns. *Archiv fuer d Anatomie und Physiologie, Leipzig,* 300–322.

Galaburda, A. M., & Mesulam, M. M. (1983). Neuroanatomical aspects of cerebral localization. In A. Kertesz (Ed.), *Localization in neuropsychology* (pp. 21–61). New York: Academic Press.

Galin, D., & Ornstein, R. (1972). Lateral specialization of cognitive mode: An EEG study. *Psychophysiology, 9,* 412–418.

Gazzaniga, M. S. (1970). *The bisected brain*. New York: Century & Crofts.

Gazzaniga, M. S. (1983). Right hemisphere language following brain bisection: A 20-year perspective. *American Psychologist, 38,* 342–346.

Gazzaniga, M. S., & LeDoux, J. E. (1978). *The integrated mind*. New York: Plenum Press.

Geschwind, N. (1965). Disconnexion syndromes in animals and man. *Brain, 88,* 237–294, 585–644.

Geschwind, N., & Levitsky, W. (1968). Human brain: Left-right asymmetries in temporal speech regions. *Science, 161,* 186–187.

Glassman, R. B. (1978). The logic of the lesion experiment and its role in the neural sciences. In S. Finger (Ed.), *Recovery from brain damage*. New York: Plenum Press.

Gloning, I., Gloning, K., Haub, G., & Quatember, R. (1969). Comparison of verbal behaviour in right-handed and non-right-handed patients with anatomically verified lesions of one hemisphere. *Cortex, 5,* 43–52.

Goldman-Rakic, P. S. (1988). Topography of cognition: Parallel distributed networks in primate association cortex. *Annual Review of Neuroscience, 11,* 137–156.

Goldstein, K. (1948). *Language and language disturbances*. New York: Grune & Stratton.

Goltz, F. (1881) In W. MacCormac (Ed.), *Transactions of the 7th International Medical Congress* (Vol. 1, pp. 218–228). London: J. W. Kolkmann.

Goodglass, H., & Kaplan, E. (1972). *Assessment of aphasia and related disorders*. Philadelphia, PA: Lea & Febiger.

Head, H. (1926). *Aphasia and kindred disorders of speech*. Cambridge, England: Cambridge University Press.

Hier, D. B., Mondlock, J., & Caplan, L. R. (1983). Behavioural abnormalities after right hemisphere stroke. *Neurology, 33,* 337–344.

Hill, T. C. (1980). Single-photon emission computed tomography to study cerebral function in man. *Journal of Nuclear Medicine, 21,* 1197–1199.

Hinton, G. E., & Anderson, J. A. (Eds.). (1981). *Parallel models of associative memory*. Hillsdale, NJ: Erlbaum.

Hubel, D., & Wiesel, T. (1968). Receptive fields and functional architecture of monkey striate cortex. *Journal of Physiology, 195,* 215–243.

Humphreys, G. W., & Riddoch, M. J. (1984). Routes to object constancy: Implications from neurological impairments of object constancy. *Quarterly Journal of Experimental Psychology, 36A,* 385–415.

Ingvar, D. H., & Schwartz, M. S. (1974). Blood flow patterns induced in the dominant hemisphere by speech and reading. *Brain, 97,* 273–388.

Irle, E. (1987). Lesion size and recovery of function: some new perspectives. *Brain Research Reviews, 12,* 307–320.

Jackson, H. J. (1878). On affections of speech from disease of the brain. *Brain, 1,* 304–330.

Kazdin, A. E. (1982). *Single case research designs.* New York: Oxford University Press.

Kertesz, A. (1979). *Aphasia and associated disorders: Taxonomy, localization and recovery.* New York: Grune & Stratton.

Kertesz, A. (1988). The clinical spectrum and localization of visual agnosia. In G. Humphreys & J. Riddoch (Eds.), *A cognitive neuropsychological approach* (pp. 175–196). London: Erlbaum.

Kertesz, A., & Dobrowolski, S. (1981). Right hemisphere deficits, lesion size and location. *Journal of Clinical Neuropsychology, 3,* 283–299.

Kertesz, A., Harlock, W., & Coates, R. (1979). Computer tomographic localization, lesion size and prognosis in aphasia. *Brain and Language, 8,* 34–50.

Kertesz, A., & Sheppard, A. (1981). The epidemiology of aphasic and cognitive impairment in stroke—age, sex, aphasia type and laterality differences. *Brain, 104,* 117–128.

Kertesz, A., Sheppard, A., & MacKenzie, R. A. (1982). Localization in transcortical sensory aphasia. *Archives of Neurology, 39,* 475–478.

Kinsbourne, N., & Warrington, E. K. (1963). A study of visual persevertion. *Journal of Neurology, Neurosurgery, and Psychiatry, 26,* 468–475.

Kutas, M., & Hillyard, S. A. (1980). Reading between the lines event-related brain potentials during natural sentence processing. *Brain and Language, 11,* 354–373.

Landis, T., Graves, R., Benson, D. F. & Hebben, N. (1982). Visual recognition through kinaesthetic mediation. *Psychological Medicine, 12,* 515–531.

Landis, T., Regard, M., Bliestle, A., & Kleihues, P. (1988). Prosopagnosia and agnosia for noncanonical views. *Brain, 111,* 1287–1297.

Lashley, K. S. (1938). Factors limiting recovery after central nervous lesions. *Journal of Nervous and Mental Disease, 88,* 733–755.

Levine, D. N., & Sweet, E. (1983). Localization of lesions in Broca's motor aphasia. In A. Kertesz (Ed.), *Localization in neuropsychology* (pp. 185–208). New York: Academic Press.

Lichtheim, L. (1885). On aphasia. *Brain, 7,* 443.

Low, W., Wada, J. A., & Fox, M. (1973). Electroencephalographic localization of the conative aspects of language production in the human brain. *Transactions of the American Neurological Association, 98,* 129–133.

MacKay, D. M. (1978). The dynamics of perception. In P. A. Buser & A. Rougeul-Buser (Eds.), *Cerebral correlates of conscious experience* (pp. 53–68). Amsterdam, Netherlands: Elsevier.

Marinesco, G., Sager, O., & Kreindler, A. (1936). Etudes electroencephalographiques; electroencephalogrammes dans l'aphasie. *Bulletin de l Academie de Medecine* (Paris), *116,* 182.

Mateer, C. (1983). Localization of language and visuospatial functions by electrical stimulation. In A. Kertesz (Ed.), *Localization of neuropsychology* (pp. 153–183). New York: Academic Press.

Mazziotta, J. C., & Phelps, M. E. (1984). Human sensory stimulation and deprivation: Positron emission tomographic results and strategies. *Neurology, 15* (Supp), 550–60.

McGlone, J. (1977). Sex differences in the cerebral organization of verbal functions in patients with unilateral brain lesions. *Brain, 100,* 775–793.

McLelland, J. L., & Rumelhart, D. E. (1986). *Parallel distributed processing: Explorations in the microstructure of cognition, Vol. 2: Psychological and biological models.* London: MIT Press.

Mehler, J., Morton, J., & Jusczyk, P. W. (1984). On reducing language to biology. *Cognitive Neuropsychology, 1,* 83–116.

Merzenich, M. M. (1981). Some recent observations on the functional organization of the central auditory nervous system. In Y. Katsuki, R. Norgren, & M. Sato (Eds.), *Brain mechanisms of sensation* (pp. 1–19). Chichester, England, John Wiley.

Merzenich, M. M., Kaas, J. H., Wall, J., Nelson, R. J., Sur, M., & Felleman, D. (1983). Topographic reorganisation of somatosensory cortical areas 3b and 1 in adult monkeys following restricted deafferentation. *Neuroscience, 8,* 33–55.

Mesulam, M. M. (1981). A cortical network for directed attention and unilateral neglect. *Annals of Neurology, 10,* 309–325.

Mishkin, M. (1978). Memory in monkeys severely impaired by combined but not by separate removal of amygdala and hippocampus. *Nature, 272,* 297–298.

Mohr, J. P. (1976). Broca's area and Broca's aphasia. In H. Whitaker & H. A. Whitaker (Eds.), *Studies in neurolinguistics* (Vol. 1, pp. 201–236). New York: Academic Press.

Mohr, J. P., Watters, W. C., & Duncan, G. W. (1975). Thalamic hemorrhage and aphasia. *Brain and Language, 2,* 3–17.

Mountcastle, V. B. (1957). Modality and topographic properties of single neurons of cat's somatic sensory cortex. *Journal of Neurophysiology, 20,* 408–434.

Mountcastle, V. B. (1978). An organizing principle of cerebral function: The unit module and the distributed system. In G. M. Edelman & V. B. Mountcastle (Eds.), *The mindful brain.* Cambridge, MA: MIT Press.

Munk, H. (1881). *Ueber die Funktionen der Grosshirnrinde. Gesammelte Mitteilungen aus den Jahren 1877–1880.* Berlin: Hirschwald.

Murray, E. A., & Mishkin, M. (1985). Amygdalectomy impairs crossmodal association in monkeys. *Science, 228,* 604–606.

Naeser, M. A., Alexander, M. P., Helm-Estabrooks, N., Levine, H. L., Laughlin, S. A., & Geschwind, N. (1982). Aphasia with predominantly subcortical lesion sites: Description of three capsular/putaminal aphasia syndromes. *Archives of Neurology, 39,* 2–14.

Neville, H. J., Kutas, M., & Schmidt, A. (1982). Event-related potential studies of cerebral specialization during reading. I. Studies of normal adults. *Brain and Language, 16,* 300–315.

Ojemann, G. A., & Mateer, C. (1979). Human language cortex: Localization of memory, syntax and sequential motor-phoneme identification systems. *Science, 250,* 1401–1403.

Ojemann, G. A., & Whitaker, H. A. (1978). Language localization and variability. *Brain and Language, 6,* 239–260.

Pasik, T., & Pasik, P. (1980). Extrageniculostriate vision in primates. In S. Lessell & J. T. W. van Dalin (Eds.), *Neuro-ophthalmology, 1980* (Vol. 1, pp. 95–119). Amsterdam, Netherlands: Excerpta Medica.

Pearlman, A. L., Birch, J., & Meadows, J. (1979). Cerebral colour blindness: an acquired defect in hue discrimination. *Annals of Neurology, 5,* 253–261.

Penfield, W., & Roberts, L. (1959). *Speech and brain mechanisms.* Princeton, NJ: Princeton University Press.

Peterson, S. E., Fox, P. T., Posner, M. I., Mintun, M., & Raichle, M. E. (1988). Positron emission tomographic studies of the cortical anatomy of single-word processing. *Nature, 331,* 585–589.

Phillips, C. G., Zeki, S., & Barlow, H. B. (1984) Localization of function in the cerebral cortex. *Brain, 107,* 327–361.

Posner, M. I., Petersen, S. E., Fox, P. T., & Raichle, M. E. (1988). Localization of cognitive operations in the human brain. *Science, 240,* 1627–1631.

Raichle, M. E., Herscovitch, P., Mintun, A. M., Martin, W. R. W., & Power, W. (1984). Dynamic measurements of local blood flow and metabolism in the study of higher cortical function in humans with Positron Emission Tomography. *Neurology, 14,* 48–49.

Ross, E. D. (1981). The aprosodias: Functional-anatomic organization of the affective components of language in the right hemisphere. *Archives of Neurology, 38,* 561–569.

Sanides, F. (1962). *Die architektonik des Menschlichen Stirnhirns.* Berlin: Springer-Verlag.

Sejnowski, T. J., & Rosenberg, C. R. (1987). *Complex Systems, 1,* 145–168.

Semmes, J., Weinstein, S., Ghent, L., & Teuber, H. L. (1960). *Somatosensory changes after penetrating brain wounds in man.* Cambridge, MA: Harvard University Press.

Shelburne, S. A. (1972). Visual evoked responses to word and nonsense syllable stimuli. *Cortex, 12,* 325–336.

Smith, A. (1966). Speech and other functions after left (dominant) hemispherectomy. *Journal of Neurology, Neurosurgery and Psychiatry, 29,* 467–471.

Sperry, R. W., Gazzaniga, M. S., & Bogen, J. E. (1969). Interhemispheric relationship: the neocortical commissures; syndromes of hemispheric disconnection. In P. J. Vinken & G. W. Bruyn (Eds.), *Handbook of clinical neurology* (Vol. 4, pp. 273–290). Amsterdam, Netherlands: North-Holland.

Strub, R. L., & Geschwind, N. (1983). Localization in Gerstmann Syndrome. In A. Kertesz (Ed.), *Localization in neuropsychology* (pp. 295–321). New York: Academic Press.

Sweetland, J., Kertesz, A., Prato, F. S., & Nantau, K. (1987). The effect of magnetic resonance imaging on human cognition. *Magnetic Resonance Imaging, 5,* 129–135.

Szentagothai, J. (1978). The neuron network of the cerebral cortex: a functional interpretation. *Proceedings of the Royal Society, B, 201,* 219–248.

Ter-Pogossian, M. M., Ficke, D. C., Mintun, M. A., Herscovitch, P., Fox, P. T., & Raichle, M. E. (1984). Dynamic cerebral positron emission tomographic studies. *Annals of Neurology, 15* (Suppl.), S46–47.

Tikofsky, R. W., Kooi, K. A., & Thomas, M. H. (1960). Electroencephalographic findings and recovery from aphasia. *Neurology, 10,* 154–156.

Turner, B. H., Mishkin, M., & Knapp, M. (1980). *Journal of Comparative Neurology, 191,* 515.

Van Buren, J., Fedio, P., & Frederick, G. (1978). Mechanism and localization of speech in the parietotemporal cortex. *Neurosurgery, 2,* 233–239.

von Monakow, C. (1914). *Die Lokalisation in Grosshirn und her Abbau der Funktionen durch cortikale.* Herde, Wiesbaden, Germany: Bergmann.

Warrington, E. K., & Taylor, A. M. (1973). The contribution of the right parietal lobe to object recognition. *Cortex, 9,* 152–164.

Wolpert, I. (1924). Die simultanagosie: Storung der Gesamtauffassung. *Zeitschrift fur die gesamte Neurologie and Psychiatrie, 93,* 397–415.

Woolsey, T., & Van Der Loos, H. (1970). The structural organization of layer IV in the somatosensory region (S1) of mouse cerebral cortex. *Brain Research, Amsterdam, 17,* 205–242.

Yarnell, P. R., Monroe, M. A., & Sobel, L. (1976). Aphasia outcome in stroke: A clinical and neuroradiological correlation. *Stroke, 7,* 516–522.

Zaidel, E. (1976). Auditory vocabulary of the right hemisphere following brain bisection or hemidecortication. *Cortex, 12,* 187–211.

Zeki, S. M. (1983). The distribution of wavelength and orientation selective cells in different areas of monkey visual cortex. *Proceedings of the Royal Society, B, 217,* 449–470.

Zihl, J., von Cramon, D., & Mai, N. (1983). Selective disturbance of movement vision after bilateral brain damage. *Brain, 106,* 313–340.

Zulch, K. J., Creutzfeldt, O., & Galbraith, G. C. (1975). *Cerebral localization.* New York: Springer-Verlag.

Chapter 7

Special Abilities of Idiots Savants, Hyperlexic Children, and Phenomenal Memorizers: Implications for Intelligence Theory*

Frances A. Conners

University of Alabama

Intimately involved in the issue of intelligence as one or a combination of characteristics is the fact that virtually all mental tasks intercorrelate. People high in one measured ability are likely to be high in other measured abilities, and people low in one ability are likely to be low in other abilities. It is easy to

* Preparation of this chapter was supported in part by Grant No. HD-07176 from the National Institute of Child Health and Human Development. I would like to thank Earl Hunt for his very helpful comments on an earlier draft of the chapter.

deduce that the reason mental tasks intercorrelate is that they all have one quality in common. This one quality is general intelligence ("g").

There are individuals whose patterns of abilities do not coincide with the usual correlations, however. For example, learning-disabled children perform poorly on certain mental tasks but average on most tasks. Other individuals perform exceptionally well at certain tasks but poorly or average on most tasks. It is easy to deduce from these ability discrepancies that mental abilities are conceived and develop independently from one another.

Thus, two disparate logical conclusions can be made easily. One is based on robust statistical findings, the other on consideration of relatively rare individuals. Much has been written about the robust statistical findings and about general intelligence. Little attention has been devoted, however, to the implications discrepant abilities hold for intelligence theory. It is the intent of this chapter to do so.

This chapter will focus on individuals who are of average or low general mental ability but perform exceptionally well on tasks involving specific abilities. It will also include discussion on phenomenal memorizers, whose abilities are surprising despite typically high intelligence. The chapter is organized in six sections. The first three deal with idiots savants, hyperlexics, and phenomenal memorizers, respectively. In each of these sections, general characteristics, literature, and theory pertaining to the particular group will be discussed. The fourth section integrates theories related to the three groups; the fifth section compares the applicability of "g" theories and independent abilities theories of intelligence to savant, hyperlexic, and phenomenal memory abilities; and the final section concludes the chapter.

IDIOTS SAVANTS

Characteristics

Idiots savants (referred to in this chapter as *savants*) are individuals who have a clearly outstanding ability or talent in spite of being mentally retarded and often autistic. Their talent or ability is far above that expected in nonretarded individuals. Hill (1974) reviewed the literature on savants from 1898 to 1974 and concluded that there were seven major categories of savant skills—calendar calculation, fine sensory discrimination, artistic talent, mechanical dexterity, musical talent, memorization of obscure facts, and mathematical ability. Other, less-common special abilities have also been reported, such as pseudoverbal, coordination and movement, sense of direction, "extrasensory perception," poetry writing, and knowledge of specific subjects (see Cain, 1970; Hermelin & O'Connor, 1983; Rimland, 1978). Further, savants may have more than one special ability. Rimland (1978) reported that multiple skills of autistic savants tended to cluster. Music and memory for obscure facts formed the most common combination in his sample.

Occurrence in the population. The prevalence of savants was estimated in the mid-1970s at .06% of mentally retarded people institutionalized at the time (Hill, 1977). Prevalence seems to be higher among autistic individuals, however, and has been estimated at 9.8% of autistic individuals (Rimland, 1978).

Most savants are male. Among savants institutionalized for mental retardation, the estimated ratio is near 6 males to 1 female (Hill, 1974). Among autistic savants, the ratio is near 3 males to 1 female—approximately the sex ratio in the autistic population (Rimland, 1978). Thus, savant abilities are linked with sex as well as with autism, but independently.

Etiology. Little data are available concerning the etiologies most commonly associated with savants. Hill (1978) suggested that, according to case report studies, brain injury may be the most common etiology, particularly if the injury occurred after a period of normal development. However, he noted that cases of savants with Down Syndrome, congenital syphilis, and other developmental causes of mental retardation have been reported.

Literature

Probably because of the low prevalence of savants, there are very few experimental studies of the cognitive strengths and weakness of savants that may contribute to their unusual abilities. Most of the literature consists of case studies and reviews of case studies. The present section reviews two types of studies—(a) those examining group strengths and weaknesses on psychometric tests, and (b) those investigating the process of calendar calculation in groups or individuals.

Psychometric Profile. Hill (cited in Rimland & Hill, 1984) compared WAIS subtest scores of 19 institutionalized savants with those of 111 retarded nonsavant individuals. Six savants were skilled in rote memory, five in calendar calculating, four in music, and four in art. Although the two groups were similar in Full Scale IQ, subtest scores were not all similar. Savants performed higher than nonsavants on Information, Arithmetic, Digit Span, and Block Design (presumably they performed lower on at least some of the remaining subtests, although this information is not available). Savants skilled in memory and calendar calculating tended to perform equally on Verbal and Performance scales. Those who were musically talented did better on the Verbal than the Performance scale, and those who were artistically talented did better on the Performance than the Verbal scales (Rimland & Hill, 1984). These results suggest a relationship between savant abilities and underlying ability patterns.

High performance on Digit Span by savants was also reported by Spitz and LaFontaine (1973). They found digit spans of savants to be comparable to those of a nonretarded control group, and to be significantly higher than an educable mentally retarded control group. Some case studies reported exceptionally high (Steele, Gorman, & Flexman, 1984) or average (Hill, 1975) digit span scores as well. Others, however, reported digit spans consistent with mental retardation (see Hermelin & O'Connor, 1983). It may be that good digit span performance is associated with some special abilities but not others. However, at this time there is not enough evidence available to make a distinction.

Calendar Calculation. Much of the savant literature is devoted to determining how some savants go about calculating calendar days. To be explained is the remarkable speed as well as the impeccable accuracy with which calendar calculators determine the day of the week of a given date in a given year. There are at least five possible methods by which one could calculate calendar dates. These will each be discussed briefly.

Calculation. One manner in which calendar dates could be determined is by executing complicated calculations aided by a table based on principles of a perpetual calendar. There is evidence suggesting that it is possible, through many hours of practice, for a person of normal intellectual ability to do this. In a study by Addis and Parsons (cited in Rimland, 1978), a graduate student was able to replicate the accuracy and eventually the speed with which "target" savants performed calendar calculation.

There are some difficulites with the calculation theory, as Hill (1978) pointed out. Most important (a) calender calculators typically perform poorly on tests of mathematical ability (Hill, 1975; Horwitz, Kestenbaum, Person, & Jarvik, 1965), suggesting that they would not be capable of complex mathematical computations; and (b) when questions are worded so as to be difficult to answer using the formula, accuracy does not break down and speed is not affected.

Calculation from a reference date. A related possible method of calendar calculation is using mathematical formulae as described above but to simplify the process by using an anchor or reference date. Experiments testing the reference date explanation look for (a) differences in accuracy or response time (RT) related to year, month, date, or day; and (b) decreased accuracy or increased RT for dates in leap years, which would need an additional mental operation to complete.

Hoffman (1971) found differences in accuracy and response time related to the year. His subject's accuracy was perfect, and RT "almost instantaneous," for dates in the years near testing, but they were less accurate and slower for dates in other years. Two leap years were represented, one of which showed a decrease in accuracy. However, this year was also in the future and may have been more difficult for that reason. Verbal report from the subject corroborated the anchor date explanation.

Hill (1975) tested one calender calculator on 168 dates on odd years between 1943 and 1969 (no leap years). There were few significant differences in accuracy or speed between days at the beginning and the end of the week or of the month, or between years. The only differences were due to poorer accuracy and speed in the years 1949 and 1969 (each of which began on a Wednesday) than in other years. Thus, there was some evidence of reference date use, but no particular reference date could be isolated.

O'Connor and Hermelin (1984) tested eight calender calculators on dates in several years in the past, present, and future. Responses were quickest and most accurate in the present year and increasingly slower and less accurate in years in the past or future. There was no RT difference, however, between the first, second, and third four months of the year. Thus, although the data suggest that the current year may have served as a reference, there was little support for a more specific reference date.

In perhaps the most complete investigation of the use of reference dates, Rosen (1981) studied two calendar calculators. He tested them on one randomly chosen date in each month in each of 16 years. RTs of the two subjects correlated significantly across dates. The RT variance shared by the two subjects was related to the year and month together (but to neither separately), indicating that what was similar about how the two subjects calculated involved the year and month. Because December had the fastest RT and perfect accuracy by both subjects, Rosen suggested that this month might have been used as a reference. In support of this hypothesis, he found that, for both subjects, the day of the week on which December 1 fell accounted for a significant proportion of total variance in RT. Rosen's results generally support the reference date explanation. However, contrary to the explanation, he found no systematic effects on accuracy or RT related to leap year.

Rote memory. A third possible method of calculating calendar dates is by using rote memory of dates and their corresponding days of the week. Some case studies reported subjects having good long-term memory (e.g., Rosen, 1981). This method is not well supported, however, because there are no investigations directly testing the role of rote memory in calendar calculating. Also, there would be no good explanation for more accurate calculating in current years than in past years or for the ability to calculate dates in the future.

Interest in dates. Also suggested by O'Connor and Hermelin (1984) is a method by which a strong interest in dates facilitates memory. For example, one of Horwitz et al.'s (1965) subjects reportedly spent hours at the age of 6 looking at an almanac that had a perpetual calendar printed in it. O'Connor and Hermelin, however, found no difference in savants' memory of a story involving dates and a story of a shipwreck.

Knowledge of the calendar. A final possible method of calendar calculation is the use of information about the regularities and irregularities of the calendar to figure dates. The only evidence supporting this explanation is anecdotal. For example, O'Connor and Hermelin's subjects made comments such as "April 1 and July 1 are the same day—on the same day" (O'Connor & Hermelin, 1984, p. 805). Both of Rosen's (1981) subjects displayed extensive knowledge of the calendar system. For example, they each knew that September and December always corresponded in the days of the week on which dates of the month fall.

Rosen (1981) suggested that his subjects "keyed off" from a certain day in December of a certain year, used their knowledge of the calendar, their good long-term memory and concentration, and simple calculations. His interpretation suggests that a search for one single method of calendar calculation may be misled.

Theoretical Explanations

Hill (1978) reviewed the major theories of savant phenomena (see also Goldberg, 1987). He presented two general types of theories, the first emphasizing the deficits of savants compared with everyday people and relating special abilities to these deficits, and the second emphasizing the special abilities of savants compared with other mentally retarded or developmentally disabled individuals and attempting to account for such unusual development. The theories discussed by Hill are discussed here. However, more recent perspectives have been added to the discussion to shed new light on theoretical distinctions. Assuming that humans have a finite potential for various mental tasks, and that this potential is more or less achieved with development and training, to be explained are (a) how savants are physiologically able to perform such outstanding feats, and (b) under what circumstances such potential can be developed. It should be noted that none of the existing theories has much data directly supporting it. This is not because a great deal of research has failed to support the theories; it is because direct tests of theories have not been carried out.

Comparisons with Nonretarded People.

Concrete thinking theory. Concrete thinking theory (see Hill, 1978) suggests that savants are individuals with essentially normal cognitive ability, but who have one deficiency—they are unable to think abstractly. It is this inability that makes them appear mentally retarded. To adapt to their limitation, they compensate with concrete thinking, usually employing rote or sensorimotor memory. Reinforcement of their displays of concrete thinking enhances development of a special skill.

There are two weaknesses of this theory. One is that it makes no suggestion about *why* savants might have impaired abstract thinking. Could such a defect occur normally in a proportion of the population? Could it be related to a genetic defect? Could it be related to brain damage? Nurcombe and Parker (1964) suggested that maternal or sensory deprivation, brain damage, or autism might cause the loss of abstract thinking for various psychodynamic reasons which they specify but which will not be discussed here (see also Rimland's, 1978, related ideas concerning abnormal attentional allocation in the next section).

A second criticism of concrete thinking theory that has been made is that it is not widely applicable. Though it may account for skills of some savants, there are numerous cases to which it does not easily apply. It suggests that special skills displayed by savants involve concrete thinking. Mechanical ability, calendar calculation, and memory of obscure facts may in fact involve concrete thinking, but artistic or musical ability probably involve abstract thinking to some extent. Savants have been described who displayed abstract thinking in limited areas. For example, Viscott (1970) described a musical savant who harmonized, improvised, and played in different composers' styles—she could think abstractly in the area of music but not in other areas. Also, Steel et al. (1984) discussed a mathematical savant who, though he could not reason linguistically, could reason mathematically.

Sensory deprivation theory. A second theory in this category is sensory deprivation theory. Hoffman (1971) suggested that development of a special skill is a stimulation-seeking activity resulting from the extreme isolation of institutions. He compared institutional isolation of mentally retarded individuals to that of prisoners in solitary confinement. In each case, there is a need to find mental stimulation that is lacking in the environment (autistic withdrawal constitutes an analagous type of isolation). Individuals' motivation to seek stimulation is channeled into certain responses, and there are few normal activities available to interfere. It is under these conditions that a special ability is developed to a phenomenal level.

This explanation is consistent with the compulsive nature of the behavior of some savants when engaged in their special talent (Jones, 1926; Steel et al., 1984) as well as with the co-occurrence of savant abilities and autism. However, it is difficult to believe that such complicated mental functions as calendar calculation could be performed by a mentally retarded person simply out of need for stimulation. In addition, sensory deprivation theory only considers the conditions under which a special ability might develop, and says little about how mentally retarded individuals are physiologically capable of outstanding abilities.

Procedural memory theory. Recently, Goldberg (1987) proposed a new theory of savant abilities. He suggested that savants' procedural memory systems are dysfunctional, whereas their declarative memory systems are relatively intact. Procedural memory involves sequences of actions (e.g., getting dressed), motor movements (e.g., riding a bicycle), and automatized functions (e.g., reciting the alphabet). Declarative memory involves retrieval of stored facts and knowledge. Procedural memory is believed to be located in the basal ganglia, and declarative memory in the diencephalic and bitemporal regions of the brain.

Goldberg noted that many savants have good retrieval of digits and word strings. However, adaptive action sequences such as dressing and washing are often disrupted, whereas maladaptive ones such as stereotypies and rituals are often present. Specifically, Goldberg suggested a dissociation of procedural and declarative memory—an inability to apply declarative knowledge to action sequences.

The theory is important because it explains (a) why savants often have abnormal behavior patterns, and (b) how discrepancies may exist in related abilities. However, many savant abilities involve procedural memory. Musical, artistic, and mechanical abilities certainly do, and calendar and lightning calculation probably do. Further, the theory does not explain the level of expertise at which savant abilities are expressed and, as Goldberg pointed out, why so many savants would develop the same skill (e.g., calendar calculating).

Compensation theory. Compensation theory holds that savants are individuals with uneven abilities and that they compensate for weak abilities by developing their strong abilities to expert levels. Lindsley (1965) compared this type of compensation with that occurring in blind people, who develop their hearing to very acute levels in order to compensate for their lack of sight.

He suggested that compensation could occur in individuals with uneven abilities because (a) the competition from other abilities for the individual's time and energy is minimized; (b) reinforcement becomes ineffective in other less successful domains, but becomes more effective in the special domain; (c) heavy reliance on the better abilities leads to increased discrimination in favored skills; (d) strong skills can be developed from an early age, because it is clear early in life which skills are strong; and (e) there are few behaviors that must be inhibited in order for the skill to blossom.

It is plausible that individuals have uneven abilities—that they could have better artistic ability than verbal ability, or better memory for obscure facts than conceptual understanding. It is also plausible that better abilities could be nurtured and developed (e.g., Lindsley, 1965; Morishima, 1974). Even in regard to calendar calculating, it is plausible that some individuals may have better—whatever abilities underly calendar calculating—than other abilities. But who knows how individuals discover they have such a skill in order to display it, be reinforced for it, and nurture and develop it?

A more biologically based view of compensation was presented by Selfe (1977). She pointed out that "if one area [of the brain] is destroyed neuronal connections can be established which can mediate a certain function in another area of the brain" (Selfe, 1977, p. 128). She suggested that, in the case one young autistic artist, damage to the parietal lobe language function may have adaptively caused increased development of her perceptual system. However, few language-impaired children display such artistic ability. There must have been some other important characteristic of this savant that distinguished her from other language-impaired autistic children.

Comparisons with Nonsavant Retarded People.

Genetic theory. The second type of theory compares savants with other mentally retarded individuals and tries to explain how retarded and/or autistic people could display such talents. Genetic theory states that savants are simply the rare individuals who, due to genetic predisposition, fall at the low extreme of the intelligence continuum and at the same time at the high extreme of the continuum for a specific ability. Their unique patterns of abilities are the manifestation of this unusual endowment. For example, suppose musical talent is a trait genetically transmitted independently of intelligence. A musical savant might then be a person who inherited both low general intelligence and high musical ability. The theory assumes that to realize a genetically based talent does not require average intelligence.

If genetic theory holds, then we would expect to find other incidences of artistic ability in the families of artistic savants, mathematical talent in the families of mathematical savants, and so on. We would also expect mental retardation in families of savants. Calendar calculation has been identified in identical male twins (Horwitz et al., 1965) as well as in a paternal uncle (cited from Hill, 1978). Surprisingly, little is known about instances of mental retardation in families of savants.

The frequency of brain damage among savants, however, suggests that it is more likely that mental retardation concurrent with talent results from brain injury on top of genetic endowment or from unique patterns of brain injury. The case of a mechanical savant who barely could read and write his own name but could take apart and rebuild multigear bicycles (Brink, 1980) illustrates this position. The savant may have had a genetic predisposition toward mechanics, since his father had outstanding mechanical ability. His history revealed that he had normal intelligence until a gunshot wound damaged his left cerebral hemisphere. He lost left hemisphere functions related to verbal, calculative, and abstract thinking skills, but retained right hemisphere functions of motor learning, visualization, and spatial ability. Brink suggested that the subject's savant pattern of abilities was the result of genetic endowment for mechanical ability along with the loss of left brain functioning.

Steel et al. (1984) described an autistic individual brain damaged at birth who had an overall IQ of 91 but had very discrepant and savant-like abilities. In spite of retarded adaptive behavior and verbal abstract ability, the savant had exceptional mathematical ability. His intelligence test subtest scores ranged on an IQ-equivalent scale from 40 (Similarities and Differences, Free Recall, Painted Cubes) to 160 (Digit Span). Neurological testing and behavioral signs strongly suggested impairment of the frontal lobe and verbal abstract ability. Also, highly developed posterior hemisphere function was implied on the basis of high scores on tests measuring mathematical/spatial ability.

Unfortunately, little information is provided about the intellectual ability of the savant's parents or siblings. It is possible that he would have been highly intelligent or mathematically inclined by genetic endowment, but specific damage to his frontal lobe left him autistic and impaired in several mental capacities. In his odd, autistic way he incessantly made up math problems and solved them, thereby exercising and strengthening one of the outstanding abilities he had at his disposal.

Memory theory. Memory theory and concentration theory (discussed next) both postulate the existence of specific mechanisms that would allow development of a savant ability in a mentally retarded person.

Spitz and LaFontaine (1973) suggested that inherited special abilities of savants may be allowed to develop by way of unimpaired immediate memory. As already mentioned, there is some evidence for normal or superior short-term memory functioning in savants as measured by digit span tests (Spitz & LaFontaine, 1973; Steel et al., 1984).

Alternately, savants could be capable of their feats because they are capable of eidetic imagery, or photographic memory. In spite of studies reporting higher incidences of eidetic imagery in brain-injured mentally retarded individuals than in the general population (Giray, Altkin, & Barclay, 1976; Siipola & Hayden, 1965; Symmes, 1971; cf. Richardson & Cant, 1970), there is little evidence for this explanation other than scattered case studies. Also, some case studies have systematically rejected the hypothesis of eidetic imagery (e.g., Hill, 1975).

Concentration theory. Hill (1978) described a concentration theory that he said was not a theory at all, but rather a necessary condition for the development of a savant ability. He noted that savants tend to concentrate for hours and hours on their special capacity, and that, because of the intense concentration, they learn something.

Rimland (1978) offered a more sophisticated theory of concentration or attention. He suggested that, along with whatever other intellectual characteristics savants have, they have a biochemically mediated abnormal attentional allocation. This abnormality causes savants to devote an inordinate amount of attention to physical attributes of stimuli and extremely little attention to the more conceptual or abstract aspects of stimuli. In Rimland's words, they have an abnormal tendency to "fine tune." In fact, they are virtually unable to detach attention from certain stimuli or topics. Because of their attention to concrete aspects of stimuli, and their tendency to concentrate, they develop abilities to high levels utilizing concrete aspects of stimuli. Concrete aspects of stimuli are utilized in any mechanical or rote abilities.

This theory accounts for the phenomenal fidelity to form and detail present in the artwork, music, and memorization of savants, but not for ability to compose music (Rimland, 1978) or create abstract artistic designs (Lindsley, 1965). Yet to be elaborated in this theory is a hypothetical biochemical mechanism that would result in such abnormal attentional allocation. Rimland suggested the reticular formation as a possible target area, but did not specify a hypothetical mechanism.

HYPERLEXICS

Characteristics

Hyperlexic children display an ability to read words in isolation at a level substantially higher than their typically low level of general verbal functioning (Silberberg & Silberberg, 1967). Often this reading ability is acquired between 2 and 4 years of age without instruction.

Along with unexplained superior word recognition, hyperlexic children usually have a language-related deficiency, including disturbance of expressive or receptive spoken language (Healy, Aram, Horowitz, & Kessler, 1982), and poor comprehension of written material (Graziani, Brodsky, Mason, & Zager, 1983; Healy, 1982; Healy et al., 1982; Richman & Kitchell, 1981). Thus, hyperlexic children excel in reading recognition despite various forms of verbal deficit.

In addition, several case studies reported high spelling proficiency (deHirsch, 1971; Mehegan & Dreifuss, 1972; Silberberg & Silberberg, 1968) and number recognition ability (Graziani et al., 1983; Healy, 1982) accompanying hyperlexia (but see Siegel, 1984). Behavioral abnormalities also usually exist, such as hyperactivity, echolalia, and autistic characteristics.

Occurrence in the population. No attempts have been made to determine the prevalence of hyperlexia in the general population. Two studies reported the prevalence of hyperlexia in inpatient or outpatient hospital populations, however. Whitehouse and Harris (1984) found one hyperlexic for every 750 children treated at a hospital, and one for every three autistic children. Cobrinik (1974) reported identifying as hyperlexic "less than 10%" of all seriously disturbed children in residence at a children's hospital.

Most hyperlexic children are boys. Combining studies involving samples of eight or more hyperlexic subjects, the ratio of boys to girls in study samples is 9.0 to 1. Elsewhere it has been estimated at about 10 to 1 (Goldberg, 1987). In addition, hyperlexia has been observed in brothers (Healy et al., 1982; Silberberg & Silberberg, 1967; Whitehouse & Harris, 1984) and in male twins (Silberberg & Silberberg, 1967).

Etiology. Because of the sex ratio of hyperlexics and the existence of hyperlexic brothers and male twins, it has been suggested that hyperlexia may be a genetic abnormality, possibly x-linked (Healy, 1982; Healy et al., 1982; Whitehouse & Harris, 1984). Adding to the circumstantial genetic evidence, Healy et al. reported that there was evidence of language or learning problems related to reading in the immediate paternal relatives of 11 of 12 subjects and in male or female siblings of seven subjects.

There is also evidence that hyperlexia may be related to organically based abnormalities. Besides being found in autistic children (Cobrinik, 1974; Frith & Snowling, 1983; Snowling & Frith, 1986; Welsh, Pennington, & Rogers, 1987; Whitehouse & Harris, 1984), hyperlexia has been found in brain damaged children (Mehegan & Dreifuss, 1972), in children who have severe developmental language disorder (Richman & Kitchell, 1981; Welsh, Pennington, & Rogers, 1987), and in children in whom other neurological conditions exist. For example, Mehegan and Driefuss (1972) found labor or delivery complications in 6 of 12 of the children they studied (see also Huttenlocher & Huttenlocher, 1973), abnormal cranial configurations in 4 of 12, and abnormal neurological examinations of all children, with signs including hyperactivity, abnormal movements and tics, and lack of hand domination (see also Elliott & Needleman, 1976; Graziani et al., 1983). However, it is also evident that extremely advanced and precocious word reading occurs in children without neurological complications or brain damage (e.g., Pennington, Johnson, & Welsh, 1987).

The Syndrome

Research with hyperlexic children has indicated that these children have several characteristics in common besides their word reading. Healy and her colleagues have led others in discussing hyperlexia as a syndrome including exceptional word reading, disordered language and cognitive ability, and behavioral abnormalities.

Word reading ability. The major identifying characteristic of the syndrome, of course, is exceptional word reading. There is spontaneous and intense early interest in letters and words resulting in the development of extensive word recognition prior to age 5. The ability to read words is usually well above that expected for the child's general ability level and is often done in a compulsive and ritualistic manner (Mehegan & Dreifuss, 1972; Huttenlocher & Huttenlocher, 1973). Until recently, no systematic discrepancy criterion has been established, and two to three grade levels above the grade level expected for age and general ability has been used as an acceptable criterion (e.g., Richman & Kitchell, 1981; Silberberg & Silberberg, 1968). Recently, however, a reading quotient criterion has been established, which is a proportion of a reading age score (based on single-word reading) to mental age (Pennington et al., 1987; Welsh et al., 1987). Paralleling criteria for identifying dyslexics, the criterion for hyperlexia is .20 over the expected proportion, or 1.20.

Language skills. Second, there are disordered language processes. Deficiencies may occur in spoken and written language.

Spoken language. One type of language skill deficient in hyperlexics is spoken language. Of 22 published case and group studies on hyperlexia reviewed for this chapter, 20 mentioned disturbance of spoken language—either expressive or receptive or both—as a common characteristic of the subjects (for a review of case studies, see Goldberg, 1987). Some subjects had complete absence of speech (Elliott & Needleman, 1976; Mehegan & Dreifuss, 1972) or complete absence followed by emergence of full language capacity (Cobrinik, 1974). Most commonly, expressive speech was virtually limited to echolalia (e.g., Cobrinik, 1974 [5 of 6 cases]; Goldberg & Rothermal, 1984 [8 of 8 cases]; Healy et al., 1982 [9 of 12 cases]; Huttenlocher & Huttenlocher, 1973 [2 of 3 cases]. Still others showed dysnomia (Welsh et al., 1987) or little understanding of spoken language (Cobrinik, 1974).

Healy et al. (1982) measured several types of language functioning in 12 hyperlexic children aged 5 to 11. Language measures included the following subtests of the Test of Language Development—Picture Vocabulary (point to the picture corresponding to a spoken word), Grammatic Understanding (read a word or sentence and match it with a picture), Oral Vocabulary (define simple words), Grammatic Completion (complete a sentence with a syntactically correct word), and Sentence Imitation (repeat a sentence verbatim). As a group, hyperlexic children performed 1.3 to 1.9 SD below average on each subtest (mean −1.6 SD across subtests). Thus, the general ability to deal with language was substantially below average in this sample. This level of proficiency, however, is about the same as would be expected on the basis of the children's overall ability scores (about −1.7 SD).

Written language. Comprehension of written language, or reading comprehension, has also been identified as an area of weakness in hyperlexics. On standardized reading comprehension tests, hyperlexics in several studies scored at or below the expected level, but nowhere near their reading recognition level (Graziani et al., 1983; Healy, 1982; Healy et al., 1982; Richman & Kitchell, 1981).

Frith and Snowling (Frith & Snowling, 1983; Snowling & Frith, 1986) studied several comprehension processes in autistic and nonautistic hyperlexics. Their purpose was to determine exactly what aspects of reading comprehension posed a problem for hyperlexics. Their research found no evidence for specific deficits in utilizing syntactic information (see also Goldberg & Rothermal, 1984) or accessing meanings of individual words (see also Goldberg & Rothermal, 1984; Welsh et al., 1987). The reading comprehension deficits that were found involved using semantic context and integrating story information with existing knowledge.

Frith and Snowling's (1983) sample included eight autistic hyperlexics and 10 normal readers matched for word reading ability. Half of the hyperlexics had average intelligence, but all of them had language-related cognitive deficits. In spite of the reading age match, comparison subjects were as a group slightly younger than hyperlexics.

In their study, two experiments indicated that hyperlexics have difficulty using semantic sentence context for comprehension. In the first, subjects were asked to read paragraphs containing homographs—words that have two different pronunciations corresponding to two different meanings (e.g., *bow* and *bow*). Hyperlexic children made more errors on homographs than did comparison readers, tending to pronounce words according to their most frequent pronunciation regardless of sentence context. The results were replicated within a low verbal ability group in a study comparing nonautistic hyperlexics with autistic hyperlexics and reading level comparison subjects (Snowling & Frith, 1986).

In another experiment, hyperlexics performed worse than reading controls in a cloze task that required completing sentences by filling in blanks with words as well as in a cloze-type story task (see Siegel, 1984, for a similar finding). In this task, stories were provided with some words missing. Subjects chose, from three alternatives, the word that best fit the context. The alternatives all were plausible syntactically, but only one was plausible semantically.

In the authors' replication of the story task (Snowling & Frith, 1986), two of the three alternatives were semantically as well as syntactically plausible. However, one was plausible only in the context of the sentence, and the other was plausible in the context of the sentence as well as in the larger context of the story. In the low verbal ability group, autistic and nonautistic hyperlexics performed more poorly than normal readers.

Finally, Snowling and Frith (1986) examined integration of text with existing knowledge. Children read stories and then answered questions on facts specific to the story and questions that could only be answered by using existing knowledge alone or in combination with story facts. In the low-ability group, hyperlexics performed worse than nonhyperlexics.

It is important to note that, in Snowling and Frith's (1986) study, there were no differences in utilization of semantic context or application of prior knowledge to story information for subjects high in verbal ability. This may imply division on which hyperlexics can be subtyped, or, as the authors point out, it may suggest that the "true" hyperlexics are those with low verbal ability.

Behavioral Abnormalities. Hyperlexia is also usually accompanied by behavioral abnormalities of some kind, such as autistic withdrawal, hyperkinesis, and stereotypy. As previously stated, there is a higher incidence of hyperlexia among autistic children than among nonautistic children. Even among hyperlexics not identified as autistic, social withdrawal and problems with interpersonal relationships are prevalent. For example, all of Healy's 12 subjects had problems with interpersonal relationships.

Hyperactivity is at least as prevalent among hyperlexics as autistic withdrawal. For example, five of Richman and Kitchell's (1981) ten subjects were originally referred for psychological services for hyperactivity, distractibility, or inattention. All of Mehegan and Dreifuss' (1972) 11 subjects, all of Huttenlocher and Huttenlocher's (1973) three cases, and half of Goldberg and Rothermal's (1984) eight subjects had signs of hyperkenesis, distractibility, or short attention span (see also Elliott & Needleman, 1976).

Stereotypy was noted in a few reports—bouncing, whirling, hand and arm flapping (Healy, 1982), pacing and waving (Mehegan & Dreifuss, 1972), and fingering surfaces (Cobrinik, 1974). Other deviant behavior reported includes self-injurious behavior such as head banging and self-biting (Cobrinik, 1974; Goldberg & Rothermal, 1984; Siegel, 1984) and violent outbursts (Cobrinik, 1974; Goldberg & Rothermal, 1984; Mehegan & Dreifuss, 1972).

Underlying Abilities

A large portion of the hyperlexia literature had been devoted to examining the abilities that would manifest in exceptional reading recognition. A couple of studies examined memory in hyperlexics. A greater number of studies, however, bear on the distinction between phonological and orthographic processing in word reading. A popular model of reading holds that normal readers use a combination of at least two and possibly three processing routes to gain meaning from print. The phonological route involves "sounding out"—mapping grapheme–sound correspondance to come up with a pronounceable word which is then referred to an internal lexicon for meaning. The orthographic route does not involve sounding out, but instead associating or matching the visual pattern of letters of a word with a pronounceable word or word segment which is then referred to the lexicon. The semantic route, believed less common, involves making a direct association between the pattern of letters in a word and its meaning. Recently, this theory has been criticized (e.g., Humphreys & Evett, 1985), and other models have gained attention, but phonological and orthographic skills are still believed to underly reading skill. Research indicates that, despite low intelligence, hyperlexics probably have both phonological and orthographic skills at least as readily available to them as they are to individuals of average intelligence.

Phonological Processing. Evidence for intact and perhaps superior phonological processing by hyperlexics has been amassed in two ways. The first is by examining pseudoword reading or nonword reading. The second is by error analysis of oral reading.

Four different studies investigated nonword reading, two of which used standardized tests. Using the Reading of Symbols subtest of the Goldman-Fristoe-Woodcock Auditory Skills Test Battery (GFW), Healy and her colleagues (Healy, 1982; Healy et al., 1982) found that 9 of 12 subjects scored at or above their age-appropriate grade level, and four of these scored three to five grades ahead. The remaining three subjects scored one grade below their age-appropriate grade level, at a level consistent with their general ability. Using the Woodcock Word Attack subtest, Welsh and her associates (Welsh et al., 1987) found that each of five children performed at a level higher than his or her general intelligence and consistent with his or her single-word reading.

The other two studies used laboratory nonword reading tasks. Frith and Snowling (1983) found no significant difference in nonword reading accuracy between hyperlexics and reading-matched controls. The fact that there was no difference suggests that hyperlexics' phonological coding was at a level consistent with their exceptional word reading.

Also, hyperlexics showed the same superiority in reading regular words over irregular words showed by normal readers, which suggests a dependence to some extent on phonological processes.

Goldberg and Rothermal (1984) used several nonword reading tasks. The first required subjects to read one and two syllable nonwords. Subjects demonstrated their phonological skill by reading an average of 55% correctly. In a second task, subjects read a nonword, and then the experimenter said four nonwords from which subjects chose the one that was the same as the written word. Five of the eight subjects performed well, with about 75% of items correct. However, the other three could not perform the task at all. In a third task, the experimenter said a nonword and the subjects indicated which of four written words corresponded. All subjects were able to do this, and the accuracy rate was about 66%.

In still another nonword task, subjects read a pseudohomophone—a nonword that sounds the same as a real word—and chose the correct pictorial analogue out of four alternatives. Subjects averaged about four out of every seven correct.

The Healy, Welsh et al., and Goldberg and Rothermal studies all reported error analyses of oral reading. Again, Healy used a standardized test—the Reading Miscue Inventory—in which children read aloud fourth-, seventh-, and twelfth-grade text passages. When errors were analyzed in terms of graphic relationships to the correct words, 67.6% were classified as high graphic similarity (e.g., *and* for *any*) as opposed to medium and low graphic similarity. When errors were analyzed in terms of sound relationships to the correct words, 63.6% involved confusions of high sound similarity (e.g., *Annie* for *any*) as opposed to medium and low sound similarity. Errors related to semantic confusions were very rare. The pattern of errors indicated that subjects were using orthographic processing and phonological processing to read words.

The Welsh study results showed that the greatest number of errors that were classifiable were coded as phonological, followed by visual, followed by semantic (only .03 for one subject). However, Goldberg and Rothermal reported more visual than phonological errors in their tasks. In any case, error analyses indicated the use of both phonological and orthographic processing. Emphasis on one or the other is what distinguishes study results.

Results from three other tasks administered by Goldberg and Rothermal (1984) indicate that hyperlexics are effective in phonological processing. In one task, the authors paired words that used the same grapheme clusters to represent different sounds, such as *march* and *monarch*. On the average, hyperlexics read only three word pairs out of 10 correctly (most often missing the exception word), suggesting that they were primarily dependent on a phonological rule-based process. There is an alternate explanation, however, that subjects were simply not familiar with the irregular words they were asked to read. However, their errors consisted mostly of misapplication of phonological rules (.57) rather than visual confusions (.24). It should be noted, however, that some subjects did read word pairs in spite of their inconsistent grapheme–sound correspondences, which suggests such subjects were using orthographic as well as phonological processes.

Goldberg and Rothermal also found that subjects' word reading was generally not disturbed by changes in visual appearance of words by horizontal misalignment of letters, inconsistent case, inconsistent spacing of letters, and unusual orientation (e.g., vertical). Only when plusses were inserted between letters did reading accuracy suffer (about 33% vs. about 83%). These results may indicate the relative unimportance of the visual pattern of the word relative to the phonological processing strength of hyperlexics (unless the appearance of words is changed drastically enough to break the flow of attention necessary for phonological processing). They may also indicate that hyperlexics' orthographic processing is abstract and flexible.

Finally, in another Goldberg and Rothermal task, subjects were given a target word and three alternative words, each of which was either orthographically similar, phonetically similar, or semantically similar. Subjects chose the word that was most "like" the target. They chose phonetically similar words most often, but the difference among type did not quite reach significance.

Orthographic processing. If hyperlexics read words well primarily because their orthographic processes are well developed, (a) word familiarity would make a difference in their reading accuracy; (b) irregularly spelled words would not necessarily pose a problem; and (c) they might be good at pattern recognition tasks in general. There is evidence for all three of these.

Goldberg and Rothermal (1984) found that their subjects read high-frequency words better than low-frequency words, suggesting that word familiarity is related to hyperlexics' reading ability. Further, when meaningful, errors on this task consisted mostly of visual (orthographic) confusions rather than phonological confusions. The results of this error analysis were replicated in another test of long vs. short words.

In another task that measured orthographic skill, words with irregular spellings posed little difficulty for hyperlexics, who had a success rate of about 75%. If subjects were using primarily phonological processing to read the irregular words, they would miss most all of them. In Welsh et al.'s study, however, all hyperlexics read more regular than irregular words (as well as more consistent than inconsistent words) accurately, suggesting that phonological processing was dominant. Both studies, though, show evidence of the capability of hyperlexics to process words orthographically, even if it is not the preferred or stronger skill.

Cobrinik (1982) demonstrated that hyperlexics may have exceptional visual processing skills, allowing them to quickly synthesize parts of stimulus and then process the whole. Hyperlexics might quickly synthesize letters into a word and then process the word as an orthographic unit.

He compared the performance of five mentally retarded and emotionally disturbed hyperlexics 9 to 13 years of age with that of nonretarded nonhyperlexic children of the same age on a task in which subjects read degraded words. Two lists of the same 14 familiar words were made up. In one list the words were complete; in the other they were degraded by deleting identifying aspects of letters. The complete words were paired with words similar in structure for use in a priming procedure. These intact words were presented first, and subjects were asked to read them. Then, the degraded words were presented, and subjects were asked to read them. The priming procedure served to increase subjects' probability of identifying the degraded words. The use of structurally similar words in the priming procedure was meant to "discourage premature recognition on the basis of superficial detail" (Cobrinik, 1982, p. 573).

Hyperlexics read significantly more words within the allowed 15-second time segments, and also read more words within 1 second. On words in which misperceptions were made, hyperlexics made only one error for every nine errors made by comparison subjects. Because misperceptions indicate an analytic approach to word decoding, Cobrinik suggested that hyperlexics process visual stimuli globally (they tried to decipher the entire word as a whole), whereas most children in this age range process analytically (they tried to decipher letter by letter). Compelling though this explanation may be, it cannot account for the ability of hyperlexics to read nonsense words they have never seen before and which they would have to sound out letter by letter.

Although the literature on phonological and orthographic processing by hyperlexics is not crystal clear, reasonable conclusions can be made. Goldberg and Rothermal (1984) suggested that hyperlexics have both phonological and orthographic routes available to them. Whether errors tend to be of the visual or phonological type probably depends on task characteristics (e.g., contrast their nonword task with their inconsistent pairs task). It is possible that some hyperlexics depend on one processing route more than the other, or that some use one route exclusively, whereas others may use the other. Also, it is possible that early accurate word reading results in good phonological and orthographic skill in hyperlexics, instead of (or in addition to) the inverse (see Wagner & Torgusen, 1987). Most evident is that better-than-expected phonological AND/OR orthographic processing skills accompany hyperlexic reading.

Memory. A final cognitive ability that has been investigated as an underlying ability related to hyperlexia is memory. There is evidence that, relative to their general intelligence, hyperlexics have superior memory for sound–symbol relationships and for unrelated items, but not superior recognition memory or memory for sentences.

Kistner, Robbins, and Haskett (1988) hypothesized that underlying hyperlexics' well-developed phonological coding was superior memory for sound–symbol relationships. They found that four hyperlexics all scored substantially higher than their IQs on two relevent subtests of the GFW. One of these subtests (Sound–Symbol Association) provides verbal nonsense labels for abstract visual symbols and then requires children, either immediately or after a delay, to pick out the symbol corresponding to a label given by the tester. The second subtest (Visual–Auditory Learning) requires the sequential memorization of English verbal labels for novel symbols which, when "decoded," form a sentence. In this study there was no evidence of exceptional performance on the Memory for Sentences subtest or the Recognition Memory Test subtest.

Three studies showed the strength of hyperlexics in rote or repetition memory. First, in the Kistner et al. (1988) study just discussed, subjects performed at a level higher than their IQs on the Numbers Reversed subtest of the GFW.

Second, Richman and Kitchell (1981) tested repetition memory using the Hiskey-Nebraska Test of Learning Aptitude and compared it with IQ. Repetition memory subtests included Bead Patterns, Memory for Colors, and Visual Attention Span (choose a series of pictures from memory). They found that repetition memory was higher than IQ. In addition, in a control group comparison, hyperlexics significantly outperformed age-matched nonhyperlexic controls on the Rey Auditory Learning Test, which requires learning a list of 15 words over five trials.

Finally, Healy et al. (1982) found that McCarthy Scale of Children's Abilities subtests that measured repetition memory—Pictorial Memory, Tapping Sequence, Verbal Memory I, and Numerical Memory I and II—were all relative group strengths except Verbal Memory I, which was a relative weakness. It consisted of two parts—repeating words and repeating sentences. Though subjects repeated words well, they repeated sentences poorly enough to lower their subtest scores. Thus, when memory could have been aided by comprehension, subjects performed poorly. Performance discrepancies between memory for unrelated items and memory for sentences were also seen in the Kistner et al. (1988) study.

Theoretical Explanations

Cobrinik (1974) described three types of theoretical explanations accounting for the discrepant abilities of hyperlexics—(a) psychodynamic/experiential, (b) plasticity, and (c) deficit. According to Cobrinik, psychodynamic explanations would implicate causes such as parental pressure, "attempts to achieve mastery through circumscribed activity, and the conjunction of a significant dynamic event and the origin of a given ability" (Cobrinik, 1974, p. 164). Plasticity theories are based on the assumptions that lag and acceleration may exist within the same individual, that wide interindividual variability exists, and that various abilities may develop independently of one another. Deficit theories attempt to explain isolated word reading abilities within the context of deficit. Plasticity and deficit theories will each be described, as well as theories that combine the two orientations. Readers interested in psychoanalytic theory are referred to Cain (1970).

Plasticity. At least three authors have offered theoretical explanations of hyperlexic abilities that rest on the assumption that abilities can develop at different rates and to different levels. These authors have said little about the literature in the normal population showing robust correlation among mental ability measures.

Physiological variant. The simplest of the plasticity explanations is that of Silberberg and Silberberg (1968, 1971). They suggested that word calling is an ability independent of verbal comprehension or intelligence and, like intelligence, is distributed normally in the population. Those at the low end of the word-calling continuum whose intelligence is average or above average are labeled dyslexic. Those at the high end of the word calling continuum whose intelligence is low or average are labeled hyperlexic.

To test this contention, the Silberbergs collected WISC verbal IQ scores and reading recognition scores from 97 third graders (Silberberg, Iverson, & Silberberg, 1969). They found that most children's word reading scores were near their verbal IQ scores. However, a proportion of children scored exceptionally low on reading in comparison to their verbal IQ scores, and a similar proportion scored exceptionally high on reading in comparison with their verbal IQ scores. It should be pointed out that the data do not suggest two completely independent distributions—there was a correlation of .32 between reading recognition and verbal IQ. However, a parallel was drawn between hyperlexia and dyslexia.

The Silberbergs adopted the simplest, most obvious explanation of hyperlexic abilities. The explanation falls short, not because it is simple, but because it raises more questions than it answers. For example, if verbal intelligence and word reading ability are each independently normally distributed in the population, then why do the two correlate? If word reading ability is independent of verbal intelligence, then wouldn't other (complex) abilities be independent of verbal intelligence as well? For example, other abilities requiring similar mental processes? The Silberbergs' early "hyperlexic" subjects did not have all of the characteristics of the hyperlexia syndrome identified in later research, and it is possible that the Silberbergs were referring to children essentially different from those referred to in later work.

Accelerated skills. Elliott and Needleman (1976) contended that it is a specific heightened ability to deal with linguistic symbols (phonological skill) that allows hyperlexics to read words. They used terms such as *super ability* and *hyperdevelopment* to describe word reading, which they suggested is the product of a specific innate capacity for dealing with linguistic symbols. They contended that ability to recognize written words and translate them into spoken words is not merely intact, but is in fact superior. Evidence from studies of nonword reading support this notion (Frith & Snowling, 1983; Healy, 1982; Healy et al., 1982). However, phonological skill is not the only one at which hyperlexics are advanced (see Cobrinik, 1982; Kistner et al., 1988; Richman & Kitchell, 1981).

Deficit explanation: specific language deficit. The most detailed deficit explanation was put forth by Huttenlocher and Huttenlocher (1973). Their theory suggested that hyperlexia represents a developmental difficulty in associating speech sounds with meaning. It was based on the observation that hyperlexics could (a) recognize and retain speech sounds and relate them to words, and (b) identify letter groups and translate them to spoken words. However, they seemed unable to associate the spoken word with the concept represented by the word.

The theory suggested that a defect in word comprehension makes hyperlexics look retarded in most cognitive activities. However, in cognitive activities not requiring association of spoken word with meaning, they are "normal." Remember that hyperlexia is defined (in part) by reading recognition far beyond one's own general intellectual ability level, not necessarily far beyond the ability of most people. According to the Huttenlochers' theory, hyperlexics develop these "normal" abilities to a special level because they are among the few skills available to them.

According to the theory, hyperlexics should perform as well as intellectually average children on tasks requiring no verbal instructions and no association of spoken words with meaning.

The Huttenlochers found that a similar symptom configuration can be found in brain-injured adults whose speech/language areas are intact, but whose (parietal) cortex is lesioned (see also Mehegan & Dreifuss, 1972). They suggested that hyperlexia may be an abnormality in development of parietal lobe function, probably a "subtle defect in the formation of connections in parietal lobes, and possibly in other cortical areas" (Huttenlocher & Huttenlocher, 1973, p. 1114). The defect probably has several causes resulting in a similar group of symptoms (e.g., x-linked genetic defect, perinatal, or postnatal injury).

Two important weakness of the Huttenlochers' theory must be recognized. First, it is based on the assumption that hyperlexics have little comprehension of individual words. Snowling and Frith (1986) have since shown that hyperlexics can access word meanings similarly to nonhyperlexics (see also Goldberg & Rothermal, 1984), and that their comprehension deficit probably lies at the phrase or story level rather than the word level. These new findings considered, however, the Huttenlochers' theory need only be slightly revised.

Another flaw in the theory was discussed by Elliott and Needleman. Elliott and Needleman questioned why children would be fascinated with reading when they could play or do other things. For example, they could use other abilities available to them (those not requiring association of spoken word with meaning).

Combination Theories

Specific language deficit with superior abilities. Three explanations of hyperlexic abilities combine the plasticity and the deficit theoretical approaches. Richman and Kitchell (1981), for example, suggested, as the Huttenlochers did, that hyperlexia results from a specific form of language disorder—one in which only verbal associative ability is impaired. Because verbal associative ability is central to intellectual functioning, many other abilities seem impaired as well. Language abilities related to word calling, however, are not impaired. These abilities are developed to an elevated level because they provide a source of reinforcement and satisfaction for the individual. Unlike the Huttenlochers, Richman and Kitchell also suggested that the specific language disorder is accompanied by superior isolated memory (visual memory and paired-associate learning), since their hyperlexics outperformed normal children on an auditory memory task.

Behavior disorder with superior abilities. Whitehouse and Harris (1984) suggested that hyperlexic children are developmentally disabled children who have (a) good audiovisual association ability (phonological skill), (b) good memory, and (c) a particular behavioral phenotype expressed as a compulsion to utilize written material. They stress the behavioral disorder, noting that compared with younger subjects, older subjects showed less compulsion toward written material as well as diminished (but still relatively high) word recognition.

PHENOMENAL MEMORIZERS

Phenomenal memorizers are individuals who display feats of memory far beyond those displayed by the average person. They have average or above-average intelligence and may or may not excel in other areas of mental activity. Their memories may be exceptional in capacity or in structure.

Research on phenomenal memorizers is even less common than research on savants and hyperlexics. Only cases studies exist, and many conclusions are based on verbal reports of the subject. More recent accounts have used experimental procedures in addition to verbal reports in order to obtain more detailed and objective information. Case studies of four phenomenal memorizers are discussed, although others exist that are not discussed in detail in this chapter (see Ericsson, 1985, for a comprehensive review).

Case 1: S

Characteristics. The most famous memorizer is S, who was described by Luria (1968). S grew up in a small Russian Jewish community around the turn of the 20th century. He had many siblings, some of whom were intellectually gifted. His father and mother displayed good memory for specific information, and his nephew reportedly also had remarkable memory. As a child he demonstrated musical talent and was sent to a special music school. He would have been a violinist by profession had he not experienced hearing loss after an illness. Instead he became a newspaper reporter. He impressed his editor by repeating the assignments for all of the reporters. It was his editor who first noted S's amazing memory and sent him to Luria's lab to have his memory tested. S eventually became a professional mnemonicist, earning his living by displaying his memory.

Luria set out to find the limits of S's memory only to find that it seemed to have no limits. S could repeat up to seventy items (numbers, words, letters, nonsense words) presented orally or in written form without error, backward or forward, and could give the item preceding or following any other item. Upon subsequent testing, it seemed his memory had limitless duration (at least 16 years).

In spite of S's exceptional ability, he had areas of cognitive deficiency. For example, he complained he had a poor memory for faces, he demonstrated poor story or paragraph comprehension, and he had difficulty with certain aspects of language (metaphors, synonyms, homonyms) as well as with abstract thinking.

Explanations. According to Luria, S's phenomenal memory was characterized by three qualities—(a) eidetic imagery, (b) synesthesia, and (c) mental manipulations. His memory was qualitatively different from that of most people.

Eidetic imagery. Luria concluded that S used eidetic imagery in recalling tables of numbers. According to S's verbal reports, he continued to see matrices he was asked to memorize, and then read them out.

Corroborating S's verbal reports is his performance on a 52-digit matrix. Not only was S able to produce the entire matrix without error, he was also able to produce without error missing numbers, missing series of numbers in reverse order, vertical rows, diagonals, and a multidigit number formed from all the digits in the matrix. Also, it took about the same amount of time to recall digits in vertical rows (40 seconds) as it took to recall in horizontal rows (50 seconds). It also took about the same time to recall the second vertical column from top to bottom (25 seconds) as it took to recall the same column from bottom to top (30 seconds). It was apparent that S did not use a memory strategy that utilized sequential order of the numbers.

It was also apparent that S did not use obvious logical methods of recall. When he was given lists of words to remember containing several types of birds or liquids, he did not categorize or cluster words to aid recall as most people would. Although he recalled the words with perfect accuracy, he did not even notice the category clusters until after recall. When he was given a table of logically ordered numbers to memorize (1 2 3 4, 2 3 4 5, 3 4 5 6, 4 5 6 7, etc.), he recalled accurately but was unaware of the logical order.

Synesthesia. In addition to eidetic imagery, however, S reportedly experienced environmental stimuli synesthetically—with more than one type of sensation at a time. Visual images mixed with tastes and textures to produce a unique multisensual experience for each stimulus. Luria presented S with various tones, and S described different visual images for each one, accompanied by taste, touch, and/or pain sensation.

If a word was familiar and concrete, it would evoke a visual image synesthetic sensations. However, if the word was unfamiliar or abstract, it was represented visually as a series of colors, splashes, splotches, and lines related to the sound of the word.

As might be imagined, this caused problems for S in a number of areas. For example, story comprehension was difficult, because, as he read or heard words, he was barraged with images appearing so fast they were difficult to sort out conceptually. Any words not represented by a visual picture appeared as colors, splashes, and lines. Also, S had trouble keeping track of alternate meanings of homonyms, as well as understanding metaphors (some words are used to mean other things, and S always interpreted words literally). He also had trouble accepting that two very different-sounding words could have the same meaning (synonyms). S had difficulty understanding abstract ideas as well. He expressed this difficulty, stating, "'I can only understand what I can visualize' " (Luria, 1968, p. 130). It seemed impossible for him to "cross that 'accursed' threshold to a higher level of thought" (p. 133) which was abstract thinking. Finally, S's poor memory of faces is consistent with synesthesia. S reported that he saw faces as fluctuations of light and dark, always changing. Upon seeing a face he had seen before, he would see a new set of fluctuations of light and dark. There were too many fluctuations to match.

Mental manipulation. Although S could generally remember things simply by the images they evoked, when he became a professional mnemonicist, he had to deal with great volumes of material without confusing it. People gave him the most difficult series to memorize they could think of, including series of meaningless items. S developed a system for handling these difficulties in which he manipulated his mental images.

Normally, to remember lists of words, each of which evoked an image, he arranged the images along a familiar road or room, and, to recall, took a "mental walk." To recall in reverse order, he would take a walk in the opposite direction. Occasionally he omitted a word because he had "placed" it in a location in which it would be difficult to see (e.g., placing an egg on the wall and the wall happens to be white, or placing an item in a poorly lit area). His mistakes in recall were related more to perception than to memory.

For his professional endeavors, S modified his procedure. He manipulated his images so that he would no longer omit items that were difficult to see. For example, he visualized a very large egg that would be easier to see, and created better lighting by adding a street lamp. He also decreased the detail of his images by using representative details of images rather than complete images. Rather than picture "restaurant" as an entranceway with people inside, an orchestra tuning up, and so on, he simply pictured a storefront with a door and something white inside. He also symbolized words that were less conducive to visual images. He symbolized "America" as Uncle Sam. Finally, he converted senseless words into meaningful images by breaking them down into syllables and associating each syllable with a meaningful word. This system allowed him to eliminate the series of color, splotches, and lines he would see for meaningless word sounds.

Conclusions. Luria concluded that S's memory was qualitatively different from most people's memories. Besides his unusual eidetic imagery, synesthesia, and mental manipulations, S's memory had no measurable limits of capacity, durability, or duration. Stimulus traces did not inhibit each other as they do in normal memory, memory traces did not diminish over time, and he showed no primacy or recency effects—his errors were related to perceptual flaws in images and not to order in the list.

Luria attributed S's exceptional memory to two factors. The first and most important was unusual characteristics Luria believed to be innate and possibly genetically determined. The second factor was the use of technique along with these characteristics.

Case 2: Aitken

Characteristics. Alexander Aitken was a distinguished scholar who had won many awards (Hunter, 1977, 1982). He not only had an exceptional memory, but also was an outstanding mathematician, mental calculator, and violinist (see Hunter, 1962, for an account of Aitken's calculating ability). He was born in New Zealand in the 1890s and, at the time of Hunter's case reports, lived in Scotland.

Aitken could recall a great deal of detailed information and could quickly learn new information that interested him. As a boy he memorized the decimal equivalent of 1/97 to 96 digits. In World War I, when his platoon's roll book was missing, he recalled it in entirety—each full name and corresponding information. He remembered by heart whole books and he could recite verse, produce facts, recall musical compositions, and recall details of events. Aitken's memory was exceptional in range, precision, duration, and speed.

Aitken's short term memory had a greater capacity than most people's, though, unlike S's, it did have limits. Sutherland (cited in Hunter, 1977) asked Aitken to repeat sequences of items presented at a rate of two items per second. Aitken's auditory memory span was 10 for letters and 13 for digits; his visual memory span was 15 for digits. Hunter reported that Aitken's knowledge base also had limits—he knew little about sports.

In other experiments, the precision and duration of Aitken's memory was tested. Aitken was asked to repeat 25 unrelated words presented auditorily. In the first trial he recalled 12 words, and by the fourth trial he had perfect accuracy. One week later his accuracy dropped to two words, where it remained at testing 3 months later. However, after another 15 months, accuracy increased again to 24 words. Twenty-seven years later, recall was perfect.

Aitken was asked to remember a list of 16 three-digit numbers. His recall increased steadily to perfect performance on the fourth trial, continued near perfect after 24 hours, and dropped to 12 after 4 years and to 11 after 24 years. Clearly, the precision and duration of Aitken's memory was outstanding, although, as in normal memory, repetition aided his recall and time lapse decreased accuracy.

There is also anecdotal evidence that Aitken's memory was consolidated faster than most. For example, when he was a teacher he could remember all 35 names of his students after reading the roster only once.

Explanations. Hunter attributed Aitken's memory to three factors—(a) a tendency to extract properties of stimuli and relate them to other stimuli, (b) an intense interest in the meaning of the material, and (c) relaxation as opposed to concentration in the information-assimilation process.

Patterns of multiple properties. Aitken seemed to code material in terms of several properties, many of which other people would not even recognize. One type of information especially easy for him to memorize was music. Picking out multiple and unusual properties of the music (e.g., meter, rhythm, tune, harmony, emotion, meaning, etc.) aided his memory of the music. He believed that musical memory can be developed to a finer degree than other memory.

Because of his fondness for music, Aitken often coded stimuli in terms of their musical properties. For example, as a boy he was able to memorize the decimal equivalent of 1/97 to 96 digits by "memory of an auditory or rhythmic kind"—not by working them out quickly in his head. Aitken also reported coding the series of 16 three-digit numbers by its auditory-rhythmic properties (see also Hunter, 1962).

Meaning and interest of the material. One quality distinguishing what Aitken remembered and what he did not was his interest in the material. If he found the material meaningful and interesting, he would have no trouble remembering it. If he found it dull, however, he would not remember it. Evidence lies in the types of material Aitken could recall. He recalled musical pieces and mathematical theory. However, he detested memorizing numbers for memorization's sake, and, according to Hunter, would have been a mediocre mnemonicist. Hunter suggested that interest aided in focusing attention on the material, which was crucial in storing it in memory.

Relaxation. Finally, relaxation was a key to Aitken's memory. When trying to memorize something, Aitken "cleared his mind and relinquished the job to his vast cognitive system, allowing it to work largely autonomously and in whatever way came most naturally" (Hunter, 1977, p. 158). Often this meant that the auditory—rhythmic properties of the material would "sink in." Aitken did not consciously memorize or consciously use mnemonic techniques.

Conclusions. Hunter concluded that Aitken's memory was not qualitatively different from most people's memory, but was quantitatively different. His memory was limited in short-term capacity, though his capacity was larger than most. His long-term memory was richer in areas of his special interests as is that of most people, but he remembered more of what he read and learned than most people. Also, he had an "overall larger and more finely articulated cognitive system" (Hunter, 1977, p. 162).

Case 3: VP

Characteristics. Hunt and Love (1972, 1982) first recognized VP as a person of exceptional ability because he could play up to seven simultaneous chess matches blindfolded or up to 60 chess matches not blindfolded using no notes. Through psychometric testing, Hunt and Love discovered that VP was above average in intelligence but not outstandingly so (IQ = 136), and his WAIS performance subtests were not outstanding. However, he performed near the ceiling on any test involving memory.

VP's childhood reveals precocious development. An only child "in an intellectual home" (Hunt & Love, 1972, p. 238), he was born in Latvia in Eastern Europe. At 3.5 years old he started to read. At age 5 he memorized the street map of a large city, railroad timetables, and bus schedules. At 8 he began to play chess. At 10, he memorized 150 poems for a contest. During 5 years of his childhood he lived in a post-World War II Displaced Persons Camp in Germany, where he attended a school that provided no books or other materials. As an adult he is fluent in English, Latvian, German, and Russian and has reading knowledge of most other modern European languages. At the time the study took place he worked as a store clerk.

Explanations. Hunt and Love made several systematic investigations of VP's cognitive abilities in order to pinpoint the sources of his extraordinary memory. They explored his use of eidetic imagery and mnemonics as well as his mode of information processing and attention to details.

Eidetic imagery. Several tests distinguished between the use of eidetic imagery and the use of mnemonics. It was determined that VP's memory performance was not attributable to eidetic imagery, but rather in part to elaborate and continued use of verbal and conceptual associations.

Two tests determined that VP was not using eidetic imagery. In the first, VP could not identify a Santa Claus face when shown one half of the picture followed by the second half. People with eidetic imagery can identify the face when they see the two halves within 24 hours of each other.

In the second test, VP was asked to recall visually presented number matrices. The columns in the matrices were either lined up or misaligned and spaced irregularly. The latter ('staggered') matrix took longer to read than the former ('normal') matrix. VP recalled the staggered matrix as accurately and quickly as the normal matrix. If he were reading out from eidetic images of the matrices, it would take him longer to read the staggered matrix.

Linguistic associations. Evidence in favor of VP's use of linguistic associations rather than eidetic imagery were that (a) VP could remember chess boards with more accuracy when they consisted of legal as opposed to illegal moves, (b) his recall for high-imagery words was better than his recall for low-imagery words, and (c) in free recall, he clustered words semantically rather than by physical similarity (shape or directional orientation). The first finding suggested that VP used already-acquired knowledge in his recall strategies. The second two findings suggested that VP used word meanings in his recall strategies. Further, VP was able to increase his visual digit span by using verbal associations—he "translated" numbers into weights, dates, or other transformations that were conducive to verbal elaboration.

Parallel processing. Linguistic association was not the only special skill related to memory to be revealed in VP. His performance on a few tasks suggested that he may have processed information in parallel under conditions in which most people process information serially. Alternately, he simply may have demonstrated serial processing many times more efficient than that of most people.

For example, VP completed a Sternberg short term memory (STM) search task in which he first heard a list of one to six digits. Following this "memory set," a probe digit was presented visually, and VP indicated whether or not it was a member of the memory set he had just heard. Typically, response time increases as memory set increases, indicating that STM is searched in a serial (sequential) manner rather than a parallel (simultaneous) manner, although there have been alternative explanations of the data (see Sternberg, 1975) VP's response times varied from set size to set size, but in no systematic way. His data indicated parallel search of STM or extremely efficient serial search.

Further supporting the parallel processing hypothesis are VP's data on a Brown-Peterson auditory STM task. This task was designed to measure decay of STM when rehearsal is not available as a memory strategy. VP was asked to recall trigrams. On each trial, a trigram was presented auditorily followed by a three-digit number. VP counted backwards by threes from the three-digit number until signalled to recall the trigram. The time interval between presentation and recall of the trigram was varied. Most people experience a decrease in recall accuracy as the retention interval increases. VP, however, experienced very little decrease in recall accuracy at all (despite the fact that his accuracy was under 100%). Although the task was designed to prevent rehearsal of items or other memory strategy by keeping subjects otherwise mentally occupied, VP reported that he did use verbal associations to aid recall. If this in fact explained his superior performance, then it is apparent that he was able to do two significant mental tasks at once. VP's ability to play several chess games at once is consistent with this explanation.

Attention to details. A final capacity of VP allowing for his exceptional memory is his acute attention to detail—perceptual, semantic, and linguistic. Hunt and Love asked VP to read several stories and reconstruct various portions of the stories after varying intervals of time up to 6 weeks. VP was able to recall the stories nearly verbatim, regardless of the time elapsed. Since other tests showed that VP does not rely on eidetic imagery, he must have coded and stored story details in memory. Details VP reproduced pertained to content as well as syntax.

VP also excelled at a task in which he looked at two strings of digits and determined whether they were the same or different. His accuracy on this task was vastly superior to that of all control subjects. This discrepancy demonstrates his ability to rapidly pick out visual or structural details.

Conclusions. Hunt and Love concluded that two factors were responsible for VP's phenomenal memory. The first is an ability to notice details quickly, especially those in verbal material. The second is an ability to associate virtually any material with something meaningful, and to do it very rapidly. They suggest that one reason there are very few phenomenal memorizers is that there is no great value placed on memorization as there was in VP's childhood schooling.

Case 4: SF

Characteristics. SF was an undergraduate student who participated in an experiment in which he learned to memorize long strings of numbers (Ericsson, Chase & Faloon, 1980; see also Ericsson & Chase, 1982; Ericsson, 1988). He reportedly had average memory ability and average intelligence for a college student. He practiced memorizing about 1 hour per day, 3–5 days per week, for more than 1½ years. During these sessions, he was read sequences of random digits at a rate of one digit per second, and he attempted to repeat the sequences immediately. If he repeated a sequence correctly, the following sequence was increased by one item. If he repeated incorrectly, the following sequence was reduced by 1 digit.

SF steadily improved his digit span from 7 to 79 digits. He also increased his ability to recall the series after the session from virtually zero to over 80% of the session's digits. Six months into the experiment SF did the 50-digit matrix task that both S and VP had done. "SF's study times and recall times were at least as good as those of the lifetime memory experts" (Ericsson et al., 1980, p. 1181).

Explanations. How could an individual like SF, who had normal memory and intelligence, perform as well as S, Aitken, and VP? The use of mnemonic associations and a hierarchical retrieval structure were probably responsible for transforming SF's memory abilities.

Mnemonic associations. Mnemonic associations were said to be the most important aspect of SF's memory. According to SF's own reports, whenever possible, he categorized three- and four-digit groups as running times for various races, since, being a good long distance runner, he was familiar with categories of races. When he could not code digits as a running time, he coded them as an age. He coded nearly 90% of digits as either running times or ages.

SF's verbal reports were verified by two methods. A computer simulation of his reported chunking method replicated it 85%–95% of the time. Also, when SF was given digits that would be difficult to classify as running times, his digit span dropped almost to his starting level; when again given digits encodable as running times, his digit span increased.

Hierarchical retrieval structures. Evidence also showed that SF organized running times hierarchically for easier retrieval. SF said that he first learned to code the first six digits in two running times while holding the last four to seven numbers in his rehearsal buffer. He could remember up to 18 digits this way (three four-digit running times plus six single digits in the buffer).

For more than three or four running times, though, SF had trouble keeping the order straight. To mitigate the problem, he subgrouped his running times, leaving four to six digits in the buffer. He started with two groups of two running times and expanded two groups of three running times and two groups of four running times. He was able to remember about 30 digits using this system. Next, he used a three-level hierarchy (e.g., two sets of two groups of running times) and was able to remember close to 80 digits.

Speech patterns provided evidence consistent with SF's verbal reports. SF tended to recall digits at a rate of one per second. However, he paused about 2 seconds between groups and longer between supergroups. Also, his intonation fell consistently between supergroups.

Pause times indicated that SF was grouping digits. However, it was possible that he was using associations between groups to remember them, rather than using the supergroup hierarchy. To check this possibility, Ericsson his colleagues asked SF to give the three- or four-digit string (running time) that preceded or followed a particular three- or four-digit string. If SF were using associations among groups, his RTs would be the same whether or not his answers required crossing so-called supergroup boundaries. If he were using hierarchical organization, his RTs would be longer when the answers required crossing supergroup boundaries than when they did not require such crossing. In fact, SF took twice as long to recall the string if it required crossing a supergroup boundary than if it did not, suggesting he was using hierarchical organization.

Conclusion. Although SF was able to increase his memory *performance* to the level of the famous mnemonicists, Ericsson and his associates concluded that SF did not actually increase his memory *capacity*. Theoretically, short-term memory has a working capacity limited to three to four items and a rehearsal buffer limited to six to seven items. Consistent with this short-term memory model, SF's (a) groups were always three to four digits, (b) rehearsal groups hardly ever exceeded six digits, and (c) supergroups were almost always three groups. Also, SF displayed no transfer from digits to letters—he only remembered six consonants—indicating that his memory span was dependent on well-learned mnemonics specific to numbers. Ericsson et al. suggested that with an "appropriate mnemonic system and retrieval structure, there is seemingly no limit to improvement in memory skill with practice" (Ericsson et al., 1980, p. 1182).

Theoretical Explanations

Two theories of phenomenal memory are dominant. One can be called *superior ability theory* and is more or less implicit and informal. The other, recently formulated, is *skilled memory theory*.

Superior memory theory. Superior memory theory holds that individuals such as S, Aitken, and VP have, by constitution, memory capacities that are superior to those of average human beings. The specific capacities of each individual may be different, but in each case the result is phenomenal memory.

The case study that best fits this theory is that of S. S's memory was qualitatively different from the average memory. He did not show any of the usual constraints on memory, nor did he show influence of any of the factors that typically influence recall (e.g., categorical grouping, primacy, and recency). He apparently had eidetic imagery as well as synesthesia.

VP's memory was governed by most of the usual constraints on memory, and was for the most part qualitatively similar to others' memories. However, he seemed able to process much information simultaneously, attend to detail, and quickly apply linguistic associations at a keener level than most people. According to the theory, these are exceptional abilities that resulted in VP's superior memory capacity.

Similar to VP's, Aitken's memory was ruled by the usual constraints (e.g., capacity limitation and decay over time) and was aided by the usual influences. However, he could remember more information quicker than most people, and for a longer time. Also, he had the ability to attend to details along multiple dimensions, which served storage and retrieval of material.

Skilled memory theory. SF's case instigated the formulation of skilled memory theory (Ericsson & Chase, 1982; Ericsson, 1985). This case indicated that a person of normal memory ability can learn techniques that will increase his or her memory performance to an exceptional level. Skilled memory theory maintains that there is no constitutional basis for exceptional memory. Rather, it is achieved through practice and mnemonic technique. Existing knowledge in long-term memory (LTM), such as running times, music, or language, is used as a structure for encoding material to be memorized. Material is stored in LTM rather than in STM as originally thought. Also, related and structured retrieval cues are used to organize the recall of information stored in LTM.

Ericsson and Chase believe that memory feats of all of the phenomenal memorizers can be accounted for by skilled memory theory (Ericsson, 1985; see also Gordon, Valentine, & Wilding, 1984). It is true that the mnemonicists discussed here probably had a great deal of memorization practice. VP went to a school that emphasized memorization. Both he and Aitken memorized books, poems, and lists from childhood. Though S claimed not to expend any effort which remembering matrices, he consciously modified his methods when he became a professional mnemonicist. Although it is fairly certain that S's memory was not attributable to learning alone, it is possible that Aitken's and VP's memories were. Both had above average general intelligence and both used systems for aiding memory.

CONSOLIDATION OF THEORIES

Theoretical explanations offered to account for special abilities have already been described. The present section summarizes the theories as they relate to the "g" vs independent abilities controversy. The theories can be grouped into four categories—those that explain unique patterns of abilities in terms of (a) select special abilities, (b) impairment of select abilities, and (c) uneven abilities, and (d) theories not related to cognitive abilities.

Select Special Abilities

One set of theories maintains that savants and hyperlexics have low general intellectual ability except for one or two areas of great competence. In one view, abilities displayed by savants and hyperlexics normally vary independently of general intellectual level (Hill, 1978; Silberberg & Silberberg, 1967, 1968, 1971). As intelligence is distributed normally, so are specific abilities. The rare individuals who fall at the low extreme of the intelligence continuum and at the same time at the high extreme of the continuum for a specific ability are those identified as savants or hyperlexics. Similarly, those whose memory capacities are at the extreme high end of the distribution yet have average or above-average intelligence are identified as phenomenal memorizers.

Abilities that have been proposed to vary independently of intelligence include word recognition (Silberberg & Silberberg, 1971); immediate memory (Spitz & Lafontaine, 1973); ability to deal with written linguistic symbols (Elliott & Needleman, 1976); and visual memory, visual recall, and pattern recognition (Fontenelle & Alarcon, 1982). Also, Hunt and Love (1972) suggested that VP had extraordinary perceptual speed and attention to details.

Specific Impairment

Another type of explanation maintains that only specific cognitive capacities are impaired. Intact capacities either may seem impaired because their function depends on the impaired capacities or may seem elevated compared to those capacities directly or indirectly affected.

One theory suggested that savants are unable to think abstractly; otherwise they are of normal cognitive ability. To adapt to their limitation, they compensate with concrete thinking, usually employing rote or sensorimotor memory. They are reinforced for displays of concrete thinking skill.

A similar process might occur if abstract thinking were limited by one's environment. VP suggested that, where he grew up and went to school there was a great emphasis on rote learning and memorization beginning from a very young age. Memorization was one of the few avenues through which children could gain recognition and approval. In fact, VP recalled that several children he knew could recite as well if not better than he could.

Huttenlocher and Huttenlocher (1973) suggested that hyperlexics have a specific difficulty associating speech sounds with meaning. Resulting difficulty in language comprehension makes them appear mentally retarded. Functions that don't require associating speech sounds with meaning, however, are not impaired and may be developed to proficient levels. Richman and Kitchell (1981) also suggested that hyperlexia results from a specific form of language disorder in which only verbal associative ability is impaired. However, they suggested that this specific impairment is accompanied by superior memory.

Another theory applicable to both savants and hyperlexics maintains that procedural memory is dysfunctional, but declarative memory is intact (Goldberg, 1987).

Uneven Abilities

Another type of explanation holds that savants and hyperlexics are individuals with uneven abilities and that they compensate for weak abilities by developing their strong abilities to expert levels. Uneven abilities could occur naturally or because of brain damage.

Lindsley (1965) suggested behavioral reasons that compensation could occur. Selfe (1977) viewed compensation in terms of neurological function (see also Welsh et al., 1987).

Also, it has been suggested that abilities of savants are usually associated with the right hemisphere, which is linked with simultaneous as opposed to sequential function (Rimland, 1978). Thus, left hemisphere impairment may be compensated for (or overcompensated for) by right hemisphere function. In Cobrinik's (1982) study in which hyperlexics read degraded words with more accuracy than nonretarded nonhyperlexics, he concluded that hyperlexics process globally (simultaneously) rather than analytically (sequentially). Interestingly, one of the unusual capabilities contributing to the exceptional memory of VP was the ability to process simultaneously information that most people process successively.

Other Theories

Attention. A theoretical explanation for special abilities not related to distribution of abilities and impairment within the individual is a theory of biochemically mediated abnormal attentional allocation (Rimland, 1978). This theory maintains that savants (and possibly hyperlexics) devote an inordinate amount of attention to physical attributes of stimuli and extremely little attention to more conceptual or abstract aspects of stimuli. The mnemonics Aitken and VP both demonstrated keen attention to details, but were also able to attend to abstract and conceptual aspects of stimuli.

Behavioral abnormality. Finally, savant and hyperlexic phenomena may be explained as a behavioral abnormality. For example, Hoffman (1971) suggested that development of a special skill is a stimulation seeking activity resulting from the extreme isolation of institutions. Also, Whitehouse and Harris (1984) suggested that hyperlexics read isolated words so well, not only because they have good memory and audiovisual association, but also because they have an abnormal compulsion to use written material. Goldberg's (1987) procedural memory theory suggests that abnormal-patterned behaviors may result from the same dysfunction that disables other normal functions related to procedural memory.

Conclusion

Although several theories have been proposed to explain the outstanding and isolated abilities of savants and hyperlexics, they have been proposed in a speculative light. No one has proposed a theory with much confidence or empirical backing. The fact is that, for all theories proposed, several cases can be found to provide rebuff. The individuals of interest make up an extremely heterogeneous group, and it is quite possible that several theories apply, but for different subgroups or individuals.

The theories reflect a general willingness to accept the notion of independently functioning and separately distributed abilities. The acceptance of this notion is not surprising given the descriptions of savants and hyperlexics, but it is surprising, given the tradition of "g."

"g" VS. INDEPENDENT ABILITIES

At the beginning of this chapter it was suggested that, if one considered the widely discrepant abilities of savants, hyperlexics, and phenomenal memorizers, one would easily conclude that intelligence is not a unitary characteristic, but rather a set of independently functioning abilities. How do "g" theories of human intelligence compare with independent abilities theories in accounting for special abilities? The analysis presented in this section indicates that, although "g" theories can account for special abilities in many cases, their applicability is not as broad as that of independent abilities theories.

The discussion that follows outlines three generic theoretical viewpoints on intelligence—(a) extreme "g," (b) modified "g," and (c) independent abilities. Although the viewpoints may be more or less associated with particular theorists, they are treated as prototypical rather than specific positions. Each viewpoint includes two components related to applicability to special abilities—(a) basic mental ability or constitution or potential, and (b) development of potential. This distinction is similar to Intelligence A and Intelligence B of Hebb (1949), which he described as biologically based ability and intelligence actually shown. Each position is described and evaluated on three criteria—(a) applicability to cases

Table 1. Applicability of Three Generic Intelligence Theories to Special Abilities Phenomena

	Intelligence Theory		
Special Ability Type	***Extreme "g"***	***Modified "g"***	***Independent Abilities***
Savant—brain damaged			
Would-be high intelligence	yes	yes	yes
Would-be low intelligence	no	maybe	yes
Savant—not brain damaged	no	no	yes
Hyperlexic—brain damaged			
Would-be high intelligence	yes	yes	yes
Would-be low intelligence	no	maybe	yes
Hyperlexic—not brain damaged	no	no	yes
Phenomenal Memorizer	no	yes	yes

with or without brain damage, (b) applicability to individuals of various levels of overall ability, and (c) necessity for an explanation for hyperdevelopment of basic ability. The evaluations are summarized in Table 1.

Three Positions

Extreme "g". Both "g" positions suggest that individual differences in all mental abilities are determined in great part by individual differences in general intellectual ability. The extreme "g" position holds that there is a general intellectual potential ("g"), probably related to neurological functioning, that determines the outer limits of one's abilities. Further, "g" determines the *development* of abilities, and as a result, all the abilities of an individual develop to a similar level.

Modified "g". The modified "g" position maintains that general intelligence determines the potential of mental abilities, but that abilities develop independently. Thus, abilities start out at approximately the same level, but some may be developed to a greater extent than others as a result of interest, reinforcement, and so on. As a result, a person's abilities may be expressed at different levels, but only within the limits of his or her "g"-determined intellectual potential.

Independent abilities. From this viewpoint, mental abilities are conceived independently. During normal mental activity they combine their functions and work as a system. It is generally thought that the independent abilities are closely related to neurological function, and develop only to a limited extent. The higher-level mental functions they combine to produce, however, develop through practice.

Applicability

Literature shows that special abilities are exceptional compared to equivalent abilities in the average person, occur in individuals with and without brain damage (and other neurological abnormalities), and occur in individuals of various general mental ability levels. How well can each of the viewpoints account for all of these specifics?

Extreme "g" theory. Even the most extreme "g" theory must allow that abilities are able to *function* independently, based on many, many cases of brain-injured patients who lose some but not all of their abilities. Thus, "g" is not a physical entity that can be impaired by brain damage (although, if "g" is linked with neurological functioning, it may be considered damaged by general brain damage during early brain development).

Extreme "g" theory can account for special abilities in cases of brain-damaged individuals who would otherwise be highly intelligent. For example, brain damage could leave many mental functions impaired, but some intact. If this were to happen in a highly intelligent person, then the intact functions could appear outstanding compared with other impaired functions, as well as compared with that function in other people of average intelligence. In other words, a person of would-be outstanding intelligence would appear mentally retarded (or of average intelligence), having one or a few extraordinary abilities.

Extreme "g" theory cannot explain special abilities in brain-damaged individuals who would otherwise not be highly intelligent. If the type of brain damage described above were to occur to this type of person, intact functions would probably not be considered special abilities. This is a minor point, because it is possible that all of the brain-damaged savants and hyperlexics otherwise would be highly intelligent.

A more serious shortcoming of the extreme "g" viewpoint is that it cannot account for special abilities in the absence of brain damage. Minor discrepancies in mental abilities are expected by "g" theory, because some abilities are more saturated with "g" than others. Highly "g"-saturated abilities should be less discrepant than less "g"-saturated abilities, which are more affected by non-"g" sources of variance. Differences in "g" saturation, however, cannot explain why some abilities can be extremely discrepant.

Modified "g" theory. Modified "g" theory fares better than extreme "g" theory in accounting for special abilities of savants, hyperlexics, and phenomenal memorizers. It applies to cases with or without brain damage. However, it requires an additional explanation to account for superdevelopment of potential.

Modified "g" theory applies to cases with brain damage in the same way that extreme "g" theory does. However, it not only applies to brain-damaged individuals who would otherwise be highly intelligent, but also to those who would otherwise be of average or low intelligence. It applies because it supposes that abilities *develop* independently of one another and of "g." It would be possible for an intact ability to be developed to a greater degree than the individual's would-be average observed ability level, and appear as a special ability.

Independent development of abilities also leaves open the possibility that, *within limits of potential,* some abilities naturally may be more highly developed than others. An intelligent person with no brain damage could conceivably have a recognized special ability (e.g., phenomenal memorizers). Because of the limits placed on development of abilities by general intellectual potential, it would be unlikely that a non-brain-damaged person of average or low intelligence would have a special ability. The modified "g" theory cannot explain non-brain-damaged, low-intelligence special ability cases without specifying an explanation of superdevelopment of abilities.

Independent Abilities Theory. The independent abilities position applies to cases with and without brain damage and cases of any level of intelligence. Further, it does not require a theoretical explanation of superdevelopment of abilities.

Because from this perspective mental abilities are conceived independently from one another, some may have greater capacity than others. Because the higher-level functions they combine to carry out develop independently, some of these may be better practiced than others. Thus, there are two sources of variance in measurable ability. This means that measurable mental abilities may be very discrepant. If a particular measured ability (e.g., digit span) requires basic abilities that are of high capacity, and if that measured ability has been highly developed, then a special ability (e.g., phenomenal memorizing) may result naturally without brain damage. This could happen in people who have average or little ability in other less developed spheres in which these especially high basic abilities are not required.

The independent abilities theory applies to brain damaged cases of special abilities as well (the following explanation also applies to similar configurations of abilities arising from natural discrepancies in abilities). If brain damage occurs, damaging some basic abilities and not others, the way in which the basic abilities combine determines the pattern of more complex and measurable abilities. Some high-level abilities will be impaired, whereas others will not. If the high-level abilities that are impaired are those required for school success or intelligence test performance (e.g., comprehension, knowledge acquisition), then the individual may appear to be mentally retarded despite having some fully functioning capabilities. If the basic abilities underlying these fully functioning capabilities are strong ones, and these capabilities are well developed, they may appear as special abilities. Superdevelopment of abilities through motivation, extended practice, and reinforcement is allowable in this theory, and is reasonable, given that development of other abilities is limited by impairment of basic abilities.

CONCLUSION

This chapter reviewed research and theory on three groups of individuals who have cognitive abilities that are outstanding compared with their average level of abilities and compared with abilities of other people. In general, theories were consistent with an independent abilities theory of intelligence. Further, when the independent abilities theory was compared with extreme and modified "g" theories in its capacity to explain special abilities, it was more successful.

Independent abilities theory cannot be accepted, however, on the basis of the abilities of a few sets of unusual people. It still must explain the robust finding of intercorrelations among mental tests without pointing to a single common source of variance such as "g." Various theorists have rationally explained psychometric "g" through independent abilities analysis in very plausible ways (e.g., Detterman, 1982, 1986), although they have not claimed to have found the very abilities that are proposed to be independent.

"g" theory, on the other hand, can actually cite data supporting it. However, it does not account for as wide a variety of phenomena as does independent abilities theory. Further, the data (patterns of correlations) supporting "g" theory would also be expected from independent abilities theory. Independent abilities theory is in the unique position of being able to theoretically explain more mental phenomena, but without any substantial supporting data.

There are several areas of ambiguity in the research on savants, hyperlexics, and phenomenal memorizers that, if cleared up, would shed light on the "g" vs. independent abilities controversy at least within this narrow realm. For example, it is thought that, although many cases of savants and hyperlexics have brain damage or neurological abnormalities, not all cases do. Is this true, or is it only that brain abnormalities in some cases have gone undetected? Are individuals with special abilities only individuals who would otherwise have high average intellectual ability, or could they otherwise have any level of average ability? Investigations of family intellectual patterns might be enlightening. Can a distinction be made between capacity and development of an ability, and if so, which is more responsible for the expression of special abilities?

It is evident that it will take a long time before these questions are answered, due to the scarcity of people with special abilities. Perhaps posing the questions, however, will stimulate some researchers in the field of savant, hyperlexia, and mnemonic phenomena to conduct their research with intelligence theory in mind, and some researchers in the field of mental retardation and human intelligence to include investigations of special abilities in their theory-related work.

REFERENCES

Brink, T. L. (1980). Idiot savant with unusual mechanical ability: An organic explanation. *American Journal of Psychiatry, 137,* 250–251.

Cain, A. C. (1970). Special "isolated" abilities in severely psychotic young children. In S. Chess & A. Thomas (Eds.), *Annual progress in child psychiatry and child development* (pp. 417–435). New York: Brunner/Mazel.

Cobrinik, L. (1974). Unusual reading ability in severely disturbed children. *Journal of Autism and Childhood Schizophrenia, 4,* 163–175.

Cobrinik, L. (1982). The performance of hyperlexic children on an "incomplete words" task. *Neuropsychologia, 20,* 569–577.

deHirsch, K. (1971). Are hyperlexics dyslexics? *The Journal of Special Education, 5,* 243–245.

Detterman, D. K. (1982). Does "g" exist? *Intelligence, 6,* 99–108.

Detterman, D. K. (1986). Human intelligence is a complex system of separate processes. In R. J. Sternberg & D. K. Detterman (Eds.), *What is intelligence?* (pp. 57–61). Norwood, NJ: Ablex Publishing Corp.

Elliott, D. E., & Needleman, R. M. (1976). The syndrome of hyperlexia. *Brain and Language, 3,* 339–349.

Ericsson, K. A. (1985). Memory skill. *Canadian Journal of Psychology, 39,* 188–231.

Ericsson, K. A. (1988). Analysis of memory performance in terms of memory skill. In R. J. Sternberg (Ed.), *Advances in the psychology of human intelligence* (Vol. 4, pp. 137–179). New York: Academic.

Ericsson, K. A., Chase, W. G., & Faloon, S. (1980). Acquisition of a memory skill. *Science, 208,* 1181–1182.

Ericsson, K. A., & Chase, W. G. (1982). Exceptional memory. *American Scientist, 70,* 607–615.

Frith, U., & Snowling, M. (1983). Reading for meaning and reading for sound in autistic and dyslexic children. *British Journal of Developmental Psychology, 1,* 329–342.

Fontenelle, S., & Alarcon, M. (1982). Hyperlexia: Precocious word recognition in developmentally delayed children. *Perceptual and Motor Skills, 55,* 247–252.

Giray, E. F., Altkin, W. M., & Barclay, A. G. (1976). Frequency of eidetic imagery among hydrocephalic children. *Perceptual and Motor Skills, 43,* 187–194.

Golberg, T. E. (1987). On hermetic reading abilities. *Journal of Autism and Developmental Disorders, 17,* 29–45.

Goldberg, T. E., & Rothermal, R. D., Jr. (1984). Hyperlexic children reading. *Brain, 107,* 759–785.

Gordon, P., Valentine, E., & Wilding, J. (1984). One man's memory: A study of a mnemonist. *British Journal of Psychology, 75,* 1–14.

Graziani, L. J., Brodsky, K., Mason, J. C., & Zager, R. P. (1983). Scores and prognosis in children with hyperlexia. *Journal of the American Academy of Child Psychiatry, 22,* 441–443.

Healy, J. M. (1982). The enigma of hyperlexia. *Reading Research Quarterly, 17,* 319–338.

Healy, J. M., Aram, D. M., Horowitz, S. J., & Kessler, J. W. (1982). A study of hyperlexia. *Brain and Language, 17,* 1–23.

Hebb, D. O. (1949). *The organization of behaviour.* New York: Wiley.

Hermelin, B., & O'Connor, N. (1983). The idiot savant: Flawed genius or clever Hans? *Psychological Medicine, 13,* 479–481.

Hill, A. L. (1974). Idiots savants: A categorization of abilities. *Mental Retardation, 12*(6), 12–13.

Hill, A. L. (1975). An investigation of calendar calculating by an idiot savant. *American Journal of Psychiatry, 132,* 557–560.

Hill, A. L. (1977). Idiot Savant: Rate of incidence. *Perceptual and Motor Skills, 44,* 161–162.

Hill, A. L. (1978). Savants: Mentally retarded individuals with special skills. In N. R. Ellis (Ed.), *International review of research in mental retardation* (Vol. 9, pp. 277–299). New York: Academic Press.

Hoffman, E. (1971). The idiot savant: A case report and a review of explanations. *Mental Retardation, 9*(4), 18–21.

Horwitz, W. A., Kestenbaum, C., Person, E., & Jarvik, L. (1965). Identical twins—"idiot savants"—Calendar calculators. *American Journal of Psychiatry, 121,* 1075–1079.

Humphreys, G. W., & Evett, L. J. (1985). Are there independent lexical and nonlexical routes in word processing? An evaluation of the dual route theory of reading. *The Behavioral and Brain Sciences, 8,* 689–740.

Hunt, E., & Love, T. (1972). How good can memory be? In A. Melton & E. Martin (Eds.), *Coding processes in human memory* (pp. 237–260). Washington, DC: Winston.

Hunt, E., & Love, T. (1982). The second mnemonist. In U. Neisser (Ed.), *Memory observed* (pp. 390–398). San Francisco, CA: W. H. Freeman.

Hunter, I. M. L. (1962). An exceptional talent for calculative thinking. *British Journal of Psychology, 53,* 243–258.

Hunter, I. M. L. (1977). An exceptional memory. *British Journal of Psychology, 68,* 155–164.

Hunter, I. M. L. (1982). An exceptional memory. In U. Neisser (Ed.), *Memory observed* (pp. 418–424). San Francisco, CA: W. H. Freeman.

Huttenlocher, P. R., & Huttenlocher, J. (1973). A study of children with hyperlexia. *Neurology, 23,* 1107–1116.

Jones, H. E. (1926). Phenomenal memorizing as a "special ability". *Journal of Applied Psychology, 10,* 367–376.

Kistner, J., Robbins, F., & Haskett, M. (1988). Assessment and skill remediation of hyperlexic children. *Journal of Autism and Developmental Disorders, 18,* 191–205.

Lindsley, O. R. (1965). Can deficiency produce specific superiority: The challenge of the idiot savant. *Exceptional Children, 31,* 225–232.

Luria, A. R. (1968). *The mind of a mnemonicist* (L. Solotaroff, trans.). New York: Basic Books. (Original work published 1965)

Mehegan, C. C., & Dreifuss, F. E. (1972). Hyperlexia: Exceptional reading ability in brain-damaged children. *Neurology, 22,* 1105–1111.

Morishima, A. (1974). "Another VanGogh of Japan": The superior art work of a retarded boy. *Exceptional Children, 41,* 92–96.

Nurcombe, B., & Parker, N. (1964). The idiot savant. *Journal of the American Academy of Child Psychiatry, 3,* 469–487.

O'Connor, N., & Hermelin, B. (1984). Idiot savant calendrical calculators: Maths or memory? *Psychological Medicine, 14,* 801–806.

Pennington, B. F., Johnson, C., & Welsh, M. C. (1987). Unexpected reading precocity in a normal preschooler: Implications for hyperlexia. *Brain and Language, 30,* 165–180.

Richardson, A., & Cant, R. (1970). Eidetic imagery and brain damage. *Australian Journal of Psychology, 22,* 275–286.
Richman, L. C., & Kitchell, M. M. (1981). Hyperlexia as a variant of developmental language disorder. *Brain and Language, 12,* 203–212.
Rimland, B. (1978). Savant capabilities of autistic children and their cognitive implications. In G. Serban (Ed.), *Cognitive defects in the development of mental illness* (pp. 43–65). New York: Brunner/Mazel.
Rimland, B., & Hill, A. L. (1984). Idiot Savants. In J. Wortis (Ed.), *Mental retardation and developmental disabilities* (Vol. 13, pp. 155–169). New York: Plenum.
Rosen, A. M. (1981). Adult calendar calculators in a psychiatric OPD: A report of two cases and comparative analysis of abilities. *Journal of Autism and Developmental Disorders, 11,* 285–293.
Selfe, L. (1977). *Nadia: A case of extraordinary drawing ability in an autistic child.* New York: Academic.
Siegel, L. S. (1984). A longitudinal study of a hyperlexic child: Hyperlexia as a language disorder. *Neuropsychologia, 22,* 577–585.
Siipola, E. M., & Hayden, S. D. (1965). Exploring eidetic imagery among the retarded. *Perceptual and Motor Skills, 21,* 275–286.
Silberberg, N., Iverson, I., & Silberberg, M. (1969). A model for classifying children according to their reading level. *Journal of Learning Disabilities, 2*(12), 634–643.
Silberberg, N. E., & Silberberg, M. C. (1967). Hyperlexia: Specific word recognition skills in young children. *Exceptional Children, 34,* 41–42.
Silberberg, N. E., & Silberberg, M. C. (1968). Case histories in hyperlexia. *Journal of School Psychology, 7,* 3–7.
Silberberg, N., & Silberberg, M. (1971). Hyperlexia: The other end of the continuum. *Journal of Special Education, 5,* 233–242.
Snowling, M., & Frith, U. (1986). Comprehension in "Hyperlexic" readers. *Journal of Experimental Child Psychology, 42,* 392–415.
Spitz, H. H., & LaFontaine, L. (1973). The digit span of idiot savants. *American Journal of Mental Deficiency, 77,* 757–759.
Steel, J. G., Gorman, R., & Flexman, J. E. (1984). Neuropsychiatric testing in an autistic mathematical idiot-savant: Evidence for nonverbal abstract capacity. *Journal of the American Academy of Child Psychiatry, 23,* 704–707.
Sternberg, S. (1975). Memory scanning: New findings and current controversies. *Quarterly Journal of Experimental Psychology, 27,* 1–32.
Symmes, J. (1971). Visual imagery in brain-injured children. *Perceptual and Motor Skills, 33,* 507–514.
Viscott, D. S. (1970). A musical idiot savant: A psychodynamic study and some speculations on the creative process. *Psychiatry, 33*(4), 494–415.
Wagner, R. K., & Torgusen, J. K. (1987). The nature of phonological processing and its causal role in the acquisition of reading skills. *Psychological Bulletin, 101,* 192–212.
Welsh, M. C., Pennington, B. F., & Rogers, S. (1987). Word recognition and comprehension skills in hyperlexic children. *Brain and Language, 32,* 76–96.
Whitehouse, D., & Harris, J. C. (1984). Hyperlexia in infantile autism. *Journal of Autism and Developmental Disorders, 14,* 281–289.

Chapter *8*

Unitary and Modular Approaches to Human Memory

Robert L. Greene

Case Western Reserve University

Scientific arguments at times arise, not from conflicting interpretations of data, but rather from conflicting views of the nature of science itself. Science is not a single enterprise but is rather a single name for a number of different methods of enquiry. Conflicts may arise when scientists approach the same subject material with very different ideas as to what science "really" is.

There are two methods of scientific enquiry that are particularly relevant to the present discussion. The first can be considered taxonomic. This method sees as its goal the discovery of natural categories. According to this approach, science can be viewed as the discovery of nature's structure. The work of Linnaeus is an obvious example in biology. The painstaking classification of mental illnesses embodied in typologies such as DSM-111 (American Psychological Association, 1980) is perhaps another. An alternative method of scientific investigation is to discover general principles that underlie a large number of different phenomena.

The work of Darwin, who sought to explain countless numbers of observations with the single principle of natural selection, and Einstein, who devoted the latter part of his life to a quest for a unified theory of natural forces, can be considered examples of this approach. A psychological example might be Freud, who sought a unified account for phenomena as disparate as dreams, history, mental illness, works of art, and slips of the tongue.

Clearly, it is not the case that one of these approaches is wrong and the other is right. They are asking different sorts of questions. Still, these two approaches do make different implicit assumptions about nature. The taxonomic approach assumes that natural categories of phenomena exist, and that it is possible to discover the cutting points of reality. This approach sees nature as being essentially modular. The approach emphasizing the discovery of general principles assumes that the apparent cutting points are, at least in part, illusionary, and that it is possible to discover principles that unite widely differing phenomena. This approach takes a unitary view of natural phenomena.

The field of memory has been studied by proponents of both of these approaches. Although William James may be an exception, the emphasis of early researchers was on the discovery of general principles. In fact the whole research program of the Behaviorists can be seen as an attempt to discover general laws of learning that apply to all sorts of information and all species. This program was greatly successful, leading to a dramatic expansion of our knowledge about learning processes. Among psychologists working on verbal learning by human subjects, the complex set of principles known as interference theory can be seen as another relatively successful attempt to construct a general set of laws of learning.

By the 1960s, however, this approach seemed to have outlived its usefulness. Psychologists were discovering categories of learning and memory that seemed to follow distinctive sets of principles. This had several effects. The first was the separation of human and animal research into separate camps, with relatively little interaction. Recognizing the importance of species differences was easy when the quest for general principles was abandoned as impossible. The second effect was a redefinition of the goals of memory researchers: No longer was the formulation of general principles the goal; rather, it was the discovery of distinct forms of memory. In other words, classification replaced unification as the goal of experimental psychology. Although this approach was evident in animal research as well, research on human memory increasingly came to supply most of the important insights.

In the 1960s, a typology of human memories was developed. According to this typology, there are three general classes of memories. The first is the brief persistence of relatively raw, perceptual information in sensory stores. These sensory memories are *precategorical;* that is, they have not yet been classified meaningfully. The second general class is the temporary storage of a small amount of postcategorical information in some sort of short-term memory buffer.

The final general class is the (relatively) permanent storage of information in long-term memory.

This typology became amazingly popular. Even to this day, it is repeated in introductory textbooks with no hint of uncertainty. The taxonomic approach to human memory became dominant to a whole generation of psychologists. In fact, many of these researchers argued strongly against even the possibility of finding general principles. For example, Mandler (1979) called for memory researchers to "abandon the promised land of simple principles and return to the complexities of the human mind" (p. 305). Baddeley (1978) argued that "the most fruitful way to extend our understanding of human memory is not to search for broader generalizations and 'principles', but is rather to develop ways of separating out and analyzing more deeply the complex underlying processes" (p. 150). Tulving (1985) claimed that a taxonomic approach to human memory is the only possible approach, because "no profound generalizations can be made about memory as a whole, but general statements about particular kinds of memory are perfectly possible" (p. 385).

A sociologist of science would be better trained than a psychologist to explain why the taxonomy of memory developed in the 1960s proved so attractive. Still, this popularity seems to be a result of the discovery of several striking laboratory phenomena that were easily explained by the postulation of separate memory stores. It would be impossible to explain why the concept of visual sensory memory, for example, became so widespread without referring to Sperling's (1960) partial-report procedure. Likewise, the concept of a short-term store has become inextricably linked with research on serial-position effects in recall and rapid forgetting of information during a period of distraction. To evaluate how necessary it is to keep this taxonomy, one must determine whether it is possible to explain these phenomena without reference to separate memory stores.

I turn now to a consideration of the dominant taxonomy of memory and determine how well it fits the empirical pattern it was designed to explain. Two classes of memories (sensory and short-term) have been proposed as representing fundamentally different kinds of information than standard (i.e., long-term) memory. I will review the literature to determine how necessary that proposal is in the light of current knowledge. Then I will discuss several general principles that have been suggested as alternatives to this taxonomy.

SENSORY MEMORIES

According to the modal model of memory developed in the 1960s (e.g., Atkinson & Shiffrin, 1968), information is first maintained in a relatively raw, precategorical form in a sensory memory store. A sensory store is believed to have a large capacity but to persist for only a brief period of time. The two sensory stores that have received the most attention theoretically and empirically are those for vision (iconic memory) and audition (echoic memory).

Iconic Memory

It is undeniable that visual information persists over time. The human nervous system is constructed so that patterns of neural stimulation do not immediately switch on and off. A classic demonstration was performed by Haber and Standing (1969), who presented an array of letters and asked subjects to set a brief "click" to coincide with the onset and offset of the array. Subjects tended to misjudge the offset of the array by approximately 250 ms. According to Haber and Standing, these errors were due to the persisting visual information. Subjects mistook the icon for the original stimulus.

Duration-of-stimulus studies of this sort are convincing demonstrations that temporal resolution in the visual system is not perfect. Of course, since performance on no psychological test is perfect, this is hardly a dramatic conclusion. What is unclear is whether this sort of phenomenal persistence is used by people to remember events that happened in the past. In other words, is this really memory? Can this sort of information be retrieved and used by people to answer questions? Haber (1983) has argued that visual persistence would not be useful in everyday life. I would be willing to consider a less demanding criterion. I would be happy to consider this sort of persistence "memory" if any task (no matter how artificial) could be constructed in which this sort of information is useful in remembering events that happened in the past. Two paradigms have been cited most often as evidence for this.

Partial-report task. Sperling (1960) initiated modern interest in the persistence of visual information. In his research, an array of letters would be displayed on a screen for a brief period of time (e.g., 50 ms). In one condition, subjects would be required to report all of the letters in the array. In another condition, subjects would have to recall only letters from one row. Tones of varying pitches were used as signals to indicate which row had to be reported on each trial. Sperling found that subjects recalled a higher proportion of items correctly in the partial-report condition than in the whole-report condition, and that this partial-report advantage decreased as a function of the delay of the cue.

Sperling (1960), as well as most later investigators, interpreted this pattern of results as evidence for a rapidly decaying visual sensory store. If this interpretation were true, this would meet reasonable criteria for memory, since this information was clearly of aid to people in a laboratory task requiring recall. The information that subjects had to report was no longer physically present and therefore had to be retrieved from some sort of memory store.

However, a partial-report superiority in and of itself is no evidence for visual sensory store. The proportion of items recalled correctly always decreases as a function of the number of items that have to be reported. This can be explained through the mechanism of interference, which is as general a principle of forgetting as can be imagined. Rather, other aspects of Sperling's (1960) data are critical. Coltheart (1975) lucidly explained the reasoning behind the iconic-memory interpretation of Sperling's results. According to Coltheart, two crucial pieces of evidence were that partial-report superiority was only found when selection of items to be reported could be done on the basis of a physical dimension (e.g., location, color) and that this superiority decreased as a function of delay. If the partial-report superiority simply represented interference, then it should not be dependent on delay or on the particular dimension used to select items.

Coltheart's arguments were extremely compelling. Unfortunately, as Coltheart (1983, 1984) himself now admits, they are also wrong. It turns out that a partial-report advantage that decreases as a function of delay can also be found when selection is based on the semantic, rather than the physical, properties of the items (Duncan, 1983; Merikle, 1980). Such a finding is inconsistent with an account based on a precategorical memory store. Also, recent evidence suggests that an alternative approach is needed to explain the decay of partial-report superiority as a function of delay. Mewhort, Campbell, Marchetti, and Campbell (1981; see also Mewhort & Leppmann, 1985; Mewhort, Marchetti, Gurnsey, & Campbell, 1984; Townsend, 1973) have found that partial report is hurt by cue delay only because subjects lose track of the location or order of the items. However, they remember what items were in the display, no matter when the signal is given. If iconic memory was being used here, delay would lead to a fading of the icon and a subsequent inability to report what items were in the display.

How then should the results from the partial-report paradigm be explained? It seems likely that the partial-report advantage is just another example of a list-length effect, that is, that people recall a greater proportion of items from short lists than long lists. This effect can be explained using the general principle of interference between different items in memory. The partial-report advantage decreases as a function of delay, because people begin to forget the order of the items. Memory for order is required in the partial-report condition but not in the whole-report condition. Order or location information is usually forgotten at a much faster rate than item information (Bjork & Healy, 1974). In short, far from revealing distinctive processes, performance in the Sperling (1960) task is best explained by the use of general principles that apply to all memory tasks.

Visual masking. Another task that has been used to support the concept of iconic memory is visual masking. Masking occurs when one stimulus interferes with identification of another stimulus. Of particular interest to memory theorists is backward masking, where the masking stimulus is presented after the offset of the target stimulus that must be identified. A standard account assumes that the icon is used to process briefly presented targets. The mask can interfere with the icon of the target stimulus, leading to decreased identification.

The interpretation of masking is far more difficult than this simple account implies. After all, almost any event occurring shortly after a target stimulus will interfere with memory for the target. Masking by itself is no evidence for an icon. Particularly important is Marcel's (1983) demonstration that pattern masking interferes only with conscious awareness of the presence of a stimulus, and not with semantic processing of the stimulus. Such a finding is difficult to reconcile with the notion of a mask somehow obliterating a target.

Echoic Memory

As is the case with visual information, auditory stimulation persists in the nervous system. Subjects are not able to judge perfectly the offset of auditory events (Efron, 1970). In other words, temporal resolution is no more perfect in the auditory system than it is in the visual system. As was the case with vision, this does not necessarily mean that there is an auditory sensory memory store, that is, a store from which it is possible to retrieve useful information. However, there are three different paradigms that have been widely used and have been interpreted as evidence for such a store.

Partial-report task. One of the studies most often cited as evidence for an auditory sensory store was a series of experiments carried out by Darwin, Turvey, and Crowder (1972). This study was an attempt to construct an auditory analogue to Sperling's (1960) visual partial-report task. Of course, the recent evidence that has cast doubt upon the sensory-store interpretation of the visual data should make one hesitate to interpret the auditory data in this fashion.

Darwin et al. (1972) followed Sperling's (1960) example of presenting more information than the subject can categorize in the time allowed. Three lists of three items each were simultaneously presented to the left, middle, and right sides of the head. In the whole-report condition, subjects were required to recall as many items as they could. In the partial-report condition, a visual signal would indicate which of the three lists was to be reported. The partial-report signal was presented either immediately after offset of the lists or following delays of 1, 2, or 4 seconds. The results showed that the proportion of items recalled correctly was higher in the partial-report condition than in the whole-report condition. Also, this partial-report advantage decreased as a function of delay. These results parallel those found in vision by Sperling.

Since the visual partial-report tasks do not seem to measure sensory memory, it is reasonable to question the relevance of the auditory partial-report data. Later evidence has been consistent with this suspicion. Massaro (1976) demonstrated that semantic category cues were as effective as location cues in facilitating partial-report performance. Selection on the basis of category would not be possible from a precategorical store such as auditory memory. As is the case with vision, the auditory data may simply reflect interference effects and the rapid forgetting of position information.

Auditory masking. Just as visual masking has at times been cited as evidence for iconic memory, auditory masking has been used to support echoic memory. The most well-studied version of this approach is the auditory backward recognition masking paradigm used by Massaro and his colleagues (see Massaro, 1975, for a review). In this paradigm, a subject is asked to identify a target sound (usually a single pure tone) when a second sound is presented shortly after the target. Identification of the target sound is impaired if the second sound (the mask) is presented within 250 msec of the offset of the target. Massaro and his colleagues have used this pattern of data to argue for the existence of an auditory sensory memory store in which information decays within 250 msec.

Unfortunately, the evidence for this 250 msec estimate is very weak. Masking studies can give no information about the maximum duration of information in storage. All we know from these studies is that auditory masks do not hurt performance if they occur 250 msec after stimulus offset. Massaro argued that masks become ineffective after 250 msec, because echoic information has decayed by then. Alternatively, it is possible that the subject has already analyzed the target stimulus within 250 msec. In this case, the absence of a masking effect would not mean that the memory trace wasn't there anymore after 250 msec, but simply that it was no longer needed.

There is evidence to support this latter interpretation of Massaro's masking studies. Massaro (1972) varied the duration of a target tone from 40 to 440 msec. Identification of the tone improved with increases in the tone's duration only up to 250 msec. Even when the target tone is physically present for a relatively long time, analysis of it seems complete within 250 msec. This suggests that no information about the maximum duration of the information used by subjects in these experiments can be determined. It is possible that the information subjects use here is not from a temporary buffer system at all, but is instead from long-term memory.

Modality and stimulus-suffix effects. The previous two paradigms discussed in this section had clear parallels in vision. However, the most common way of studying echoic memory has utilized a singularly auditory set of phenomena. When subjects have to recall a list immediately after presentation, they do much better on the last few items if they heard the items rather than saw them. This advantage for auditory presentation at the end of a list is known as the *modality effect.* This phenomenon can be eliminated if an irrelevant sound (a stimulus suffix) occurs after presentation of the last item. The standard interpretation of modality and stimulus-suffix effects attributes them to echoic memory (Crowder & Morton, 1969). According to this account, auditory sensory memory persists for at least several seconds after the offset of a stimulus. This persisting echoic trace can then be used to recall the last item on an auditory list unless it is masked by a subsequent sound.

In the last few years, it has become clear that the echoic-memory account of modality and stimulus-suffix effects is wrong. One of the more decisive findings has involved the study of lipread material. Lipreading of silently mouthed material leads to modality and suffix effects formerly believed to occur only with auditory stimulation. For example, Greene and Crowder (1984b, Experiment 3) performed an experiment in which subjects were required to recall lists of nine digits in order. All lists were presented via videotape. For half of the lists, subjects were able to hear the items. For the remaining lists, the sound was removed from the tape, and subjects had to lipread the list items. In addition, each list was followed either by no suffix, by a suffix that the subject heard, or by a suffix the subject lipread. The predictions of the echoic-memory theory are clear. Hearing the list items should lead to enhanced recall of terminal items, but lipreading them should not. The auditory advantage should be eliminated by an auditory suffix but not by a lipread suffix. In reality, the results showed a completely different pattern. Lipread stimuli exhibited patterns of data essentially identical to those found with auditory presentations. Both auditory and lipread presentation exhibited enhanced recall of terminal items. This pattern was eliminated for both kinds of stimuli by either an auditory suffix or by a lipread suffix. Lipread information is not the only sort of nonauditory information to display modality- and suffix-like effects. Recall of information presented visually that the subject has to mouth silently also leads to patterns of recall just like auditory presentation (Greene & Crowder, 1984b, 1986), Modality and suffix effects cannot therefore be due to a purely auditory system like echoic memory.

Another set of disconfirming evidence for the echoic-memory account comes from studies examining the duration of modality and suffix effects. It turns out that auditory advantages in recall may persist for much longer than formerly believed (Greene & Crowder, 1986). This conflicts with attempts to attribute modality and suffix effects to a temporary store such as echoic memory.

At present, there is no explanation of any sort that can be considered satisfactory for modality and suffix effects. Still, it is clear that the echoic-memory account is wrong. Thus, there is no support here for a special kind of memory store. The evidence in fact suggests that modality and suffix effects are based on much more permanent sources of information.

Conclusions

The evidence used to argue for the existence of separate sensory memory stores has been reviewed. It now appears likely that none of the evidence actually reflects the operation of sensory stores. To the extent that satisfactory explanations are available, it seems that this evidence is better explained through the use of general memory principles than through the invoking of specialized memory stores.

SHORT-TERM MEMORY

Perhaps the most famous distinction that memory theorists of a taxonomic bent have made is between short-term (or *primary*) memory and long-term (or *secondary*) memory. Short-term memory is seen as a limited-capacity buffer system capable of holding about two to seven items for a period of approximately 20 seconds in the absence of rehearsal. The concept of short-term memory gained so much notoriety because it was a useful explanation for a number of striking phenomena. In recent years, however, it has no longer been clear that the short-term memory construct has been useful at all. To demonstrate this, I will review the four sets of findings that have been most closely associated with the concept of short-term memory.

The Brown-Peterson Paradigm

The distractor task developed independently by Brown (1958) and Peterson and Peterson (1959) was the first paradigm seen as tapping a separate short-term memory store. In this task, the subject is presented with a short sequence of items to be learned, followed by a rehearsal-preventing distractor task that takes varying amounts of time. Then, the subject is asked to recall the sequence of items in order. The standard finding is that probability of correct recall is a decreasing function of the duration of the distractor task. This rapid decline in memory performance was seen as evidence for a short-term memory store that decays rapidly in the absence of rehearsal.

This interpretation was challenged almost immediately by Keppel and Underwood (1962). They demonstrated that the effects of the retention interval were dependent on the number of previous trials the subject had been tested on. Keppel and Underwood found that there was no sign of forgetting over the course of the retention interval on the first trial in an experiment. The negative effects of the duration of the retention interval developed over the course of the first three to six trials. If decay from short-term memory were responsible for forgetting in this task, it is not clear why it would not occur on the first few trials in an experiment.

If decay from short-term memory is not the cause of the forgetting found on later trials in a Brown-Peterson experiment, what is the cause? Keppel and Underwood (1962) claimed that proactive interference (i.e., interference from previous lists) was responsible. When no previous lists had yet been learned, interference is negligible, and no forgetting is found. When several previous lists had been learned, proactive interference becomes much more powerful. The increase in forgetting as a function of the retention interval reflects the fact that interference increases as a function of delay (Postman, Stark, & Fraser, 1968).

The implication of Keppel and Underwood's (1962) finding is that we do not need to posit a separate short-term memory store in order to explain the basic patterns of data found in the Brown-Peterson task. Rather, these data are explainable on the basis of general principles of proactive interference originally derived to explain forgetting over much longer periods of time. As Waugh and Norman (1965) pointed out, Keppel and Underwood's results do not prove that a short-term memory store can not be involved in Brown-Peterson performance under some circumstances. However, positing such a store does not seem necessary, and the law of parsimony would seem to demand that we accept the use of multiple stores only when they are needed to explain the data.

Coding

At one time, it seemed possible to assign acoustic coding exclusively to short-term memory, and semantic coding to long-term memory (Baddelely & Dale, 1966; Kintsch & Buschke, 1969). This sort of absolute difference in coding format would constitute an important difference between the two memory stores. However, it has become clear that this simple assignment of coding formats is wrong. It is quite possible to take tasks associated with short-term memory and find evidence for semantic (e.g., Crowder, 1978; Shulman, 1971) or visual coding (e.g., Shepard & Metzler, 1971). Similarly, in tasks typically considered long-term, there is evidence for acoustic (Craik & Kirsner, 1974; Geiselman & Glenny, 1977) and visual (Paivio, 1971) coding. The issue of memory stores is quite orthogonal to the question of coding format.

Memory Scanning

The memory-scanning task, developed by Sternberg (1966), is perhaps the most studied (or most overstudied) paradigm in memory research. In this task, subjects are given a small set of items to remember and are then given a test item. Subjects have to indicate as rapidly as possible whether the test item was a member of the set. The central finding is that reaction time is an increasing linear function of set size. This function has equal slopes but different intercepts for positive and negative trials.

Sternberg (1966) interpreted his results as evidence for an exhaustive, serial-scanning process. According to this account, subjects scan each item in the memory set, one item at a time, and compare each item with the test stimulus. This accounts for the linear increase in reaction time as a function of set size. All items in the memory set are always scanned, leading to equal slopes for positive and negative trials. This interpretation suggests that the results found here are specific to short-term memory. After all, to scan every single trace in long-term memory one at a time would take an unimagineably long time.

Of course, this claim that short-term and long-term memory must have different retrieval mechanisms holds true only if the serial, exhaustive account of Sternberg's (1966) is accurate. There are several problems with this account, however. There are many different theories that make exactly the same predictions as Sternberg's account about mean reaction times. These theories can assume a serial, self-terminating scan (Theios, Smith, Haviland, Traupmann, & Moy, 1973), a parallel exhaustive scan (Taylor, 1976), a parallel self-terminating scan (Ratcliff, 1978), or no scanning process at all (Baddelely & Ecob, 1973; Pike, Dalgliesh, & Wright, 1977). It is simply too easy to make up a theory to account for mean reaction times. Any pattern of times is consistent with a large number of different classes of theories.

This indeterminacy of mean reaction times has led theorists to seek more conclusive data on performance on this task. For example, Reed (1976) used the response-signal procedure in which subjects are told to respond immediately when a certain signal is given. This allows the experimenter to plot the growth of information over time by varying the delay of the signal. Ratcliff (1978) studied the distributions of reaction times, as well as their means. Several theories that can account equally well for mean reaction times may make radically different predictions about the shape of the reaction-time distributions. This new evidence has turned out to be more decisive than the mean reaction times were. After a lengthy review, McNichol and Stewart (1980) concluded that only the models of Pike et al. (1977) and Ratcliff (1978) do a reasonably good job of accounting for the complete pattern of data. What is particularly important for our purposes is that the models of Pike et al. and Ratcliff are as applicable to long-term recognition as to immediate recognition. In fact, Ratcliff has even applied his model to semantic-memory tasks, such as classification (Ratcliff & McKoon, 1982). It is not necessary to assume that different retrieval processes are used on short-term and long-term memory in order to account for the results found by Sternberg (1966). In fact, the models that are most successful in accounting for the whole range of data are those that are also applicable to long-term memory situations.

Recency Effects in Recall

The phenomenon most closely associated with the concept of short-term memory is the recency effect in free recall (see Greene, 1986b, for a review). When subjects are given a list of items to remember, they typically are much more likely to recall the last few items than the other items on the list. According to the dual-store account (e.g., Atkinson & Shiffrin, 1968; Glanzer, 1972; Waugh & Norman, 1965), the last few items are still present in short-term memory at the time of recall. Since retrieval from short-term memory is so much easier than retrieval from long-term memory, there is a marked advantage in recall for terminal items. The evidence most often used to support this interpretation is the finding that the recency effect is eliminated if a filled retention interval is inserted between presentation and the last item and the beginning of recall (Glanzer & Cunitz, 1966).

In recent years, considerable evidence has been collected that recency effects in free recall can occur in situations where short-term memory could not be responsible (e.g., Baddeley & Hitch, 1977; Roediger & Crowder, 1976, Rundus, 1980; Watkins & Peynircioglu, 1983). The most well studied of these situations is in the continuous-distractor paradigm developed by Bjork and Whitten (1974). In this paradigm, the presentation of each pair of words is preceded by a period of distractor activity. The last pair of items is followed by another period of distractor activity that would be sufficient to eliminate the recency effect, using the conventional method of presentation. When this paradigm is used, large recency effects can be obtained even though the distractor activity should have occupied short-term memory.

Of course, if the long-term recency effects found in the Bjork and Whitten (1974) paradigm result from different processes than those found in immediate free recall, they would be entirely irrelevant to discussions about short-term memory. However, there is good reason to believe that the recency effects found in both of these paradigms result from common processes. Variables such as word frequency, list length, semantic similarity, and presentation modality have equivalent effects on the serial-position curve in immediate free recall and in the Bjork and Whitten paradigm (Greene, 1986a).

If short-term memory is not responsible for the recency effect in free recall, what is? A number of authors (e.g., Baddelely & Hitch, 1977; Bjork & Whitten, 1974; Glenberg et al., 1980) have argued that temporal or contextual cues are used to retrieve terminal items from short-term storage. The effectiveness of these cues is dependent in part on the temporal arrangement of the items. Greene and Crowder (1984a, 1988) have reported tests of this interpretation of recency effects.

Conclusion

This review suggests that the concept of short-term memory is simply no longer needed to explain any of the phenomena that are typically attributed to it. Short-term memory itself has rarely been directly challenged. However, as Crowder (1982) has noted, it is almost never used as an explanatory construct anymore. Whether a separate short-term store exists is something we could all speculate about. However, at present, we have no evidence that demands such a store, and memory theorists are tending more and more to ignore the concept entirely.

UNITARY APPROACHES TO HUMAN MEMORY

This review suggests that the general taxonomic structure developed in the 1960s is no longer adequate to cope with the empirical discoveries made by many researchers. In particular, the empirical phenomena that at one time seemed to demand this sort of taxonomy have now been reinterpreted and can be explained better by general principles of memory functioning than by assuming the existence of separate memory stores.

Of course, just because the 1960s taxonomy that became so popular is wrong doesn't mean that a taxonomic approach to memory is necessarily incorrect. In fact, many memory theorists have argued that we ought to be spending our time developing better taxonomies. Often, these revised taxonomies involve dividing up the different memory stores. For example, Coltheart (1980) and Long (1980) have suggested that the visual sensory memory store should actually be broken up into several stores. Cowan (1984) argued that there are several different auditory sensory stores. Baddeley (1983) has suggested that short-term memory should be conceptualized as consisting of at least four different stores.

There have also been proposals for dividing long-term memory into separate systems. Tulving's (1983) distinction between episodic and semantic memory is one example. However, there is strong evidence against this distinction (McKoon, Ratcliff, & Dell, 1986). Hasher and Zacks (1984) drew a distinction between automatically encoded and effortfully encoded information in memory, but this approach has also failed to find empirical support (e.g., Greene, 1984). Perhaps the only distinction in memory that seems promising is the distinction between explicit memory (that is, the conscious awareness of retrieving a particular past event) and implicit memory (the effect an earlier event may have on behavior even in the absence of conscious awareness of retrieval). There is evidence that explicit and implicit memory may be affected differently by a number of manipulations (see Schacter, 1987, for a review). Even here, however, some of the most promising theoretical accounts have seen explicit and implicit memory as representing separate facets of retrieval from a single memory system and have tried to account for differences between implicit and explicit remembering through the use of general principles (e.g., Jacoby, 1983; Roediger & Blaxton, 1987). Therefore, even this implicit/explicit distinction does not provide strong evidence for the existence of more than one memory system.

An alternative approach is to give up the search for separate memory stores and instead concentrate on developing general principles of memory processes. In my opinion, this approach has proven to be fruitful over the course of the last decade. Three principles in particular seem to be able to account for the preponderance of findings in the literature.

Levels of processing. Craik and Lockhart (1972) suggested that processing of stimuli goes through several different levels of complexity and that later memory performance will depend on the level to which a particular stimulus has been processed. In recent years, however, less emphasis has been paid to the notion of a fixed hierarchy of levels (Kolers & Roediger, 1984). Still, although this proposal has been reworded several times, there is now considerable evidence that this general approach can account for many of the findings in the literature (Cermak & Craik, 1979).

Encoding specificity. The levels-of-processing approach is clearly incomplete, because it deals only with events happening during the initial encoding of the stimulus. However, memory performance will also be affected by conditions present during the time of retrieval. In fact, it is particularly important that the conditions at retrieval be as similar as possible to the conditions that prevailed at the time of encoding. In other words, it is crucial that there be a match between encoding and retrieval environments. Tulving (1983) and his colleagues have called this the *encoding-specificity principle.*

There are numerous examples of the encoding-specificity principle in action (see Tulving, 1983, for a review). For example, people are much more likely to recall a list of words correctly if they are tested in the same room in which they learned the words (Smith, 1979). Also, subjects who memorize items under the influence of a certain drug are most likely to remember the items if they are tested under the influence of that same drug (Eich, 1980).

The encoding-specificity principle is needed to correct some of the faulty predictions made by the levels-of-processing approach. For example, it has been demonstrated that the type of processing that will lead to the greatest retention depends upon the information that will be available at the time of testing. If subjects are given words that rhyme with the memorized items to use as retrieval cues, they are better off having performed structural processing of the list items initially, rather than semantic processing (Fischer & Craik, 1977).

Associative interference. Not all cues are equally effective. Cues have to direct memory search specifically to the desired items. For example, imagine that a subject receives a list of words containing the items *LION* and *TIGER*. If the subject is told at the time of test that the items that must be recalled are words, this will not be very useful information. The items the subject is looking for are indeed words, but there are millions of words that did not occur on the list. The information would not help the subject to narrow memory search very effectively. Telling the subject that two of the items were the names of animals would be more effective. Even better would be the information that the two items are wild, ferocious animals. The effectiveness of a cue in leading to retrieval of a particular event is a negative function of the number of events to which that cue is associated. This principle is actually nothing more than that of interference and was the focus of most experimental work on memory until the 1960s. It has appeared more recently under such names as the *fan effect* (Anderson, 1983) or the *cue-overload principle* (Watkins & Watkins, 1975).

It is possible that these three principles could be reduced to two or possibly one. For example, it has been suggested that level of processing affects memory only because subjects tend to rely on semantic retrieval routes. Level of processing could then be considered an example of encoding specificity. Still, it is impressive that a few principles are capable of explaining so much of the literature on memory. Essentially all of the phenomena discussed earlier in respect to the multistore approach are now most often explained with one or more of these principles. It is worthwhile to note that the three mathematical models that seem to explain the most data in respect to memory rely heavily on these principles (Anderson, 1983; Raaijmakers & Shiffrin, 1981; Ratcliff, 1978).

IMPLICATIONS FOR INDIVIDUAL-DIFFERENCES RESEARCH

This chapter will probably seem unusual to those who have read the other chapters in this volume. I have not discussed a single experiment examining individual or group differences in memory. This is not just an oversight on my part. Frankly, studies of individual or group differences have had almost no impact at all on the development of theories of memory. Rather, memory theories have typically been influenced only by laboratory phenomena that are exhibited by almost all populations of subjects. If any evidence is needed for this assertion, the reader can have a look at any of the major theoretical statements made by memory researchers in the last 30 years; one is hard pressed to find references to individual differences in any of them (e.g., Anderson, 1983; Anderson & Bower, 1973; Atkinson & Shiffrin, 1968; Craik & Lockhart, 1972; Crowder & Morton, 1969; Kolers & Roediger, 1984; Melton, 1963; Morton, 1970; Murdock, 1982; Raaijmakers & Shiffrin, 1981; Ratcliff, 1978; Sperling, 1960; Tulving, 1983; Underwood, 1969; Waugh & Norman, 1965). Studies on individual or group differences have followed along the path set by current memory theory, and not vice versa. Once a memory theory is established, then numerous studies are reported showing how it is compatible with patterns of individual or group differences. Proponents of particular theories of memory have been more than happy to use group or individual differences as evidence for their accounts but have generally not been influenced by them when constructing their theories.

Moreover, I believe that this relative neglect of research on individual differences is reasonable, because this research is unlikely to tell theorists anything about the structure of memory. Any pattern of individual differences that is found would be equally consistent with a unitary or a modular approach. For example, let us take the finding that intelligence correlates significantly with recall of prerecency items in free recall, but not with recall of recency items. This finding can be interpreted for the claim that recall of early items on a list is from long-term memory and recall of later items is from short-term memory. However, this finding is also consistent with any theory that claims that subjects do not use exactly the same processes in encoding and retrieval of items from different parts of a list. All theories of memory suggested in the last 25 years have assumed that.

To start choosing between these theories, one must test the predictions made by specific theories through the manipulation of carefully controlled variables. The study of individual differences is rarely useful here.

Research on special populations has also had minimal impact on the development of theories of memory. There are two major reasons for this. The first is the knowledge that these populations are special precisely because their cognitive systems do not function in the same way as those of most people. This introduces a certain amount of skepticism about how confidently one can generalize from special populations to normal subjects. The second reason for this neglect is simply that patterns of differences between populations, like patterns of individual differences, can be interpreted in many different ways. To find an illustration, one need only look at the countless interpretations of amnesia that have been developed.

Given that work on general memory theory has more influence on work on individual differences than vice versa, what trends should we expect to see in individual-differences research in the next few years? One possibility is that less effort will be spent in documenting the many ways in which special populations of subjects differ from controls, and more effort will be invested in finding ways in which these special populations perform normally. This trend is already clear in the area of amnesia (e.g., Graf, Squire, & Mandler, 1984) and in the study of memory attributes that seem to be encoded well by all subjects (Hasher & Zacks, 1984). In other words, it is possible that the next few years will see a resurgence of interest in principles of memory that generalize across individual and populations.

CONCLUSION

It might be assumed on the basis of my arguments thus far that I believe that a unitary approach to memory emphasizing the search for general principles is the correct path to take. Actually, this is not quite true. Rather, I am merely trying to point out two conclusions. The first is that the standard taxonomy of memory stores that is still covered in all of our introductory textbooks can no longer be considered tenable. The second is that the greatest contributions to knowledge in this field over the last 15 years or so have been made by scientists emphasizing the search for general principles.

It is almost certain that all of the theories we develop in cognitive psychology will turn out to be wrong. Taking this into account, it seems absurd to argue about which kind of theory we ought to develop. However, it is not absurd to ponder what sort of theory seems most likely to lead to the greater accumulation of knowledge in the immediate future. It is clear in retrospect that a taxonomic approach was the most fruitful path to take in the 1960s. The multistore approach led to a huge outpouring of research and a virtual explosion of effort into the study of memory. The alternative was the system of general principles developed by verbal-learning researchers. By this time, those general principles were dependent on numerous epicycles and questionable assumptions, and this approach had lost whatever claims it once had on parsimony. There were some people who tried to defend verbal-learning principles from the new onslaught (e.g., Melton, 1963), but these had limited influence. The time was right for new approaches.

The multistore approach has now similarly met its limitations. It is no longer able to explain even the basic phenomena that led to its formation. It is now the general-principles approach that seems to be leading to the greatest gain in knowledge. This does not mean that this approach is correct in any absolute sense. However, it has been the most useful approach to take in the recent past and will probably continue to be so for the immediate future.

What sort of evidence would be required to decide whether the unitary or modular approach is correct? I believe that no evidence could possibly be relevant to this issue. All classes of psychological theories are formally equivalent; for every prediction made by a theory of a certain class, one can find another theory from the contrasting class that makes the same prediction. This has already been proven mathematically in several specific domains (e.g., Anderson, 1978; Townsend, 1971). Specific theories in each class can be tested. However, a class of theories (such as unitary class or a modular class of memory theories) is not subject to disproof. All researchers who claim to be testing whether mind is modular or unitary are actually only contrasting specific theories of the two classes. In a similar fashion, I have criticized one particular kind of modular theory in this chapter but have not presented any evidence at all against modular theories in general. Any researcher who claims to have disproven either the unitary or modular approach is simply wrong. We should not base our research on the false hope of resolving this issue. Rather, we should be asking ourselves which approach will be most useful in a particular domain in the future. In the case of memory, I believe that it is the unitary approach.

REFERENCES

American Psychiatric Association. (1980). *Diagnostic and statistical manual of mental disorders* (3rd ed.). Washington, DC: American Psychiatric Association.

Anderson, J. R. (1978). Arguments concerning representations for mental imagery. *Psychological Review, 85*, 249–277.

Anderson, J. R. (1983). *The architecture of cognition*. Cambridge, MA: Harvard University Press.

Anderson, J. R., & Bower, G. H. (1973). *Human associative memory*. Washington, DC: Winston.

Atkinson, R. C., & Shiffrin, R. M. (1968). Human memory: A proposed system and its control processes. In K. W. Spence & J. T. Spence (Eds.), *The psychology of learning and motivation* (Vol. 2, pp. 89–105). New York: Academic Press.

Baddeley, A. D. (1978). The trouble with levels: A reexamination of Craik and Lockhart's framework for memory research. *Psychological Review, 85,* 139–152.

Baddeley, A. D. (1983). Working memory. *Philosophical Transactions of the Royal Society of London, B, 302,* 311–324.

Baddeley, A. D., & Dale, H. C. A. (1955). The effect of semantic similarity on retroactive interference in long- and short-term memory. *Journal of Verbal Learning and Verbal Behavior, 5,* 417–420.

Baddeley, A. D., & Ecob, J. R. (1973). Reaction time and short-term memory: Implications of repetition effects for the high-speed exhaustive scan hypothesis. *Quarterly Journal of Experimental Psychology, 25,* 229–240.

Baddeley, A. D., & Hitch, G. J. (1977). Recency re-examined. In S. Dornic (Ed.), *Attention and performance VI* (pp. 647–667). Hillsdale, NJ: Erlbaum.

Bjork, E. L., & Healy, A. F. (1974). Short-term order and item retention. *Journal of Verbal Learning and Verbal Behavior, 13,* 80–97.

Bjork, R. A., & Whitten, W. B. (1974). Recency-sensitive retrieval processes in long-term free recall. *Cognitive Psychology, 6,* 173–189.

Brown, J. (1958). Some tests of the decay theory of immediate memory. *Quarterly Journal of Experimental Psychology, 10,* 12–21.

Cermak, L. S., & Craik, F. I. M. (Eds.). (1979). *Levels of processing in human memory.* Hillsdale, NJ: Erlbaum.

Coltheart, M. (1975). Iconic memory: A reply to Professor Holding. *Memory & Cognition, 3,* 42–48.

Coltheart, M. (1980). Iconic memory and visible persistence. *Perception & Psychophysics, 27,* 183–228.

Coltheart, M. (1983). Iconic memory. *Philosophical Transactions of the Royal Society of London, B, 302,* 283–294.

Coltheart, M. (1984). Sensory memory: A tutorial review. In H. Bouma & D. G. Bouwhuis (Eds.), *Attention and performance X: Control of language processes.* Hillsdale, NJ: Erlbaum.

Cowan, N. (1984). On short and long auditory stores. *Psychological Bulletin, 96,* 341–370.

Craik, F. I. M., & Kirsner, K. (1974). The effect of speaker's voice on word recognition. *Quarterly Journal of Experimental Psychology, 26,* 274–284.

Craik, F. I. M., & Lockhart, R. S. (1972). Levels of processing: A framework for memory research. *Journal of Verbal Learning and Verbal Behavior, 11,* 671–684.

Crowder, R. G. (1978). Memory for phonologically uniform lists. *Journal of Verbal Learning and Verbal Behavior, 17,* 73–89.

Crowder, R. G. (1982). The demise of short-term memory. *Acta Psychologica, 50,* 291–323.

Crowder, R. G., & Morton, J. (1969). Precategorical acoustic storage (PAS). *Perception & Psychophysics, 5,* 365–373.

Darwin, C. J., Turvey, M. T., & Crowder, R. G. (1972). An auditory analogue of the Sperling partial-report procedure: Evidence for brief auditory storage. *Cognitive Psychology, 3,* 255–267.

Duncan, J. (1983). Perceptual selection based on alphanumeric class: Evidence from partial report. *Perception & Psychophysics, 33,* 533–547.

Efron, R. (1970). Effects of stimulus duration on perceptual onset and offset latencies. *Perception & Psychophysics, 8,* 231–234.

Eich, J. E. (1980). The cue-dependent nature of state dependent retrieval. *Memory & Cognition, 8,* 157–173.

Fisher, R. P., & Craik, F. I. M. (1977). Interaction between encoding and retrieval operations in cued recall. *Journal of Experimental Psychology: Human Learning and Memory, 3,* 701–711.

Geiselman, R. E., & Glenny, J. (1977). Effects of imagining speakers' voices on the retention of words presented visually. *Memory & Cognition, 5,* 499–504.

Glanzer, M. (1972). Storage mechanisms in recall. In G. H. Bower & J. T. Spence (Eds.), *The psychology of learning and motivation* (Vol. 5, pp. 129–193). New York: Academic Press.

Glanzer, M., & Cunitz, A. R. (1966). Two storage mechanisms in free recall. *Journal of Verbal Learning and Verbal Behavior, 5,* 351–360.

Glenberg, A. M., Bradley, M. M., Stevenson, J. A., Kraus, T., Tkachuk, M. J., Gretz, A. L., Fish, J. H., & Turpin, B. M. (1980). A two-process account of long-term serial position effects. *Journal of Experimental Psychology: Human Learning and Memory, 6,* 355–369.

Graf, P., Squire, L. R., & Mandler, G. (1984). The information that amnesic patients do not forget. *Journal of Experimental Psychology: Learning, Memory, and Cognition, 10,* 164–178.

Greene, R. L. (1984). Incidental learning of event frequency. *Memory & Cognition, 12,* 90–95.

Greene, R. L. (1986a). A common basis for recency effects in immediate and delayed recall. *Journal of Experimental Psychology: Learning, Memory, and Cognition, 12,* 413–418.

Greene, R. L. (1986b). Sources of recency effects in free recall. *Psychological Bulletin, 99,* 221–228.

Greene, R. L., & Crowder, R. G. (1984a). Effects of semantic similarity on long-term recency. *American Journal of Psychology, 97,* 441–449.

Greene, R. L., & Crowder, R. G. (1984b). Modality and suffix effects in the absence of auditory stimulation. *Journal of Verbal Learning and Verbal Behavior, 23,* 371–382.

Greene, R. L., & Crowder, R. G. (1986). Recency effects in delayed recall of mouthed stimuli. *Memory & Cognition, 14,* 355–360.

Greene, R. L., & Crowder, R. G. (1988). Memory for serial position: Effects of spacing, vocalization, and stimulus suffixes. *Journal of Experimental Psychology: Learning, Memory, and Cognition, 14,* 740–748.

Haber, R. N. (1983). The impending demise of the icon: A critique of the concept of iconic storage in visual information processing. *The Behavioral and Brain Sciences, 6,* 1–54.

Haber, R. N., & Standing, L. (1969). Direct measures of short-term visual storage. *Quarterly Journal of Experimental Psychology, 21,* 43–54.

Hasher, L., & Zacks, R. T. (1984). Automatic processing of fundamental information: The case of frequency of occurrence. *American Psychologist, 39,* 1372–1388.

Jacoby, L. L. (1983). Perceptual enhancement: Persistent effects of an experience. *Journal of Experimental Psychology: Learning, Memory, and Cognition, 9,* 21–38.

Keppel, G., & Underwood, B. J. (1962). Proactive inhibition in short-term retention of single items. *Journal of Verbal Learning and Verbal Behavior, 1,* 153–161.

Kintsch, W., & Buschke, H. (1969). Homophones and synonyms in short-term memory. *Journal of Experimental Psychology, 80,* 403–407.

Kolers, P. A., & Roediger, H. L., III. (1984). Procedures of mind. *Journal of Verbal Learning and Verbal Behavior, 23,* 425–449.

Long, G. M. (1980). Iconic memory: A review and critique of the study of short-term visual storage. *Psychological Bulletin, 88,* 785–820.

Mandler, G. (1979). Organization and repetition: Organizational principles with special reference to rote learning. In L. G. Nilsson (Ed.), *Perspectives on memory research: Essays in honor of Uppsala University's 500th anniversary.* Hillsdale, NJ: Erlbaum.

Marcel, A. T. (1983). Conscious and unconscious perception: Experiments on visual masking and word selection. *Cognitive Psychology, 15,* 197–237.

Massaro, D. W. (1972). Preperceptual images, processing time, and perceptual units in auditory perception. *Psychological Review, 79,* 124–145.

Massaro, D. W. (1975). *Experimental psychology and information processing.* Chicago, IL: Rand McNally.

Massaro, D. W. (1976) Preperceptual processing in dichotic listening. *Journal of Experimental Psychology: Human Learning and Memory, 2,* 331–339.

McKoon, G., Ratcliff, R., & Dell, G. (1986). A critical evaluation of the semantic episodic distinction. *Journal of Experimental Psychology: Learning, Memory, and Cognition, 12,* 295–306.

McNicol, D., & Stewart, G. W. (1980). Reaction time and the study of memory. In A. T. Welford (Ed.), *Reaction times.* New York: Academic Press.

Melton, A. W. (1963). Implications of short-term memory for a general theory of memory. *Journal of Verbal Learning and Verbal Behavior, 2,* 1–21.

Merikle, P. M. (1980). Selection from visual persistence by perceptual groups and category membership. *Journal of Experimental Psychology: General, 109,* 279–295.

Mewhort, D. J. K., Campbell, A. J., Marchetti, F. M., & Campbell, J. I. D. (1981). Identification, localization, and "iconic memory": An evaluation of the bar-probe task. *Memory & Cognition, 9,* 50–67.

Mewhort, D. J. K., & Leppman, K. P. (1985). Information persistence: Testing spatial and identity information with a voice probe. *Psychological Research, 47,* 51–58.

Mewhort, D. J. K., Marchetti, F. M., Gurnsey, R., & Campbell, A. J. (1984). Information persistence: A dual buffer model for initial visual processing. In H. Bouma & D. G. Bouwhuis (Eds.), *Attention and performance X: Control of language processes* (pp. 287–298). Hillsdale, NJ: Erlbaum.

Morton, J. (1970). A functional model of memory. In D. A. Norman (Ed.), *Models of memory* (pp. 203–254). New York: Academic Press.

Murdock, B. B., Jr. (1982). A theory for the storage and retrieval of item and associative information. *Psychological Review, 89,* 609–626.

Paivio, A. (1971). *Imagery and verbal processes.* New York: Holt, Rinehart, & Winston.

Peterson, L. R., & Peterson, M. J. (1959). Short-term retention of individual verbal items. *Journal of Experimental Psychology, 58,* 193–198.

Pike, R., Dalgleish, L., & Wright, J. (1977). A multiple-observations model for response latency and the latencies of correct and incorrect responses in recognition memory. *Memory & Cognition, 5,* 580–589.

Postman, L., Stark, K., & Fraser, J. (1968). Temporal changes in interference. *Journal of Verbal Learning and Verbal Behavior, 7,* 672–694.

Raaijmakers, J. G. W., & Shiffrin, R. M. (1981). Search of associative memory. *Psychological Review, 88,* 93–134.

Ratcliff, R. (1978). A theory of memory retrieval. *Psychological Review, 85,* 552–572.

Ratcliff, R., & McKoon, G. (1982). Speed and accuracy in the processing of false statements about semantic information. *Journal of Experimental Psychology: Learning, Memory, and Cognition, 8,* 16–36.

Reed, A. Y. (1976). List length and the time course of recognition in immediate memory. *Memory & Cognition, 4,* 16–30.

Roediger, H. L., III, & Blaxton, T. A. (1987). Retrieval modes produce dissociations in memory for surface information. In D. S. Gorfein & R. R. Hoffman (Eds.), *Memory and cognitive processes: The Ebbinghaus centennial conference* (pp. 349–379). Hillsdale, NJ: Erlbaum.

Roediger, H. L., III, & Crowder, R. G. (1976). A serial position effect in recall of United States presidents. *Bulletin of the Psychonomic Society, 8,* 275–278.

Rundus, D. (1980). Maintenance rehearsal and long-term recency. *Memory & Cognition, 8,* 226–230.

Schacter, D. L. (1987). Implicit memory: History and current status. *Journal of Experimental Psychology: Learning, Memory, and Cognition, 13,* 501–518.

Shepard, R. N., & Metzler, J. (1971). Mental rotation of three-dimensional objects. *Science, 171,* 701–703.

Shulman, H. G. (1971). Similarity effects in short-term memory. *Psychological Bulletin, 75,* 399–415.

Smith, S. M. (1979). Remembering in and out of context. *Journal of Experimental Psychology: Human Learning and Memory, 5,* 460–471.

Sperling, G. (1960). The information available in brief visual presentations. *Psychological Monographs, 74* (Whole No. 11).

Sternberg, S. (1966). High-speed scanning in human memory. *Science, 153,* 652–654.

Taylor, D. A. (1976). Stage analysis of reaction time. *Psychological Bulletin, 83,* 161–191.

Theios, J., Smith, P. G., Haviland, S. E., Traupmann, J., & Moy, M. C. (1973). Memory scanning as a serial self-terminating process. *Journal of Experimental Psychology, 97,* 323–336.

Townsend, J. T. (1971). A note on the identifiability of parallel and serial processes. *Perception & Psychophysics, 10,* 161–173.

Townsend, V. M. (1973). Loss of spatial and identity information following a tachistoscopic exposure. *Journal of Experimental Psychology, 98,* 113–118.

Tulving, E. (1983). *Elements of episodic memory.* New York: Oxford University Press.

Underwood, B. J. (1969). Attributes of memory. *Psychological Review, 76,* 559–573.

Watkins, M. J., & Peynircioglu, A. F. (1983). Three recency effects at the same time. *Journal of Verbal Learning and Verbal Behavior, 22,* 375–384.

Watkins, O. C., & Watkins, M. J. (1975). Build-up of proactive interference as a cue-overload effect. *Journal of Experimental Psychology: Human Learning and Memory, 1,* 442–452.

Waugh, N. C., & Norman, D. A. (1965). Primary memory. *Psychological Review, 72,* 89–104.

Author Index

H

I

J

Subject Index